VITAL STRIFE

VITAL STRIFE

SLEEP, INSOMNIA, AND THE EARLY MODERN ETHICS OF CARE

BENJAMIN PARRIS

CORNELL UNIVERSITY PRESS
Ithaca and London

First published 2022 by Cornell University Press

Library of Congress Cataloging-in-Publication Data

Names: Parris, Benjamin, 1977– author.
Title: Vital strife : sleep, insomnia, and the early modern ethics of care / Benjamin Parris.
Description: Ithaca [New York] : Cornell University Press, 2022. | Includes bibliographical references and index.
Identifiers: LCCN 2022003211 (print) | LCCN 2022003212 (ebook) | ISBN 9781501764509 (hardcover) | ISBN 9781501764523 (pdf) | ISBN 9781501764516 (epub)
Subjects: LCSH: Literature, Modern—15th and 16th centuries—History and criticism. | Literature, Modern—17th century—History and criticism. | Sleep in literature. | Sleep—Philosophy.
Classification: LCC PN731 .P37 2022 (print) | LCC PN731 (ebook) | DDC 809/.933561—dc23/eng/20220331
LC record available at https://lccn.loc.gov/2022003211
LC ebook record available at https://lccn.loc.gov/2022003212

To the oikos *we care for: Nandi, Homer, and Kleos*

All our labour is for rest, all our trauell for ease, all our care to auoide care.

Richard Mulcaster, *The First Part of the Elementarie*, 1582

Somne, quies rerum, placidissime Somne Deorum, Pax animi, quem cura fugit, qui corpora duris Fessa ministeriis mulces, reparasque labori.

O sleep, repose of all things, Sleep, serenest of gods, / and peace of mind, you, shunned by care, you, who soothe / all bodies made weary with service and restore them for toil.

Ovid, *Metamorphoses*, 8 AD

The first appetite of a living creature is to preserve itself, this being from the beginning proper to it by nature, as Chrysippus in his first Book of Ends, who affirms that the care [of] our selves, and the consciousness thereof, is the first property of all living Creatures.

Thomas Stanley, *The History of Philosophy*, 1656

Contents

Acknowledgments

I am grateful to my mentors, colleagues, and friends for their support over the years spent working on this book. I owe much to Richard Halpern, who gave me essential guidance in the early stages of this project during my time at Johns Hopkins. His generosity and sustained attention have benefited my writing and thinking immeasurably. I also thank Drew Daniel and Frances Ferguson for their faithful support and insight, as well as Amanda Anderson, Sharon Cameron, Jonathan Kramnick, Chris Nealon, and Mark Thompson for encouragement at essential moments while navigating the perils of graduate study. I had the good fortune to spend the 2014–2015 academic year as a society fellow at Cornell's Society for the Humanities, which served as a catalyst to some crucial developments in this book. I thank the society for its support, Tim Murray for his contributions as director and his confidence in my project, as well as Emily Parsons and Paula Epps-Cepero for their expertise at A. D. White House. Verity Platt set me on the path to Stoic *oikeiôsis*; Amanda Jo Goldstein was a valuable interlocutor on ancient materialisms; Anne Cvetkovitch helped me to see how my book could reach beyond early modern studies. I thank them, along with Lauren Berlant, Susanna Siegel, Christine Balance, Munia Bhaumik, Ida Dominijanni, Andrew McGonigal, Dana Luciano, Saida Hodzic, Annette Richards, Rebecca Kosick, Johannes Wankhammer, Diana Allan, Maria Flood, Paul Miller, Erin Obodiac, and Nathan Pilkington for making my year at Cornell such a wonderful experience. Jenny Mann has my deepest gratitude for her friendship and support in Ithaca and beyond. Other friends in Ithaca deserve thanks for making life there so memorable, including Rayna Kalas, Phil Lorenz, Alex Livingston, and Merike Andre-Barret. Though I first met Anna Watkins Fisher and Antoine Traisnel in Ithaca, I am delighted that they have become close friends through many meaningful conversations since.

Colleagues in the Haverford College Department of English made my time there immensely rewarding and fun. Laura McGrane was the best chair I could have hoped for, and a true friend. Tina Zwarg, Maud McInerney, and Gus Stadler were excellent company, both in Woodside Cottage and at the dinner table.

I thank Colby Gordon for his generosity and wisdom, from which I have benefited tremendously. I am grateful to Pearl Brilmyer and Filipo Trentin, who amplified life in Philadelphia with their quick minds and good humor. Joe Campana invited me to think and write alongside a group of early modernists whose work I greatly admire for a special issue of *SEL: Studies in English Literature*; both he and Graham Hammill responded thoughtfully to those efforts in ways that have improved this book. I thank them, as well as Russ Leo, for their insightful comments. I also thank Margaret Simon and Nancy Simpson-Younger for their invitation to contribute to a wonderful collection of essays on early modern sleep. I am grateful to *Shakespeare Studies*, *Modern Philology*, and Penn State University Press for permission to use previously published material: an earlier version of chapter 3 appeared as "'The body is with the King but the King is not with the body': Sovereign Sleep in *Hamlet* and *Macbeth*," in *Shakespeare Studies* 40 (2012): 101–142; parts of chapter 4 appeared as "'Watching to banish Care': Sleep and Insomnia in Book 1 of *The Faerie Queene*," in *Modern Philology* 113, no. 2 (2015): 151–177; parts of chapter 4 also appeared as "Life and Labor in the House of Care: Spenserian Ethics and the Aesthetics of Insomnia," in *Forming Sleep: Representing Consciousness in the English Renaissance*, ed. Margaret Simon and Nancy Simpson-Younger (Penn State University Press, 2020).

Mahinder Kingra at Cornell University Press has my deepest gratitude for his insightful recommendations and support of this book. Chris Pye has been an encouraging interlocutor whose clear-sighted and generous responses I value deeply. I have also benefited from Will Miller's enthusiasm for this project over several years, as well as his helpful advice in its final stages. Steven Swarbrick gave shrewd commentary on the introduction at a crucial moment. A new friend, Danielle St. Hilaire, and an old, Maggie Vinter, were kind enough to provide incisive comments that have made the chapter on Milton's *Paradise Lost* stronger. Will Rhodes offered perceptive and helpful readings of several chapters, as well as essential encouragement. Unhae Langis appeared in my life quite unexpectedly, and has given generously expert guidance on this book's investments in ancient wisdom traditions and the fascinating cosmology of the Stoics. I am most grateful to her, and truly pleased that the web of causes brought us together. For many years, Garrett Sullivan Jr. has provided intellectual inspiration and support—both professional and personal—which I deeply appreciate. Elisha Cohn has been a dear friend at each step along the way, and a fellow traveler in somnolent thought. It is not an exaggeration to say that this book would not exist were it not for the care and brilliance of Julia Reinhard Lupton, and I am immensely grateful to her for all she has done.

My parents, Mark and Marsh Parris, have my heartfelt thanks for drawing me into a love of reading at an early age. They smoothed my passage through tumultuous times that were also made easier with the support of my sister, Whitney Parris-Lamb, and my brother-in-law, Chris Parris-Lamb. Both my father's untimely passing and my mother's fierce optimism have left their stamp on this book. Finally, I thank Nandi Theunissen for her constant companionship and monkey business; she reminds me to look for the good amid all the turbulence. This book is for her.

Introduction

Vital Strife

This book is about the close yet puzzling relationship between sleep and the early modern ethics of care. Its first epigraph, from Richard Mulcaster's pedagogical treatise, the *Elementarie* (1582), captures an important paradox concerning the nature of care as it was understood by Renaissance humanists: the care put into the work of reading, writing, and learning each day is for the sake of avoiding cares that assail our souls with worry and distress. These are cares that, as Ovid's *Metamorphoses* (8 AD) suggests in the second epigraph, are best alleviated by the restorative solace that sleep brings to laboring and exhausted bodies. Sleep annuls care, because sleep removes us from ourselves. It thus dissolves our attachment to the form of care, *cura sui*, that Seneca describes as being "prior to everything else" by letting us—temporarily, at least—escape the physical and cognitive vestiges of our daily toil.[1] For Mulcaster and other Renaissance humanists well versed in Ovid's poetry and in Seneca's letters, care was a curiously ambivalent thing. A highly malleable facet of human agency and expression, care was recognized as a necessary catalyst to any pursuit of ethical or literary virtue. But because care could slide so easily into feelings of distress and suffering, it was itself an object of anxious concern and therapeutic attention.[2] Too little care in one's endeavors showed sloth and negligence, while a surplus of care threatened to harm souls overly attached to virtue. And yet, as Cicero writes, "the devotees of learning are so far from making pleasure their aim, that they actually endure care, anxiety and loss of sleep, in the exercise of the noblest part of man's nature, the divine element within us (for so we must consider the keen edge of the intellect and the reason)."[3] Humanist pedagogues like Mulcaster shared Cicero's vision of the deep value of intellectual activity by cultivating attention, bodily rigor, and affective devotion in their classrooms as care for and among their students through the reading and translation of classical texts by Ovid, Seneca, and of course, Cicero himself.

Grounded in habits that promoted the mutually reinforcing ends of diligent study and ethical care so valued by classical Roman writers, humanist pedagogy also drew support from models of political-theological vigilance and spiritual care foregrounded in the epistles of St. Paul (c. 50–64 AD) and extended by thinkers such as Desiderius Erasmus. His manual on the life of the Christian soldier, *Enchridion Militis Christiani* (1501), begins with a chapter titled, "We must watche and loke aboute us euer more, whyle we be in this lyfe."[4] To watch is to extend a care that refuses sleep, while sustaining a commitment to vigilance for as long as we inhabit our mortal bodies. After all, it takes hard work and wakefulness to know the good, and our creaturely proclivities toward idleness, sloth, and most essentially the escape from care afforded by sleep all seem to work against our ethical and spiritual interests in that regard. Erasmus's understanding of human life further clarifies the political-theological valences of sleep and care. For if the sovereign's care for his subjects is in some sense modeled on the constant care that God manifests in watching over his creation—the God "that keepeth thee . . . [and] that keepeth Israel shall neither slumber nor sleep" (Psalms 121:3–4, King James Version)—then the rupture in attention caused by sleep inevitably threatens the integrity of the monarch's watch over the body politic, just as it threatens to derail the humanist commitment to virtue in the classroom and beyond. For early modern monarchs, teachers, and students alike, sleep would seem to embody a paradigmatic form of carelessness, one that temporarily dissolves the psychosomatic territory on which Renaissance humanism proudly planted its flag.

Yet despite these humanist and political-theological antipathies toward sleep and related states of idleness, inaction, and carelessness, the works at the heart of this book—by Jasper Heywood, William Shakespeare, Edmund Spenser, and John Milton—show signs of what I call "humanist fatigue": a sense of intellectual weariness and skepticism concerning the body's capacity to sustain the forms of vigilant care and self-discipline that govern the moral psychologies of Renaissance humanism and Pauline political theology. Instead, these writers value the unconscious motions of physical life, giving credence to the mysterious yet vital power of sleep—a power that in early modern literature curbs the self-instrumentalizing ends of humanism and offers shelter from the harms of sovereign domination. Through sleep, we care for life, even as we abandon life's cares. So it is with every human soul, whose physical foundation is acknowledged each night by a return to slumber that dissolves our connection to the world while renewing the body that upholds it. In this way, sleep and sleeplessness form the emblematic center of a fascination with paradoxes of ethical care in early modern literature, drawing attention to a mounting concern with the nature of physical life and its recovery—a concern that I argue is biopolitical in that it attributes ethical value and political significance to states of dormancy. Succinctly put, early modern writers are sensitive to a biopolitical conundrum, or paradox, that sleep presents for the care of the early modern self and others: to sleep is to care for the bodily life that sustains waking attention, but only insofar as sleep abandons the forms of wakefulness that promote ethical and spiritual care.

In the chapters that follow, this form of care submerged in carelessness is taken as a sign of shifting value in early modernity, one that literary thinking is uniquely disposed to capture in the wake of Renaissance humanism and its cultures of vigilant attention.[5] In its most extreme guise, the idealization of vigilant care shared by humanism and Christian political theology takes an allegorical form articulated in the epistles of St. Paul: sleep is the face of death, and thus an anticipatory figure for the end of an earthbound, creaturely life that demands constant vigilance in its struggles with sin.[6] Against this allegorical capture of the living body and the forceful assertion that death is the deeper meaning of sleep, early modern dramatists and poets give rise to a poetics of care that draws attention to the strange vitality of somnolence. This moment, I argue, owes much to the literary absorption of ancient Stoic ethics and cosmology in sixteenth- and seventeenth-century England, partly routed through the English translations of Senecan drama collected in Thomas Newton's edition of *Seneca: His Tenne Tragedies* (1581). More particularly, Jasper Heywood's rendering of Hercules's cosmic swoon at the center of Seneca's *Hercules Furens* (c. 50 AD), which depicts sleep as a restorative benefit to the corporeal soul and a therapeutic salve to the hero's fury, sets into motion a literary icon of sleep to which early modern English writers return time and again.[7] As if bearing witness to a primal scene where the life and sustaining relations of the *oikos* are annihilated yet somehow must be remade, early modern writers reanimate and configure anew the event of Hercules's sleep and his tragic reawakening through their own literary approximations of sleeping life and the early modern ethics of care. From Spenser's Redcrosse knight to Shakespeare's King Lear to Milton's Adam, these and other creations of English writers follow the figure of Seneca's Hercules in foregrounding the palliative virtues of sleep and its essential role in the ethical care for life. In its emphasis upon the physical body's self-sensation as the necessary foundation and starting point for the path to virtue, ancient Stoicism serves as a touchstone for what this book argues constitutes an emergent form of value in early modernity, one that is housed in physical life and its autopoietic capacities for restoration through sleep.

In this way, sleep begins to shed its political-theological trappings of spiritual vulnerability, carelessness, and threatening isolation from the Christian community. Instead, for early modern writers trained under the precepts of humanism, the event of sleep marks a gathering point of interest in an experience that eludes the forms of vigilant care and attention on which the ends of Renaissance humanism depend, even as it constitutes a distinctive form of care for the embodied life that underpins such efforts. This form of care—first disclosed by the living being's innately sensed and favorable disposition toward itself as a physically constituted being—is what the ancient Stoic philosopher Chrysippus (c. 279–206 BC) describes as the first principle of life, an idea that is reproduced in my final epigraph and which informs Seneca's dramatic depiction of Hercules's restorative slumber. Taken from Thomas Stanley's *History of Philosophy* (1656), the passage describes Chrysippus's view of care as both a natural impulse and the first property of living creatures. Over the course of this book, I will show how ancient Stoic physicalism and its foundational theory of care are reanimated through early modern works that turn to the unconsciously regenerative processes of life and the subtler, stranger sensations that emerge in sleep: from psychosomatic slackness to perceptual drift and other such liminal experiences at the boundaries of conscious thought and intentionality. Central here is the Stoic concept of *oikeiôsis*, which lacks a precise English translation but includes senses of dearness, affiliation, appropriation, and belonging. Oikeiôsis names the ethical development of animal life from an incipient mode of care for its organic physical constitution into a fully realized ecological cosmopolitanism among living beings. For the Stoics, we are all citizens of a thriving cosmic whole, striving to find our place in it. Sleep plays a distinctive role in this process by relaxing the perceptive tension that animates thought and action, which restores the foundational balance of the soul's ruling principle and harmonizes its motions with the *pneuma*, or the active principle of reason that permeates all physical entities in the Stoic cosmos. Drawing on the Stoic model of oikeiôsis and the therapeutic role it conceives for sleep, early modern writers rethink the place of sleep in their own literary constructions of ethical care and domestic affiliation. In short, they are captivated by the seemingly paradoxical yet recalcitrant truth that while sleep is an experience defined by carelessness, it also discloses a distinctive form of care on which human life depends. For these writers, sleep constitutes an immanent virtue and a norm-positing capacity for psychosomatic restoration. Meanwhile, they view the condition of sleeplessness as a harmful and often involuntary amplification of waking cares, which becomes a much greater threat to the ethical flourishing and cohesion of persons and polity alike.

This latter point is crucial to the arc of the book. It is borne out by the etymology of a word representing a special kind of hell that plagues many a modern soul: *insomnia*. While the word "sleep" can be traced to Old English texts as early as the ninth century, "insomnia" does not frequently appear in print until the eighteenth century. Henry Cockeram's *English Dictionary* (1623) contains an entry for "Insomnie" that defines it as "watching, want of power to sleepe," which suggests that in its earliest uses, the term could mark both a specific lack—a "want of power"—on the part of the self as well as a commitment to nocturnal vigilance connoted by the word "watch."[8] Before "insomnia" was regularly used in print, writers typically employed some variant of "sleepless" to describe the condition of not sleeping when one was supposed to do so, though even this term only appears for the first time in print during the fifteenth century.[9] Such a sketch of its lexical history gives credence to the notion that insomnia begins to emerge as both a distinctive historical concept and an ethical problem for the care of early modern embodied life—meaning the bodies of self and others, as well as the social body of the polity—and that this moment represents a shift away from longstanding political-theological wisdom asserting the necessary and mutually reinforcing relationship between vigilance and care in models of governance. In other words, both sleep and sleeplessness undergo a significant and mutually affecting transformation during the early modern period: while sleep does not entirely shed its associations with spiritual peril and deathliness, it is increasingly valued for its restoration of the laboring body burdened with cares, while the debilitating threat of insomnia is seen as a vital concern in the care for physical life.

One might think that in this way my argument stretches to attribute a secular view of the care for physical life and its value to depictions of sleep in early modern literature. That is not the case, though my readings of sleep and insomnia will tiptoe between sacred and secular determinations in assessing the early modern valuation of physical life, as well as its standing in relation to the norms of vigilance that shape prominent figurations of sovereign and spiritual care. Following Graham Hammill's characterization of early modern political theology as "an ongoing entanglement and antagonism between two discrete discourses and styles of thinking—politics and theology," I understand the literary writers whose works I discuss to articulate a tense, sometimes contradictory, yet often productive relationship between the ethical demands of physical life and spiritual virtue, or between political and theological calculations of the care for human life.[10] In so doing, these writers show their disdain for the shared commitments to martial and spiritual vigilance that guide much political-theological and Renaissance humanist wisdom on the virtues of care. While Heywood, Shakespeare, Spenser, and Milton may at times attribute a sacred significance to the dormant life that guards against corrosive forms of excessive wakefulness, they also understand the reproductive capacities and value of that life to be grounded in the *physis* of the unconscious material body. In other words, their aim is to deny in both ideological and practical terms the paradigm of vigilance that shapes early modern understandings of ethical life and virtuous activity. And insofar as these writers articulate a view of sleep's restorative power that is immanent to living bodies—and, indeed, acts as a source of shelter from the harms of sovereign domination and the self-instrumentalizing ends of humanism—we can say that sleep for them constitutes a form of bio-power that may or may not be sacralized, but which need not be taken as a theological notion in itself.

Because this vital power of sleep is amenable to—and in some cases, directly modeled upon—the pagan cosmology of ancient Stoic thought, it also affords a broader view of what theology might mean in early modernity as writers strain beyond the confines of humanist Christian doctrine in assessing the life of sleep. For the Stoics, Zeus is pneuma: the rational and active body that is thoroughly blended with all passive matter throughout the cosmos, forming its hylozoic and panpsychic unity. When Margaret Cavendish argues that Nature is a single, organic whole and recognizes an "innate matter" that acts as "a kind of God or gods to the dull part of matter, having the power to form it,"[11] or when she suggests that "innated matter, is the soul of nature" and the "dull part of matter, the body," she affirms ancient Stoic principles that imbue physical matter with a cosmic rationality that is both an active principle and a body in its own right.[12] From one angle, then, the accounts of physical life and sleep in this book might be drawn into the circle of arguments made by critics whose readings of early modern literature track processes of secularization in western Europe: the valuation of physical life looks ahead to a world of medical and biological norms that treat the body in merely, if not purely, physical terms.[13] But from another vantage, the restorative physis of sleeping life and its conceptual debt to the Stoic doctrine of the pneuma would seem to retain an unavoidably theological or at least spiritual quality that resists a decisive narrative of secularization. Without attempting to reconcile this impasse, the readings I pursue hold open possibilities afforded by both secular and theological strands of thought, hewing closely to the sort of openness concerning panpsychism and nature that is staked out by Thomas Nagel in *Mind and Cosmos*. Nagel's recent work sustains a set of philosophical convictions that are given life in the early modern period by the writers at the heart of this book. Like Nagel, they are unconvinced that purely materialist understandings of the physical cosmos—such as those elaborated by Epicurean atomism—can fully account for sentience and mental life, or that teleology should have no bearing upon our understanding not only of the actions and orientations of living beings but also the physical matter that circulates through the cosmos. Such positions guide this book's recovery and reactivation of what I see as critically underappreciated and often misunderstood aspects of Stoicism, and fuel my hope to restore a fuller understanding of Stoic thought in early modern studies and in humanistic inquiry more broadly.

From Stoic Physicalism to English Vitalism

By tracking an intellectual current from the resurrection of Senecan drama and Stoicism in sixteenth-century English humanist thought to the later seventeenth-century vitalisms of John Milton and Margaret Cavendish, this book makes a novel case for the role of Stoic cosmology and ancient virtue ethics in early modern literature and in the so-called new philosophy. Milton and Cavendish are widely recognized for their contributions to the period of English materialist thought that John Rogers has aptly dubbed the "Vitalist Moment,"[14] but I am arguing that in some sense these writers mark the fulfillment of roughly a century's worth of English literary engagement with ancient Stoic physicalism in its conviction that ethical life is constituted through knowledge of physical bodies, and with the Stoic project of articulating a "vital cosmology" that serves as the natural foundation of ethical and political attachments to the self and others.[15] And it is precisely when turning our attention to sleep and the ethics of care in late sixteenth- and early seventeenth-century literature that these connections appear, first taking shape in Jasper Heywood's seminal 1561 translation of Seneca's *Hercules Furens*, and followed by William Shakespeare's *Hamlet*, *Macbeth*, and *King Lear*, Edmund Spenser's *The Faerie Queene*, and John Milton's *Paradise Lost*. A chapter is devoted to each of these writers and their respective works, while this book's coda situates the treatment of sleep, sensation, and corporeal life in Margaret Cavendish's *Observations upon Experimental Philosophy* in light of her dismissals of Cartesian thought. This final juxtaposition of Cavendish with Descartes allows me to clarify how the latter's mechanistic physiology and his ethical valuation of the sheer longevity of bodily life sever the intimate connections among corporeal life, teleology, and care that the Stoics developed, and which are taken up anew by vitalist thinkers like Cavendish in her investigations of the inherent capacities of physical matter.

Early modern literary studies has seen a recent effulgence of brilliant monographs on ancient materialism and early modern literature, yet the predominant focus has been on the assimilation of Epicurean atomism by way of Lucretius's *De Rerum Natura* (c. 50 BC).[16] Among the growing number of conversations on the nature of matter and life in early modern thought, however, we lack a sustained and coherent account of the place of Stoic physicalism. The doctrine of oikeiôsis most likely emerged as a direct challenge to Epicurean moral psychology and its atomistic cosmology of the swerve, so it is all the more apparent that a revaluation of ancient Stoic physicalism and its ethical cosmology is timely and appropriate.[17] Chapter 1 offers an account of physical life and sleep in Jasper Heywood's translation of *Hercules Furens* that addresses some of the field's influential yet incomplete characterizations of Stoicism as a doctrine advocating either the radical separation of self and world or the virtuous elimination of all feeling as a basis for action, through a focus on Hercules's careworn body and his collapse into sleep. The sixteenth- and seventeenth-century writers I discuss in the following chapters further reveal the limitations inherent to the dominant image of Stoic thought when they explore the subtle physiology of sleep and the nature of corporeal bodies in light of some core Stoic insights: that an ethical life is lived in accordance with physical nature and its teleological orientations, and that caring for self and others involves an intimate understanding of the corporeal mixtures that generate and sustain both life and virtue in the cosmos—itself understood as a living physical organism to which we relate affectively as parts of an organic whole.

Humoralism of course provides the predominant early modern framework for assessing the influence of corporeal mixtures upon states of illness and health, as well as prescriptive measures conducive to the latter, including good sleep.[18] Sixteenth-century medical treatises, for instance, imagine very real and potentially unsettling correspondences between the physical position and horizontal extension of the sleeping body, its cycles of humoral recuperation, and the dissolution of mind that submerges waking consciousness at night. Physicians of body and spirit link disease, distemper, and even susceptibility to demonic meddling with improper practices of sleep. From sleeping while sitting upright, to not sleeping at noon, to avoiding "veneryous actes before the fyrste slepe, and specially [to] beware of suche thynges after dyner or after a full stomacke," the body's placement and position, its recent activities, and its customary diet were all thought to affect its humoral balance and to determine whether one slept well or whether one's sleep could potentially compromise good health.[19] To some, a sleeping body looked suspiciously like a dead body, and this reinforced a spiritual concern for the apparent ease with which sleep could slide into death. A treatise on health published in 1567 by Andrew Boorde actually lists a series of afflictions due to immoderate sleep, and suggests that physiological disease is deeply entangled with theological concerns and the multifaceted "powers of man":

> moderate slepe is acceptable in the syght of God. . . . And contraryle immoderate slepe and sluggysshenes doth humecte and maketh lyght the brayne, it doth ingendre rewme & impostumes, it is evyl for the palsy whyther it be universal or partyculer, it is evyl for the fallynge syckenes called Epilencia, Analencia, & Cathalencia, Appoplesia, Soda, with all other infyrmytyes in the heade. . . . And shortly to conclude it doth perturbe the naturall, and anymall, and spyrytuall powers of man. And specially it doth instigate and leade a manne to synne, and doth induce and infer brevyte of lyfe, & detestably it displeaseth God.[20]

Boorde's stark assessment of the perils of sleep underscore an early modern worry over the ways that bodily decay and death creep into life, since humoral spirits are at any moment capable of a sudden shift in inflection that harms both physiological and spiritual health. Hence, discussions of health and bodily practice also emphasized techniques for maximizing good sleep and guarding against its immoderate or evil forms. William Vaughan's *Approved Directions for Health, Both Naturall and Artificial* devotes three of its nine chapters to this problem, beginning by identifying the "*commodities of sleepe*" as follows: "Moderate sleepe strengtheneth all the spirits, comforteth the body, quieteth the Humours and pulses, qualifieth the heat of the liuer, taketh away sorrow, and asswageth furie of the minde."[21] By invoking sleep's capacity to calm psychic fury, Vaughan's musings also reflect longstanding associations of the perils of Herculean *ira* with the restorative salve of slumber—a view which Alastair Blanshard's character study of Hercules attributes to numerous early modern physicians and to their classical predecessors alike.[22] Vaughan goes on to recommend less sleep for sanguine and choleric men, and more sleep for men who are melancholic or phlegmatic; he offers prescriptions for sleep aids, alongside warnings against sleeping at noon or while wearing one's shoes, since the "thickness of the leather at the soles doth returne the hurtfull vapours of the feet (that else should vanish away) in the head and eyes."[23] Early modern sleep is a site of strategic self-care and evaluation, requiring an individualizing knowledge based on humoral type and physiological disposition that often takes aim at quelling eruptions of anger, fury, obstinacy, and distress.

The historian Sasha Handley has in fact argued that between the sixteenth and eighteenth centuries, "No other daily activity was so heavily governed by principles of good health, nor consumed as much time, money, and labour as did sleep."[24] Handley's book provides a valuable archive of cultural practices and habits bent toward caring for sleep during this period of transition, corroborating the notion that early modern sleep is increasingly drawn into the calculations of governance and productive activities that sustain modern biopolitical states. In the first volume of his *History of Sexuality*, Michel Foucault describes an intimate link between capitalism and the rise of biopolitics that depended upon a bourgeois consolidation of class consciousness around the life of the physical body during the eighteenth century.[25] But this valuation and discursive proliferation of techniques aiming at an "indefinite extension of strength, vigor, health, and life" does not simply spring ready-made into existence, as Foucault himself acknowledges throughout his College de France lecture series. More particularly, in his remarks on the Christian pastorate, Foucault treats pastoral power as a crucial precursor to biopolitics, arguing that "pastoral power is a power of care" routed through the figure of the shepherd who watches constantly over the flock. "Pastoral power initially manifests itself in its zeal, devotion, and endless application. . . . The shepherd is someone who keeps watch . . . above all else in the sense of vigilance with regard to any possible misfortune."[26] If the life of the physical body and the techniques of care that aim to support it during the sixteenth and seventeenth centuries are a concrete predecessor to biopolitics, then it is clear that sleep occupies a crucial position in those discursive formations—both as a potential threat to the constant watch of pastors and those who seek to emulate them, and as a necessary source of bodily restoration and a vital benefit to life.

Yet in the midst of mounting concerns with the practical aspects of sleep that seek to corral its restorative powers into more reliably virtuous habits, the sixteenth- and seventeenth-century writers I discuss also value sleep precisely for its mysterious inability to be tamed—in other words, for the seemingly paradoxical fact that its capacity to cure the physical ailments of work and the psychic toil of distress necessarily dissolve the psychosomatic foundations upon which waking care and spiritual vigilance depend. For that very reason, the restorative power of sleep is an ultimately ungovernable event that asserts the primacy of the physical body and the cosmic forces that engender it. It is perhaps this aspect of sleep that makes it most notable in the genealogy of biopolitics and ethical care: sleep invariably eludes efforts to capture and control it, a situation that affirms, from a different angle, Foucault's thought that even under regimes of biopower life is not "totally integrated into techniques that govern and administer it; it constantly escapes them."[27] While his claim is a helpful reminder that the biopolitical mastery over life encounters limits to its successful application, in this passage Foucault means limitations of the sort that arise through continued instances of famine, disease, and other forms of biological risk that threaten the reproduction and proliferation of species life. My point concerning early modern sleep and biopower is different. It is that the autopoietic capacities of the living physical body depicted in early modern literature are both ontologically and historically prior to the modes of biopolitical governance and care that Foucault describes, and that the restorative power of sleep is an inherently intractable form of biopower—one that early modern writers recognize as a site of shelter and resistance to the vigilant core of political theology and the norms of humanist care.[28]

Physiology, Normativity, and Biopower

I have given a fairly broad sketch of how the early modern valuation of sleep has a place in literary histories of ethical care, along with some of its biopolitical implications. But there is more to say about the relationship between ethical norms, biopower, and the philosophical and literary histories this book seeks to recover. Early modernists have for some time looked to Giorgio Agamben's conceptual and historical revisions of Michel Foucault's theories of biopower and biopolitics as a way of grappling with the significance of biological life vis-à-vis early modern political theology and ethical norms.[29] For Agamben, biological life is always captured by a transcendent *dispositif* of sovereignty and is thereby ineluctably placed in a relation of subordinate dependence to ethical and political activity. Moreover, he argues that this structure has been in operation since the political community of the ancient Greeks, though the course of history in the West has seen the separation of *bios* from *zoé* become less salient or successful as a political strategy for organizing human life. The advent of modern biopolitics marks a kind of inversion by which *zoé* has instead become a regular domain of political activity, and human life more thoroughly inscribed by the structure of an exception separating bare life from political belonging. Lying dormant in the natural life of every citizen, the exceptional status of the sacred can be reawakened at any moment through the exercise of sovereignty. As Agamben writes in *Homo Sacer*, "Bare life is no longer confined to a particular place or a definite category. It now dwells in the biological body of every living being."[30] For this reason, Agamben argues that the task of ethico-political thinking, if not thinking per se, is to escape the grasp of the biopolitical machine of sovereignty.

Against this line of thought, I am suggesting that ancient Greek ethics and its grounding in life's teleological orientations afford other possibilities for understanding the normative and biopolitical significance of physical life—a claim that is in solidarity with Julia Lupton's incisive readings of the biopolitical valences of action and virtue in *Thinking with Shakespeare*, and with Garret Sullivan's argument in *Sleep, Romance, and Human Embodiment* that early modern sleep summons virtues that Aristotelian thought ascribes to the nutritive soul.[31] In assessing the biopolitical significance of early modern sleep and the ethics of care, however, this book's philosophical bedfellows are the Stoics. Building on premises established by Aristotle, the Stoics envision not simply a conciliation but rather a direct passage of growth from physical life and sensation into ethical normativity, one that eschews the logic of Agamben's biopolitical machine and offers underappreciated resources for thinking how the "flexible crease between *bios* and *zoē*" that Lupton describes as an abiding concern of Shakespearean drama is taken up by other sixteenth- and seventeenth-century writers captivated by sleeping life and its ethical significance.[32] The Stoics view both the impulse to survive and the capacity to restore life as virtues in themselves—in the language of biopolitics, they articulate a nascent disposition of *zoé*, or physical life, to care for itself and to develop care more broadly as the telos of a life whose embodied pneuma participates in the cosmic web of causation. For the Stoics, *zoé* is not constrained to the fate of an inclusionary exclusion ultimately dominated by the sovereignty of *bios*, and so the sleeping life that Agamben argues is merely another instance of a hidden biological "stowaway" accompanying us on our biopolitical journey is in fact a condition that elucidates our ontological and normative foundations in physical life—foundations that we share with other living organisms that are also bodily parts of the organic being that is the cosmos at large.[33] Within this cosmic framework sleep relaxes the psychosomatic tension by which living souls grasp their own constitution as well as the natural order of the cosmos, yet in doing so sleep also brings them into closer contact with the vitalistic foundations of care that sustain the living whole.

This Stoic conception of physical life in its organic disposition toward care bears some striking affinities with the thought of Georges Canguilhem, the French philosopher of science and teacher of Michel Foucault. More specifically, the Stoic ethical theory of oikeiôsis as the natural impulse and first principle of life finds a modern analogue in his theory of biological normativity, which is also an intellectual precursor to Foucault's conception of biopower. For Canguilhem and the Stoics alike, there is a deep connection between physiological activity and value that serves as the basis of their understanding of the life principle. While he does not engage Stoicism explicitly, Canguilhem's interest in ancient virtue ethics and biology are clear from writings in which he describes Aristotle's conception of life as an inherently "plastic power" that in turn informs Canguilhem's own vitalism.[34] For Canguilhem, this power of life manifests in the positing of biological norms, which life generates as it struggles against whatever "obstructs its preservation and development taken as norms."[35] As he argues in *The Normal and the Pathological*,

> life is a polarity and thereby even an unconscious position of value; in short, life is in fact a normative activity. *Normative*, in philosophy, means every judgment which evaluates or qualifies a fact in relation to a norm, but this mode of judgment is essentially subordinate to that which establishes norms. Normative, in the fullest sense of the word, is that which establishes norms. And it is in this sense that we plan to talk about biological normativity. We think that we are as careful as anyone as far as the tendency to fall into anthropomorphism is concerned. We do not ascribe a human content to vital norms but we do ask ourselves how normativity essential to human consciousness would be explained if it did not in some way exist in embryo life.[36]

In this remarkable passage, Canguilhem contends that life is defined by an organic, norm-positing capacity that extends through conscious and unconscious forms of activity, or through sleeping and waking life alike. According to Canguilhem, life abides by physiological constants that provide a functional foundation—beginning even with embryonic life—which he describes as "habitual norms" that are made and remade anew by the organism. Through habit, physiological constants become malleable sites of agency as they respond to individual and social forms of influence, yet nonetheless draw their inherent power from what Canguilhem describes as "man's functional plasticity, linked in him to vital normativity."[37] Biological norms thus aim, first and foremost, at the fundamental preservation of a given entity's organic life and its capacity to posit norms on terms most amenable to it. For this reason, he asserts that "physiological constants must be definable, other than metaphorically, as virtues in the old sense of the word, which blends virtue, power and function. . . . The physiological constant is the expression of a physiological optimum in given conditions among which we must bear in mind those which the living being in general, and *homo faber* in particular, give themselves."[38] In other words, Canguilhem is concerned to show that what is good for a particular organism involves norms shaped both consciously and unconsciously through the biological processes that sustain it, and which cannot be entirely captured by medical or scientific forms of knowledge that situate individual cases in light of socially preestablished norms.

In aiming to reactivate this "old sense" of the virtues, Canguilhem's language also aligns his theory of vital normativity with ancient Greek conceptions of the intimate relationship between virtue and physical life—a relationship that has been severely underplayed in the work of Agamben through his insistence upon a decisive separation between spheres of biological and ethico-political life, or *zoé* and *bios*. Canguilhem's account of life's plastic power and habitual norms shares the naturalist insight of the Greeks, a view of life as function that is present in Aristotle's writings and in the ethical cosmology of the Stoics. The Stoics take this view to its logical and conceptual limit by arguing that the cosmos itself is a living body whose functional activities are guided by the agential and rational motions of the pneuma. While the Stoics are also the source of the familiar claim against Aristotle that virtue is itself sufficient for *eudaimonia*, the explanation behind this idea involves a sophisticated vision of the normative significance of organic life, and the extent to which virtue amounts to acting in accordance with a natural and physical disposition of the soul's ruling principle, or *hêgemonikon*. More particularly, the Stoic theory of oikeiôsis provides the first principle and conceptual foundation on which this ethical system rests, and the doctrine shares Canguilhem's conviction that natural life, or *zoé*, posits value and thereby posits norms in the activity of living.[39] The essential point here is that the core affinities between Canguilhem and the Stoics elucidate early modern conceptions of the ethical and biopolitical significance of sleep. Early modern writers are informed by a Stoic cosmological virtue ethics that ascribes a norm-positing capacity to the physiological activity that sustains life, even in its embryonic forms, and which contends that the orientation to one's embodied constitution is inherently a political matter. The Stoics, that is, are uniquely biopolitical thinkers whose principles animate the early modern biopolitics of sleep.

This claim calls for some principled explanation, which begins with Stoic physics. Stoics contend that all material entities, from dirt to rocks to animals, are a combination of physical matter and pneuma. The two cannot exist without each other, and insofar as matter and pneuma are ontologically inseparable, the Stoics do not countenance the familiar dualism of body and soul. They rather adhere to a form of monism that is both cosmological and cognitive. On the one hand, the cosmos is an organic living whole and each of its parts is physically existent as a semiautonomous entity. Yet on the other hand, each physical entity that constitutes a single part of this whole is infused to a certain degree with the presence of the pneuma, constituting the basis of a vitalistic panpsychism that distributes various capacities among the individual parts of the cosmic whole. Rocks, for instance, indicate the presence of the pneuma through their basic physical cohesion; the pneuma generates the minimal degree of tension or *tonos* necessary for them to hold together as rocks. For other kinds of physical entities, the pneuma provides other sorts of capacities. For animal beings, the *tonos* generated through the motions of the pneuma makes sensation possible, and for human beings this tension also provides a capacity for conceptual understanding that can grasp the finely grained order of the cosmos and its web of causes. But in all cases, these varying capacities result from the particular activity and degree of tension established by the tug and pull that occurs between the pneuma and the physical material that it shapes. So while it is important to recognize that the pneuma is itself rational and present in all physical bodies, it does not provide all entities with the ability to grasp the rational workings of the cosmos—or with the knowledge that virtue is synonymous with achieving this understanding of nature and bringing one's actions into alignment with it. Humans are provided with this capacity by nature, but they must work to develop it properly and to its fullest expression by training their souls. This point is at the heart of Stoic virtue ethics and its ancient conception of care. Yet unlike Plato or Aristotle, who hold similar views concerning the need to care for the soul, the Stoics are cognitive monists in that they do not think the human soul is divided into different domains, potentially at war with each other. Instead, the soul is a unity whose natural function simply is, in the case of human animals, reason. Passion is nothing more than an unnatural agitation of the rational corporeal soul, rather than an upheaval or rebellion by a lower part of the soul against its higher intellective function.

Of course, my account of Stoic ethical cosmology thus far has been silently guided by the ideal framework handed down to us through writings and fragments attributed to the school's chief thinkers. The question of passion invariably raises the specter of human error, and the possibility of failing to abide by the rational motions of the pneuma that guide the actions of the Stoic sage. Much more will be said on this matter in chapter 2, with respect to the apparent dilemma it presents for realizing the Stoic paradigm of virtue, and the question of how a cosmos supposedly permeated by the spirit of reason can give rise to passionate and irrational judgments. But here it is sufficient to note that the Stoics presume the course of human life will in fact be beset by error and failure, and that their model of virtue ethics in no way implies easy success. The cosmos is an organic whole, but the play of forces spread across its many parts makes for a reality of turbulent and volatile physical mixtures. This point holds true for human bodies as well as others, meaning that physical transformations can temporarily agitate and pervert the motions of reason, in effect bringing the illness of passion to an otherwise healthy body. As Seneca writes in his ethical treatise on the passion known as *ira* or anger, "Prolonged assistance is needed against constant and prolific evils, not so they cease, but so they don't gain the upper hand."[40] Such susceptibility is precisely why the Stoic ethics of care seeks to develop therapeutic measures by which life might actively adjust itself to the challenging conditions it faces in order to achieve the good. For the Stoics, passion twists the corporeal soul into an unnatural and confused state that the pursuit of *eudaimonia* aims to correct. And the cosmic volatility that leads passion to grip the embodied human soul takes center stage in Senecan tragedy—as it does in those early modern works inspired by the Stoic playwright's vision of a tumultuous physical environment, through which passion circulates as a material body that constantly threatens to derail the pursuit of virtue.

This brief recapitulation of some core principles of Stoic physics and ethical psychology suggests the systematic nature of the school's philosophy, which prepares us for the tense encounter in Senecan drama between the turbulent reality of bodily mixtures in the Stoic cosmos and the normative ideal of the sage who masters them.[41] But what is most important to this book's argument concerning the Stoic ethics of care are the key features of its doctrine of oikeiôsis and the latter's connection to sleep. Oikeiôsis begins with the fundamental grasping of self-constitution that emerges in all sentient beings upon birth—it is an immediate disposition toward care that is given to all embodied life and which results from the motions of the pneuma. The earliest use of the term oikeiôsis is typically attributed to Zeno, the founder of the ancient Stoic school in Athens.[42] Sharing the same root as *oikos*, the Greek word for home, it has no direct English translation, but various renderings include affiliation, affinity, attachment, appropriation, domestic instinct, familiarization, and being near and dear.[43] These variations show the difficulty of finding a precise contemporary term that sufficiently captures the ancient Greek sense of a process that is at once ethical and natural, political and cosmological, and which orients the living being toward its proper objects of care beginning with itself. For the Stoics, animal life is born with an innate understanding of its constitution as a living being endowed with certain physical capacities, and as it grows into the sort of organism it is, these capacities further develop and expand to include concentric circles of care proper to the life of the being from which they extend. This process is the ongoing activity of oikeiôsis, and the Stoics envision its ultimate telos as a community of cosmic citizens whose polis is the organic, living whole of the universe and whose nomos is revealed to them through the natural motions of the pneuma. To be a good citizen is to grasp the ultimately rational motions of the cosmos and to live and act in accordance with them. As Hans Blumenberg rightly suggests, Stoic reason is a cosmic reason of care, a *divina cura* that flows through the living cosmos and through each entity that is part of that whole. And the pneuma that is the rational soul of the cosmos provides the impulse through which oikeiôsis first emerges in animal life as a nascent sense of its own constitution.[44] Along such lines, Daniel Heller-Roazen argues based on passages from Seneca's ethical letters that "the living being, [as Seneca] repeats, senses before all else its 'constitution.' If it adapts itself to itself in caring for itself, it does so because of this primary sensation alone, which refers not to itself but to its nature."[45]

And what of sleep? We might expect the Stoics to follow their ancient Greek predecessors in viewing sleep as a function of the living soul that occurs entirely outside of its rational activity.[46] Yet the Stoic view of sleep is not prone to such sharp distinctions, as it reflects a conviction that even in sleep our souls are bound up with the rational motions of the cosmos as they continue to embody a disposition toward care. The Stoics define sleep as a slackening of the perceptive tension that animates living beings. Because life is constituted by the tension between pneuma and physical body, a complete slackening of this tension amounts to the death of the organism, whereas sleep merely reduces the degree of psychosomatic tension that constitutes life. As the Stoics reportedly argued, "Sleep occurs when the sensory tension is relaxed in the ruling part of the soul."[47] While one consequence of this slackening is the temporary suspension of rational cognition and clarity in sensorial awareness, Stoic texts also note that oikeiôsis continues even while animals are asleep, and the sleeping Hercules is in fact a paradigmatic example. In his treatise *Elements of Ethics* (c. 150 AD), Hierocles the Stoic mentions Hercules clutching his club as a perfect instance of oikeiôsis in sleep. He notes that if part of our body becomes cold while we are asleep, we draw the blanket closer to us; likewise, if we are wounded we keep those parts of our body free from pressure, "even if we are sleeping profoundly, as though we were employing, if I may put it this way, a fully awake attention . . . so will signs of their disposition filter through the bodies of those who are sleeping. Thus, for example, Heracles too sleeps grasping his club in his right hand."[48] The physical disposition toward care continues even while we sleep, because the activity of the pneuma itself continues. Such activity in sleep shows that the motions of the pneuma are disposed by nature to act in accordance with reason, even when our embodied souls are not sufficiently tense to cognitively grasp those motions. The broader implication here is that through sleep, the embodied soul participates in a kind of virtue, insofar as sleep restores the foundational tension that orients it toward the vital rationality of the cosmos. And Hercules clutching his club serves as a paradigmatic figure for this uniquely Stoic notion of a care for life that continues to hold onto that which is dear even when our souls slumber.

This point is consistent with the philosopher Jacob Klein's broader account of Stoic oikeiôsis as a baseline of self-perception that disposes the animal soul's hêgemonikon toward care but also reveals its connection with a larger, living ecology of interconnected ends. As he explains, "What seems clear from oikeiôsis accounts . . . is that the doctrine of self-perception supplies a crucial link, within the Stoic system, between cosmic teleology and psychological theory . . . [it is] a motivational theory that aims to explain appropriate action in both animals and humans on the basis of self-awareness and accurate cognition."[49] Tension within and among bodies draws them together into a cosmic web of causes that spreads to infinity. Yet the foundational tension that allows physical entities to cohere and which animates living beings is the same in kind, though different in degree, as that which causes the cognitive grasping of concepts by certain souls. Accordingly, Klein describes the Stoic theory of impulse (*horme*), or the natural inclination of the hêgemonikon to act, as "a characteristically Stoic extension of a Socratic point, one that applies a cognitive theory of motivation—remarkably—to a much wider analysis of living organisms."[50] All organic beings perceive cognitively, in the sense that perception is an event presenting an image of the world to the percipient, whether or not said picture also involves a conceptually structured and rational understanding. But the point Klein makes here is intended to illustrate the common foundation of all life, indeed of all physical entities, in the Stoic cosmos. The basis upon which normative judgments are consciously made is the same natural basis upon which the unconsciously rational motions of the cosmos circulate and bring about the particular ends that are proper to any given entity, ranging from the cohesion of a simple physical body and its orientation toward preserving that cohesion to a full and conceptually structured grasping of the workings of the cosmos. To return to the paradigmatic example of Hercules, the grasping of his club in sleep is constituted by a tension that is same in kind yet different in degree as that which leads him to perform virtuous actions in waking life.

These aspects of Stoic thought reveal the sense in which I argue the Stoics are biopolitical thinkers: they forge a unique theory of the mutually reinforcing relationship between the physical motions that sustain biological life and the forms of ethical care and political belonging that grow naturally from that foundation. Sleep is a condition that illustrates these fundamental presuppositions of Stoic ethical psychology by revealing the distinctive connection between physical life and care articulated in the school's theory of oikeiôsis. But these Stoic principles are also worth uncovering because the two thinkers whose work has indelibly shaped our contemporary understanding of biopolitics—Foucault and Agamben—have both responded to Stoic thought quite differently, and in terms that tend to ignore or even obscure the ideas I want to foreground. As is well known, in his investigations of the history of the care of the self, Foucault engages with a range of ancient philosophical thinkers that includes the Stoics as well as their Athenian predecessors, Socrates, Plato, and Aristotle. Foucault looks in *The Care of the Self* to numerous examples of Stoic ethical thought culled from Greek and Roman thinkers who underscore the Socratic obligation to care for one's soul by establishing an ethical and practical relation of the self to the self. Foucault is no doubt correct in drawing our attention to the Socratic legacy of this idea and the place of Stoic philosophy within it. But in his book's account of Stoicism he only briefly mentions the Stoic conviction that the proper care of the self does not isolate the self from its social relations. It is easy to miss this point as it arrives at an early moment in his text, and more so given the book's emphasis upon ancient notions of self-oriented activities of careful regulation and attention to the individual body and soul. Yet as Foucault acknowledges, ancient societies placed individuals within "strong systems" of interpersonal dependence. "Furthermore," as he writes,

> it should be noted that the doctrines that were most attached to austerity of conduction—and the Stoics can be placed at the head of the list—were also those which insisted the most on the need to fulfill one's obligations to mankind, to one's fellow-citizens, and to one's family, and which were quickest to denounce an attitude of laxity and self-satisfaction in practices of social withdrawal.[51]

Foucault is right to describe contempt for social withdrawal as a central feature of Stoic ethics, though this facet of the school's thought is more often than not forgotten in contemporary discussions.[52] Yet while he acknowledges the social, if not cosmic, orientation of the Stoic good in *The Care of the Self*, Foucault's book by and large focuses on the individually practical aspects of Stoic ethical thought, drawing most of its examples from texts by Epictetus, Galen, Seneca, and Marcus Aurelius.

However, in his 1981–1982 College de France lectures published as *The Hermeneutics of the Subject*, Foucault takes further steps toward assessing both the social and cosmic dimensions of Stoic ethical thought. He contends that for Seneca the goal of Stoic ethics can only be achieved "at the cost of the knowledge of nature that is, at the same time, knowledge of the totality of the world."[53] Foucault goes on to unpack this Senecan unification of ethics and cosmology at it appears in his ecological treatise, *Natural Questions* (c. 62 AD), noting the philosopher's claim that freedom is rooted in the law of nature and that our reason is of the same kind as the divine reason that permeates the cosmos. According to the Roman Stoic, Foucault argues,

> what is actually involved in this real investigation [of the soul] is understanding the rationality of the world in order to recognize, at that point, that the reason that presided over the organization of the world, and

> which is God's reason itself, is of the same kind as the reason we possess that enables us to know it. To reiterate, this discovery that human and divine reason share a common nature and function together is not brought about in the form of the recollection of the soul looking at itself, but rather through a movement of the mind's curiosity exploring the order of the world.[54]

Though he does not mention the concept explicitly, Foucault's analysis of Seneca's text reveals the logic of oikeiôsis and its central role in Stoic ethical thought. It is through a natural orientation to cosmic reason that the hêgemonikon, or ruling principle of the soul, is capable of the sort of exploration that Foucault sees working in Seneca's cosmological treatise. For the Stoics, the proper care of the self means that one is preserving one's natural self-constitution and therefore maintaining the functional state of the hêgemonikon, which allows for the grasping of the natural order and leads to right action. This is oikeiôsis, as the care for one's self expands into ever-widening circles to include the care for others and for the cosmos at large. This integration of the self with the cosmos through the care of the self, as Foucault suggests, aims at a communion with the Stoic God of reason, allowing us "to find ourselves again, the text says, '*in consortium Dei*': in a sort of co-naturalness or co-functionality with God. That is to say, human reason is of the same nature as divine reason."[55] It is for this reason that Seneca contends in his ethical letters to Lucilius, as Foucault remarks, that "the virtuous soul is a soul which is in contact with the whole universe and which carefully contemplates everything making up its events, activities and processes."[56] To be virtuous is to be a natural scientist and sage at once, turning one's attention to the physical motions of the living cosmos and to one's own physical position as part of that organism and its living processes. Yet apart from these passages reflecting on Seneca's *Natural Questions*, Foucault does not further explore the cosmological and physiological basis of Stoic ethics, nor does he explicitly mention the doctrine of oikeiôsis.

Meanwhile, Giorgio Agamben, the other biopolitical thinker whose work has been most widely taken up among early modernists, has written briefly on Stoic ethics and the concept of oikeiôsis in *The Use of Bodies*, the most recent and final volume in his *Homo Sacer* series. Agamben's discussion of Stoic oikeiôsis is inflected by his book's overarching aim of establishing a political ontology of use, or *chresis*, which he argues is the key to comprehending oikeiôsis. Perhaps unsurprisingly, Agamben's interpretation of Stoic oikeiôsis does not address the role of reason or the underpinning tension between the physical body and the pneuma that establishes the corporeal soul's hêgemonikon. He instead approaches the doctrine from a phenomenological perspective, arguing that its deepest significance is the Stoic revelation that selfhood consists in a relation between the fundamental sense of self and the use to which that sense is put; the self is therefore nonsubstantial and more like a process disclosed by the immediate relation between use and awareness. As Agamben writes,

> if use, in the sense that we have seen, means being affected, constituting-oneself insofar as one is in relation with something, then use-of-oneself coincides with *oikeiosis*, insofar as this term names the very mode of being of the living being. The living being uses-itself, in the sense that in its life and in its entering into relationship with what is other than the self, it has to do each time with its very self, feels the self and familiarizes itself with itself. The self is nothing other than use-of-oneself.[57]

One advantage of Agamben's reading is that it captures the subtlety of the relation that the Stoics conceive between impulse and care—we are thrown, to appropriate a Heideggerian formulation, into our care to the extent that as living beings we immediately sense our physical constitution as such and are disposed to care for and to act in natural accordance with it. But Agamben also identifies this baseline sensation and orientation toward care with a mode of nonrational awareness, which I would argue is in the unstated interest of preserving its affinity with his own concept of inoperativity, which is the value he attributes to the refusal or suspension of the political instrumentalization that Agamben views as an apparatus of sovereignty. Hence he claims, based on a reading of Seneca's letter 121, that "the familiarity and self-sensation of which the Stoics speak [as the basis of oikeiôsis] do not entail a rational consciousness but seem to be obscurely immanent to the very use-of oneself."[58] There is a kind of murkiness in Agamben's formulation here, which the account of oikeiôsis that I have been developing reveals as a real limitation. By "rational consciousness" I imagine Agamben means something like a fully awake and alert attention that conceptually grasps a state of affairs and which must therefore be opposed to the immanently obscure sensations and mode of awareness he attributes to oikeiôsis. Yet as I have shown, Stoic thinkers do not only argue that oikeiôsis carries on even during sleep and—we must presume—other experiences that similarly slacken the perceptive tension of the pneuma without dissolving it completely. The Stoics also contend that even these unconscious physical motions and states of sensation, for all their fuzziness and obscurity, are manifestations of a cosmic reason whose fundamentally physical nature is in kind no different from the rationality that characterizes human cognition in its sharpest and most lucid form. The point here is that Agamben wants to draw lines or conceptual caesurae where, at least as far as the Stoics are concerned, there are none. So while his interpretation of oikeiôsis aims to transcribe the concept into terms that are amenable to the contours of Agamben's own ontological-biopolitical machine—with the aim of rendering it inoperative—there are reasons to resist that maneuver. If animal oikeiôsis, human and otherwise, is inherently a rational and physical process at once, then Agamben's assessment of Stoic ethics elides the normative grounds on which the concept rests, and misses a foundational sense in which the Stoics articulate a biopolitical conception of the care for life that is continuous with cosmic reason.

Herculean Aesthetics

A book dedicated to works of drama and epic poetry would be lacking without a clear articulation of the relationship between its philosophical and aesthetic stakes. Insofar as sleep dissolves the virtuous coupling between wakefulness and the good held dear by humanist thought, it brings the human being into contact with a form of impersonal yet creative cosmic reason whose activity holds both ethical and aesthetic implications. In his ethical letters, Seneca returns to an ancient Stoic image of poetry as a superior means of activating sensation and drawing the human soul into a transformative encounter with such forces. Seneca attributes the original image to Cleanthes (c. 330–230 BC), second head of the Stoic school in Athens. Poetry is a uniquely constraining and productive medium, according to the Athenian Stoic, because it extracts and sharpens perceptions in a manner superior to that of mere prose:

> As our breath produces a brighter sound when a trumpet drives it through the narrows of an extended channel and spreads it at last through a wider opening, so our perceptions are rendered brighter by the narrow constraints of verse. The same material, when expressed in prose, meets with little interest and is less effective. But where verse accedes, and well-defined meters sharpen and expose the sense, that perception acquires the thrust of a hurled javelin.[59]

The passage provides us with a lucid instance of Stoic literary theory that unsurprisingly accords with both the systematic nature of the school's philosophy and its emphasis upon the vital breath or pneuma that generates the psychosomatic tension underpinning life, sensation, and the animal disposition toward care. Poetry at once brightens and sharpens the sensations it conveys across physical bodies, modulating the pneuma such that the perceptions it engenders pierce the auditor like a finely aimed weapon. The force of poetry in this regard resembles a striking image from Cleanthes's own "Hymn to Zeus," a work that has been described as a creative Stoic synthesis of ancient Greek literary and philosophical material ranging from Homer and Hesiod to Heraclitus and Pythagoras.[60] One passage in particular resonates with Seneca's citation of Cleanthes, in its depiction of the thunderbolt of Zeus as the creative and animating principle that guides the cosmos:

> This whole universe, spinning around the earth, truly
> Obeys you wherever you lead, and is readily ruled by you;
> Such a servant do you have between your unconquerable hands,
> The two-edged, fiery, ever-living thunderbolt.
> For by its stroke all works of nature [are guided].
> With it you direct the universal reason, which permeates
> Everything, mingling with the great and the small lights. (7–13)[61]

Zeus's thunderbolt figures the living and creative power of cosmic reason, the pneuma that also guides the javelin-like force of poetry uniquely housed—according to Cleanthes via Seneca—within the "narrow constraints of verse." Poetry does not simply reproduce or represent sensation, but draws it from the world and preserves it as a refined yet durable mode of creative being that continues to work upon and transform those who encounter it through the animating power of the pneuma.

The chapters ahead show how the literary afterlife of Seneca's sleeping Hercules renders in poetic form a field of somnolent sensations that constitute the ongoing presence and, indeed, durability of Stoic oikeiôsis as both a materially lived process and a site of aesthetic creativity. This figure of the sleeping Hercules resonates with a range of early modern works belonging to what Rolf Soellner has described as the "Hercules *furens* convention," a literary tradition long recognized for its influential reflections upon the psychosomatic and affective life of anger, not to mention the ethical consequences of indulging that passion.[62] But what has not been appreciated regarding Seneca's well-known tragedy is the strength of the connections it draws between Herculean *ira* and insomnia, as well as the crucial role played by the restorative corporeal motions of sleep and the moment of transformed awakening that follows. Herculean somnolence is a salve to the hero's mythical fury. Its curative virtues are reanimated and reconfigured by an early modern poetics of sleep and care that draws on this critically neglected aspect of the hero's legacy. I would like to suggest that the sleeping Hercules thus constitutes an aesthetic monument in the sense developed by Gilles Deleuze and Felix Guattari in *What Is Philosophy?* For Deleuze and Guattari, art thinks through percepts and affects that are extracted from the mortal physicality of lived experience to embody the timeless event. As they write, "A monument does not commemorate or celebrate something that happened but confides to the ear of the future the persistent sensations that embody the event: the constantly renewed suffering of men and women, their re-created protestations, their constantly resumed struggle."[63] A monument is not a decaying, concrete monolith of the past that endures into the present but rather a summoning of those timeless and transformative aspects of sensation that escape their temporal mooring in the physical mixtures of nature, and constitute the work of art in its struggle to emerge as such. Deleuze and Guattari thus provide an ontology and a metaphysics for the work that honors the idea (quite familiar among early modern writers) that art is a means by which life escapes its mortal constraints and participates in the eternal—a form of life whose piercing and transformative sensations accord with the ancient Stoic descriptions of the pneumatic force of poetry and of Zeus's guiding thunderbolt attributed to Cleanthes.

Yet Deleuze and Guattari's theory is no simple valorization of the artist as an inspired individual or master of their craft. It instead encompasses cosmic processes of radical deindividuation and desubjectification within a field of hyperrational activity and, in the case of literature, the genesis of a texture of resonance among artists, readers, and works across time: "It is in this way that, from one writer to another, great creative affects can link up or diverge, within compounds of sensations that transform themselves, vibrate, couple, or split apart: it is these beings of sensation that account for the artist's relationship with a public, for the relation between different works by the same artist, or even for a possible affinity between artists."[64] Along such lines, *Vital Strife* conceives the figure of sleeping Hercules from Senecan tragedy—itself a vibratory incarnation of the event in Euripides's ancient Greek tragedy *Herakles*—as an aesthetic monument that links up with the creative affects and percepts permeating early modern scenes of sleep and insomnia. In act 4 of Jasper Heywood's translation of *Hercules Furens*, the chorus prays over Hercules's prostrate form, asking that cosmic forces "Keepe him fast bounde with heavy sleepe opprest" until his sanity is restored. When Milton, nearly a century later, refers to Adam's sleep as a force of "soft oppression" in *Paradise Lost*, the affective and literary resonances across time with Heywood and, indeed, with both writers' classical predecessors emerge, and we should see the figure of Hercules's sleep living in and through Adam's. More than just a common use of words, the Herculean resonances at the heart of this book form a series of monumental figures of sleep, and a distinctive mode of literary and aesthetic life in struggle that reactivates Stoicism through a somnolent poetics of care. To be sure, Hercules lives many forms of life in early modern literature. Renaissance humanists often appeal to Hercules as a paradigm of virtue whose constant activity is to be emulated, as when Erasmus suggests in his *Adages* that "if any human labours ever deserved to be called Herculean, it is certainly the work of those who are striving to restore the great works of ancient literature."[65] Yet the Hercules I recover through Heywood's rendering of Seneca, and whose afterlife I trace among works by prominent humanist-educated writers following Erasmus, rather models the recuperative virtues of sleep as a much-needed therapy to the postures of vigilant care and exertion endorsed by Renaissance humanism in its own approximations of classical virtue ethics.

The Structure of the Book

The first chapter, "Heavy with Care," constructs a genealogy of sleep and care that provides essential philosophical, literary, and scientific materials for the book's argument, moving across a series of texts that I dub, following the Stoics, *oikeiôn*, or "dear," to early modern writers. I show that sleep occupies a compelling place in the ancient Greek philosophies of Heraclitus, Plato, and Aristotle, before moving to an account of its unique role in Stoic thought and in that school's doctrine of oikeiôsis—which is both an immediate habit into which we are born and an evolving process that naturally attaches the animal being to itself and to those things for which it rightly cares over the course of its life. I further examine implications of the Stoic argument that oikeiôsis continues even in sleep, an idea that departs from earlier Greek ethical thought which conceives a stricter separation between the life of sleep and the human good. The notion of sleep as an inferior form of life, I go on to argue, informs Christian political theologies of sleep and spiritual vigilance, from the Pauline epistles to writings of early monastic communities whose members weaponized wakefulness as a means to resist demonic temptation and fleshliness. I demonstrate how these perspectives inform Renaissance humanist theologians from Erasmus to Calvin to Luther, and that sleep is likewise seen as a condition in need of methodical discipline among English humanists and grammar school teachers including Richard Mulcaster. Such commitments to vigilant care reflect a longstanding connection between wakefulness and virtue in western thought—and a key point of departure for the writers at the heart of this book.

Chapter 2, "Hercules Asleep," elucidates the early English humanist revival of Stoicism through a case study of Jasper Heywood's translation of Seneca's tragedy, *Hercules Furens*. The play's central action hinges on a Stoic vision of the unruly cosmos and the volatile physical mixtures that constantly threaten to upend the care of the virtuous soul. Upon returning from the Underworld, Hercules and Theseus describe a living landscape of horrors and hellish sensations that seem to have remained with the hero as he massacres his family in a fit of madness. But I argue that this scene of fury and domestic annihilation is also brought on by a refusal to rest, which connects the ethics of self-care and *oikonomia* to the perils of insomnia. After murdering his kin, Hercules swoons and collapses into a fitful slumber. While he sleeps the Chorus prays that he remain "fast bounde with heavy sleepe opprest" so that "slumber deepe" might bring calm to his impassioned soul—thereby balancing its ruling principle and restoring the foundation of the hero's oikeiôsis. The argument of this chapter shows how early modern writers from Spenser to Milton could find in Seneca's tragedy a cosmological framework investing scenes of dormant life with an ethical power grounded in the therapy of rest—a power all the more remarkable in that it eludes Herculean self-mastery while nonetheless sustaining his virtuous labors. As an unconscious physical event, sleep escapes the muscular attention and purposive discipline of self-care for which Hercules is a paradigmatic figure. In *Hercules Furens*, sleep's ethical and physiological dimensions thus elaborate a tragic biopolitical friction between the life of virtue and the demands of the *oikos*, which Seneca's hero attempts to preserve against the motions of a turbulent physical cosmos.

In chapter 3, "'The Body Is with the King, but the King Is Not with the Body,'" I track Shakespeare's skepticism regarding the political theology of vigilant care that undergirds the theory of the King's Two Bodies, arguing that some of its guiding presumptions propel the biopolitical crises of state in the tragedies of *Hamlet*, *Macbeth*, and *King Lear*. In these plays, Shakespeare draws on principles of Stoic cosmology at the heart of Senecan drama by figuring sovereign sleep and insomnia as volatile events causing the physical and metaphysical transformation of the union of the King's Two Bodies. The tragedies of *Hamlet* and *Macbeth* both hinge on the violent deaths of sleeping kings and a politically chaotic aftermath, which resists the highly wrought fictions of constant vigilance, immortality, and stately perfection that buttress the doctrine of the King's Two Bodies. Kings Hamlet and Duncan alike fall prey to a form of sleep that underscores that condition's potential turn toward deathly physical mixtures and venomous environmental influence, as the sovereign succumbs to a period of careless slumber. Shakespeare's depictions of the physiological vulnerability of sleep as an ecological event illustrates his indebtedness to Seneca's depiction of Hercules's cosmological madness and swoon in particular, but I argue that the Stoic perspective of sleep as a simultaneously physiological and ethical benefit likewise informs the playwright's depictions of monarchical insomnia as a threat to the health of the sovereign's personal and political bodies. This latter point is particularly salient in the case of King Lear, whose cosmological rage and self-dissolution are only alleviated by the therapeutic virtues of sleep—a therapy that ties him explicitly to Seneca's Hercules and marks the finality of his separation from England's body politic. While Shakespearean tragedy thus exposes the outworn ideologies of the King's Two Bodies and its political theology of militant vigilance, taken together these plays more strikingly construct a vision of the emerging foundations of biopolitical governance, which rest upon the care for physical life and its immanent powers of restoration.

Chapter 4, "'Watching to Banish Care,'" turns to Spenser's epic poetry and shows how an early modern reactivation of the Stoic ethics of sleep challenges core principles of Pauline political theology. Chapter 5 of St. Paul's letter to the Ephesians is widely acknowledged as Spenser's source for the martial arms of Redcrosse knight. And Paul's epistles consistently use sleep to figure the unholy spiritual slumber from which Christians must awaken, forgoing all "fellowship" with the "workes of darknesse." If Pauline vigilance is key to Spenserian self-care and to the integrity of the ecclesiastical body, then the sleep that "melts" Redcrosse's "manly heart" in the first canto suggests a moment of dissolved fortitude that threatens to place him outside of the Pauline community. This scene has encouraged critics such as Northrop Frye and Deborah Shuger to read sleep in Spenser's epic as an existential threat, whose fluid force dissolves the psychic structures of heroic, Protestant virtue and humanist discipline. I argue that in book 1, Spenser acknowledges these valences while also aligning sleep with the restoration and recovery of Redcrosse knight's earthly life, which requires the hero to remove his armor at night. Spenser thus brings Redcrosse's physiological necessity for sleep into direct conflict with a stark approximation of the Pauline ideal of unwavering spiritual vigilance. Book 1's allegory of holiness suggests—contra Paul's paradigm—that human beings are radically unable to arise from spiritual sleep and to remain constantly vigilant due to the competing demands of physical life and waking cares. Hence, book 1 develops as its ethical paradigm a structure of mutual care modeled on Stoic oikeiôsis, and which only Redcrosse knight and Una can make whole. Meanwhile, in book 4, Spenser's turn toward forms of life and affiliation not buttressed by political theology emerges more clearly in his personification of Care as the headmaster to a team of hammering blacksmiths whose nocturnal labors keep Sir Scudamor from sleep. Care's minions circumvent sleep's vital powers of self-recovery and restoration using the hero's insomniac care to enlarge the stature of their allegorical master and exert a biopolitics of control over the animal oikeiôsis that organizes Scudamor's orientation toward self and world.

In chapter 5, "'Inhabit Lax,'" I argue that John Milton's *Paradise Lost* adapts Stoic principles concerning the nature of physical bodies, vitality, and cosmic reason, both in its depictions of the harmonious unity of slumbering prelapsarian life and in its imaginative vision of the origin of evil as a moment of insomnia. In Milton's epic, Satan's turn from God represents the primal scene of a discordance that introduces evil to the cosmos. And this original perversion takes place during a moment of sleeplessness by which Satan swerves from the harmonious motions of Heaven's slumbering angelic organism, as described by Raphael to Adam in book 5. Sleep reveals an immanent ecopolitical theology in Heaven, constituted by the physical motions of a vital spirit that flows through and gives shape to the organic corporeal unity of God's creation—consonant with the ancient Greek senses of organon as a musical instrument, a sense organ, and a tool used by an artisan. Like Seneca and the Stoics, Milton depicts sleep's slackness and regenerative powers as simultaneously physiological and ethical benefits, and the poet uses these associations to represent insomnia as a perverse threat to the living creature—and therefore an apt figure for the origin of evil. The slackening release of sleep is a sublime loosening of angelic being that opens these creatures to a deeper union with God, deindividuating their bodies and sensations in ways akin to the unconstrained union of angelic sex. And yet this slackness seems also to enable the possibility of turning away from God, upon which Lucifer acts to become the being of privation that is henceforth called Satan. Lucifer's pride becomes a vice that constrains him to wakefulness and radically divides him from the slumbering organic unity of Heaven. Insomnia thus serves as Milton's chief figure for the discordant influence of Satanic pride and rebellion, and for evil as a mode of privation from God—a figure that holds repercussions for the pre- and postlapsarian ecologies of sleep and sleeplessness shaping angelic, demonic, and human forms of life and care across the poem. The psychosomatic transformations occasioned by sleep are themselves transformed over the course of *Paradise Lost*, as sleep becomes a more desirable yet less achievable condition of release from the agonies of waking care. Ultimately, I argue that Milton's vitalist representations of sleep and care not only syncretize Stoic philosophical and Christian perspectives but also ascribe a uniquely early modern biopolitical value to the organic and unconscious processes of physical life.

Vital Strife concludes with a brief coda, "A Vital Rationality," that reveals essential connections among Margaret Cavendish's late philosophies of matter and sensation and the legacies of Stoicism. In her *Observations upon Experimental Philosophy*, Cavendish contends "that nature is a self-moving, and consequently a self-living and self-knowing infinite body, divisible into infinite parts," thereby revealing her deep affiliations with Stoic thought and its cosmological basis. I argue that Cavendish radicalizes the Stoic doctrine of oikeiôsis by attributing a mode of self-knowledge to each and every particle of nature. Cavendish imagines all matter as "belonging": according to her distinctively early modern variant of oikeiôsis, Nature rationally discloses to each physical entity an inherent understanding of its constitution as part of the whole. By insisting that knowledge of self and motion is inherent to every particle of the cosmos, Cavendish's neo-Stoicism challenges both the mechanical philosophy of thinkers such as Hobbes and Descartes as well as the seventeenth-century ascendance of Epicurean atomism and its doctrine of lifeless, inert particles whose random swerves form the foundation of life. More specifically, I show how Cavendish redresses Rene Descartes's severing of the intimate relationship between corporeality, teleology, and care first articulated by the natural philosophy of the Stoics. She offers instead a view of perpetual and rational corporeal motion as the vitalistic principle organizing the cosmos, which in turn shapes her Stoic view of sleep as an experience during which such motions continue steadily to affirm the place of bodies within the cosmic whole.

Chapter 1

Heavy with Care

Sleep and Ethical Life from Ancient Greece to Early Modern England

The notion that sleep is antithetical to the humanist pursuit of virtue features conspicuously in a canonical text of Renaissance humanism. I'm thinking of Erasmus's *The Praise of Folly* (1509), which conceives the human animal as a creature beset by forces eager to undo its steady focus and disrupt its virtuous ends. Hence, in a passage where Folly describes her comrades, Sound Sleep (*Negretos Hypnon*) appears alongside Madness (*Anoia*), Self-love (*Philautia*), and several other characters who display harmful postures and affectations ranging from slothful ease to sensual indulgence:

> This one you see with her eyebrows raised is, of course, *Philautia*, Self-love. . . . The sleepy one who looks only half-awake is *Lethe*, Forgetfulness, and this one leaning on her elbow with her hands folded is *Misaponia*, Idleness. . . . The one here with the rolling eyes she can't keep still is *Anoia*, Madness, and this plump one with the well-fed look is *Tryphe*, Sensuality. You can see there are also two gods amongst the girls; one is called *Comus*, Revelry, and the other *Negretos Hypnos*, Sound Sleep. This, then, is the household that serves me loyally in bringing the whole world under my sway, so that even great rulers have to bow to my rule.[1]

The inhabitants of Folly's *oikos* allegorize those aspects of human life that cause it to swerve from the good and fall into easy pleasures and distractions. It is unsurprising to find sleep and its kindred forms among Folly's household, as Folly suggests that such forces are a common physical fact for all human life: the "whole world . . . even great rulers" inevitably fall "under my sway." Folly's household thus gives voice to those experiences that humanism places in a subordinate relation to the pursuits of virtue because they threaten to derail ethical and political projects of attentive care, even as humanism acknowledges their inevitable pull on life. The release from care that Erasmus aligns with these attendants of Folly's household is denigrated as a lower, baser form of life that vigilance keeps at bay.[2] Such are the pleasures afforded by Sound Sleep and her domestic brethren, Idleness and Forgetfulness, whose temporary soothing of the soul must be subordinated to the work of humanist care.

Readers of Michel Foucault's *History of Madness* will likely recognize the preceding passage and recall Foucault's claim that it reflects a shift from medieval views of madness as simply one evil among many in the cluster of human vices, all of which are understood to be tragic forces of sin that grip the world. As madness dislodges from this pack to take its place as a warped refraction of the early modern "subtle relationship that man has with himself," according to Foucault, it begins to shed its cosmic and mythical skin. Folly in the Renaissance becomes a more lighthearted affair under the pen of literary humanists such as Erasmus and More: "This literary Folly is an attraction, but hardly a fascination," and "the mythological personification of madness is no more than literary artifice."[3] The Renaissance vision of Folly thus introduces a gap between madness and other forms of harm that continues to widen with an approaching modernity, a gap between the critical perspective of madness as the failure to maintain an ethical relation to the self, and the tragic view of madness as a matter of cosmic fate that essentially absolves the self of culpability. Erasmian folly for Foucault thus

> turns attention away from that madness "sent up from the underworld by avenging Furies whenever they dart forth their serpents," for the Folly that he set out to praise was of a different order. His concern is with the "most desirable" form that "occurs whenever a certain pleasant mental distraction relieves the heart from its anxieties and cares and at the same time soothes with the balm of manifold pleasures." A world of calm, without secret, that is easily mastered and fully displays its naïve reductions to the eyes of the wise, who keep their distance through laughter.[4]

Foucault's description of the psychosomatic and affective character of Erasmian folly resembles the virtuous tranquility that ancient ethical schools—Epicurean and Stoic in particular—attribute to the accomplishment of the good. It's as if Erasmus playfully imagines the ethical projects of antiquity being supplanted by the literate humanism he endorses. Foucault understands the Erasmian variant of this achievement as a measure of control granted by virtue of the humanist's critical distance from folly, a position of irony akin to the posture of an "Olympian God" looking downward and laughing at mortal fools. Erasmian irony thus provides one form of humanist security—life that is *sine cura*, or without care—through an education in classical letters and a literary approximation of ataraxia infused with ironic humor. For Foucault, Erasmus's text is less concerned with warning its readers against the forces that derail virtue than it is in giving those forces a literary form that secures humanist detachment through the mechanics of allegory: it is a paradigmatic example of humanist literary knowledge-power.

Yet the critical detachment from Folly that Foucault attributes to the Erasmian position also depends upon a strategic detachment from the self, or at the very least from the latter's most harmful guise as an overly invested *Philautia*. While it is not a line pursued in the early pages of Foucault's work, this feature of Erasmus's text is worth some thought. If Foucault is right to understand the release from care represented by the humanist's ironic position over Folly and her household as a sprezzatura-like nonchalance achieved through "literary artifice," it is one that is nonetheless secured, behind the scenes, through the attentive work of care and all its invested practices in a humanism that develops the self through reading and writing, and which owes part of its conceptual foundations in vigilant attention to the writings of St. Paul and his early Christian inheritors. Humanist care cultivates and tends to the self; yet as Foucault also contends, for Erasmian humanism, "an attachment to oneself is the first sign of madness, and it is through that attachment to oneself that man takes error for truth, lies for reality, violence and ugliness for beauty and justice."[5] The sort of attachment he means here is most pertinent to those figures of ethical harm associated with extremes of *Philautia*, and therefore with indulgent or prideful aspects of the self that inflate it beyond its proper dimensions. But the paradox remains: If the care of the self is the only way to detach from such harms and to learn the good, then how are we to understand this primary attachment to the self as potentially already harmful, an unhealthy preoccupation of care that must eventually be managed through the alienating distance of irony?

The implicit paradox that emerges from this constellation of self-attachment, care, and Renaissance humanist thought is an important point of departure for the chapters ahead, as well as a scene of arrival for this first chapter's genealogy of sleep and ethical care. For if Erasmus's *Praise of Folly* banished the Furies at the turn of the sixteenth century, in 1561 Jasper Heywood's translation of Seneca's *Hercules Furens* summoned them anew, and presented a hero whose descent into murderous rage is simultaneously a failure of his ethical attachment to himself and the result of impersonal cosmic forces that lead him to annihilate his family and the *oikos* that sustains him. Hercules swoons and falls into a fitful sleep immediately after murdering his wife and children, and early modern poets and dramatists alike enlist Seneca's figure of Herculean slumber—and principles of ancient Stoicism more broadly—to rethink some fundamental assumptions guiding the Christian humanist anthropology advanced by Erasmus and other writers of his ilk. Chief among these concerns is the supposed affinity between vigilance and virtue, or wakefulness and the good, which raises questions about how the restorative powers of sleep ought to figure in the ethical care for life. This first chapter thus provides a genealogy of sleep and care that illuminates both the humanist worries over sleep as well as the responses to such concerns constituted by works of drama and poetry discussed in later chapters—works which increasingly treat insomnia as a greater threat to ethical flourishing and psychosomatic well-being. I begin with Greek and Roman philosophical texts that take up the ethical relationship between sleep and care, turning then to consider the place of sleep in Christian political-theological writings by St. Paul and early church fathers, eventually coming back to where things began with another look at some tenets of Erasmian humanism and its English inheritors, whom I place into productive tension with the cosmological ethics of Senecan Stoicism and its valorization of sleep through the figure of the somnolent Hercules. This genealogy will obviously contain gaps, and it is not meant to be a comprehensive intellectual history of sleep or an account of the causal forces behind the shifts in thought that it maps. Rather, I have tried to give due time to thinkers whose writings on sleep, sleeplessness, and ethical care were familiar and dear—or *oikeion*, to appropriate the Stoic formulation—to the early modern writers whose works are the central focus of this book. In some cases, these classical musings on the physicality of sleep slide into figurative meanings and resonances, from the metaphorical darkness of ignorance in Platonic thought to the spiritual carelessness or distance from divinity that sleep figures for St. Paul. And throughout such reflections, we shall see competing notions of care in its ethical and ontological dimensions, as an orientation to self and world but also as a process that cannot unfold without the attentive concern for others, as both Aristotle and Seneca argue. In asking what care is, how it appears and why it seems to involve ends both beneficial and harmful to the self, these writers also display their fascination with the escape from care that is offered by the alluring fall of sleep.

Asleep in the Polis

Sleep, sensation, and care appear closely knit in the philosophical cosmology of the pre-Socratic philosopher Heraclitus. His esoteric fragments ponder the form of still and barely animate life that emerges in slumber and which places human life upon a threshold: "A man strikes a light for himself in the night, when his sight is quenched. Living, he touches the dead in his sleep; waking, he touches the sleeper."[6] In the original Greek, Heraclitus unites this series of oppositions—light-night, living-dead, waking-sleeping—with three repetitions that pun on the verb *haptetai*, which means variously "strike," "touch," "kindle," or "catch fire."[7] The fragment thus imagines that while nightfall causes us to turn away from the shared light or "fire" that mutually animates our sight, this quenching of common daily vision leads each soul to strike for itself a fainter, softer light illuminating its contact with the world of the dead.

Charles Kahn reads this fragment as a "sequence of psychic stages," which imagines human experience at night as a perceptual descent through increasing levels of darkness, and an eventual return to waking vision that retains only a faint memory of having brushed against, without fully entering, the realm of the dead.[8] Heraclitus's cosmology views the soul itself as a form of vital fire that is often seen as a precursor to the Stoic theory of pneuma. As G. S. Kirk points out, the fragment thus suggests that the "death" of the soul in sleep is but "a new becoming—either as water, or, in the case of souls of which the fiery nature has not been impaired by death, as another form of fire."[9] The touch of Heraclitean fire denotes an active inactivity, a form of experience whose uncertain phenomenological contours correlate with transitional movements between worlds. We travel from a field of public, waking vision into an enclosure of private dormancy that kindles life by quenching its outward expression and leads back again to the world of commonly animated perceptions. Yet our presence across these domains remains in contact with the world from which we have just departed, as we remain alive while touching the dead in sleep, and continue touching the sleeper when we are awake. The sense of touch is for Heraclitus a threshold sensation that orients our care across multiple registers of life as we pass through them all, sustained by the vital fire that inherently animates the cosmos and the life within us.

Plato uses the word *haptetai* in the *Phaedo* to articulate what happens when the properly trained soul encounters truth: it touches Being, or brushes up against the intelligible Forms that are the true causes of all things.[10] But this intellective touching is of a purer sort, less murky and more reliable than the sensorial thresholds imagined in Heraclitus's cosmology of vital fire and the motions of life. For Plato, embodied sensorial experiences including vision, hearing, feeling, and any other forms of contingent perceptual awareness are always part of the world of becoming—which is to say, unstable and therefore epistemologically relegated to belief or opinion. Touching truth requires abandoning the bodily constraint and imprecision of the senses in favor of contemplating Forms through the power of pure intellection—an experience potentially enabled by the condition of deep, dreamless sleep for the souls of the virtuous, as Socrates suggests in book 9 of the *Republic*. But before that moment arrives in Plato's treatise on justice, Socrates refers in book 6 to the Heraclitean fragment on sleep, when he asserts that in the present political conditions of Athens, "those who touch philosophy at all are young men just past childhood, in the interval before setting up a household and beginning to earn their own living. Just when they approach the hardest part of it, they quit. . . . With a few exceptions, as they approach old age, their light is quenched more thoroughly than the Sun of Heraclitus, inasmuch as it is not again rekindled."[11] Socrates seems to describe a trajectory from wakefulness to slumber as the potential for philosophical work and care fades with age, and the duties of household maintenance and mature citizenship come into greater focus. For this reason, Plato contends that the ripest moment for nurturing philosophical reflection is during adolescence—before young men take up their duties as head of the *oikos*, requiring them to focus on economic affairs and missing the best opportunity to begin cultivating philosophical rigor. Socrates goes on to argue that ideally, boys and young men ought to "deal with education and philosophy in a way suited to their youth, and while growing into manhood take very good care of their bodies as a support to philosophy. As age advances and the soul begins to reach maturity, they should intensify exercise of the body" (498b). So while Plato decisively locates the source of knowledge beyond bodily sensation and in the realm of intelligible Forms, he nonetheless asserts the need to care for and develop the body in ways that attune the soul properly, so that it can "kindle" and care for the spark of philosophy throughout life.

Plato's Socratic conviction that we must care for our souls is widely known. But what does the Platonic encounter with truth, this "touching" of intelligible Forms and therefore the highest sort of care, look like? It's a question worth asking, since over the course of books 6 and 7 of *The Republic*, Plato's accounts of the Form of the Good and the realm of intelligibility repeatedly figure the philosopher's encounter with truth as a superior mode of seeing: vision that is clear and just and which provides a foundation for stable political rule. This ideal mode of vision is poetically and functionally explained through an appeal to the sun and its role in the cosmos, whereas obstacles to a clear view of Being are represented as forms of sensorial constraint or confusion inflicted by darkness and akin to the experience of sleep. In numerous passages, Plato links the capacity for good governance to achieving a form of illuminated vision that grasps the good while avoiding the forms of darkness that he aligns with a misguided care for that which does not last—namely, the physical world of becoming. At the opening of book 6, for instance, Socrates argues, "It is clear . . . that a Guardian must not be blind but sharp of sight if he is to guard anything at all" (484d). He goes on to suggest to his interlocutors that they must "first agree that philosophical natures are always in love with a study which makes clear to them the nature and reality of what always is, and is not caused to wonder by coming to be and passing away" (485b). Through this course of study, the Guardians learn to care foremost for the contemplation of Forms, and eventually their vision will be properly oriented to the highest good, which is the Form of the Good itself. Once a soul is capable of contemplating the Form of the Good, "It is fixed upon what truth and reality illuminate, it conceives and knows it, and proves to possess thought. But when it is fixed upon what is mixed with darkness, upon what comes to be and passes away, it judges and becomes dull and changes opinions back and forth, and seems not to possess thought" (508d). Good thinking is stable and unified in its clarity—not subject to the deformations and occlusions of darkness, by which things shift and withdraw with the passing of time.

To further explain the Form of the Good, Socrates then constructs an extended analogy comparing its effects with the functions of the sun. Just as the sun produces the light by which all things in the world are made commonly visible, the Form of the Good is the power that "provides truth to things known and gives to the knower the power of knowing, [and so] you must say [it] is the Idea of the Good" (508e).[12] But this comparison of the Form of the Good with the sun is very much a graded analogy, as he soon confirms: "I suppose you will say that the Sun provides not only the power of being seen to things seen, but also of becoming and growth and nurture, though it is not itself becoming. . . . And say also for things known, then, not only that intelligibility is present by agency of the Good, but reality and being is also present to them by it, though the Good is not being, but even beyond being, surpassing it in respect to dignity and power" (509b). The sun's power is impressive indeed, since it provides the cosmic fuel of growth and sustenance while also making vision itself possible, which Socrates ranks as the highest of the bodily senses. But it is precisely for these reasons that, ultimately, the sun is an engine of sensations and change that constitute the world of becoming, so its value is inferior to the value of the Form of the Good and to the latter's capacity to endow the intelligible Forms with the quality of being forms.

This discussion of course leads to the allegory of the cave in book 7, which continues to use a poetics of darkness and light to describe the effects of encountering the dazzling brightness of the Forms, after having one's senses chained to the degraded perceptions and shadows of the cave of becoming. But Socrates now begins to describe the soul's impoverishment not only as a perceptual enslavement to the world of becoming but also as living in a dream. The guardians, for instance, must see the good clearly, "And in this way you will govern our city wide awake instead of in a dream, as most cities are now governed, where people fight over shadows and quarrel about office, supposing it a great good" (520d). Likewise, "Whoever cannot distinguish the Idea of the Good by reason and set it apart from all other things . . . you will claim that someone like that knows neither the Good itself nor any other good. Rather, if in some way he grasps a deficient image of it, he does so by opinion, not knowledge, and sleeps and dreams away his present life. Before he ever awakens here, he will go the place of the dead and fall asleep completely" (534c–d). While yoked to our bodily perceptions, thought is neither free nor clear, and it only "grasps a deficient image" of the good. To care for these deficient images is to care for the things of the world as they change and pass away, and thus to live one's life in an ethical stupor. Yet even this somnolent haze is merely a watered-down image of the final picture that Socrates offers us of the end of bodily life and the total sleep of death. True understanding, meanwhile, awakens thought from its slumber within the confused and dreamlike world of becoming: "Some things summon the understanding, others do not. What affects perception in opposite ways at the same time I distinguish as summoning it; what does not does not awaken thought" (524d).

While it would be wrong to claim that sleep is a major source of concern or interest in Plato's *Republic*, the above examples show that it functions as a kind of subterranean metaphor for experiences of disruptive change and haze-inducing transformation that Plato associates with the world of becoming. Plato lays important philosophical and poetic foundations that align sleep with distraction and confusion while emphasizing a close connection between wakefulness and the good. But as I have mentioned, Socrates also addresses the physical nature and condition of sleep more directly in book 9, invoking it to illustrate the power of "lawless desires" that can lead to tyranny in the unjust soul and city. After concluding their discussion of how tyrannical government develops from a democracy, Socrates and Glaucon turn to address the typology and emergence of the tyrannical man himself. Socrates then decides that he must first outline more clearly the desires that inhabit the appetitive part of the soul, because "among unnecessary pleasures and desires, some seem lawless," and while in certain persons these are mastered or disciplined by law and reason, in others they are "stronger and more numerous" (571b). For such rowdy beings, sleep becomes a monstrous event that actually "awakens" or stirs up these lawless desires,

> when the rest of the soul slumbers—the rational and gentle and ruling element of the person. But the wild and beastlike element, flown with food or drink, leaps up and shakes off sleep and undertakes to go forth and fulfill its own character. You know that in such circumstances it dares everything, supposing itself loosed from all shame and released from all wisdom. For it does not shrink from attempting sexual intercourse with a mother, as it supposes, and anyone else among men, gods, or beasts; or from committing any murder; and it abstains from no food. In a word, it falls short of no extremity of madness or shamelessness. (571d)

If Socrates identifies justice by analogizing individual souls and political constitutions, then the condition of being ruled by the frenzied desires unleashed in sleep represents the lowest plane conceivable for the human soul and the polity alike.

It is also worth noting that the passions Socrates imagines sleep stirring up are the stuff of ancient tragedy—urges of incest and parricide, cannibalism, and an "extremity of madness or shamelessness" that would aptly describe the victims and archvillains of tragic drama, whose stories upend the social and political mores of their worlds. That is why Socrates immediately contrasts this example with the sleep of the virtuous man, who is "self-possessed and healthy and temperate," striking an ideal accord between appetite, spirit, and reason. The just man

> goes to sleep after awakening his own rational part and feeding it with excellent reasoning and inquiries, he arrives at self-awareness and self-understanding, giving neither excess nor deficiency to the appetitive part, so that it may be lulled to rest, and not by its pleasure or pain provoke disturbance in what is best, but allows it to inquire alone by itself and to desire something in singleness and purity, and to perceive what it does not know, whether past or present or to come. He also tames the spirited element in like manner: he does not go to his sleep with spirit roused, or moved to anger against anyone. Having thus quieted these two forms but stirred and moved the third, in which intelligence is present, he thus goes to his rest, and as you know, in such circumstance he most especially touches the truth, and the visions which appear in his dreams are then least lawless. (572a)

In the case of unjust persons, sleep only amplifies and unleashes the desires that are already problematically ascendant in their souls; for the just man, however, sleep leads to visions by which "he most especially touches the truth" because he has managed, through the care of the self, to subordinate both appetite and spirit to reason. Sleep thus serves as a diagnostic measure for the condition of the soul. But in the case of the virtuous man who has properly cared for himself, it actually enables a peerless encounter with truth, when the soul is unencumbered and not distracted by the feelings and sensations of the body.

Both following and expanding upon several Platonic principles concerning sleep and care, a range of Aristotelian texts examine the effects of sleep on embodiment, sensation, and virtue. While sleep is not a major source of concern for Aristotle's models of the ideal governance of self and society, it does represent a point of serious recurring interest for the philosopher. Book 1 of Aristotle's *Nicomachean Ethics* contains a brief discussion of the ethical and political repercussions of sleep, and the *Eudemian Ethics*, *Metaphysics*, *Parva Naturalia*, and *Generation of Animals* all treat sleep as a phenomenon worthy of investigation for overlapping ethical, biological, and metaphysical reasons. In a basic sense, for Aristotle sleep raises questions about the ontological consistency of the human, the biological and physiological transformations undergone by the sleeping body and soul, and a range of metaphysical questions concerning causality, form, and matter. Moreover, Aristotle's naturalist orientations toward the biological life of animate beings and the processes that sustain them anticipate to some extent Stoic teleologies of organic life and virtue. Aristotle shares with the Stoics a sense that care is a virtuous activity undertaken among living human beings and grounded in our mutual capacities for sensation, intellection, and virtue. Yet as we shall see, the Peripatetic and Stoic schools part ways in their differing accounts of sleep's psychosomatic effects upon the human and its capacities for virtue.

Plato's premise that sleep unfetters the rational faculty of virtuous men does not hold for Aristotle, though much like Plato he does argue that virtuous men are more likely to have better dreams.[13] While his theory of the tripartite human soul and his writings on sleep share some core elements with Platonic notions of sleep, there is a sharp distinction in that Aristotle contends that sleep suspends or constrains the rational faculty of the soul, which is unique to the human being. This difference is subtle, but nonetheless important—not simply for clarifying distinctions between Platonic and Aristotelian moral psychology and their respective views of sleep but also because the question of how exactly sleep affects the sensorial and rational faculties of the soul appears in numerous early modern speculations on the matter that are clearly informed by both thinkers. For Aristotle, sleep is the logical opposite of wakefulness, and sensation is at the core of this basic dialectic. Both sleep and waking depend upon and are in fact defined by the soul's capacities to sense and to have sense suspended, and so Aristotle holds that only animal and human souls can sleep. But what exactly happens to the human soul when it sleeps, from a metaphysical or even ethical perspective? Aristotle claims in book 1 of the *Nicomachean Ethics* that a sleeping human soul temporarily loses that which makes it properly human: namely, the ability to exercise the power of reason. This means that the sleeping human soul is temporarily reduced to its most basic, primary grade of actuality, and so while the ethical disposition of a virtuous person does not entirely disappear while they sleep, "It is possible for the disposition to be present and yet to produce nothing good, as for example in the case of the person who is asleep, or in some other way rendered inactive, but the same will not hold of the activity: the person will necessarily be doing something, and will do (it) well."[14] Sleep does not in itself present an ethical dilemma, since it is both perfectly natural for the human body and soul to sleep, and because the nonrational, nutritive element of the soul (the first principle of life) is most active during sleep. Sleep in fact actualizes an inherent good or excellence of the soul, which is that part concerned with the nutritive sustenance and reproduction of life. But here is where things become a bit less clear: for Aristotle, the nonrational element of the soul is "divided" with respect to the rational element, since the "plant-like aspect of soul does not share in reason in any way, while the appetitive and generally desiring part does participate in it in a way, i.e. in so far as it is capable of listening to it and obeying it."[15] Both the nutritive and the appetitive functions of the soul are nonrational, yet the appetitive aspect of the soul bleeds into the domain of reason, and can thus be tamed or disciplined in the interest of attaining virtue. This point is essential to Aristotle's theory of developing ethical habit. But the soul's appetites can also struggle against, confuse, and override the rational aspect, leading to unethical action. Hence, sleep is analogized to the situation of a person suffering from *akrasia*, or the "un-self-controlled" type of individual who has some awareness of proper, virtuous action but who does not entirely have such knowledge as mastery, since they act in a manner contrary to its prescription. In other words, as Aristotle puts it, "Under 'having but not using' we observe a distinction in 'having,' such that a person both has knowledge in a way and does not have it, as with someone asleep, raving, or drunk."[16]

It is crucial to recognize that the analogy Aristotle makes here between sleep and *akrasia* is limited and based on a metaphysical resemblance; he uses it simply to explain how it can be possible simultaneously to "have" and "not have" virtue. It is not the case that sleep causes, brings about, or even encourages *akrasia* in Aristotle's system—sleep simply renders the human virtues into a state of potential that can only be made actual upon the return to waking life. This detail too will take on greater significance in the arguments ahead, because medieval and early modern thinkers draw upon Christian traditions identifying sloth, idleness, and acedia as sin, to suggest that sleep can in some instances actually corrupt spiritual and bodily well-being and aggress the physical conditions of virtue. But for Aristotle, the idea that sleep could biologically harm or ethically degrade the condition of one's body or soul (presuming a basic foundation of good health) makes no sense. Although he compares the condition of sleep to that of *akrasia* in one respect, he only slightly devalues or derides sleep itself, insofar as it prevents us from temporarily pursuing what is best in life, as he observes in the *Eudemian Ethics*:

> No one would prefer life for the pleasure of sleep; for what difference is there between sleeping without ever waking from one's first day to one's last, over a period of ten thousand years—or however many one likes—and living the life of a plant? Certainly plants seem to have a share in some such sort of life, as do infants. Babies indeed when they first come to be inside the mother exist in their natural state, but asleep all the time. So all this makes it clear that what the well and the good is in life eludes those who investigate the subject.[17]

For Aristotle, the highest good for humans is synonymous with virtuous activity that exercises the intellect, so sleep's suspension of both sensation and thought cannot actualize what is best in human life.

Aristotle's theory of friendship between virtuous persons reflects the same metaphysical underpinnings, and here too Aristotle uses the example of sleep to make his point: "But just as with the excellences predicating 'good' of people sometimes refers to disposition, sometimes to activity, so it is with 'friendship' too; for some are friends in so far as they delight in living together and provide the relevant good things for each other, while others, because asleep or separated by geographical distance, are not actively friends but are disposed so as to be active in that way—it is not friendship, unqualified, that location dissolves, only its activity."[18] These claims lead to Aristotle's later discussion of friendship and sensation in book 9 of the *Nicomachean Ethics*, where he asserts that the virtuous person could not live in isolation, because virtue requires that benefits be bestowed upon others, and because "man is a civic being, one whose nature is to live with others."[19] Aristotle bases this point on the insight that at its most fundamental level of being alive, the human animal's "primary sense seems to be perceiving or thinking" and that this "being alive is something that is good and pleasant in itself."[20] The innate awareness of our sensation and thought—the fact that we perceive that we are feeling, sensing, and thinking—registers the function of the common sense organ. This functioning is also a fundamental good that encourages us both to care for ourselves and for others. Sleep's isolation removes the human from its capacities to sense, to exercise the intellect, and to actualize its community of beneficence, through which the good is actualized in caring for friends and citizens. Simply put, we cannot care while we sleep.[21]

As we have seen, Aristotle uses sleep to elaborate the conceptual and metaphysical underpinnings of his ethical system, and to clarify how his notion of the good is realized between friends by bestowing benefits through care. But elsewhere he discusses sleep in biological terms that hold sway in early modern science and medicine. He devotes an entire treatise to sleeping and waking in the *Parva Naturalia*, which provides the basic template of an interwoven humoral physiological and psychic process that many early modern thinkers adopt but also critique or adjust to accommodate their own theological and philosophical investments.[22] In the Aristotelian system, sleep follows a kind of thickening and cooling in the bodily mixtures that sustain life, when the "corporeal element" in blood that typically rises to the head and makes human beings stand upright is forced downward as part of the process of nutrition:

> Sleep is not co-extensive with any and every impotence of the perceptive faculty, but this affection is one which arises from the evaporation attendant upon the process of nutrition. The matter evaporated must be driven onwards to a certain point, then turn back, and change its current to and fro, like tide-race in a narrow strait. Now, in every animal the hot naturally tends to move upwards, but when it has reached the parts above, it turns back again, and moves downwards in a mass. This explains why fits of drowsiness are especially apt to come on after meals; for the matter, both the liquid and the corporeal, which is borne upwards in a mass, is then of considerable quantity. When, therefore, this comes to a stand it weighs a person down and causes him to nod, but when it has actually sunk downwards, and by its return has repulsed the hot, sleep comes on, and the animal so affected is presently asleep.[23]

This passage sketches the core physiological process that materially causes sleep in human beings, but Aristotle also discusses sleep and waking in the *Parva Naturalia* with respect to the soul, and in fact claims that sleep only exists with regard to the soul's capacity to sense, even if it depends upon the body as a material cause. Because "the exercise of sense-perception does not belong to soul or body exclusively," he argues, "it is clear that its affection is not an affection of soul exclusively, and that a soulless body has not the potentiality of perception."[24] But "sleep is, in a certain way, an inhibition of function, or, as it were, a tie, imposed on sense-perception, while its loosening or remission constitutes the being awake."[25] Sleep binds the human soul insofar as it renders its sensing actuality into a mere potentiality. Here, too, we see that Aristotle's biological account of sleep bleeds into his ethical and metaphysical presumptions, since this suspension of sense-perception both defines sleep and makes the human soul temporarily incapable of exercising the form of waking, rational thought that is a necessary precondition of virtuous action. Sleep is a limiting constraint upon many potentialities of the human being that are essential, in Aristotle's thought, to its pursuits of truth and the good—despite the fact that sleep inherently actualizes the virtues of the nutritive soul that nourish life and provide the means for its ongoing reproduction.[26]

Aristotelian philosophy thus takes up some basic premises of Plato's moral psychology of sleep, but expands and develops them across ethical, political, metaphysical, and biological domains of inquiry. Sleep is a phenomenon worthy of investigation, as well as an apt figure for approximating various psychosomatic states of being, for clarifying metaphysical principles, and for theorizing the foundations of the care of the self and the polity. These Platonic and Aristotelian views of sleep and the embodied human soul of course inform and intrigue early modern writers, who adopt them partially in order to explore classical humoralism and its implications for defining the corporeal life of humankind. But for the early modern dramatists and poets at the heart of this book, the scenes of sleep and sleeplessness they construct owe more to Stoic philosophical fragments collected by Diogenes Laertius and Stobaeus, or to scenes of sleep from Roman literature composed by Seneca and Ovid. These Stoic visions of sleeping life and care differ sharply from their Platonic and Aristotelian predecessors with respect to key ethical and metaphysical suppositions. Stoic thinking about the constitution of the self and its place within the natural world leads to quite different assessments of the physical life of sleep, not to mention its role in the care of the self and the life of virtue. The reanimation of Stoic thought is especially visible in the cosmological orientation of early modern English literature as it is concerned with the environmental flux of the nocturnal world and its implications for the psychosomatic composition of the self. The life of sleep thus takes center stage in early modern works whose ecologies of care creatively reimagine the grounds of ethical normativity and physical vitality. But to lay bare those features that make the Stoic perspective and its early modern variants so uniquely compelling—and which set Stoicism apart from its philosophical predecessors—will require a bit more conceptual clearing.

The Tension of Care

According to the ontological schema of the ancient Stoics, bodies are physically existent entities bearing force and tension, which act as causes to other bodies. In fact, only bodies can act as causes to other bodies in the Stoic cosmos, and therefore all change is purely physical—whether it be the growth and decay of a living being, or the movement from ignorance to wisdom that comes about through learning. A body that is cut by another body is caused to have the physical attribute of being cut, rather than the cut being an effect that is brought about by the causal interaction between the body of the knife and the body of the flesh. Because all causality is physical for the Stoics, sensation is also a particular sort of bodily tension, or *tonos*, which occurs through processes of material constriction and release that physically impress images upon the corporeal soul that is capable of grasping them. Likewise, passions [*pathē*] such as anger, dread, and madness are all physical bodies according to the Stoics—so too is reason. Yet technically not everything in the cosmos is a body, even though everything that acts as a cause is. Alongside physical bodies there is another, more puzzling sort of ontological order: four modes of incorporeality that spread upon the surfaces of being and subsist as purely "logical or dialectical attributes."[27] These four Stoic incorporeals are Time, Place, the Void, and "sayables," or *lekta*. Strictly speaking, they are nonexistent entities. Only bodies actually exist in space and time, establishing a vast cosmic chain of fate through interlocking causal mixtures. But the incorporeals subsist or inhere by forming an essential reciprocity with existing physical mixtures, so they are known to the Stoics under the ontological category of "something," which is the primary genus that includes physical bodies, incorporeals, and fictional entities.[28] D. J. T. Bailey describes the Stoic position as "identifying the fundamentally real as the bodily," and as that which grounds the incorporeals in the sense that they cannot subsist without it.[29]

Stoic physicalism is thus a quasi physicalism, a cosmic system in which corporeality is the mark of existence that provides the only explanatory foundation for causation and change, though physical mixtures also form reciprocal relations with incorporeal entities articulated through language. Stoicism's esoteric explanations of causation and change obviously mean that physical existence has a priority in the Stoic cosmos that is at odds with the ontological foundations of other ancient philosophies, most especially the Platonic doctrine of Forms. But the idea that bodies provide the ontological bedrock of the real also has direct implications for the Stoic theory of the good and the pursuit of knowledge. Hence, the Stoics divide philosophy into three categories: physics, ethics, and logic. Yet in keeping with the Stoic commitment to physicalism, these distinctions are not simply epistemological abstractions; they pertain in fact to the physical body that is philosophy, and to the understanding that rightly grasps the nature of that body—and which is a bodily disposition as well. According to Diogenes Laertius, the Stoics "say that philosophical doctrine has three parts: the physical, the ethical, and the logical. . . . They compare philosophy to an animal, likening logic to the bones and sinews, ethics to the fleshier parts, and physics to the soul."[30] To understand the causal motions of this living animal body is to arrive at a particular physical condition that provides, through the corporeal tension of the pneuma, the soul's hêgemonikon with an accurate cognitive grasping of them. For Stoic thinkers, ethics thus necessarily involves intimate knowledge of the nature and tendencies of physical bodies and their mixtures. Passion and reason alike are bodies; this means that achieving virtue is at once a physical and cognitive state according to which the tension of the corporeal soul is correctly attuned to the natural order of the cosmos and therefore capable of grasping it—which in turn provides the physical basis for judgments concerning right action. Sensation plays an essential role in this process, because for rational beings the hêgemonikon supervenes to shape impulse "like a craftsman," thus determining whether any given perception indeed constitutes a truthful grasping of the world, or a *kataleptike phantasia*.[31] Reason naturally guides the motions of the pneuma such that the impulses received are sorted accordingly by the hêgemonikon, and the human animal either does or does not assent to the impressions made on the soul in the event of perception. Those who have attained virtue (which is synonymous with reason for the Stoics) "aim genuinely and vigilantly for their own improvement by making a practice of concealing base things and bringing to light whatever is good."[32] Being virtuous means being capable of attending to and perceiving the good by physically embodying the mode of vision that can recognize the natural order of the cosmos. The Stoics thus provide an ancient model of natural judgment that is at once cognitive, physical, and ethical, and for which a careful empirical and sensorial engagement with the world is essential—a scientific naturalism rooted in the pneumatic tension of embodied sensation. The harmful effects of passion are first and foremost due to its clouding of the powers of judgment, because it unnaturally twists and agitates the otherwise naturally balanced tension of the soul's hêgemonikon.

What happens, then, to this ruling principle of soul when the Stoic body succumbs to sleep? Zeno reportedly held that "sleep occurs when the sensory tension is relaxed in the ruling part of the soul."[33] The *tonos* or tension of which Zeno speaks is responsible for a cosmic spectrum of capacities in physical bodies, running from their basic cohesion to the rational grasping that arises in human souls. When bodies that sense fall asleep, the pneuma that animates them relaxes and therefore slackens the perceptive tension that otherwise allows them to receive the imprint of the world. This view is propagated by Hierocles the Stoic in his treatise *Elements of Ethics*, in which he argues that all animals are a composite of body and soul, "each of which is touchable" and exerts a steadily reciprocal force upon the other. But Hierocles resists the easy notion that body contains or holds soul in the way that a jug holds wine. Instead, the two are thoroughly inmixed, or as he puts it, "wondrously blended and wholly intermingled, so that not even the least part of the mixture fails to have a share in either of them. . . . Thus, too, what pertains to shared affect [συμπάθεια] is total for both. For each shares the affects of the other, and neither is the soul heedless of bodily affects, nor is the body completely deaf to the torments of the soul."[34] Sleep slackens this tensional motion that permeates body and soul in such a thoroughgoing manner, which in turn reduces the living animal's sensorial grasp on the world and, to some extent, itself. Hence, Hierocles argues that "if ever an animal becomes wholly insensible of itself, this invariably happens above all in time of sleep. But we see that even then—in a way not very easy for most people to follow—an animal nevertheless perceives itself."[35] Remarkably, Hierocles goes on to claim that even during sleep there is a part of the animal that continues to perceive itself, insofar as a minimum degree of tension must exist in order for life to continue. He cites the hero Hercules as proof: "Thus, for example, Heracles too sleeps grasping his club in his right hand" (5.20). Some awareness of our proper being goes on working, "even if we are sleeping profoundly, as though we were employing . . . a fully awake attention" (5.5). In other words, there is a form of care that carries on during our slumber, and which cannot be dissolved despite sleep's compromising effects on the human's capacity to exercise its attachment to reason.

This is why, for the Stoics, sleep and death exist along a continuum, on which death is a total release or complete slackening of the perceptive tension that constitutes the attachment to self-awareness, or oikeiôsis. The Stoic theory of oikeiôsis contends that all animal beings (including humans) are born into a reflective awareness of themselves as embodied, sensing entities. And so long as a body lives, oikeiôsis continues even in moments of relatively fuzzy or confused perception, such as sleep. Through the ongoing process of oikeiôsis, an animal learns during its waking life to conduct itself in the world amid various forms of attachment and alienation, which depend upon an organism's developing sense of the ends that are proper to its being. Learning to know the good and also to recognize what is not good are the essential poles that organize this ethical and physiological development. As Alex Dressler observes, in the case of the human animal, "their attachment to themselves entails an additional attachment to reason, no less a corporeal part of themselves, according to Stoic physics, than their gross body."[36] Stoic ethics thus emphasizes a teleological process of development that is continuously physical and mental, depending upon a successful yet ongoing orchestration of body, environment, and cosmic reason by virtue of the pneuma that flows through all bodies and directs the tensional motion of change, the cognitive grasping of nature, and of course the process of oikeiôsis that immediately orients the animal being toward care for its own constitution.

In fact, Seneca argues in his ethical letter devoted to the topic of animal instinct that the human animal's relationship to *cura* is such that "my concern for myself is prior to everything else [*ante omnia est mei cura*]."[37] But this "self" is less a robust, ego-driven image than we might expect, and its ontological basis in Senecan thought and in Stoicism more broadly recalls the Aristotelian notion of the common sense that serves as the basis for self-awareness and the virtues of care. The key difference, however, is that the Stoics abide by a psychological monism that views the motions of the soul as articulations of a single active principle, the pneuma that pervades all physical entities and whose particular actions are determined by its ruling hêgemonikon, which in turn depends upon the particular nature of the living being. Sensation and reason alike are movements of the pneuma in its more active form, which for ensouled beings involves an immediate apperception of their condition as living beings. In Daniel Heller-Roazen's words, "The thesis he [Seneca] consistently advances is the one proposition that seems, by all accounts, to have also been that of Chrysippus: the living being, he repeats, senses before all else its 'constitution.' If it adapts itself to itself in caring for itself, it does so because of this primary sensation alone, which refers not to itself but to its nature."[38] This inner sense "is that for which every living thing, to be and to preserve itself, must 'care,' that which each being, rational or not, incessantly senses and never knows."[39] Heller-Roazen goes on to suggest a core affinity between Aristotelian and Stoic thought concerning the human animal's attachment to itself through the sense of sensing, though his account elides some of the foundational differences between Stoic and Peripatetic psychology that I have mentioned. If we recall that Aristotle aligns sleep's suspension of the common sense organ with a form of binding or constriction, another important distinction from the Stoics emerges. In the *Parva Naturalia* he contends that "sleep is, in a certain way, an inhibition of function, or, as it were, a tie, imposed on sense-perception, while its loosening or remission constitutes the being awake" (454b). For the Stoics, however, being awake entails a perceptive constriction and tightening that prepares the corporeal soul to receive impressions, whereas sleep is a condition of slackness that loosens the tension by which thoughts and sensations arise in the soul. Ideally, this moment of perceptive slackening occurs in a soul guided by reason, whose influence allows both body and soul to achieve calm tranquility. Hence, Seneca's contention that "there is no restful calm but that which is settled by reason. Night doesn't take away our cares; rather, it exposes them to view, exchanging one anxiety for another. . . . Only as the mind develops into excellence do we achieve any real tranquility."[40] Virtue extends its calming powers into sleep and wakefulness alike, effectively curing the cares that assail us at night.

Yet given Seneca's claim that for human beings, the good is perfected by care (*cura*), sleep's suspension of the capacity to care would also seem to situate sleep as a lower form of the good, and thus to constitute a minimal expression of ethical life.[41] In *De Beneficiis*, Seneca chastises an Epicurean image of pleasurable inaction and "sluggish ease" while asserting that attaining virtue is in fact a labor of vigilant care that bestows superior pleasures of benefit:

> Your idea of pleasure is to give your contemptible body over to idle sloth, to seek a freedom from care tantamount to sleep, to hide out in thick shade, to divert the torpor of a lethargic mind with the softest thoughts, which you call "tranquility," and to stuff bodies pallid from idleness with food and drink in privacy of your garden. Our idea of pleasure is to confer benefits even if they involve effort, provided that they reduce the efforts of others; even if they involve danger, provided they rescue others from danger; even if they strain our finances, provided they relieve the wants and hardships of others.[42]

In other words, Seneca argues, to care for another human animal is to exercise and develop the good by both bestowing benefit and in turn benefiting from its pleasures, while indulging in one's own bodily pleasure is a habitual harm best to avoid. In both his emphasis on the virtues of care and its realization in the interpersonal care that nurtures others, Seneca's formulations recall the Aristotelian assessment of friendship's virtue and its basis in the shared sense of sensing that the friend is another self. But for Stoics such as Seneca, this means that the friend is naturally to be accommodated within the expanding circles of one's oikeiôsis, in an expansive ecology of care that actualizes the cosmic good. Seneca's references to sleep and sluggishness in this passage mean to identify forms of life that misdirect or pervert care by corralling it into an enclosure of self-satisfying ease that forestalls its naturally cosmopolitan inclinations. And while sleep may technically constitute a lesser form of life in the sense that it does not encompass the broadest possible circle of our care, it is nonetheless an experience during which the care that fundamentally defines oikeiôsis carries on.

Calcidius, a fourth-century commentator on Plato's *Timaeus*, recognizes this Stoic view of reason and suggests that both Heraclitus and the Stoics understand sleep as a condition that potentially brings our reason closer to that which permeates the cosmos: "Indeed, Heraclitus, and the Stoics with him, associate our reason with the divine one which governs and controls everything in the world. On account of the indissoluble union of the two, our own reason is made acquainted with that which cosmic reason has resolved, and reveals to us the future while our mind is resting from sensation."[43] So long as the corporeal soul maintains the balanced *tonos* that allows its hêgemonikon to function naturally and in attunement with cosmic reason, sleep will both restore and revive the physical body made weary from toil and daily cares. As the Chorus in Seneca's *Agamemnon* reminds its audience, sleep is the "tamer of cares" that eases our waking woes. Likewise, Seneca contrasts the easy sleep of the golden age with the sleepless nights of high-ranking men who labor and worry over imperial Rome: "We toss and turn with anxiety on our purple bedclothes, kept awake by the sting of our cares. How softly those people slept on the hard ground!"[44] Seneca's ethical letters and dramatic corpus thus bring into focus principles animating the early modern paradoxes of care introduced at the beginning of this book. Sleep relaxes the psychic tension that shapes care into its virtuous and wakeful formations, even as such an escape from the tension of care is necessary to the ongoing recovery of human life. Hence, Richard Mulcaster's humanist concern with the constant labors of care that seek to avoid care. But before turning in earnest to the writers whose works amplify in an extreme form the paradoxes suggested by Seneca's treatment of sleep and care, a final step remains. We must assess the place of sleep in Christian political theology, and especially within the Pauline exhortations of vigilant spiritual care and constant wakefulness on the part of Christian soldiers.

Body, Flesh, Vigilance: Pastoral Care and the Political Theology of Sleep

When reconstructing a political theology of sleep for the early modern world, the turn to biblical characterizations of sleep yields mixed results. On the one hand, God apparently sleeps. Hebrew descriptions of Yahweh in Genesis 2:2 suggest that sleep is a divine prerogative after the work of creation, and that God's rest on the seventh day follows naturally from that activity. There are analogues to this moment of divine leisure in earlier religious texts, such as the Egyptian "Theology of Memphis" that tells of the creator god, Ptah, "who rested after he made everything, including the divine order," as well as Mesopotamian myths that describe the proper state of ruling gods as one of divine leisure and repose—whereas humans have been created so as to work and provide the gods with nourishment.[45] In the Babylonian Atrahasis epic, the god

Enlil is disturbed and awakened by the rebellious cries of humans who lament their oppression in laboring purely for the benefit of the gods. As Bernard Batto shows, godly sleep in these ancient sources is both a divine prerogative and a sign of supreme rule, and the interruption of the deity's sleep calls upon him to master forces of rebellion or chaos—a motif we see repeated in texts deemed sacred by Jewish and Christian faiths alike. God is depicted as sleeping not only after the act of creation in Genesis, but also in the context of personal and political laments by the Israelites. Psalm 44:23 enters a plea with Yahweh to awaken and rouse himself in light of his people's suffering, and the plea to administer justice against the enemies of his people is repeated throughout the book of Psalms as it is in the book of Isaiah. Yet rather than a sign of fallibility or inattentiveness, Batto suggests, these images of God asleep emerge from the ancient cultural and religious views of divine sleep as a sign of supreme sovereignty. As he writes, "The appeal to Yahweh to 'wake up,' far from being a slur on the effectiveness of divine rule, was actually an extension of Israel's active faith in Yahweh's universal rule even in the midst of gross injustice and manifest evil."[46] Yahweh's sleep is akin to that of the Egyptian Ptah or the Babylonian Enlil in that it denotes his supreme power and ability to master chaos through creation and order, though of course for the Israelites that superiority derives from a monotheistic foundation that is lacking in earlier versions.

On the other hand, it seems that God never sleeps. Alongside these images of a slumbering God, we find the notion of an unsleeping deity whose protection over the world is a constant guarantee. Psalm 121 describes the God that "keepeth Israel" as one who "will neither slumber nor sleep," which reinforces his absolute sovereignty through the attribution of a sleepless and perpetual watch. This image of God as an ever-vigilant caretaker also has ancient analogues, such as the Egyptian hymn to Amun-Ra that describes the god "at night wakeful while all sleep, / Seeking good for his flock."[47] Such invocations of godly care as perpetual wakefulness cast divinity in the mold of pastoral power, the form of care that Michel Foucault attributes to the figure of the shepherd who protects and guides his flock, and which the French thinker argues emerges in ancient cultures as a modality of power that distinguishes itself from the nexus of divine sovereignty and law. As Foucault tracks images of pastoral power from ancient eastern sources to Greek political thought and on to medieval and early modern European reformers, he returns to the constant theme that the pastor remains ever vigilant in his care for the flock, and that his power manifests not in a display of absolute authority but rather as "zeal, devotion, and endless application. . . . The shepherd is someone who keeps watch."[48] In other words, pastoral power supplements the authority given by the form of law that is handed down by a supreme divinity (whether monotheistic or not), and is more immediately and intimately concerned with the care for life in its practically ethical, spiritual, and physical dimensions. And insofar as pastoral care is a power of zealous devotion and constant application, its successful exercise is antithetical to sleep.

For early and early modern Christians alike, one of the most important scriptural variants of this logic of vigilant care is found in the epistles of Paul, whose shepherding of the early church took the form of epistolary exhortations to communities across the Mediterranean world just after Christ's death. Paul's epistles establish a crucial figural link between sleep and sin, and more broadly with any form of the worldly "darkness" that characterizes living outside of Christian fellowship. He exhorts believers to leave behind such darkened perspectives and to be joined, through the grace of the spirit, to the universal body of Christ. In 2 Thessalonians 5:2, Paul warns the faithful to be vigilant, because "the day of the Lord shal come, euen as a thefe in the night." He goes on to characterize believers as "children of light, and the children of the day: we are not of the night nether of darkenes. Therefore let vs not slepe as do others, but le vs watch and be sober."[49] And being vigilant, sober, and in the light is typically compared with wearing the armor of faith that God provides, which keeps believers not only from having "fellowship with the unfruteful workes of darkenes" but also girds the faithful "euen to reproue them" (Ephesians 5:11). Likewise, Paul's letter to the Romans describes God's once chosen people as being misled from God's love because "their foolish heart was full of darkenes" (Romans 1:21), and so he urges, "It is now time that we shulde arise from slepe: for now is our saluation nerer, then when we beleued it. The night is past, & the day is at hand: let us therefore cast away the workes of darkenes, and let vs put on the armour of light, So that we walke honestly, as in the day: not in glotonie, and dronkennes, neither in chambering and wantonness, nor in strife and enuying" (Romans 13:10–13). Yet despite their negative valences, these and other Pauline images of sleep are not immediately concerned with its physiological or bodily effects. Instead, Paul uses sleep to figure a lapse in spiritual vigilance, increased vulnerability to assaults by the Devil, or a refusal to awaken from spiritual slumber and join the Christian community. Sleep thus serves as a metaphor for the human tendency to live "for the world," as John A. T. Robinson puts it, and to be ruled by the inclinations of the flesh. And while this Pauline perspective suggests that the inevitability of spiritual struggle might be likened to the inevitability of sleep, Paul's epistles construct an ideal of constant, vigilant faith that forgoes the "workes of darkenes" and arises from spiritual slumber. Passionate, fleshly strife is to be abandoned in favor of putting complete trust in God's newly given transcendent and universal law of love. For Paul, all human bodies are fleshly, but the body (*soma*) is not quite the same as the flesh (*sarx*). Robinson gives a helpful account of Paul's concept of the flesh in his study of the role of the body in Pauline theology: "One could describe the situation by saying that σάρχ [*sarx*] as neutral is man living in the world, σάρχ as sinful is man living for the world: he becomes a 'man of the world' by allowing his being-in-the-world, itself God-given, to govern his whole life and conduct. . . . It is to be 'careful for the things of the world' rather than 'for the things of the Lord.'"[50] Robinson also shows that for Paul, the body is not something that a person has, like an eye, a hand, or a head of hair; it is rather something that a person is, and much like Paul's concept of the flesh, the body has the potential to be disposed either for God or for the world.[51] But the key difference between body and flesh is as follows: "While σάρχ stands for man, in the solidarity of creation, in his distance from God, σωμα [*soma*] stands for man, in the solidarity of creation, as made for God."[52] Proper care for the body is thus central to Pauline theology, because the body, not the flesh, is that which is resurrected to God, and it is through Christ's embodied life that God's spirit enters the fallen world to quicken the bodies of believers.

Early monastics and patristic writers expand upon Paul's doctrines of body and flesh as well as his allegorical figurations of sleep in their writings and lived practices, in ways that increasingly presume the experience of sleep actually aggravates the fleshly body, or the condition of depravity that defines the human being according to Pauline theology. Sleep becomes an essential site of monastic discipline, playing its part in a Christian *oikonomia* that illustrates the ongoing centrality of pastoral care and vigilance to the physical life of the pastorate. Often drawing on Greek and Roman philosophical discourses that we have seen aligning sleep with a retraction or suspension of the intellect, early monks developed techniques of sleep deprivation, discipline, and even "watchful sleep" over the course of the first five centuries of the Christian *koinonia* as a key weapon in their wars against spiritual temptation and demonic assault. Giving physical heft and shape to St. Paul's allegorical armor of light and spiritual wakefulness, these early Christians weaponized their bodies and souls in order to resist or modify the need for sleep and thus master their temporary descent into darkness. Biographical writings describe Pachomius the Great, a fourth-century North African monk and founder of cenobitic monasticism, as especially vigilant in such endeavors. While many of the early desert monks lived in isolation and transmitted their practices via one-on-one relationships, Pachomius founded a monastic *koinonia* that provided mutual support among its inhabitants in their stringent ascetic practices. As the historian of early Christian monasticism David Brakke notes, "For him, care for others formed the heart of Christianity."[53] Pachomius's particular innovation was to produce a daily regimen and set pattern for monastic life in a community setting, one that each monk followed regularly and which was codified into a written rule. This rule was put to use within a hierarchical structure of households watched over by a head monk, all of whom were responsible to an overarching father monk.[54] According to biographical texts, Pachomius's teacher, the monk Palamon, urged him to "stay awake, Pachomius, lest Satan tempt you, for many have fallen asleep in their affliction because of the heaviness of sleep."[55] Brakke notes that the "virtue of wakefulness and the danger of sleep are frequent themes in Pachomian exhortations," and Pachomian communities were known for sleeping on upright reclining seats that did not allow for deep and lengthy periods of slumber but instead cultivated an "antidemonic vigilance" that promoted the *koinonia*'s chief ends of "vigilance and mutual care."[56]

Pachomius's codifications of monastic life and community served a role in the eastern Church analogous to that of Benedict of Nursia's *Rule of St. Benedict* in western Christian monasteries, a text which shares the Pachomian commitment to sleep discipline as a key technique of pastoral care. According to the *Rule*, a series of strict orders must be observed with respect to the sleeping arrangements of monks. These include separate beds located within the same space, but always "under the watchful care of seniors." The monks must also "sleep clothed, and girded with belts or cords; but they should remove their knives, lest they accidentally cut themselves in their sleep. Thus the monks will always be ready to arise without delay when the signal is given. . . . On arising for the Work of God, they will quietly encourage each other, for the sleepy like to make excuses."[57] Benedict's elaboration of strict, all-encompassing rules had a tremendous influence on monastic life across medieval and early modern Europe, including England.[58] It reveals close connections between pastoral care and an ideal of ongoing vigilance on the part of shepherding ministers entrusted with the spiritual guardianship of the flock, as well as the potentially derailing effects of sleep on those efforts. It moreover shows that even among those monks who succumb to the inevitable need to sleep, the wearing of their habits is both a symbolic and practical measure of their spiritual devotion and readiness.

The word "habit" of course also calls up the history of ethical self-care and discipline (the Greek *ethos* can be translated as habit), and here it suggests that the vulnerability of the physical body in sleep need not compromise the soul's integrity in its commitment to the life of the spirit for early Christians. Hence, John Chrysostom calls in his homily on Paul's first epistle to Timothy for a disciplined form of sleep among the members of his congregation, which resembles the resting state of the Benedictine monks remaining vigilant even during slumber:

> No one calls for his servant, for each waits upon himself: neither does he require so many clothes, nor need to shake off sleep. For as soon as he opens his eyes, he is like one who has been long awake in collectedness. For when the heart is not stifled within by excess of food, it soon recovers itself, and is immediately wakeful. The hands are always pure; for his sleep is composed and regular. No one among them is found snoring or breathing hard, or tossing about in sleep, or with his body exposed; but they lie in sleep as decently as those who are awake, and all this is the effect of the orderly state of their souls.[59]

Chrysostom's vision of a watchful sleep that preserves the integrity of the well-governed soul resembles the Platonic vision of a virtuous sleep in book 9 of *The Republic*. Yet it more closely knits the care of the physical body through dietetics to the maximization of the soul's inherent watchfulness, in keeping with other early Christian ascetic accounts of sleep and pastoral care that likewise direct attention to the disciplining of physical life by way of nutrition and sensation. As we have seen, sleep is largely regarded as an unfortunate necessity that should be minimized and managed in ways that aim at eliminating its problematic aspects. Sleep's place in the monastic ecologies of care and pastoral power among early Christians seemingly confirms Gregory of Nyssa's contention that sleep is a reversal of the natural hierarchy by which the intellect rules over human life: "In sleep the supremacy of these faculties is in some way reversed in us, and while the less rational becomes supreme, the operation of the other ceases indeed, yet is not absolutely extinguished."[60] Accordingly, the natural aim of an ethical relation to sleep becomes the preservation of the intellect's inner light and the formation of a vigilant psychic core that guards against the demonic onslaught described by St. Paul as the works of darkness.

In the work of some early Christian writers, this onslaught is conceived in specific relation to concupiscence and the ethical dilemma presented by nocturnal emissions. The issue was especially pertinent for early Christian monks who worried whether experiencing a nocturnal emission should prohibit them from receiving communion.[61] John Cassian's *The Conferences* features a conversation on nocturnal emissions whose participants attribute the experience to a range of possible causes that include gluttonous diet, spiritual laxity, and demonic meddling. And should a monk experience emissions due to an infernal agent who "deceives the sentinels of our slumbering mind" and "provokes a natural emission compelled by necessity," then the monk should still participate in holy communion and can rest assured that he has not defiled the communal body of Christ.[62] Augustine of Hippo, meanwhile, extends the Pauline associations of sleep with spiritual peril by reading the letter to the Romans as a commentary on divided will that emerges in the passionate strife of fleshly sleep. He laments in *Confessions* that "images of acts" are "fixed" in his memory by "sexual habit," and "while I am awake they have no force, but in sleep they not only arouse pleasure but even elicit consent." He asks God "to cure all the sicknesses of my soul and, by a more abundant outflow of your grace, to extinguish the lascivious impulses of my sleep."[63] For Augustine, as for so many early Christian writers, sleep renders the self even more susceptible to the fleshly stirrings of concupiscent passion. And alongside the patristic writings on sleep that appear before his time, Augustine's texts serve as an important hinge between Paul's figural uses of sleep on the one hand and early modern worries over the entangled spiritual and corporeal aspects of sleep on the other. During sleep, our carnal nature temporarily but more thoroughly binds the sleeping body, and the retraction of reason underscored by ancient pagan thinkers such as Plato and Aristotle becomes a perfect conceit among early Christian writers for a wayward and fleshly form of life given over to the ways of the sinful world.

This is the life that Christians must fight to escape, and it correlates in the early modern world with both Lutheran and Calvinist perspectives on the care for spiritual and bodily life. According to Martin Luther's reading of Paul's doctrine of the flesh, the flesh defines our very being, so reason as well as passion, body, soul, and spirit are all subjected or bound to the power of carnality. As Richard Strier writes, "Fleshliness or carnality, from this point of view, is fundamentally the condition of egotism or self-regard—the condition of being, as Luther wonderfully put it in Latin, '*incurvatus in se*' (curved in upon oneself). Being 'spiritual,' from this point of view, would be a matter of being turned away from self-regard."[64] Sleep may represent, from such a Lutheran vantage, the most fleshly of all bodily mixtures or dispositions; not so much because of its thickening effects with respect to the earthy substances of humoral embodiment but because it amplifies to an absolute extreme the turning inward of the self that Luther chastises—a turning inward so complete that even self-regard loses the capacity to regard as such. The utter fleshliness and depravity of sleep can be understood, in theological and phenomenal terms, as a radical incapacity to look outward, which equates to lack of concern for others in the world, and especially for the spiritual community—hence, Paul's exhortations in Romans 13:10 to "arise from slepe" and leave the "workes of darkenes" behind. To return to the way of the flesh is to fall back into the unholy sphere of spiritual and bodily sleep, because the body is the key pathway for the spirit of God to enter and infuse the fleshly self with grace.

In their discussions of sleep and vigilance in the Pauline epistles, both Luther and Calvin extend Paul's distrust of spiritual slumber, but they articulate the force of his conceit in even more individualizing and moralistic terms that share the spirit of early Christian pastors and their commitment to vigilant care. Luther's commentary on Romans holds that "scripture speaks of sleep in at least a threefold sense," which can denote literal bodily sleep, as well as spiritual sleep that is either holy or unholy, depending on the condition of faith: "What is night for the former (*the believer*) is day for the latter (*the unbeliever*). What the former regards as an awakening, the latter looks upon as sleep, and vice versa."[65] So spiritual slumber leads unbelievers both to live for the world and to believe they are spiritually awake, despite actually being "asleep in the lusts of the flesh."[66] To guard against these proclivities, Luther writes, "The Apostle desires that Christians should take care of their bodies in such a way that no evil desires are nurtured thereby. . . . We should not destroy the body, but crucify its vices or evil passions."[67] Thus Luther concludes his discussion of Romans 13 with a perceived emphasis on the vigilant care of the embodied self, as dictated by Paul.

In his own commentaries on Romans 13, John Calvin likewise insists upon a personal responsibility to remain vigilant: "By *awakening out of sleep*," he writes, Paul "means that we are to be armed and ready to do what the Lord requires of us . . . Paul says, *armour* rather than works, because we are to fight in the service of the Lord."[68] And with respect to Paul's image of the armor of light in Ephesians 6, Calvin writes, "To make us more vigilant, he tells us that we must not only engage in open warfare, but that we have a crafty and insidious foe, who attacks us secretly in ambushes."[69] Both Luther and Calvin present us with subtle yet meaningful variations on a core theme of Pauline theology: Paul's concept of the body of Christ radically deindividuates the fallen bodies of believers, only to reconstitute them corporeally and existentially as members of Christ's body, which is the body of the Church infused with God's spirit.[70] Paul thus sets the terms for Luther's emphasis on turning outward toward the faithful community and the spiritual gift of grace, just as he does for Calvin's emphatic Christian militancy. But while the political-theological role of sleep in Paul's epistles is acknowledged in kind by Luther and Calvin, both inflect Paul's allegorical treatment of sleep with a heightened sense of personal obligation in obedience to God and to the holy community, further elaborating the models of pastoral care and vigilance that we have seen cultivated among early monastic communities and patristic writers. The obligatory turning outward of the self to receive the spirit becomes a paradigm for godly living and even militant battle, to which the darkened isolation of sleep stands in an antithetical relation.

But Calvin also considers the dictates of Pauline Christianity vis-à-vis humanist philosophical and metaphysical questions inherited from classical thinkers such as Aristotle and Seneca. Near the beginning of *The Institutes of the Christian Religion*, Calvin launches into a critique of those who give "an indirect turn to the frigid doctrine of Aristotle, to employ it both for the purpose of disproving the immortality of the soul, and robbing God of his rights."[71] In this passage, the mind's powers prove the soul's immortality, insofar as they continue to manifest while the body sleeps:

> The swift and versatile movements of the soul in glancing from heaven to earth, connecting the future with the past, retaining the remembrance of former years, nay, forming creations of its own—its skill, moreover, in making astonishing discoveries and inventing so many wonderful arts, are sure indications of the agency of God in man. What shall we say of its activity when the body is asleep, its many revolving thoughts, its many useful suggestions, its many solid arguments, nay, its presentiment yet of things to come? What shall we say but that man bears about with him a stamp of immortality which can never be effaced. . . . Shall some remains of intelligence continue with us in sleep, and yet no God keep watch in heaven?[72]

These musings may recall the Platonic notion that virtuous souls dream of truth, but Calvin follows early Christian monks in clearly attributing this imprint of the good to the fact of man's soul being created and stamped by the Christian God. He goes on in the *Institutes* to associate those who are misled by false belief with a propensity to be influenced by the poetry of Virgil and Lucretius, arguing that both of these writers imagine a pantheistic, "universal mind animating and invigorating the world," which results in the formulation of "an unsubstantial deity" and a banishing of "the true God whom we ought to fear and worship."[73] The soul must, for Calvin, always retain and reflect the fact that its immortality is divinely created, and likewise gird Christians against the influence of pagan cosmologies. When the body sleeps, the soul's continuing sensations simply affirm the truth of its divine foundation.

Likewise, in his attack on the heresy of soul sleep, *Psychopannychia*, Calvin cites Tertullian's claim that "the soul of the soul is perception," and he argues that because the soul, unlike the body, cannot truly die it can never completely cease to sense.[74] Oddly enough, Calvin's assessment of ongoing sensation in sleep and death relies on Tertullian's attempted synthesis of Christian doctrine with the pagan Stoic theory of oikeiôsis in its emphasis on the perceptive attachment to the soul's ruling principle or hêgemonikon—as is evident in Tertullian's frequent appeals to the Stoics in chapter 5 of his *De Anima*, where he cites Zeno, Cleanthes, and Chrysippus for their insistence upon the corporeality of the soul and the physical basis of its powers of sensation and intellect.

But Tertullian's relatively early position among patristic writers helps to account for his more positive estimation of Stoic doctrine, and for his less stringent view of sleep in relation to psychosomatic care. On the whole, Calvin extends the view of sleep more commonly held among later patristic writers who are extremely wary of its compromising effects on the intellect and its opening of the self to spiritual peril. For Calvin, along with the powers of reason comes a fundamental opportunity that is also a responsibility: Do we look outward and upward in hope of receiving God's grace, or do we look toward ourselves, to the pleasures of a fallen world and the pursuits of an ungodly life? Put another way, the question might be: Do we indulge in the pleasures of reading Aristotle, Virgil, Lucretius, Ovid, and Seneca, or do we resist such temptation in favor of diligent biblical study and exegesis? For Calvin the answer is obvious, and his contention regarding the immortality and power of the soul goes a long way in explaining an overarching suspicion of sleep, in both early modern Northern humanist culture and in the Christian humanist theologies of early modern England.

Erasmian humanism is particularly salient in its yoking of political-theological ends to the vigilant care of the self and a corresponding distrust of sleep. While his *Praise of Folly* gives a comedic face to these humanist convictions, in his *Enchiridion Militis Christiani*, Erasmus more stringently describes "the lyfe of mortal men" as a "perpetuall exercise of warre" that demands our resistance to laxity and carelessness. Hence, the first chapter of the *Enchiridion* is titled, "We must watche and loke aboute vs euer more, whyle we be in this lyfe," and it goes on to characterize the life of most men as one lacking "care and circumspection . . . how ydelly we slepe / now vpon the one side / and now vpon the other / whan without ceasing we are beseged with so great nombre of armed vices."[75] And in the second chapter of this work, Erasmus urges his readers that our "wepons be alway redy at hande / leest thyne so subtyle an enemy shuld take the sleper and vnarmed . . . as longe as we kepe warre in this body / may departe from our harneys, and wepons no ceason / no not (as the sayeng is) one finger brede . . . Therefore let thy first care be, that thy mynde be not vnarmed."[76] His Christian humanist rhetoric of watchful care as the psychosomatic foundation of a perpetually martialized soul is clearly modeled on the Pauline epistles—especially those to the Romans and the Ephesians, which as we have seen idealize the militant spiritual self in its commitment to vigilance while eschewing the carelessness figured by slumber. But Erasmian thought is also a crucial vehicle that extends this vision from Christian theology to the educational enterprises of English Renaissance humanism, which shares some version of the notion—running from Platonic ethics to early modern political theology—that sleep compromises the rule of reason and the habits of vigilant care that are essential to our pursuits of the good. Hence, Erasmus insists that

> the chefe care of christen men ought to be applyed to this poynte / that their chyldren streyght waye from the cradle / amongest the very flaterynges of the noryses, and kisses of the parentes / may receyue and suck vnder the handes of them whiche are lerned / opynyons and perswasyons mete and worthy of Christe: bycause that nothing eyther synketh deper or cleaueth faster in the mynde, than that, whiche (as Fabyus saythe) in the yonge and tender yeres is poured in.[77]

The Erasmian humanist vision of the child as a naturally eager learner, apt to receive and imitate models of virtue from its caretakers is well attested. Yet as Richard Halpern suggests, Erasmus views the child not as a purely passive object to be molded by parents and teachers but rather as a "quantum of energy that seeks of its own accord to be bound and shaped; it desires to invest itself in a governing model."[78] To adapt a formulation closer to my own purposes, the child's own care is a potential waiting to be harnessed and directed through careful instruction; it is drawn into an educational milieu of reading, writing, bodily habit, and disciplinary practice while being watched over by a master whose care for his pupils oscillates between gestures of support and physical coercion. For in seeking to capture and direct the child's care toward productive ends, humanism must find ways of resisting—and encouraging the child himself to resist—the natural propensities to fatigue, careless distraction, and above all else, sleep in the classroom.

English Humanist Ecologies of Care

Not long after its founding in 1480 by William Waynflete, an anonymous teacher at the Magdalen School of Oxford recorded a series of around four hundred passages used for teaching Latin translation to young boys. Written in English prose, the passages featured in the Magdalen *vulgaria* describe the sort of ordinary, everyday events and practices that the average schoolboy might encounter, from talk in the schoolroom to food and drink to morning rituals. Such *vulgaria* were indispensable in early humanist schoolrooms, and the Magdalen School played a particularly influential role in transforming the educational practices of English grammar schools during the first half of the sixteenth century.[79] Its teachers and alumni supplied many of the texts adopted by English humanists during this time, who were following the school's founding emphasis on grammar, largely inspired by Erasmus. The Dutch humanist in fact likely stayed at Magdalen College during his visit to Oxford in 1498 and 1499, further indicating the close ties between Erasmian humanism and the school's pedagogical values.

The Magdalen School compilation is of particular interest here for its descriptions of the early beginnings of a typical English schoolboy's day. As William Nelson suggests in his introduction to a print version of the *vulgaria* found in the Arundel manuscript, the passages being used for translation purposes were written so as to assist the schoolboys in their efforts to stay focused on the task at hand. This explains why the *vulgaria* often featured brief commentary on daily routines and tasks that were familiar to the students, and in some cases offered a bit of levity to an otherwise tedious task. A look at the Magdalen School's *vulgaria* gives us a sense of the quotidian life of humanist schoolboys, as well as the frustrations and affective resistances they faced with the tedium of translation and the long hours devoted to the intellectually and physically demanding work of humanist care. In one remarkable passage worth excerpting at length, the fictional speaker is a schoolboy lamenting the rough transition from life at home to boarding at the Magdalen School, and it appears that what he misses most are the pleasures of laxity and late sleeping that his early childhood had once afforded him:

> The worlde waxeth worse every day, and all is turnede upside down, contrary to th'olde guyse. for all that was to me a pleasure when I was a childe, from iij yere olde to x (for now I go upon the xij yere), while I was undre my father and mothers kepyng, be tornyde now to tormentes and payne. For than I was wont to lye styll abedde tyll it was forth dais [late in the day], delitynge myselfe in slepe and ease. . . . Ther durste no mann but he were made awake me oute of my slepe upon his owne hede while me list to slepe. at my wyll I arose with in treatese, and whan th'appetite of rest went his way by his owne accorde, than I awoke and callede whom me list to lay my gere redy to me. . . . But nowe the worlde rennyth upon another whele. for nowe at fyve of the clocke by the monelyght I most go to my booke and lete slepe and slouthe alon. and yff oure maister hape to awake us, he bryngeth a rode stede of a candle. Now I leve pleasurs that I hade sumtyme. here is nought els preferryde but monyshynge [admonishing] and strypys. brekfastes that were sumtyme brought at my biddynge is dryven oute of contrey and never shall cum agayne. I wolde tell more of my mysfortunes, but thoughe I have leysure to say, yet I have no pleasure, for the reherse of them makyth my mynde more hevy. I sech all the ways I can to lyve ons at myn ease, that I myght rise and go to bede when me liste oute of the fere of betynge.[80]

The passage speaks for itself concerning the young scholar's fond memories of indulgent sleep and idleness in distinction from his daily regimen and the guiding expectations of the Magdalen School's humanist agenda. He has been forced to exchange the pleasures of slumber for regular "monyshynge and strypys," or admonishments and lashes from his rod-wielding masters. Should he fail to rise precisely at five in the morning, he risks a beating from his house master. Yet even if he does manage to wake of his own accord, he must turn immediately to his "booke and lete slepe and slouth alon," risking yet another beating from his schoolteacher if his work is not finished on time. As his melancholic memory of childhood ease suggests, the entry into humanist learning demands the cultivation and regular exercise of a vigilant attention whose economy is boosted by the regular threat of physical violence waiting to be delivered at the very outset of the day.

Numerous passages from the Magdalen *vulgaria* reinforce the simultaneously ethical and intellectual stakes of wakefulness and the humanist devotion to learning. "It is pite to cheryshe such scolars as slepyth styll all the mornynges, taking no thought how moch tyme thei losse," reads one, while another affirms the benefits of rising early and the harmful consequences of too much sleep: "It is a worlde to se the delectacioun and pleasur that a mann shall have which riseth erly in thes summer mornynges, for the very dew shal be so confortable to hym that it shal casuse hym inwardely to rejose. . . . Who wolde than lye thus loterynge in his bedde . . . and gyve hymself only to slepe, be the which thou shalt hurt greatly thyself and also short the tyme of thy lyff? It shal cause the furthmore to be full and voide of connynge, without which lyff and deth be both onn."[81] The proximity of sleep and death is a well-worn classical trope at least since Homer's Odyssey, so it is unsurprising to find this notion reproduced in a humanist *vulgaria*. And we find in the same collection the mutually reinforcing implication that a life spent in wakefulness and an active resistance to sleep in the interest of learning is both a desirable aim and a sign of living virtue. In an imagined exchanged between pupil and master, the child tells his teacher, "I wolde desire iij thynges of you: onn that I myght not wake over longe of nyghtes, another that I be not bett when I com to schole, the thirde that I myght every emong go play with me." In response, he is told, "Gentle scholar, I wolde that ye shulde do iij other thynges: onn that ye ryse betyme of mornynges, another that ye go to your booke delygnetly, the thirde that ye behave yourself against gode devoutly, all menn honestly, and then ye shall have youre askynge."[82] The child's chief complaint regarding the diligence being demanded of him is that it spills over into the time of sleep, requiring him to work well into the night and yet, as his master reminds him, also wake early in the morning. And of course the threat of physical punishment remains a constant presence in the pedagogical dynamic between them, helping to ensure that the young pupil will succeed in resisting the allure of slumber.

The grammatical exercises originating from the Magdalen School show that sleep and wakefulness are crucial considerations in the practical and relational dynamics of care that structure humanist pedagogy. Just as the master's care for his students and their development shapes their sleeping habits and encourages (if not physically coerces) them to commit to long hours and wakeful nights of study, the student's intellectual and ethical care is guided to value vigilant attention to the exercises that shape mind and self, while eschewing the laxity of sleep—which in turn is coded as an unproductive, slothful, and potentially harmful condition when indulged. Garrett Sullivan has shown that the idea of harmful sleep is in fact common in early modern literary, medical, and theological texts, and that immoderate amounts of sleep were imagined to result in negative consequences enfolding ethical and biological forms of life with Christian spirituality.[83] Sullivan's descriptions of the potential harms of sleep are especially revealing for the pedagogical apparatus of humanism, in its insistence upon the cultivation of and dedication to vigilant and attentive forms of care. Yet the pupil's consistent pleas across the pages of the Magdalen *vulgaria* register not only the difficulties inherent to realizing such aims but also the fact that in all likelihood students simply never managed to sleep as much as they wanted or needed in order to feel restored and ready to face each morning's tasks. In other words, the practical need and desire for more sleep combined with the coding of such desire as both a transgression and a failure in living up to the master's expectations makes sleep a charged site of potentially contradictory yet nonetheless intense affective and emotional investments. Here, I extend Lynn Enterline's argument in *Shakespeare's Schoolroom*, which counters the notion that humanist classrooms efficiently and unambiguously produced docile subjects of learning—a position that Rebecca Bushnell develops from a different angle in *A Culture of Teaching*.[84] Bushnell suggests that early modern humanism's inherently ambivalent pedagogical theories and practices complicated its relationship to disciplinary authority, while Enterline argues that in the literature penned by humanist-educated writers like Shakespeare, we find "ambivalent and contradictory" symptoms of the disciplining effects of humanist pedagogy despite the theoretical pronouncements of its schoolmasters.[85] Along such lines, I suggest that the resistances to sleep and the cultivation of vigilance as a humanist paradigm for care in the early modern classroom and beyond made sleep all the more compelling as a site of literary creativity and ethical concern for writers trained under such pedagogical and ethical norms. Renaissance humanism, that is, elicits a specific form of humanist fatigue that enfolds physical and symbolic aspects of life caught up in its ecology of care. As Jeff Dolven eloquently observes of English poets trained by humanist pedagogues, "Their skepticism and self-doubt smolder at the historical roots of English humanism."[86]

Some compelling images of humanist care and fatigue have been handed down to us by a well-known advocate and practitioner of English humanism closer to the end of the sixteenth century. In Richard Mulcaster's *Elementarie* (1582), the headmaster of the Merchant Taylors' School offers five master principles essential to the education of children—reading, writing, drawing, singing, and playing—which he affirms will lead them along a proper course of development to virtue in both public and private forms of life. "Doth not this Elementarie then make childern most capable of vertew in elder years," Mulcaster asks his readers, "for whose growing it is so carefull in their tender age, both by precept and performance?"[87] Mulcaster doesn't shy away from the inherent difficulty of this project; if anything, he is eager to remind us, as he does in the opening pages of the *Elementarie* and throughout, that "good things grow on verie hardlie at their first planting."[88] And while the labors directed by his five principles eventually bring great benefit, the path is one that Mulcaster describes as a thorny and careworn route:

> Againe doth not all our learning conceiued by the eie, and vttered by the tung confesse the great benefit which it receiueth by reading? Doth not all our deliuerie brought furth by the minde, and set furth by the pen acknowledge a dewtie to the principle of writing? Doth not all our descriptions, which figur in the thought, and pictur to the sense both preach & praise the pencill, which causeth them to be sene? Doth not all our delite in times not bisied (as all our labour is for rest, all our trauell for ease, all our care to auoide care) protest in plane termes, that it is wonderfullie endetted to either part of Musik, both by instrument and voice?[89]

The schoolmaster's guiding principles train the student's integrated psychosomatic being—the activities of eye, tongue, hand, and sense—to accomplish his ends with skill. Mulcaster's principles even offer means for achieving the pleasures of relaxation, through training in music. Education in instrument and voice, he tells us, prepares the student for "delite in times not bisied." Mulcaster's humanist teleology thus instrumentalizes the self, though it would be unjust to view that process only as a crudely manipulative disciplining. For one thing, the ultimate telos here is an experience of "delite" in a time of rest; that notion in itself suggests that the schoolmaster has a refined understanding of classical virtue ethics and shares with it some version of the notion that the right sort of contemplative ease is of great value and benefit to the embodied soul. This point reappears in his Peroration, where Mulcaster sums up his view of learning: "First for my generall care to the hole course of learning, I haue thus much to saie. The end of euerie particular mans doings, for his own self: & of the hole common weal for the good of vs all, is so like in consideration, and so the same in natur, as the one being sene, the other nedes small seking: Euerie priuat man traueleth in this world to win rest after toil, to haue ease after labor, and not to trauell still as being a thing exceeding vncomfortable, if so be it were endlesse."[90] The work we do is to provide us with the means to rest, but not simply for those parts of ourselves that need physical restoration or material sustenance; we also work to accomplish ends that, once accomplished, confer a sense of wellbeing that is synonymous with ease. Once we recognize this simple fact we will understand a good deal not only about ourselves but also the political community we inhabit and for whose good we also struggle. Mulcaster's humanism thus aims at cultivating our inherent capacity to achieve that state—both personal and political—whereby a sense of peaceful ease is bestowed upon us.

These lines come from the concluding section of Mulcaster's work, and they shed light on his earlier claim, remarkable in its succinct formulation of an apparent paradox at the heart of humanist thought: "all our care [is] to auoide care."[91] Mulcaster figures care as a humanist project of personal and political development that begins in youth and carries on until we perfect the good, which in turn prevents us from becoming overly entangled in the cares that might be harmful to us, or which derail our efforts at accomplishing virtue. But in a telling passage where Mulcaster searches for a just metaphor to describe the care that tends to children in their earliest years along their path to virtue, he lands upon sleep. Young children are like the sleeping general Timotheus of Athens from the fourth century BC, who is described by Plutarch as being painted asleep while Fortune hovers over his head, "bringing cuntries, towns, and victories vnto him in a net, meaning thereby, that he became such a conqueror, more by hap then by cunning, more by his enemies want, then by his own wit." Sleepers are without care, and so their temporary removal from the world figures for Mulcaster the condition of children who avoid care simply because they are oblivious to it, not yet capable of recognizing the goodly care that tends to them. As he writes,

> Childern which be well trained in their youth be like to sleping Timotheus, preferred by their frinds, ear themselues can perceiue it: and their frinds like to fortun, which furnish them so well, ear themselues can discern, what good is don vnto them. But when theie com to years, and ar once awaked, then with open eies theie behold, their frinds care,

> their own conquest, and fortun fishing for them, naie Gods prouidence verie carefull for them, by the ministerie of parents, masters, and frinds, while theie were fast a slepe, and could not themselues, either help themselues, or iudge right of their helpers.[92]

Mulcaster imagines an ecology of care distributed among roles of parent, teacher, and friend; it tends to children at home and school alike, at their desks and in their sleeping chambers, cultivating their own capacities for care so that they might become properly awakened. Here, sleep is not so much an image of alarming spiritual carelessness or even a direct threat to the humanist project; it instead figures the natural potential that humanism will draw out and sharpen, causing the child eventually to awaken fully into their own. Until that point, they are given over to the care of others, remaining blissfully unaware of the worries and concerns that form the web of their world's caretakers. But this situation of course prepares the child to take on the burdens of self-care as well as the care of others, in keeping with a core paradigm of European humanist thought since Petrarch's fourteenth-century vision of *animi cura*, itself modeled on Senecan positions and grounded in practices of reading and writing that tend to the soul.[93]

Mulcaster's comparison of children in their early years with the figure of a sleeping Timotheus conjoins sleep with carelessness, though with less of the didactic vehemence that informs the author of the Magdalen School grammar in his handling of sleep. Nonetheless, the overall point holds true for English humanism and humanist thought more broadly: sleep is antithetical to the cultivation of virtue, and a force whose inherently downward pull risks collapsing the aspirational project of self-care that so crucially begins at an early age and in the earliest hours of waking life, extending over the course of each day's toil and often well into the evening. We may see in the above depictions of humanist practice among students and teachers as well as in the pedagogical theory espoused by Mulcaster some shared features of the nexus of vigilance and pastoral care that defines early Christian attitudes toward sleep.[94] Mulcaster was known for being a particularly demanding master who was "intolerant of idle pupils" and unafraid to exercise the rod as he deemed necessary, even as he emphasized the cultivation of love for learning among students.[95] In one account of the teacher, it seems that Mulcaster remained a model of the vigilant care and constant attention so valued by humanist pedagogues, even when his body demanded rest. In his *Worthies of England* (1662), Thomas Fuller describes Mulcaster's daily habit as follows: "In a morning he would exactly and plainly construe and parse the lessons to his scholars; which done, he slept his hour (custom made him critical to proportion it) in his desk in the school; but woe be to the scholar that slept the while. Awaking, he heard them accurately; and Atropos might be persuaded to pity, as soon as he to pardon, where he found just fault."[96] Whether or not Fuller's depiction of Mulcaster is entirely to be believed, at the very least it constitutes an instructive urban legend of English humanism. Denying to others the restorative release from care that he seems temptingly to manifest before them, Mulcaster in fact retains his awareness of their scholarly endeavors and is quite ready to call out any errors they make. The vigilant schoolmaster maintains his watchful care over the classroom, even as he sleeps.

Impair and Repair

English humanists, in their emphasis upon vigilant and wakeful attention as the normative foundation of care, sought to instrumentalize the attribute of sensate life that Cicero describes in *De Finibus* as "the desire, most evident in humans but also present in animals, for constant activity."[97] Aristotle, too, notes the inherent pleasures and value of ongoing psychic activity in the eleventh book of his *Metaphysics*, where he argues that the operation of the intellect is the highest pleasure for those beings who are capable of exercising it. He thus describes the prime mover as a divine intellect that is always active and must never sleep: "For if this mind knows nothing, what dignity does it have? It is like one asleep."[98] These classical valorizations of constant sensorial and intellectual activity fold easily into humanist paradigms of vigilant care and virtuous exertion, which in turn resonate with Hans Blumenberg's suggestion that the "mania for work [that] seized postmedieval man" accompanied a certain Cartesian shift in philosophical and scientific thought. Namely, with the promise of knowing nature with greater certainty, humanity also began more earnestly to envision "the prospect of exclusively determining the quality and possibly even the quantity of [its] life."[99] Blumenberg thus attributes to Descartes a newfound emphasis on knowing the physical machinations of life as a means to promoting its longevity, a "medicine for the lengthening and optimizing of organic life" derived from the knowledge of physical nature.[100] For Descartes, such knowledge depends upon the properly trained and steady uses of the intellect in accordance with the new method he develops.[101] But given Aristotle's account of the tendencies of the intellect, and Cicero's sense of a natural proclivity—indeed, a "craving"—for constant activity that is common to sensate life, not to mention the subsequent project of sharpening such psychosomatic capacities in accordance with the norms of Renaissance humanism, perhaps the mania that Blumenberg describes in *Care Crosses the River* is part of an even longer history that has been the central focus of this chapter. That history turns on the cultivation of care as a form of vigilant exertion and attentiveness to self and others, whose extreme and ultimately harmful guise in early modern literature is a pathological form of watch that becomes known as insomnia.

As we turn to the works of drama and poetry at the center of *Vital Strife*, we will see the writers I discuss grapple with the mixed effects of sleep and insomnia in ways that reveal both their indebtedness to humanist models of virtue and ethical care as well as skepticism regarding humanist and political-theological valorizations of vigilance. In these works, the concept of insomnia as an ethically and spiritually harmful outgrowth of vigilant care is increasingly accompanied by worries over its depriving the physical body of the restorative virtues of sleep. Insomnia becomes, in early modern literature, an ethical problem that makes the care for physical life a biopolitical concern. Early modern representations of insomnia suggest that the human animal remains bound to the natural world in fundamentally material ways, and must return each night to a state of unconscious abandon—giving itself back to the care of nature, or what the Stoics call *cura divina*—in order to recover from the accumulated cares of waking life. In this way, insomnia takes on greater meaning as a sign of physical life that is overexerted, fatigued, and in need of recovery—all of which runs counter to the established political-theological and humanist wisdom that sleep compromises ethical and spiritual integrity. Put simply, sleep is a symptom of the human's inseparability from and need to care for its physical nature, while insomnia is the symptom of an excessive care that estranges the human from its physical constitution and self-regenerative capacities. Such powers are, for the writers ahead, grounded in the unconscious bodily processes and subtle transformations occasioned by sleep, and often accompanied by unexpected virtues of perceptual fuzziness and careless lapses in attention. Still, these writers remain intrigued by—and in some instances, committed to—the notion that reason is essential to the care for human life, and may even inhere within its obscure physical foundations. And in this regard, they also look to Seneca's tragedy and to the Stoic figure of the sleeping Hercules as a therapeutic treatment for humanist fatigue. The well-worn Renaissance image of Hercules at the crossroads emblematizes the active choice of a life of virtuous hardship in pursuit of the good, and to that extent he is an apt figure for the constant activity and the coupling of vigilance and virtue valorized by humanist thought.[102] But Seneca's figure of the hero's collapse into the restorative rhythm of sleep, which begins the process of therapeutically balancing his impassioned soul, more emphatically marks the consequences of an overly vigilant commitment to virtue and of the hero's refusal to rest. In that regard, Seneca's Hercules is poised at a different sort of crossroads between sleep and wakefulness, and the shape of his struggles can be tracked across the range of early modern works of drama and poetry that form the core of this book.

Chapter 2

Hercules Asleep

Stoic Oikeiôsis in Jasper Heywood's *Hercules Furens*

In Jasper Heywood's 1561 translation of Seneca's *Hercules Furens*, the protagonist's psychic descent into fury and subsequent slaughter of his family are followed by yet another descent.[1] Immediately after dismembering his wife and children, the hero swoons and collapses onto the earth. His mortal father, Amphitryon, stands by uncertainly: Has Hercules simply fallen, he asks, "to sleepe and quietness . . . or els to death doth thee betake / The self same rage, that hath sent all thy famyly to death?"[2] Has the fury that led Hercules to annihilate the sustaining bonds of his *oikos* now turned itself inward, only to consume the hero at his very core? Or is it that sleep has seized his corporeal soul and could potentially bring solace to the passion that rages in his breast? Amphitryon soon has his answer when he discerns the movements of breath in his son's chest, and then sees him awaken to the tragic reality of his crimes with his sanity restored—albeit somewhat precariously—as his rage cools into a melancholic despair. This process culminates in a suicidal impulse that Amphitryon only manages to restrain by threatening to take his own life and thereby further staining Hercules with the crime of patricide. Under such duress, Hercules relents, and commits himself anew to the task of living on in full knowledge of having massacred his own wife and children.

How exactly did the hero come to this point? The simplest answer is that Juno's furies are responsible for whipping him into a cosmic frenzy, and so readers might reasonably view Hercules's murderous rampage as an unavoidable matter of fate, or at least as the outcome of plotting by a vehement and vengeful goddess whose powers outmatch those of the demigod. Hercules would seem to bear little, if any, responsibility for his apparent crimes. But the tragedy situates this event within a Stoic cosmos, where the seething volatility of physical mixtures makes ethics a matter of understanding the subtle nature and causal interaction among bodies—even as the play suggests that constantly maintaining the corporeal soul's grasp on virtue is a virtually impossible task for even the mightiest of heroes and the most discerning of natural scientists. The Stoic theories of *krasis*, or coextensive blending, and *sumpatheia*, or mutual affection, mean that bodies are radically permeable and liable to mix unpredictably, generating sudden and extreme transformations, the cause of which often remains opaque to human understanding. The scene of Hercules's collapse is thus poised at a tragic literary intersection of Stoic idealism and Stoic realism, where the ethical norms of virtue and self-care must face up to the unruly physicality and passionate turbulence of life. *Hercules Furens* takes seriously Chrysippus's claim that the "virtues are animate bodies," by subjecting that premise to an extreme incarnation of its logical opposite—that vice, too, is a body apt to suddenly overtake the corporeal motions of the virtuous soul due to the thoroughness of blending among all bodies in the cosmos and the mutually affecting tension that interanimates them.

While the play depicts the physical causality behind Hercules's fury and its aftermath in a manner consistent with the Stoic system of corporeal ethics and volatile distributed agency, it also draws particular attention to the fact of Hercules's ethical failure to attend to his bodily need to sleep. Hercules's lack of sleep makes his corporeal soul's hêgemonikon (ruling principle) more susceptible to the harmful environmental circulations of fury, illustrating both the Stoic normative aim of a carefully sympathetic attunement of physiology with ecological milieu, and the radical difficulty of hitting that mark to maintain the body of virtue. In other words, the scene of domestic annihilation at the heart of the play is in part brought on by Hercules's refusal to rest, which connects the ethics of self-care and *oikonomia* to the perils of insomnia. An overly vigilant commitment to virtue leads Hercules into the Underworld for three days without rest, and upon returning to Thebes his careworn body draws the hero into contact with a harmful mixture of fire and air engendered by Juno's furies. This condition in turn obstructs him from selecting the right action at a crucial moment—precisely when his father insists that he must rest before offering a sacrificial homage to Zeus. Instead, the hero falls into a murderous rage, and when the Chorus prays for Hercules to remain "fast bounde with heavy sleepe opprest" so that "slumber deepe" might restore calm to his impassioned soul, it calls on the restorative chthonic virtues of the earthly matter that gives substance to Hercules's mortal being. His sleeping condition in this way foregrounds the restorative powers of the Stoic *cura regentis*, or cosmic care, which for Seneca and other Stoic thinkers is synonymous with the rational motions of the pneuma—the vital agent and originary cause that also subtends the process of oikeiôsis.

Hercules Furens thus reveals a surprising yet intimate connection between unconscious physical life and care by investing dormant life with a simultaneously ethical and physiological value. And this therapy of rest is all the more remarkable in that it eludes Herculean self-mastery while it is nonetheless essential to the hero's ongoing labors of virtue. As an unconscious physical event, sleep falls outside the muscular attention and purposive discipline for which Hercules is a paradigmatic figure in the Stoic tradition—and indeed, for which Stoicism more broadly is known in most critical discussions of its relationship to early modern thought. Yet there are Stoic ethical texts exploring the connections between sleep and physical embodiment in ways that challenge our familiar notions of Stoicism, and some even cite Hercules's sleep as an emblematic instance of the natural inclination and persistence of oikeiôsis. Seneca's Hercules is thus part of a broader affiliation in Stoic thought between the scene of sleep and the foundational *tonos* of life that discloses the living animal's care for itself. And in *Hercules Furens*, sleep constitutes a unique mode of *krasis*: it is a physical mixture that begins to restore and reorient the hero's oikeiôsis, or the rational grasping of his self-constitution that also serves as the psychosomatic core of his ethical care. For Hercules, the truly Stoic test emerges upon awakening and finding himself in an ethical quandary of how to endure life after having sent his wife and children to their untimely graves.

My reading of these ethical and physiological dimensions of sleep in *Hercules Furens* unsettles some familiar notions of Stoic ethics and its relationship to Senecan drama, especially among critics of early modern literature. But as I argue through an appeal to Seneca's prose writings as well as other Stoic ethical texts, there are compelling reasons to rethink what has become the popular understanding of the Stoic ethics of care and its relationship to Seneca's tragedies. Namely, that Senecan Stoicism exalts the isolated individual and imagines virtue as a form of radical detachment from the physical circulations and affective energies that can potentially open the door to a passion. It is beyond the scope of this chapter to examine multiple tragedies in detail, and so my argument is put to an admittedly partial test in assessing *Hercules Furens* alone. But given the compelling role of sleep in the play, alongside other Stoic writings on sleep and oikeiôsis, I think this tragedy holds a special place in the Senecan corpus, in that it lays bare the cosmological principles of Stoic ethical thought as they inform the care of the self and the ambivalent forms of *cura* that characterize Roman Stoicism in particular. While my reading of the play draws out a compelling intimacy between sleep and oikeiôsis in Stoic thought—which includes other references to Hercules asleep in works by Hierocles and Plutarch—it also looks ahead to the representations of sleep and insomnia in the early modern literary and philosophical works that form the substantial core of this book.[3] Heywood's translation of Seneca's tragedy is an important conduit for Senecan Stoicism among early modern English writers who creatively adapt materials from its figurations of sleeping life and vigilant care, and who are captivated by the idea that the descent into sleep can bring our embodied souls into deeper resonance with the vital motions of the cosmos that sustain all forms of life.

The Physics of Care

In the early decades of the twentieth-century, critics widely cited Seneca's formative influence on Elizabethan writers.[4] This initial wave of enthusiasm crested in 1927 with T. S. Eliot's republication of Thomas Newton's 1581 edition of *Seneca: His Tenne Tragedies*, which featured the English translations from Newton's original collection along with Eliot's introductory essay to the volume.[5] From there, a new trend emerged in mid-century criticism, which took to downplaying Seneca's role in favor of illustrating the importance of England's medieval and native dramatic traditions, or even the influence of other Roman playwrights such as Terence.[6] The rise of new historicist and theoretically savvy accounts of early modern literature in the 1980s brought renewed attention to the place of Senecan thinking in early modern literary culture: Gordon Braden's *Renaissance Tragedy and the Senecan Tradition* and Robert Miola's *Shakespeare and Classical Tragedy* are two notable and oft-cited works from this period.[7] Meanwhile, the centrality of Seneca has somewhat given way in more recent studies of Stoicism and early modern thought, which by and large track the ethical and political affiliations between Roman Stoicism and the intellectual and literary cultures of early modern England.[8]

Nearly without exception, however, these accounts of early modern literature's engagement with Senecan drama and Stoic ethics represent Stoicism as an obdurate ethical system of self-care, aimed at entirely eliminating the vagaries of feeling and thereby securing one's soul, citadel-like, against the undue influence of passion or the tumultuous rule of tyrants. Insofar as Stoicism champions resolution, constancy, and rational control over the passions, critics have presumed—and in some cases, argued quite forcefully—that it advocates an ethics that cleanly and completely separates the self and its rational faculties from the changing influence of the body, as if reason drew its powers from a space immune to flux and beyond physical life, somewhat akin to the unchanging realm of Platonic Forms. Geoffrey Miles, citing a fragment by Zeno of Citium on living *"homologoumenos tei physei"* (in harmony with nature), even asserts that "the Stoics' assumptions thus lead them back to the Platonic ideal of being always the same"—a notion at odds with the Stoic insistence that reason and passion alike are bodies, and with the school's cosmological understanding of corporeal mixtures as volatile sites of obscured causality that easily can and often do disrupt the physical cohesion of virtue.[9] Numerous early modernists and classicists alike have thus conceived the Stoic sage as a master of virtue who abides, much like the modern-day Superman, in a self-crafted fortress of solitude.[10]

Braden's oft-cited *Renaissance Tragedy and the Senecan Tradition* is exemplary in this regard, as it argues for a theory of "autarkic selfhood" that dominates Senecan tragedy and feeds directly into early modern literary and philosophical thought.[11] Braden views Stoicism as an ethical system that endorses, above all else, a notion of imperturbable selfhood that isolates the individual from the influence of other selves and other bodies. Stoicism is a kind of ethical dead end, because it leads inevitably "toward a breaking of ties with the exterior world."[12] Drawing the Stoic self further and further inward, Braden's account of Senecan autarky and its progeny in Renaissance literature suggests that for the Stoics, the solely valuable form of life is that of the sage understood as an individual in the absolute sense: someone who is completely withdrawn from the turbulent world and who stands "against a meaningless reality that has value only as an opportunity for proving ourselves and enjoying our self-esteem."[13] It is important to note the particulars of Braden's argument, though not only because it has had a formative hand in shaping our critical understanding of Senecan drama and selfhood. Braden also works up to the claim that Seneca's vision of a radically autonomous and alienated self leads presciently into Shakespeare's and Montaigne's "new sense of distant inwardness" which in turn opens "onto a prophetically modern subjectivity."[14] Braden may well be right in attributing an interest in Senecan autarky to early modern readers and writers, especially given the fact that the tragedies foreground insistent displays of self-assertion and feature numerous monologues in which characters scrutinize their own psychosomatic conditions while grappling with desires that motivate them to act against the dominant ethical norms of their world. But by gathering such episodes to make a case for his Senecan genealogy of modern subjectivity and radical autonomy, Braden's book neglects essential aspects of Seneca's Stoicism and misconstrues its influence on his dramatic corpus—more precisely, Seneca's particular vision of the care of the self and the conditions of virtue amid a turbulent physical cosmos, all of which indicate a deep commitment to the Stoic system and its ecological understandings of selfhood, physical life, and ethical care.

A crucial tension between Braden's reading of Stoic thought and Seneca's relationship to it in fact comes into focus by attending to the broader role of care. Care is not simply a matter of self-care for Seneca and other Stoic philosophers but a feature of human life that necessarily involves turning toward the world and acknowledging the cares that sustain living relations with other entities and with the cosmos at large. Katja Vogt notes that "the Stoics think in terms of *affiliation* with others. It is through an *affective* and *relational* disposition that we act as we should, and the task of virtue is to acquire this disposition."[15] From the ancient Stoics onward, this process of ethical development is known as oikeiôsis, and it is an unfolding that moves outward, not inward, as Braden's account suggests.[16] It begins with the most immediate mode of sensation constituted by the minimal degree of tension between the bodily matter and corporeal pneuma that combine, blend within, and animate all beings, and it relies upon the ongoing immediacy of reason and sensation over the course of a developing life. For this reason, bodily feeling and sensation are essential to the actions of the sage, and to the Stoic vision of ethical care and virtue. A passion is not to be indulged, but the exercise of virtue still very much depends upon the corporeal soul's capacity to feel and to acknowledge sensorial impressions and motions that are bound up with the physical motions of the cosmos, and which can then be determined as worthy or unworthy of assent. Seneca makes this point explicitly in his ninth letter to Lucilius, which takes issue with Epicurean and Cynic models of the sage for being overly detached from feeling and for denying the centrality of friendship to the good life. "Our position is different from theirs in that our wise person conquers all adversities, but still feels them; theirs does not even feel them."[17] Whether he is entirely right to ascribe to both Cynic and Epicurean schools such an extreme notion of affective detachment is beside the point: Seneca means to show that the Stoics embrace the fact that life naturally brings a multiplicity of affective states that are in fact necessary for and conducive to right action. Senecan virtue leads to a certain kind of self-strengthening, but only insofar as the body of virtue is sympathetically attuned to its environmental milieu in a manner adequate to grasping and acting in accordance with the feelings that arise as a result. The sage suffers to the extent that it is right to do so, understanding that suffering arises naturally from the conditions of the cosmos, just as the sage experiences a unique form of "joy [that] pertains only to the wise person, for it is the elevation of a mind towards goods that are real and its own."[18] These sorts of affective dispositions belong to the category identified by ancient Stoics as *eupatheiai*, or good feelings, which are good because they constitute worthwhile emotional responses to events in the world. The sage feels justly without indulging in the feeling and thereby twisting it into the amplified agitation that constitutes a passion.[19]

Moreover, the Stoic self is in no way an isolated individual caring only for its individual soul, but is instead quite literally part of a whole—the embodied soul of any human animal is simply one part of the whole that is the cosmos, itself a living and ensouled body. So when the body of an individual human animal senses and acts in accordance with nature, that is tantamount to acting in accordance with reason, and in harmony with the pneuma that flows through the living body of the cosmic whole. The autarkic selfhood that Braden attributes to Stoic thought would in fact amount to an erroneous understanding of the self in relation to the cosmos for any committed Stoic, and so the image of an isolated sage who rests securely with no care or sense whatsoever for the fluctuations of corporeal mixtures that sustain her own physical life is inconsistent with the school's foundational principles and ethical teachings.[20] To state the matter in terms closer to the framework adopted in my introductory discussion of Stoic virtue and ethical normativity, the sage selects her norms, but does so from an embodied condition—a balanced state of *tonos*—that allows her to grasp the workings of the cosmos as they bear upon and give rise to an immediate situation that calls for a certain and creative mode of action. The sage here is not an autarkic being, though she does embody a distinctive kind of autonomy in her capacity to select that which is truly *kalon*, or good in the philosophical sense. Yet the motions of her corporeal soul's hêgemonikon are the result of the pneuma that moves through her, and so her good actions arise upon cognitively grasping and acting in accordance with the bodily tension that harmonizes her psychosomatic being and draws it into attunement with the cosmos. The Stoic sage thus quite literally embodies reason in her physical being: reason is a body that is grounded in a state of affairs that can also be grasped as a corporeal and rational representation by the being whose capable body is so moved. It is in this sense that the Stoic sage also embodies a form of normative agency that closely resembles Georges Canguilhem's theory of vital normativity, in her capacity to posit norms that respond creatively to her ecological milieu and to the inevitable failure to uphold norms.[21] All of this relies deeply on an awareness of the sensations and feelings caused by the interaction between the physical matter and pneuma that combine to animate her as a living and thinking being and which engender the body of reason. This is what it means to care for self and world according to Stoic ethics, and so there is no strict separation between the individual body and the cosmic whole, nor between reason and physical sensation.[22]

While Seneca's prose writings do not contain so precise a discussion of these intersections of Stoic ethics, cosmology, and metaphysics, in his ethical letters he often reasserts the centrality of the care of the self in terms that orient us toward the cosmos and toward other entities, and in letter 65 he embarks upon a metaphysical discussion of causality that ultimately leads him to reassert the centrality of the Socratic notion of the care of the self.[23] Yet Seneca views the care of the self as a function of its cosmic origins in the Stoic pneuma, and as a sympathetic extension of "the care of him who governs all things," or the pneuma as Zeus, the "*cura regentis*" (58.28).[24] Our reason is a manifestation of cosmic rationality, just as our bodies are part of the substantial whole whose movements, development, and decay are bodies acting as causes to other bodies endlessly cycling through nature. In letter 65, he writes, "Our Stoic philosophers, as you know, declare that there are two things in the universe, which are the source of everything—namely, cause and matter. Matter lies sluggish, a substance ready for any use, but sure to remain unemployed if no one sets it in motion. Cause, however, by which we mean reason, moulds matter and turns it in whatever direction it will, producing thereby various concrete results." Seneca argues for "the primary and generic cause" which he ultimately identifies as "productive reason—that is, God. For all these things you have mentioned are not multiple individual causes but are dependent on one, the one that makes."[25] Like the Stoics before him, Seneca contends that all change is due to bodies acting as causes to other bodies, which when taken together express the unified rational movement of the cosmos as a whole guided by the pneuma.

The doctrine of the pneuma as ultimate cause also helps to explain the ancient Stoic concept of *sumpatheia*, according to which any one body can affect any other body across the entirety of the cosmos, because "the cosmos as a whole possesses the same kind of unity as living organisms. It is one in which given the interaction between the whole and its parts, the affections of the parts may be transmitted to other parts or to the whole."[26] Only bodies can cause other bodies to act as causes, while events themselves are incorporeal and cannot be causes, as Susan Sauvé Meyer explains: "The fundamental unanalyzed causal relation, on this picture, is that between agent and patient: one body acting on another. An event may be the product of this interaction, but not being a body itself, it cannot act on any body to produce a further event."[27] Sauvé Meyer's therapeutic language is revealing, as it resonates with Seneca's cosmological view of self-care as a microcosmic image of the active care for the cosmos embodied by the *cura regentis*—whose modulations the sage aims to embody through her own will. The sage's virtue is synonymous with the understanding of the natural scientist, because all causes are due to a unified, agential presence in matter that includes the stuff of our own bodies as it does any other body within the cosmos. In other words, virtue is a manifestation of Zeus or god as the pneuma or vital fire that animates and gives cohesion to all bodies.

But how exactly do these Stoic cosmological and ethical convictions relate to Seneca's tragedies? Why would a devotee of cosmic virtue and rationality pen so many tragedies that not only depict but at times seem even to valorize their exact opposites? One response is that the demands of literary genre require it. Thomas G. Rosenmeyer argues that the genre of tragedy both constrains and affords to Seneca certain creative opportunities, since the sequential order that typically defines classical dramatic action becomes instead a vehicle for exploring causality in "the Stoic cosmos, which is one of dynamic tension, fluid, soft, a biological and chemical field in which contrary energies are at best held in an equilibrium and at worst engaged in a constant struggle for superiority, straining toward excess and explosion."[28] The popular Aristotelian concept of tragic action depends upon a decisive yet mistaken choice that effects a reversal, which strikingly differs from this core thrust of Senecan tragedy and its vision of the life forces that determine action as such. This dramatic core likewise suggests that a Stoic metaphysics of causality underpins its biological and ethical differences from the Aristotelian model of drama, as Rosenmeyer argues:

> Aristotle's discovery of the coordinates of potentiality and actualization is itself indebted to a biological model. But while Aristotle's biological system was one of evolution and the final cause, and focused on the life curve of organisms, the Stoic model transcends the level of individual organisms and the life of the species and takes its incentive from a more radical understanding of life forces. . . . The varied and unstable fusion that animates the cosmos is played out in a matrix that is both pure "acting and being-acted-upon" and pure fluidity, extending from the elements to the smallest inanimate objects, bringing everything under the influence of the *pneuma*.[29]

Seneca's "radical understanding of life forces" is part of a broader Stoic philosophical tradition that coheres around a systematic form of ecological thought. The Stoic conception of action and agency understands both as movements that rise and fall within a web of interconnected physical bodies, no single one of which is purely responsible for the complex determinations of any given state of affairs or the event to which it gives rise. Senecan drama is therefore both a drama of cosmological forces and a drama of the power of the individual soul's *affectus*, but the virtues of constancy and rational action are themselves bodily conditions that in no way allow for a tidy separation of reason from the physical cosmos and its broader motions. While Seneca undoubtedly prizes the care of the self and a commitment to embodying virtue, his adherence to Stoic doctrines of corporeal causation, and the fact that both virtue and vice are physical conditions of the embodied soul, mean that the power of reason never detaches from the bodily mixtures that articulate movements of the pneuma: "The mind itself turns into the passion" when it is so moved, as he writes.[30] Likewise, "Reason and passion, as I said, don't have separate and distinct dwelling places but are the mind's transformation to a better and worse condition."[31] Reason and unreason are both conditions of the corporeal soul, and in a Senecan cosmos of radically distributed agency, maintaining the body of reason becomes a near-impossible exercise in ethical comportment—leading Rosenmeyer to assert that the "assumption of corporeality, that all causes are bodies in motion, is taken so seriously that it is largely a lost hope to want to isolate the rules of logic and the patterns of psychology from the material behavior of physical masses."[32] The unruly environments of Seneca's cosmic drama take center stage despite the vehement self-assertions of his protagonists, belying their histrionic insistence upon an impoverished and false conception of their own autonomy.

It isn't just that Seneca wants to call attention to the wrongheadedness of villains and their perverse commitments to vice; he also indicates the physical cosmos tends to disrupt any effort at maintaining virtue as well, so long as both positions insist upon the individual as a site of sui generis agency that fails to acknowledge and ascertain its cosmic embeddedness. In his recent work on Seneca's *Natural Questions*, Gareth Williams argues that under certain conditions, the embodiment of virtue is at least temporarily impossible: "Seneca himself concedes in moments that the struggle against vice is a lost cause".[33] But Williams goes further, noting that the ideal of "cosmic consciousness" that Seneca constructs over the course of *Natural Questions* is constantly undermined by the appearance of vice-ridden individuals—literary characters, of a sort—who draw the work's loftier ethical perspective downward, creating a kind of tug-and-pull for the reader that reflects the experience of embodied life: "Cosmic consciousness is no easy winner here, as if soaring effortlessly above the forces of vice that represent the view from below: if it appears to be winning out at any given point in the text (and the *NQ* is arguably centered on the struggle, not the result), the passions nevertheless always infect the work, as if a residual condition that continuously threatens a fresh outbreak and a new reverse."[34] While that in no way means that the self is emptied of all responsibility and need not strive to achieve virtue, it does mean that ethics cannot be grounded on anything beyond an accommodation of the self to the unpredictable physical movements of the cosmos in seeking that end.

Hence, in Senecan drama the uncertain flux of bodily passions, as well as interference in the lives of humans by cruel and jealous gods, serve as correlates of a Stoic cosmological perspective that actually de-emphasizes the powers of disciplined control and rational self-mastery. The ideal image of the Stoic sage is simply that: an image that becomes practically impossible to actualize and maintain with constancy, and from a literary perspective worthy of exploration as a tragically failed encounter—even as the norm of embodying virtue through the attunement of one's psychosomatic being to the rational bodily motions of the cosmos remains as a motivational end for ethical life. To put the matter in an even more cosmic framing, we might say that Seneca's literary endeavors are devoted to a creative exploration of what Gilles Deleuze describes as Stoic "bodies caught in the particularity of their limited presents," which are bound up with becoming in ways that occlude to human understanding the cosmic reason that guides the movements of the whole.[35] It is from within such mixtures that the limited human perspective is situated—a view that lacks the sage's powers of divination to see clearly through the present muck of cosmic flux in order to master the pestilent cycles of passion. Seneca's tragedies are consistent with the ethical and cosmological principles of Stoicism precisely because they draw attention to the cosmic failures of embodied life, and to the fact that the norms of virtue appear by way of the failure to constantly manifest and uphold them in their physical condition.

Krasis and *Ira*

Seneca writes in his essay *On Anger*, "We're all inconsiderate and careless; we're all unreliable, complaining, grasping; we're all—why conceal with euphemism the open wound we share?—wicked. Each and every one of us will find in his own breast the fault he rebukes in another. . . . And so we should be gentler with one another: we are wicked, living among the wicked."[36] To an untrained eye these lines may appear simply to repeat a familiar ethical maxim against hypocritically judging others; for a Stoic such as Seneca, however, the notion goes deeper and is given cosmological shape by the principle of *krasis*, or total blending. "A drop of wine penetrates the whole ocean"—this is the aphoristic formulation of *krasis* attributed to Chrysippus, which should be taken in its fullest sense as the logical consequence of the broader Stoic doctrine of *sumpatheia*, or "cosmic cohesiveness" and coextension.[37] Any given body in the cosmos is connected, through the tension animating the whole, with any other body that likewise forms a part of the cosmos. And bodies can and do so thoroughly blend with each other that they even occupy the same space—as is the case with respect to the pneuma and the bodily matter of any given animal, but which also holds true in more extreme cases such as the example provided by Chrysippus. Bodies contain the seeds of their opposites and are therefore liable to a sudden upsurge of growth that effectively reverses the qualitative features that define them at any given moment. In other words, Seneca's rebuke against judgment quite literally means that should we care to look, we will find within our own breasts the same failure or "wound" that we point to in others, because our bodies are so thoroughly intermixed and coextensive with those bodies we perceive to be outside of and neatly separate from our own. For the Stoics, the fundamental nature of psychosomatic being opens the ostensibly individual self to a radically permeable field of causal influence.

Senecan tragedy illustrates the darker side of this point by foregrounding a persistent and infectious power of the passions, which reflects Seneca's commitments to Stoic physicalism and its cosmic doctrines of *krasis* and *sumpatheia*. Brutal events seem to be the combined result of vengeful meddling by the gods and a lack of psychic care on the part of protagonists, but such extreme situations emerge from circulations of highly volatile physical mixtures within and among bodies. And in this world of an unpredictably changing physis, as C. A. J. Littlewood observes, "The landscape functions as an objective ethico-physical context for human action; even as it collapses into disorder it interprets tragic events coherently."[38] As an example, Littlewood cites the pestilent fire that spreads through the funereal ecology of *Hercules Oetaeus*: "The burning poison and the pyre which raises Hercules to heaven (*in astra tollunt* 1638) are ultimately caused by the flames of Deianira's passion and the imagery makes the connections immediate. . . . The poison in Hercules' body (*pestis* 1249) is Deianira herself (*pestem* 851) expressed in the medium of the robe (*pestem* 566). . . . What we see on the stage are passions in physical form. Through familiar patterns of imagery sequences of actions are reduced to successive representations of the same passion."[39] Littlewood shows that as passions move through Seneca's turbulent physical cosmos, they transform dramatic landscape, the bodily condition of characters, and physical objects alike, while retaining their essential quality and force as the above passage emphasizes in its repetition of the cognates of *pestis*. The sequence of bodily causes—from the fiery body of Deianira's passion to the burning poison of Hercules's blood-soaked tunic to the hero's poisoned body to the burning funeral pyre—form a concrete chain whose beginnings and ultimate end remain opaque to human discernment, extending indefinitely in both chronological direction and physical space. The precise moment at which Deianira's passion arises is uncertain because the passion is already coextensive with the physical mixtures that form her being, just as the drop of wine permeates the entire Chrysippean ocean. And yet the interpretive coherence and meaning afforded by Seneca's physical environment likewise suggest that while these passionate mixtures seethe and foment discord at the immediate level of bodily encounters and causes caught up in the limited present, the unified and rational causality of the pneuma still guides the grand cosmic mixture of the whole—a point that is crucial for understanding how to reconcile the dire events of Senecan tragedy with the philosopher's overarching Stoic commitment to cosmic order through the *cura regentis*.[40] To interpret tragic events coherently, pushing off from Littlewood's formulation, involves the work of divination and the grasping of cosmic order attributed to the embodied condition of the sage in virtuous synchronicity with the body of the whole. But the characters of Senecan drama, being caught up in the vicious and limited moments of their physical becomings amid the vice-ridden ecologies of tragedy, cannot but fail to embody the vision of the sage.

Taking Seneca's account of anger seriously thus means to acknowledge the very "open wound" to be found in each and every human breast, and to grasp the potential that any particular body in the cosmos has to suddenly and violently transform into an altered state that manifests a corporeal causal chain which has otherwise gone unnoticed. While the human experience and expression of anger may have distinctive features that entail a conceptual understanding of that passion, the passion itself is a body connected to a larger cosmic chain of causality that spreads across the environmental milieu shaping an individual life. And in the tragedy whose titular hero mythically embodies the wound of anger, we see a diffused physical causality that effectively disrupts the embodiment of virtue for which Hercules is recognized as both a sage and a guardian of the earth. As Gilles Deleuze remarks, "The hero of Seneca's tragedies and of the entire Stoic thought is Hercules . . . always situated relative to the three realms of the infernal abyss, the celestial height and the surface of the earth." In Hell, Hercules encounters "frightening combinations and mixtures; in the sky he finds only emptiness and celestial monsters duplicating those of the inferno. As for the earth, he is its pacifier and surveyor, and even treads over the surface of its waters."[41] Hercules's wife Megara speaks to this Stoic virtue at the opening of act 2 in *Hercules Furens*, as she hopes for her husband's return: "And th'earth well knowes the worker of his quietnes to be / Away from earth."[42] As its hero and caretaker, Hercules guards and maintains the quiet earth—he is a human-god hybrid whose stewardship manifests the *cura regentis* that is also part of his own physical being, and which is maintained through the guiding motions of his soul's hêgemonikon.

But as Megara laments at the opening of act 2, her life as wife to Hercules has been far from easy. She is instead consumed by a constant worry that she suggests mirrors the hero's own situation: "To mee yet never day / Hath careless shin'de: the ende of one affliication past away / Beginning of an other is: an other enemy / Is forthwith founde, before that hee his joyfull family / Retourneth unto: an other sight he taketh by behest: / Nor any respite given is to him nor quiet rest."[43] Megara thus gives voice to the cares that are a necessary component of Herculean virtue, but whose burdens have deeply affected both the hero and his family alike. As spokesperson for the *oikos* that sustains him but which sharply feels his absence, Megara worries over the simple yet crucial fact that Hercules's constant labors prevent him from taking rest. Her words remind the audience of Hercules's mortal half, and of the fact that his split being brings with it the necessity to attend to his own physical constitution, even as his participation in divinity both supports and encourages his virtuous labors in ways that reach beyond the sphere of mortal possibility.

In fact, the notion that Hercules's labors have enervated his mortal being, making him frantic and careworn, actually appears before Megara's speech. The Chorus of act 1 suggests that Hercules embodies an extreme version of the laborious cares that it attributes naturally to human life. As the sun rises over the countryside, "labor hard beginnes, and everye kynde / Of cares it styrres," from the shepherd who watches his flock and guides them to grass, to the sailor who goes out to sea "in doubt of lyfe" yet strives to return home safely with each day's catch. The Chorus describes these bucolic activities as bringing a daily dose of anxiety and worry, but such cares are offset by the "quiet rest" of each day's night and the contentedness of simple living. This balanced vision of life alternating between periods of activity and rest then shifts into a description of the "dreadful feares" that define city life, where the inhabitants pursue wealth and fame, many going "without the rest of sleepe."[44] In John Fitch's reading of the play, the Chorus of act 1 drives home the point "that the ambitious man lacks *secura quies* and that the fortunes of his house are insecure," echoing Megara's earlier worry that the earth lacks its guardian and, in another sense, suggesting the guardian himself lacks the security of a quiet earth due to the restlessness that occupies and enervates him. "When they draw a contrast between the quiet life and the life of ambitious activity," Fitch notes, "there can be no doubt on which side Hercules is ranged."[45] He is represented as "a man incapable of relaxing," who strives not only to conquer the challenge before him but immediately to find the next obstacle in need of clearing.[46] The Chorus thus draws attention to both the unnatural and unsustainable character of Hercules's labors, given his half-mortal composition and the brute physical fact of his need for sleep. Translated into the terms of Deleuze's Stoic spatialization of Herculean heroism, we might say that Hercules fails to realize that his movements among and mastery over the geographies of depth, height, and surface also involve the balanced care of his own corporeal soul. And it is precisely this failure to acknowledge and to care therapeutically for the physical life that underpins Hercules's heroism that the tragedy foregrounds at the moment when the furies overtake him.

That is not to argue in any single-minded sense that Hercules's madness is his own fault; it is instead to see that the play draws attention to the hero's physical life—and the need to care for it through the restorative therapy of sleep—as one crucial factor leading to a scene of mistaken perception and action that holds tragic consequences. But to see this moment of Hercules's fury and his ethical failure in properly Stoic terms, we must track the causal chain of passion that engenders it, beginning from Juno's opening screed in act 1, where the goddess rues Hercules's victories in all his labors thus far. She is embittered by the knowledge that he will soon return triumphant from Hades, and she fears his hubris will lead him to seek a place in the heavens and upend the rule of his father and her husband, Jove. Juno thus decides that since no monstrous other can defeat Hercules, he must be led to defeat himself: "Seekes thou a match t'Alcides yet? / Thers none, except hymselfe: let him agaynst himselfe rebell. / Let present be from bottome deepe upraysd of lowest hell / Th'Eumenides, let flaming lockes of theyrs the fires out flinge."[47] To provoke self-destructive rage in one's enemies represents a superior form of malevolence in the Senecan cosmos, as Heywood's earlier translation of *Thyestes* illustrates.[48] In that play, the following exchange between Atreus and his servant, Satelles, touts the rancorous power of a self-annihilating *ira* over the inferior thrust and pyrotechnics of sword and fire:

Satelles: What sworde?
Atreus: To little that.
Satelles: What fire?
Atreus: And that is yet to light.
Satelles: What weapon then shall sorow such fynde fit to worke thy wyll?
Atreus: Thyestes selfe.
Satelles: Then yre it self yet thats a greater yll.[49]

Like Atreus, Juno aims to destroy her foe by encouraging him to destroy himself. She weaponizes the body of *ira* by summoning furies from the cosmic depths that will amplify anger across the ecological milieu of Thebes, such that it overtakes the ruling principle of Hercules's soul and leads him to annihilate his own family in a fit of rage. Rosenmeyer suggests that in *Hercules Furens*, "an examination of moral action cannot be conducted without a full accounting of the various biological and environmental factors that enter into it."[50] Clearly, Juno aims to upend the balanced care of bodily self and corporeal soul attributed to

Hercules in a philosophical tradition dating back to the ancient Cynics and Stoics, who viewed the Herculean commitment to his labors as a mark of ascetic virtue and, for Seneca, a "model of the *vir sapiens*."[51] But the hero's susceptibility to Juno's nefarious intentions and the fiery motions of the furies admit of a range of psychosomatic explanations in keeping with the Stoic commitment to a "swarm of causes" (Rosenmeyer 73) that can render human perceptions inadequate to the task of arriving at full knowledge of the causal chain. We can only begin from where the play orients us in its opening pages, which is to say the Underworld, whence Juno summons the furies to their fell task.

And yet even from this starting point, complications emerge. From one angle, the furies themselves are both the causal agents and embodiments of the fiery passion that upend Hercules's sanity—demonic beings who rise from below upon Juno's summoning to bring mayhem to Thebes: "Beginne ye servantes now of hell: the fervent burning tree / Of Pyne shake up: and set with snakes her dreadful flocke to see. / Let now Megaera bring to sight, and with her mournful hand / For burning rage bring out of hell a huge and direful brand. . . . Strike through his breast, let fyercer flame, within his bosom boyle."[52] Juno seemingly directs Megara to move from the Underworld to the surface of the earth and then physically pierce Hercules's breast with her sword of fire. Yet upon summoning the furies and tasking them with whipping Hercules into a frenzy, Juno also commands them to inflame her own soul with the same fury: "That mad of mind and witles may Alcides drive bee / With fury great through pearced quight, my self must first of all / Be mad. Wherfore doth Juno yet not into raging fall? / Mee, me, ye Furyes, systers three throwne quite out of my wit / Tosse first, if any thing to do."[53] Temporally speaking, which comes first? Isn't Juno's anger at Hercules what leads her to summon the furies in the beginning, and if so, how are we to make sense of her summoning as a command that the furies first enrage Juno herself before fulfilling their task on earth?

My sense is that the scene is meant to illustrate the inscrutable physical and temporal origins of a passion. Juno's speech effectively compresses the time of the tragic action into a single moment that mythically enfolds aspects of past, present, and future. It thus confirms the Stoic principle of *krasis* from a chronological angle: Juno already contains the drop of *ira* that can be modulated and amplified into the frenzy she wishes to see overtake herself and her cosmic surroundings, as well as the corporeal soul of Hercules—whose body is likewise susceptible to the passion because Hercules is, like Juno, part of a cosmic blending that entails the presence of *ira* but which obscures the temporal and physical origin of this passion. While Juno's opening soliloquy stands as a synchronic summoning and compressed expression of the event, the action of the play that follows plots out the sequence and causal chain of the passion's tragic unfolding.[54] And in tracking the signs of physical causality that drive the tragedy, the fact that Juno commands the furies to strike at Hercules's breast is significant. According to most medical theories in classical antiquity from Aristotle to Galen, the breast is the seat of the soul's common sense organ, and the distinctively Stoic variation on this thought contends that while the pneuma is thoroughly blended throughout a given physical body, the breast houses the corporeal soul's hêgemonikon.[55] In being ordered to "strike through his breast," the furies are meant to disrupt the rational balance of Hercules's soul by attacking the foundation of his oikeiôsis—which is to say, the physical basis of his care for self and world, thereby confirming Juno's recognition that the only enemy capable of defeating Hercules is Hercules himself. This earthly aspect of his being comes into focus as the physical launching pad of Hercules's fury, because it is both the part of himself that Hercules refuses to care for therapeutically and that which is exacerbated by the vigilant commitment to virtue that his wife Megara describes.

Hercules's lack of care for his physical condition is most visible during the sacrifice that he performs as an attempt to honor the gods and bring closure to his slaying of the tyrant Lycus. Yet in his appeal to Pallas Athena, Phoebus, and "whatsoever brother else of myne doth dwell in sky," Hercules ignores the need to rinse his own hands of his enemy's blood before performing the ritual:

> HERCULES: Cast into fyres the frankincense.
> AMPHITRYON: Sonne first thy hands flowing
> With bloudy slaughter, and the death of enmy purify.
> HERCULES: Would God the bloud of hatefull head even unto Gods on hye
> I might out shed, for lycour loe more acceptable none
> Myght th'aulters stayne: nor sacrifice more ample any one
> Nor yet more plentyfull may bee to Jove above downe cast,
> Then king unjust.
> AMPHITRYON: Desyre that now thy father ende at last
> Thy labours all: let quietnes at length yet given bee,
> And rest to weary folke.[56]

Hercules's physical body betrays symptoms that demand therapeutic attention, but only his father manages to read the signs. Twice, Amphitryon cautions his son: first of the urgency to purify himself by washing the blood from his hands, and second of his bodily need for the solace of sleep. Amphitryon even offers to take up the ritual duties himself so that his son and the kingdom may rest, but Hercules stridently refuses both directives. Here, the need for ritual purification is intertwined with the need for sleep, aligning the hero's slumber with a sacral quality that makes his refusal to sleep all the more scandalous and wrongheaded.[57] Yet Hercules looks upward and outward, as if Amphitryon's words were directed to the inhabitants of Thebes rather than to his son's own agitated and weary body, and insists yet again that he is the man best suited to perform this task:

> I will thee prayers make, for mee
> And Jove ful meete in this due place let stand the haughty skye,
> And land, and ayre, and let the starres dryve forth eternally
> Their course unstayde: let restful peace kepe nations quietly,
> Let labour of the hurtles land all yron now occupye,
> And swordes lye hyd: let tempest none ful violent and dyre
> Disturbe the sea . . .
> Let poysons cease: and from hensforth let up from ground aryse
> No greevous hearbe with hurtful sappe.[58]

As he continues to pile prayer upon prayer, "let" upon "let," Hercules's offering seems more like a command spoken from the mouth of a deity than a humble request for Jove's blessing, and so our sense of his hubris mounts with each additional line of verse. But it's also crucial to see that Hercules's prayer calls for a complete end to certain manifestations of the cosmos—storms, floods, and poisonous herbs—that may have the potential to harm human life but are nonetheless part of the natural order of the whole. To call for the elimination of such things is decidedly not in keeping with the broad-minded ecology of care that defines Stoic ethics, and this indicates that Hercules has lost whatever grasp he may have had upon the form of virtuous perception embodied by the sage. Instead, the passion of *ira* has begun to manifest visible symptoms in the form of the hero's misguided judgments and his agitated affect upon the altar.

Hercules's final summons—"If to sight some other mischiefe bringe / The ground yet shall, let it make hast: and any monstruous thinge / if it prepare let it be myne"—is suddenly interrupted by an intrusion of the very "monstruous thinge" that Hercules has called for and identified as his own. Darkness gathers, the midday sun disappears, and the horrors of the depths now intrude upon his vision to engender an hallucinatory phantasm that constellates key elements of Hercules's own mythical biography and the psychosomatic wounds that he carries. Amid the midday sky's unnaturally mounting darkness, a fiery shape stands out:

> Lo here behold my laboure first ful stout
> Not in the lowest parte of heaven the Lyon shyneth bryght,

And fervently doth rage with yre, and byttes prepares to fyght.
Even now loe he some star will take, with mouth full wyde to see
He threatning standes, and fires out blowes and mane up rustleth he.[59]

At this moment, Juno's furies work their fell purpose through the bodily passions and sensations that forge a continuum between Hercules's physiology and the cosmic milieu. Hercules of course *is* the Nemean lion in both a metonymic and a more literal sense: after slaying the mythical creature by strangulation, he uses its own claws to remove its impenetrable, armor-like skin, which he then takes upon himself as both a protective covering and an emblem of virtue. According to some sources, however, the lion manages to bite off and consume one of Hercules's fingers during their battle.[60] Whether or not Seneca imagined this particular wound as part of Hercules's physical being, I would argue that the play conceives of the hero's encounter with the Nemean lion as a site of conflict that has left a psychosomatic scar, and which now gives shape to his hallucination. On the one hand, the lion's skin is an outward sign of Hercules's virtue and his wound transformed; at the same time, and in keeping with the Stoic conception of physical bodies circulating in a volatile cosmic mixture, the lion's skin is a physical cause to the strength of Hercules's body. So we might say that Hercules's physical constitution inmixes elements of an otherness by taking into the grounds of his subjective being certain powers or virtues of the creatures he has defeated, which in turn become his own. Yet such mixtures remain highly volatile and, due to *krasis*, liable to a harmful amplification toward fury that undoes the constitutional balance of the sage. From one angle, the passion that Juno's furies bring to Hercules is already part of the mixture of earthly human body and lion skin that defines him. From another, the lion's flaming mane and furious consumption of stars in the sky are physically connected to the causal chain of *ira* that Juno invokes at the opening of the play, which draws the "burning rage," the "direful brand," and the "fyercer flame" into a cosmic affiliation with Hercules's enraged soul at the sacrificial altar. This is why the sky manifests in an outwardly visible form the physical transformation and eruption of a lionlike, blazing fury that has begun to overtake the hero but which is already a subtle part of his physical constitution.

Such a reading inevitably raises questions that pit individual agency against the dictates of fate. If Hercules is already part of this passionate cosmic mixture, already fated to succumb to madness, what difference does his own action make regarding the manifestation and consequences of the passion that now moves through him? The Stoics in fact accounted for the relation between fate understood as a causal chain and the causal agency of the individual *affectus*, both of which contribute to the "swarm of causes" that radically distributes agency across an ecological milieu. As Sauvé Meyer explains in her account of Stoic fate as a bodily chain of causes, there is a crucial distinction between principal bodily causes and antecedent causes that shows up in a number of canonical discussions of Stoic causation. An antecedent cause should be understood as the "mechanism whereby the activities of individual causes are integrated into the fabric of fate. To claim that something has an antecedent cause is to affirm that its cause is part of the causal nexus."[61] In Sauvé Meyer's analysis, an antecedent cause constitutes a connection between causes in the Stoic chain of causality. When extending this idea into the domain of human action, it leads to the insight that while the soul governs the human being and its actions through the exercise of its hêgemonikon, "any particular action also has an antecedent cause" in the form of "an external body that makes an impression on the soul," and which draws that action into the causal chain of fate. But this acting upon the soul is not a one-way street: the core Stoic theory of causation as a reciprocal affection between bodies means that we are not entirely compelled by an external cause even if it does affect us, because the guiding principle of our soul is itself an agential cause made from the same physical stuff (the pneuma) as the chain of fate that impresses itself upon us. Extending this notion to the scene of Hercules's madness, we can read his enervated, careworn, and insomniac body as the source of a failure in action when he chooses not to heed the call to rest; his negligence thus constitutes a principal bodily cause that is drawn into the causal chain of *ira* whose emergence at the altar should be understood, strictly speaking, as an antecedent cause that manifests the web of fate.

To see how this Stoic framing of Hercules's fall into madness uniquely negotiates the tension between individual agency and fate requires attention to these fine-grained distinctions. The play preserves, in keeping with Stoic principles regarding physical causation and human action, a distinctive place for the human agent who is capable of acting to influence the causal nexus of which she is part, though her actions are never in a strict sense completely autonomous—they are caused by the motions of the pneuma that permeates her body, and thus by the same substance that flows through the milieu in which that body is situated. As Deleuze helpfully suggests, the aim of Stoic ethics—which may at first appear somewhat paradoxical—is to will the event into being, or to bring one's actions as guided by the hêgemonikon into perfect alignment with the fated web of bodies-as-causes, despite the extreme difficulty of that task. Here, we should recall Seneca's claim in his ethical letters that ultimately, cause is one thing: "Creative Reason," unified by virtue of its substantial nature and consistency across the cosmic whole. In a larger sense, this situation reveals how the action at the heart of the tragedy explodes the psychological unity that Aristotelian theories of action, tragedy, and, indeed, biology presume in philosophically assessing the relationship between ethical action and physical embodiment. Hercules is both a human agent capable of action and simply one body among an indeterminate number of physical bodies in the causal chain of fate. He is drawn into this web of fate because, I argue, his body is exhausted and in need of sleep, though that condition as principal cause in itself is not sufficient to have brought about the full-blown passion. The causal chain of passion, extending at least from Juno's anger and her summoning of the furies at the play's beginning, plays an essential role in drawing Hercules's body-as-cause into its web of influence and thus in confirming the chain of fate. But without Hercules's negligence and refusal to care for his physical life through sleep, such an outcome would not have been realized.

Once the fated madness fully erupts, the passion seethes into militancy, and Hercules mistakenly believes the tyrant Lycus's sons are still alive and threatening him: "But loe the stocke of enmious king doth hidden yet remayne, / The wicked Lycus seed: but to your hatefull father slayne / Even now this right hande shall you sende let nowe his arrowes light / My bowe out shoote: it seemes the shaftes to goe with such a flight / Of Hercles."[62] These children are of course not the scions of Lycus but Hercules's own, and after the enraged hero slays one child with an arrow, brains a second, and then confronts his wife Megara, she clutches their infant while pleading for him to recognize "this sonne thy countenance doth showe, / And bodyes pytche," but to no avail.[63] Hercules's failure to clearly recognize the paternal face and bodily "pytche" reproduced in his son's features is thus marked as a failure to recognize himself, further confirming the success of Juno's plot to destroy the hero by turning him against himself. And as if echoing the strange temporality of the passion and its inscrutable causal origin, Hercules's infant son is so shocked by the image of his father's *ira* that he dies before the killing blow can even be delivered: "Th'infant with fathers fyry face astonnied all for dread, / Died even before the wounde: his feare hath tooke away his life," Amphitryon laments.[64] Hercules's mortal father then responds to his son's fury by demanding that Hercules "fill up the sacrifice" and kill him, bringing the path of annihilation to an end.

But this last life is not meant to be taken; Hercules instead swoons, and Amphitryon describes his son's fainting body as it collapses into the quietus of sleep:

What meaneth this? his eyes rolle to and froe,
And heaviness doth dull his sight, see I of Hercules
The trembling hands? downe falles his face to sleepe and quietness,
And weary necke with bowed head full fast doth downeward shrynke,
With bended knee: nowe all at once he down to ground doth sinke,

As in the woods wylde Ashe cut downe, or Bulwarke for to make
A Haven in Seas. Liv'ste thou? or els to death doth thee betake
The selfe same rage, that hath sent all thy famyly to death?
It is but sleepe, for to and fro doth goe and come his breath.
Let tyme be had of quietnesse, that thus by sleepe and rest
Great force of his disease subdew'de, may ease his greeved brest.
Remove his weapons servants, least he mad get them agayne.[65]

Amphitryon calls on sleep as a cure to the pathological rage that led the hero to annihilate his family. Finally, it seems, Hercules's physical body has fully exhausted itself despite his refusal to acknowledge the demand for rest. Fitch argues that Hercules "has attempted to deny the importance of rest and death, but they will not be denied; if scorned, they will assert their power. As the Chorus sings the ode, Hercules lies mastered by sleep, and mastered in a different sense by death."[66] The notion that Hercules's collapse invokes a deathly power of sleep seems right, given Amphitryon's apparent confusion—Is it sleep or death?—along with the Chorus's ensuing assertions that sleep is the brother of "hard and pyning death" and "all mankynde loe that dreadfull is to dye, / Thou doost constrayne long death to learne by thee." But it's also clear that both Amphitryon and the Chorus ascribe to sleep a vitally restorative power and the capacity to cure Hercules of the disease of madness, whose epicenter Amphitryon imagines is located within the hero's "greeved brest." This makes perfect sense according to Stoic physiological and medical notions of both the location of the corporeal soul's hêgemonikon and its function as the ruling principle that loses its grasp upon reason when agitated into the condition of a passion—not to mention Juno's command that the furies direct their fiery assault toward Hercules's breast. Yet the idea that sleep's restorative powers involve a kind of mixing with death may seem strange, if not entirely contradictory, according to the Stoic principle of a living cosmos animated by the pneuma.

I want to argue that this situation is not as strange as it appears, if we appeal again to the notion of Stoic *krasis* as a key cosmic principle underlying these images of Herculean slumber. Sleep, like any other bodily condition according to Stoic thought, is a particular kind of physical mixture within which bodily contrarieties circulate to varying degrees. And as we have seen through the play's earlier treatment of the obscure physical and temporal origins of a passion, a Stoic view of the beginning of physical death would acknowledge that the presence of death is already blended into any living body, even if our perception of it is incomplete. Death is, for the Stoics, typically defined as an absolute slackening and release of the tension between physical matter and pneuma that is the basis of any living body's organic cohesion. So the ongoing presence of death in the Stoic body of sleep would be apparent, for instance, through the doctrine that sleep slackens the perceptive tension of the corporeal soul and temporarily releases the hêgemonikon of its functional duty. In one sense, the Stoic self "dies" into sleep because the ruling principle of the soul releases its fully conscious and conceptually clear grasp of the bodily constitution in which it inheres. This notion makes further sense of the Chorus's claim that sleep prepares human life for the event of death, in that death is only a greater slackening and release of corporeal tension that entirely dissolves the cohesion or *tonos* which holds together the constitution of any physical entity. This is also why Seneca argues in his ethical letters that a proper development of oikeiôsis in human life results in the rational grasping of death as a natural outcome of life, which will place us in the position of "caring nothing for death" and recognizing that it is a process by which "all things that seem to perish are in fact transformed."[67] We learn not to fear death by cultivating our rational capacities to grasp this truth of the natural world and its divine order.

While the Stoic theories of *krasis* and the slackening release of sleep can account for the apparent strangeness of the physical mixtures that define Hercules's collapse, there is more to say about this scene of dormancy as it bears upon Hercules's oikeiôsis. When the Chorus invokes the power of sleep as a therapeutic benefit to Hercules's soul, it also notes that the binding effects of sleep on the hero's body do not entirely subdue its motions, because Hercules still reaches for his club even while he sleeps:

> Keepe him fast bounde with heavy sleepe opprest,
> Let slomber deepe his Limmes untamed bynde,
> Nor soner leave his unright raginge breaste
> Then former mynde his course agayne may fynd.
> Loe layd on ground with full fierce hart yet still
> His cruel sleepes he turnes: and yet is
> The plague subdued of so great raging yll
> And on great club the weary head of his
> He wont to laye, doth seeke the staffe to fynde
> With empty handes his armes out casting yet
> With moving vayne.[68]

We might think that Hercules reaches for his club because the madness rages on within his breast. But it's crucial to note that the Chorus mentions that sleeping with his club is in fact the norm for Hercules—"And on great club the weary head of his / He wont to laye"—so in seeking to grasp his club as usual, the hero is instead manifesting a kind of unconscious yet vital norm that shapes his habit of physical recovery and which is part of his oikeiôsis.

The full significance of this moment risks going unnoticed without an appeal to two other Stoic texts that discuss the doctrine of oikeiôsis while citing the sleeping Hercules as a paradigmatic example. In its account of the Stoic theory of oikeiôsis as it pertains to all animal life, Plutarch's *Moralia* features a discussion of storks who clutch stones at night to keep them from sleep, thereby safeguarding the muster: "When they have descended to the ground, the sentinels that stand watch at night support themselves on one foot and with the other grasp a stone and hold it firmly; the tension of grasping this keeps them awake for a long time; but when they do relax, the stone escapes and quickly rouses the culprit. So that I am not at all surprised that Heracles tucked his bow under his arm: Embracing it with mighty arm he sleeps, / Keeping his right hand gripped about the club."[69] According to this example, Hercules preserves a minimal degree of vigilant tension by gripping his club even in sleep. Like the stork whose loss of control over the stone calls it to attention, Hercules naturally clutches his weapons. Should they slip from his grasp, he will be alerted to his potential vulnerability. Meanwhile, in his discussion of animal oikeiôsis, Hierocles the Stoic argues that certain parts of animals such as the bull's horns or the lion's claws are "congenital weapons" that form their physical constitution. An inherent understanding of how to use and maintain control over these parts of their bodies continues in sleep because the foundational tension between bodily matter and pneuma continues to disclose a basic mode of attachment to and cognitive-perceptual grasping of said constitution.[70] For instance, if part of our body becomes cold while we are asleep, we draw the blanket closer to us; likewise, if we are wounded, we keep those parts of our body free from pressure, "even if we are sleeping profoundly, as though we were employing, if I may put it this way, a fully awake attention . . . so will signs of their disposition filter through the bodies of those who are sleeping. Thus, for example, Heracles too sleeps grasping his club in his right hand."[71] For both Plutarch and Hierocles, the hero's club-clutching is not a measure taken to preserve psychosomatic tension to the degree that he doesn't fall asleep, but instead indicates that he sustains his primary attachment to his self-constitution even when he relaxes into slumber. In their examples, the club acts as a physical extension of the foundation of Hercules's oikeiôsis, which is the well-functioning hêgemonikon that rules his soul and guides his actions. The implication seems to be that as a mythical hero, the club has a special place within Hercules's expanding circles of care—it is *oikeion*, or that which belongs properly to the hero and his natural constitution. Hercules maintains a uniquely heroic oikeiôsis even while he sleeps because his body preserves the minimal degree of tension necessary to sustain his grasp upon his weapon. And it is for this reason that Hercules serves as a mythical figure for the Stoic theory of oikeiôsis as both an ethical attachment to self-constitution and a sensorial grounding in care that continues even during sleep.

Considering the play in light of these discussions, Hercules's reaching for his club is a sign that sleep has begun to restore the hero's sanity by rebalancing the foundational tension of his soul's hêgemonikon—and thus his oikeiôsis—although the Chorus also notes that this process of recovery is incomplete:

> Nor yet all rage of minde
> He hath layd down, but as with Southwind greate
> The wave once vext yet after kepeth still
> His raging long, and though the wind now bee
> Asswaged swelles, shake of theis madde and yll
> Tossinges of mynde, return let piety,
> And vertue to the man.[72]

The aftershock of the passion continues, and so while both Amphitryon and the Chorus attributed to sleep a unique capacity to restore the physical foundations of Hercules's life and his disposition toward ethical care, the tragedy does not end with his awakening into such a condition, as if his sleep had managed fully to realign the psychosomatic grounding of "vertue" in his orientation toward self and world. Rather, Hercules awakens into a state of confusion and grave concern, thinking that the carnage he sees strewn about his domicile perhaps indicates his mind has not entirely cast off its impressions of "th'infernall shapes" of Hell. He then looks for his weapons and armor, asking

> Why doth my left side lacke
> The lyons spoyle? which way is gone the cover of my backe?
> And selfe same bedde ful softe for slepe of Hercules also?
> Where are my shaftes? Where is my bow? then from my living who
> Could plucke away? who taken hath the spoyles so great as these
> And who was he that feared not even sleepe of Hercules?[73]

Shorn of his mythical arms and hesitant to assent to his waking perceptions, Hercules is marked as lacking both the material supports and the psychosomatic clarity of virtue even though his condition has improved. But his description of the lion skin as both a "cover" that protects his body and a "bedde" on which he sleeps underscores the intimate relationship between his natural body and his weapons, which the play represents as a physical mixture of bodies that ideally augments Hercules's power and his capacities for heroism. At the same time, we have seen that the skin of the Nemean lion also has the potential to act as a node in the causal chain of bodies that draws Hercules's physical body into the passion of anger and thus into the cosmic web of fate. Given such ambivalence, it is fitting that his weapons now serve as the sign that confirms his own body was the principal cause to the domestic carnage surrounding him: "Whence comes this bloud? or what doth mean flowing with death of child / The shaft imbrewd with slaughter once of Lerney monster kilde? / I see my weapons now, the hand I seeke no more to witte. / Whose hand could bend this bow but myne? or what right arme but it / Could string the bow that unto mee even scantly doth obay?"[74] Only Hercules has the power to negotiate physical mixtures of such magnitude; the fact that his bow only "scantly" obeys even his command nicely captures a sense of the Stoic principle of causation as a reciprocal tug-and-pull between bodies, and the school's distinctive conception of the will that guides human action as a force distributed among bodies in a causal web.

The play does much to establish an essential reciprocity between Hercules's bodily sense of self and his martial arms, going so far as to suggest in Stoic terms that the hero is quite literally a potent physical mixture of mutually animating bodies, whose principle causal anchor is the hêgemonikon housed within his breast. As both signs and material components of his natural virtue, the lion skin, club, and bow and arrows that Hercules carries are *oikeion* to him, and they form part of the causal web that determines his actions and facilitates his astounding labors. But after these weapons are withdrawn from his sleeping body and he awakens to see that they served as instruments in annihilating his kin, Hercules suddenly demands to have his weapons restored only so that he can break and burn them as recompense for his transgressions: "My shaftes reach hether, hither reach my mighty club also: / To thee my weapons breake I will, to thee my sonne a two / Ile knappe my bowes, and eke my clubbe, this blocke of heavy wayghts / Shal to thy sprites be burned loe: this self same quiver frayght / With Lerney shaftes to funeral of thyne shall likewyse goe. / Let all my weapons penance pay and you unhappy to / Even with my weapons burne I wil, O stepdames handes of myne."[75] Because his weapons are so intimately part of his being, this line of action constitutes an extremely punitive and self-defeating measure that soon shifts into a desire for self-annihilation. Yet while Hercules seems to think that the destruction of his martial arms is a necessary step toward atonement, Theseus and Amphitryon seek to convince him otherwise, arguing that this would in effect be cutting off his nose to spite his face. As Theseus insists, "T'is neede to be a Hercles now, this heape of yll sustayne,"[76] and Amphitryon goes further in telling Hercules that if he attempts to harm himself, Amphitryon will take his own life and hold

Hercules responsible for patricide. This drastic measure has the desired effect, as Hercules finally relents and agrees, once again with Stoic resolve, to take on a seemingly impossible burden: "My manhood yeld thy fathers will, and impery sustaine. / To Hercles labours now likewyse, let this one labour goe, / Let me yet live, lift up from ground th'afflicted lims with woe / O Theseu of my parent: for whom Godly touch doth flee / My wicked hand."[77]

Hercules's assessment of his Stoic ethical duty is seemingly in accordance with the school's writings on constancy and fortitude in the face of extreme duress. Is Hercules not known precisely for such shows of resolution in the face of adversity, and for shouldering impossible burdens? Solidifying his will to live is simply the next task in the endless line of labors thrown his way, as Hercules conceives it. But in fact, I think the play encourages a different understanding of ethical resolve that is both more complicated and more tragic than Hercules's seemingly heroic embrace of the obdurate and willful resolution to live despite his sense of shame. Clearly, Hercules believes that this is what the circumstances demand of him, as he describes his final labor of living on despite his tainted, "wicked hand" that he imagines his father can only shrink from in horror. Hercules sees himself as a monster whose actions have placed him outside the circle of human care, and he imagines that this status is simply the fate he must accept. But Amphitryon intercedes in a way that implicitly challenges his son's understanding both of himself and his ethical resolve in such terms. Amphitryon doesn't shrink from his son's touch, but tells him, "I gladly do this hand embrace to mee. By this I being slayed [supported] will goe, this moving to my brest / Ile slake my woes."[78] In reaching out and bringing Hercules's hand to his own breast, Amphitryon reverses the gesture he made earlier when threatening to take his own life and hold his son responsible: "The deadly sword throughout my breast to strike I wil apply, / Here, here the gylt of Hercules even sound of mynd shall lye."[79] Amphitryon's touch brings his son's own body into contact with the seat of his mortal father's oikeiôsis and asserts that Hercules does indeed belong to him and to his circle of care—and moreover, that both their lives are held in a mutually sustaining and reciprocal relation of care. This connection is grounded in the sensation of a therapeutic touch between their physical bodies that seeks to restore the foundation of this care. Amphitryon thus attempts to remind his son that his own physical constitution serves as the basis of his care, both for himself as an embodied being and for the relations that sustain him in life.

The tragedy here derives largely from the fact that Hercules remains oblivious to this gesture and to its ethical implications; he instead looks immediately beyond his father and the possibility of restoring his ties to kin and community. "What place shall I seeke ronnagate for rest? Where shall I hyde my self? or in what land my selfe engrave? . . . From me the world doth flee a back."[80] Hercules ignores the promise of a restored physical bond with his father and instead wonders what, if any, country would accept him in exile. In a sense, the play ends with a tragic repetition of the same mistake that Hercules made at the altar: there the hero chose to ignore the advice of his father, which was to care for the physical life and foundation of his oikeiôsis by taking rest. Here, Hercules turns away from an intimate gesture that likewise promises to restore the mortal aspect of his being and bring him again into the sustaining circles of care that serve as the physical basis of Stoic virtue. In describing Seneca's vision of the good, Rosenmeyer observes that while earlier Stoic writers such as Chrysippus and Cleanthes "had attached the greatest value to the human instinct for self-preservation, Seneca came to stress the will to live, and the will to make life worth living."[81] Hercules has fallen victim to too great an emphasis on the resolve simply to live, without recognizing the deeper ethical import of living well, which for the Stoics is a natural extension of the fundamental physical motions of life. What makes a life worth living is not simply a dogged persistence in living but an attunement of the will to the form of life that is right for the kind of being that one is. And in the case of Hercules, the tragedy drives a wedge between two visions of life: on one side, life as sheer survival committed to a mistaken, because incomplete, picture of Stoic resolve, and on the other, life as the embodied cultivation of the circles of care brought into being through oikeiôsis, beginning with the living animal's most basic sense of affiliation or dearness toward itself, and extending into the web of bodies and causes that animate the cosmos and make it an ecopolitical entity of which the human is a part. It is a presciently biopolitical vision of tragedy, because it registers a pressure to partition forms of life into seemingly irreconcilable domains. Hercules's mistaken sense is that his life no longer belongs to the ethical and political fold of cosmic reason, when in fact it quite literally reaches out to include him in its embrace. Remarkably, the play grounds the hero's final mistake in a lack of feeling that is also a failure of understanding—in the cold refusal to accept his father's gesture and to recognize the cosmopolitan inclusion of his touch. Hercules thus misrecognizes the corporeally grounded sensation of a reciprocal care that might have restored his affective disposition and allowed him to grasp that which is *oikeion* to him, making this incarnation of the Hercules myth a distinctively Stoic tragedy.

Chapter 3

"The Body Is with the King, but the King Is Not with the Body"

Sovereign Sleep in the Tragedies of *Hamlet*, *Macbeth*, and *King Lear*

In *A Paterne for A Kings Inavgvration*, James I of England advises his son Charles that the king must be "a great watchman and shepheard . . . and his eye must neuer slumber nor sleepe for the care of his flocke, euer remembring that his office, beeing duely executed, will prooue as much *onus* as *honos* unto him."[1] While drawing attention to the perils of laxity and carelessness in governance, the king's fatherly advice also suggests that the onus of rule might sometimes rob the sovereign of his ability to sleep. Kings should expect to find themselves anxiously consumed by the pressing concerns of state and the cares of the subjects who compose the body politic, and so James cautions Charles that a true king—a king devoted to the sovereign art of *imitatio Christi*—must be prepared to embody an ever-vigilant posture:

> But he must not expect a soft and easie croune, but a croune full of thornie cares, yea, of platted and intricate cares. . . . In a word, a Christian King should neuer be without that continuall and euer wakeriffe care, of the account he is one day to giue to God, of the good gouernment of his people, & their prosperous estate both in soules and bodies; which is a part of the health of his owne soule.[2]

James's allusion to Christ's crown of thorns figures the sovereign's crown and the art of "good gouernment" as a pastoral burden, a willingness to shoulder the cares of the flock and to safeguard his subjects' bodies and souls as part of the common nature they share with their sovereign. To care for the souls and bodies inhabiting the kingdom is to care for the soul of the sovereign, with all things falling under the purview of his watchful and steady gaze.

By casting the king's role as both a paternal and pastoral caretaker of English souls (including his own), James's invocation of the sovereign's "continuall and euer wakeriffe care" for the body politic also alludes to and modifies core elements of the political theology of the King's Two Bodies. As is well known to students of early modern European history, political theory, and literary studies alike, the king was held to possess a natural body common to all humans, as well as a mystical superbody that perpetuated the life of the state and lent an aura of divine perfection to the sovereign. In *The King's Two Bodies*, Ernst Kantorowicz identifies the vigilant and perpetual devotion of the sovereign with an ideal image of kingly care known as the *rex exsomnis*, or sleepless king, whose watch never ends. The *rex exsomnis* appears in a range of medieval and early modern writings on sovereignty by thinkers such as Baldus de Ubaldis, Albertus Magnus, and Francis Bacon.[3] King James's allusion to this ideal imagines a synthesis of English sovereignty with pastoral power, the form of care that Michel Foucault argues lays important groundwork for the transition from disciplinary into biopolitical societies during the early modern period.[4] Foucault describes a shift in thinking about the nature and techniques of sovereignty during the time of the Stuart monarchy, according to which sovereigns were to become more attuned to the natural life and milieu of their subjects by developing an art of political *oikonomia* that would manage their "physical and moral existence" rather than organize itself around the sovereign seizure of life and the threat of death.[5] Yet despite such a newfound emphasis on governing human life with an eye to its physical realities and vital capacities, King James's allusion to the figure of the *rex exsomnis*—like any notion of a perpetually vigilant monarch—belies the simple fact of the body natural's compulsion to sleep, which inevitably suspends the sovereign eye of care. The King must care for the physical life that underpins the exercise of sovereignty, even if that means releasing the reins of governance and falling temporarily into a vulnerable state of slumber. James's vision of the trials of sovereign vigilance and monarchical care thus raises the central question motivating this chapter's readings of Shakespearean tragedy: What happens to the body politic when the sovereign's body natural sleeps?

In the pages that follow, I track Shakespeare's explorations of the political theology of vigilant care that informs the King's Two Bodies theory, arguing that the latter's guiding presumptions propel biopolitical crises of state in the tragedies of *Hamlet*, *Macbeth*, and *King Lear*. In these plays, both sleep and insomnia impinge upon the physical life of the sovereign—and thus upon the union of the King's Two Bodies—in strange and unexpected ways. The tragedies of *Hamlet* and *Macbeth* both hinge on the violent deaths of sleeping kings and a politically chaotic aftermath that resists the highly wrought fictions of constant vigilance, immortality, and stately perfection that buttress the doctrine of the King's Two Bodies. Kings Hamlet and Duncan alike fall prey to a form of sleep that underscores that condition's potential turn toward deathly physical mixtures and venomous environmental influence, as the sovereign descends into a careless slumber. Shakespeare's depictions of sovereign sleep as an event of ecopolitical significance illustrate his indebtedness to the cosmological orientation of Senecan drama, and to the Stoic depiction of Hercules's cosmological madness and swoon in particular. But I argue that the Stoic perspective of sleep as a simultaneously physiological and ethical benefit to the corporeal soul likewise informs Shakespeare's depictions of monarchical insomnia as a threat to the health of the sovereign's personal and political bodies. This latter point is particularly salient to the case of King Lear, whose cosmological rage and self-dissolution are only alleviated by the therapeutic virtues of a sleep that also marks the finality of his separation from England's body politic.

Put simply, for Shakespeare, both sovereign sleep and insomnia constitute an "altered case"—a concept developed by Tudor jurisprudence to denote the sudden incorporation of the body politic by the newly sovereign body natural, but which I argue elucidates the playwright's visions of the King's Two Bodies transformed by the physical events of sleep and insomnia. Sleep creates an image of human imperfection in the sovereign body natural: bodily life in sleep resembles death, and so the king's physical life and mortality resurface, even though his body natural's flaws are supposedly taken up and wiped away by the presence of the body politic. In this way, Shakespeare figures sovereign sleep as a threatening moment of kingly regression, an altered case whose curious trajectory is one of decline rather than ascension. Yet with the characters of Macbeth and Lear, the playwright treats the opposite extreme of insomnia as a symptom of sovereign care that denies the life-sustaining properties of sleep and acts as a corrosive agent of madness and demise. The tragic dissolution of sovereignty in *Hamlet*, *Macbeth*, and *King Lear* suggests that sovereign sleep and insomnia not only impinge upon the monarch's ability to maintain watchful rule but also radically alter the metaphysical bonds between bodies natural and politic.

In the wake of Giorgio Agamben's work on sovereignty and biopolitics, a number of Shakespearean critics have returned to the topic of the King's Two Bodies.[6] The concept of bare life and its manifestations alongside sovereign power has opened a new path for the biopolitical analysis of early modern sovereignty and states of exception, while abandoning the once widespread critical assumption that the visual spectacle of power is its most significant or coherent locus.[7] Agamben's take on Carl Schmitt's theory of the sovereign exception, which Schmitt develops in large part by championing the work of Thomas Hobbes as a watershed moment for European sovereignty, has provided rich fodder for Shakespeareans looking to situate Renaissance drama within its political and ideological contexts.[8] Given this recent proliferation of scholarship, reading *Hamlet*, *Macbeth*, and *King Lear* in light of the King's Two Bodies and the sovereign decision may risk yet another return to near-hackneyed themes. But among the current discussions of Shakespearean drama, sovereignty, and biopolitics, none develops an account of the physiological politics of sovereign sleep—despite Shakespeare's imaginative rendering of sleep and insomnia as volatile and transformative bodily states that impinge upon the King's Two Bodies and even threaten the security of early modern sovereignty.

While such risks to the integrity of monarchical care are at the heart of his later tragedies, Shakespeare's interest in the perils of sovereign sleep clearly precedes all three of the plays that concern me here. Take, for instance, Prince Hal's famously premature donning of the crown in *Henry IV, Part 2*, which imagines his father repeating the fate of so many English sovereigns by falling prey to a deep and careless slumber while the crown rests beside his head:

> Why doth the crown lie there upon his pillow,
> Being so troublesome a bedfellow?
> O polish'd perturbation! golden care!
> That keep'st the ports of slumber open wide
> To many a watchful night! sleep with it now!
> Yet not so sound and half so deeply sweet
> As he whose brow with homely biggen bound
> Snores out the watch of night. O majesty!
> When thou dost pinch thy bearer, thou dost sit
> Like a rich armour worn in heat of day,
> That scalds with safety. By his gates of breath
> There lies a downy feather which stirs not:
> Did he suspire, that light and weightless down
> Perforce must move. My gracious lord! my father!
> This sleep is sound indeed, this is a sleep
> That from this golden rigol hath divorced
> So many English kings.
> (4.4.21–37)[9]

Hal views his father's slumbering body as a moment of biopolitical peril that manifests the troubling legacies of English sovereignty and sleep—though his description also underscores sleep's proximity to the vital breath that sustains the sovereign's physical life. Hal metonymizes the crown as the King's care, and then as a suit of armor that "scalds with safety," evoking Edmund Spenser's Herculean image of Redcrosse knight's suffering in his armor as it burns the hero's body during his battle with the dragon.[10] Kingship, like Spenser's allegory of holiness, seems to involve a fitful and unsteady alliance of the physical body with the sacred props of sovereign authority and the burdens of care they entail. But as a moment in which death appears to be present within life, the conundrum of sovereign sleep also recalls the similar paradox of disjunctive unity at the heart of the King's Two Bodies theory and its explanatory logic of monarchical succession.

Along such lines, *Richard III* stages a juxtaposition of King Richard and Henry Richmond's tents on the eve of their battle, and both sovereign and sovereign-to-be share in a dream that heralds the outcome in advance. It is as if the metaphysical transition of the body politic from one king to the next takes place while they sleep, before the physical conflict of the battlefield. Richard's spirit, overburdened with sin and melancholy, sinks before the vindictive procession of his slain rivals; meanwhile, Henry's spirit rises, blessed with good fortune in anticipation of taking the crown:

Enter the Ghosts of the two young Princes.
GHOSTS [*To Richard*]: Dream on thy cousins smothered in the Tower.
Let us be lead within thy bosom, Richard,
And weigh thee down to ruin, shame, and death.
Thy nephews' souls bid thee despair and die!
[*To Richmond*]
Sleep, Richmond, sleep in peace, and wake in joy.
Good angels guard thee from the boar's annoy.
Live, and beget a happy race of kings!
Edward's unhappy sons do bid thee flourish.
(5.3.151–157)[11]

The downward pull of melancholic despair and heavy sin weigh upon King Richard's soul, manifesting unkingly aspects of sovereign sleep as well as the burdensome tendencies of monarchical care. Shakespeare then conspicuously places this image alongside a vision of divinely sanctioned sovereignty in the figure of Henry Richmond, whose sleep is peaceful, protected, and promises a flourishing sovereignty to come. These and later Shakespearean scenes of sovereign sleep and insomnia grapple with the metaphysical and political-theological significance of the king's sleep, foregrounding the vexed issue of sovereign succession that the theory of the King's Two Bodies is meant to remedy. But alongside such considerations, the argument ahead also speaks to the form of life that sleep brings to the surface of the sovereign's body natural. It is a form of physical life sustained by volatile yet vital humoral mixtures, whose unpredictable qualities under Shakespeare's hand resonate with but also qualify Giorgio Agamben's concept of bare life and its biopolitical significance for the early modern state.

More precisely, Shakespeare's visions of life cut short in the body of sleeping kings do not reflect the logic that, according to Agamben, defines and guarantees the continuity of sovereign power. Agamben argues that the sacred life of the king is bound to the bare life of his body natural, and that it infuses the sovereign with the power to define and eradicate bare life in the bodies of his subjects. In the tragedies of *Hamlet* and *Macbeth*, however, sovereign sleep and insomnia crack open that metaphysical seal and prevent the sacred life of kingship from attaching to the body of the sovereign successor—even though both Claudius and Macbeth appear to exercise a form of the sovereign decision by drawing out and killing the natural life of the sleeping king. Taking cues from the close-knit relationship between cosmology, care, and the causal web of action in Senecan drama, Shakespeare foregrounds the humoral volatility and transformative effects of sleep in both of these plays. Yet in the case of *King Lear*, sovereign sleep takes on a strikingly different valence. In this play, Shakespeare emphasizes the restorative virtues of Lear's postsovereign slumber, modeling his therapeutic sleep on the Stoic vision of cosmic care articulated in Seneca's *Hercules Furens* and imagining a powerful yet fleeting cure to the ailments of an overly vigilant monarchical care. While Shakespearean tragedy thus exposes the conceptual and practical limits of the political theology of vigilant care that undergirds the King's Two Bodies theory, taken together these plays more strikingly construct a vision of both the foundations and horizons of biopolitical governance which rest upon the care for physical life and its immanent virtues of recovery.

The Altered Case

In March 1603, as Queen Elizabeth's aging body increasingly displayed signs of her imminent death, she told the Earl of Nottingham, "I am tied with a chain of iron about my neck . . . I am tied, I am tied, and the case is altered with me."[12] Nottingham and Elizabeth were at the time grieving the recent death of his wife, who had been a close friend of the queen's, so his visit was punctuated by mutual sadness for the Countess of Nottingham's passing, as well as for Elizabeth's own declining health. Not long after Nottingham's visit, the Earl of Northumberland discreetly sent word assuring an eager James VI of Scotland that Elizabeth had indeed taken a turn for the worse:

> Her Maiestie hathe bene euell now almoast one monthe. In the twelve first dayes it was kept secrett vnder a misprision, taking the caus to be the displeasoure she tooke at Arbella, the motions of taking in Tyron, and the deathe of her old acquentance the Lady Notinghame. Those that were nearest her did imagine these to be the reasons. Moer dais told ws it was ane indisposition of bodie; siknes was not in any maner discerned, her sleep and stomak only bereft her, so as for a 20 dayes she slept very little. Since she is growne very weak, yet sometymes gives ws comfort of recoverie, a few hours after threatnes ws with dispaire of her well doing. Phisick she will not take any, and the phisitions conclud that if this contineu she must needes fall into a distemper, not a frensie but rather into a dulnesse and lethargie.[13]

The "euell" describing Elizabeth in Northumberland's letter is an antiquated usage that denotes a state of evil health—a wretched physiological condition or a corruption of the body's humors.[14] No wonder, then, that for the first twelve days Elizabeth's sickness was kept secret, since its cause remained uncertain. But once Northumberland felt confident that Elizabeth's state was in fact "ane indisposition of bodie" and not simply a temporary psychosomatic effect of her friend's death, he found the nerve to write. Northumberland goes on to assure James of a consensus regarding her majesty's encroaching death, as well as the Scottish King's right to the throne: "Euery one almost imbraces yow, for which we that are your trew servantes are glaide of."[15] Once Elizabeth's body natural had been taken over by evil health, Northumberland suggests, the kingdom's subjects could not help but look forward to the investiture of sovereignty with James VI of Scotland.

This account of her melancholic condition and Elizabeth's own admission of her "altered case" may simply appear consistent with common early modern expressions describing life as it approaches death. The word "case" in Elizabeth's time could mean the sheath of a sword, garments covering the body, or even the body itself. Cleopatra uses this last sense to describe Antony's body—"This case of that huge spirit now is cold" (4.15.89)—once death has robbed it of its animating force and presence. But Elizabeth's choice of words with the Earl of Nottingham reflects her unique condition of sovereign embodiment. While a "chain of iron" for other humans might simply figure the physical burden of an aging and "euell" body natural, in Elizabeth's case the "chain of iron" more plausibly denotes the body politic, whose weighted interests were slowly becoming too much for Elizabeth to manage.[16]

"The case is altered with me," she tells Nottingham. Tudor jurists used the phrase "the case is altered" to designate the body natural of the monarch that was suddenly and irrevocably transformed by its incorporation of the body politic, and it became a popular proverb associated with Edmund Plowden's legal construction of the King's Two Bodies in his *Reports*.[17] The logic of the altered case also helped to account for the legal continuity of the corporative body politic with regard to the landed possessions of the king or queen, who could never relinquish a claim to property because the king or queen never truly died. While the phrase developed amid the arguments of English courtrooms, its presence in popular literature and parlance illustrates seepage into other public registers. "'The case is altered,' quoth Plowden" became a familiar expression beyond the juridical court, working its way into ballads and theatrical scripts from writers such as Whetstone, Dekker, Heywood, and Jonson—Jonson even published a play titled *The Case Is Altered*, which Thomas Nashe mentions during his parody of the red herring in *Lenten Stuffe*. As Marie Axton notes, the phrase was taken broadly in Elizabethan vernacular to designate "a change of identity which the law would recognize."[18] Still, the common character of the expression in both juridical and poetic surroundings does not entirely explain the significance of Elizabeth's usage. For one thing, Elizabeth's accession in 1558 meant that from that moment onward, her body had become an altered case, bound to the body politic and forever changed in its political, legal, and metaphysical status. For her case to be altered again, after the fact, implies a reverse trajectory, as if the body politic had already begun to depart or evacuate—an event that ought not to happen until Elizabeth's natural death.

At the moment of the monarch's bodily death, Plowden held that the body politic would immediately reinvest itself within the body natural of the new sovereign. As he argued, "Every removing of the state Royall from one body naturall to another is called in lawe *Demise Le Roy*," and this process marks the legal difference between the natural inheritance of primogeniture and the rights of royal succession.[19] The king never dies; in the state of royal demise, there is no event of complete or final death, since the body politic remains an ideally continuous presence. Instead, only a brief severing of the sovereign body natural from the body politic would take place, the latter being "instantaneously vested in his successor [since] Demise, in legal terminology, was not equivalent to death."[20] The ground of sovereign power is therefore not subject to the bodily infirmities of its possessor, but rather moves from one incarnation of the king to the next. And in fact, Plowden produced a manuscript in 1566 (which he wisely kept guarded from print, but which circulated among sympathetic jurists) titled "A treatise of the two Bodies of the king, vis. natural and politic . . . The whole intending to prove the title of Mary Quene of Scotts to the succession of the crown of England and that the Scots are not out of the allegiance of England."[21] In other words, Plowden devoted some serious legal wrangling to establishing a juridical counter against Elizabeth, challenging her claims to sovereign authority and surreptitiously looking to undermine the legitimacy of the Tudor dynasty.

It would seem, then, that Elizabeth's learned sense of irony was at play when she spoke wryly of her "altered case" approaching death. On the one hand, Elizabeth recognized the impending decay of her own body, and the inevitable legal confirmation of sovereignty upon another body—the body of James VI of Scotland, waiting hopefully in the wings. That event would ultimately represent the claim of Mary Stuart coming to fruition, against a good part of Elizabeth's political work of the past half century, and in line with Plowden's legal argument for Scottish legitimacy. But beyond a shift in legal status, the "altered case" to which Elizabeth referred was one of physiological and even metaphysical degradation, exacerbated by irregular patterns of sleep during her final months in power. It is as if she imagined the supernatural bonds between her body natural and the body politic slowly dissolving, a grim consequence of her amble towards death. Because sleep is an inevitable demand of all human bodies, it registers the persistence of the common body natural's most basic need: the renewal of physical life, which in the case of the monarch is necessary for the corporeal instantiation of sovereignty. Yet by some accounts, during her final days of life Elizabeth actually resisted sleep, despite her extremely weak and exhausted state. In defying the wishes of her physicians and counselors, Elizabeth's refusal to sleep may have constituted a final attempt to exercise sovereign authority over her own physical body and suggests her recognition of sleep's potential to slide easily into death—to finally and irrevocably sever the knot between her body natural and the body politic.[22]

When James I finally sat upon the English throne, the question of sovereign sleep may have come into more immediate focus given his notorious tendency to fall asleep during long public events, especially at the performance of plays. According to the casebooks of his personal physician, Dr. Theodore Turquet de Mayarne, James I battled mightily with insomnia, along with other physical ailments that kept him restless and uncomfortable at night.[23] James's insomnia and his propensity to fall asleep in public suggest that his sleepless nights found ways of intruding upon the king's public life and his magisterial presence, and can help to explain his preferences for shorter drama. The court masque was famously developed under the purview of James, who appreciated its formal brevity compared to the lengthy productions favored by Elizabeth.[24] Henry Paul even asserts that James's visit to Oxford in 1605 was likely present in Shakespeare's mind while writing *Macbeth*, since a firsthand account tells us that during the third evening in a row of tedious theatrical performances in his honor, King James "fell asleep and when he wakened he would have been gone saying I marvel what they think me to be."[25] What his subjects seemed to think him to be was a man and yet not a man—or at least, ideally, a king who in his magisterial nature would not succumb to the downward pull of sleep during theater performed in his honor. While the king's prerogative hypothetically meant that he could sleep when and wherever he desired, such moments of physical lapse would expose a near comic yet gravely concrete fragility to the sovereign's physical life. In different ways, then, the public personas of both Queen Elizabeth and King James registered struggles with the body natural's compulsion to sleep, despite the supposedly perfecting influence of England's body politic.[26]

Given the many biblical and classical references to sleep as an image or anticipation of death, reproduced in medical texts, philosophical writings, and literary representations of Tudor and Stuart England, sleep presented a conceptual aporia for the doctrine of the King's Two Bodies.[27] For while Plowden's juridical theory of *Demise le Roy* clearly accounted for the brief retreat and reappearance of the body politic upon the death of the sovereign's body natural, it did not offer an account of what, if anything, might happen to the body politic when the sovereign fell asleep. Admittedly, Shakespeare's knowledge of Elizabeth's final days—or of James's insomnia—cannot be ascertained with any certainty. Yet the tragedies of *Hamlet*, *Macbeth*, and *King Lear* evince an abiding interest in sovereign sleep and insomnia and the monarchical complications that these states entail. The playwright imagines both embodied conditions not simply as physical facts but as political and ecological events that impinge upon the integrity of sovereign care and the watchful gaze of the monarch. Sovereign sleep and insomnia are transformative states of becoming within an unstable ecology of bodily mixtures and obscure causal connections, which can in turn compromise both the living union of the King's Two Bodies and the transfer of the body politic from one sovereign to the next.

Discussions of the King's Two Bodies and the structures of sovereign continuity in Shakespeare typically begin with Kantorowicz's seminal work on the concept's history, which takes *Richard II* as an exemplary case—"the tragedy proper of the King's Two Bodies," as he puts it.[28] Citing the apparently contradictory language of Tudor jurisprudence, which irrationally finds two bodies to be located in one, Kantorowicz proposes that the English jurists' legal opinion of the twinned nature of the king might seem less outlandish if one reconsiders it in theological terms:

> In fact, we need only replace the strange image of the Two Bodies by the more customary theological term of the Two Natures in order to make it poignantly felt that the speech of the Elizabethan lawyers derived its tenor in the last analysis from theological diction, and that their speech itself, to say the least, was crypto-theological. Royalty, by this semi-religious terminology, was actually expounded in terms of christological definitions.[29]

Kantorowicz finds a coded meaning carried over from theology to juridical reason, a "tenor" that is buried in the diction of the Tudor jurists. In his account, Elizabethan language acts as a kind of sepulcher that "encrypts" the Two Natures doctrine of Christian theology within the secular juridical doctrine of the King's Two Bodies. Kantorowicz goes on to argue that Tudor courtrooms "applied, unconsciously rather than consciously, the current theological definitions to the defining of the nature of kingship" and that "the crypto-theological idiom was not the personal spleen of any single one among the Tudor lawyers, nor was it restricted to a small coterie of judges."[30] These points and the psychic-humoral register of Kantorowicz's metaphor will resonate with my readings of Shakespearean tragedy, but for the moment are simply meant to show that the language of Tudor jurists unconsciously based the mystical perpetuity of the body politic, and its perfecting transformation of the king's body natural, on this Christian theological precedent. Just as early church debates had framed Christ's incarnation, Tudor jurists found that the everlasting body of the king was conjoined to the sovereign body natural yet subject to no part of its fallible nature. Rather, the ideal body of the king takes up and wipes away the king's physical inferiorities, even though the king must have a "Body natural, consisting of natural Members as every other Man has, and [that] in this he is subject to Passions and Death as other men are."[31]

This common aspect of human embodiment, Kantorowicz argues, determines Shakespeare's tragic depictions of monarchical decline. While Kantorowicz finds underlying Christological and mystical influences in Plowden's writings on law, he believes that such juridical concerns are not Shakespeare's. So while his discussion of *Richard II* opens with an allusion to the proverbial life of the legal phrase "the case is altered," and he even cites Shakespeare's undoubted "familiarity with legal cases of general interest" alongside "other evidence of his association with the students at the Inns and his knowledge of court procedure," Kantorowicz then retracts the insinuation that Shakespeare's dramaturgy takes up these juridico-political dilemmas:

> Admittedly, it would make little difference whether or not Shakespeare was familiar with the subtleties of legal speech. The poet's vision of the twin natures of a king is not dependent on constitutional support, since such vision would arise very naturally from a purely human stratum. It therefore may appear futile even to pose the question whether Shakespeare applied any professional idiom of the jurists of his time, or try to determine the die of Shakespeare's coinage.[32]

Risking such futility, in the pages that follow I argue that Shakespeare's depictions of the life and death of sleeping kings are not simply visions that arise naturally from his contemplation of a "purely human stratum," bound to the sacred nature of kingship. Shakespeare rather clearly and critically recognizes the gap at which a series of discourses concerning the King's Two Bodies converge—religious, juridico-political, metaphysical, and physiological. When kings are killed in their sleep, that event generates phantasmatic reverberations that echo through the bodies and physical life of the sovereign and his subjects, spreading across the entire polity and giving rise to an ecological drama of carelessness and care. In this way, Shakespeare draws on the cosmological dimensions of Stoic thought in its concern with the power of physical mixtures, while also looking to reassess the terms binding the life of the sovereign and his subjects to the well-being of the early modern state. Through their preoccupations with sleep and insomnia, these plays draw attention to life seeking shelter and care amid turbulent realities that constrain those very possibilities. It is here that Shakespeare's drama evinces its stakes in early modern biopolitics, calling attention to the natural boundaries of vigilant care while conceiving a form of physical life whose value for sovereign and subjects alike exceeds its political-theological function as an incarnation of the sacred.

Hamlet's Stoic Phantasm

Prince Hamlet's Denmark is a polity in demise where, as Margreta de Grazia writes, the "pathology infecting the body politic is reflected in the numerous outbreaks on Danish bodies, particularly royal ones."[33] This wretched state of the kingdom is brought on by the murder of a king sleeping in his garden—a king whose body is compromised and enfeebled by the "altered case" of sleep. Rebecca Totaro has suggested that a dialectic of secure sleep and vigilant watch determines "civil, bodily, and spiritual health" in *Hamlet*'s Denmark, and that King Hamlet's sleep represents an indulgent lapse in care, which Prince Hamlet eventually recognizes as an improper and "ill maxim" for state rule.[34] "Hamlet changes it," Totaro argues, "arriving at a new conclusion: every man must watch over himself, because only in this way will his sleep be secure. If the audience imagines that Horatio's blessing over the dead body of Hamlet is answered and that Hamlet is attended by angels who sing him to his rest, perhaps this is because Shakespeare convinced them that Hamlet had become his own best watch."[35] The play thus becomes a macabre success story in Totaro's account, sanctioned by a theological reassurance: Hamlet's "successful watch" does not repeat the sins of the father, figured as the immoderate sleep to which his body and the health of the state temporarily succumb. Denmark's prince then overturns Claudius's rule and finds peace in the final, blessed sleep of death. Totaro implicitly frames this success in biopolitical terms, though her essay does not explicitly develop that line of thought. Prince Hamlet never learns how to maintain sovereign vigilance, rule a healthy kingdom, or even preserve his bloodline of succession; he rather learns how to "watch over himself," just as "every man must."

Totaro's insight speaks directly to the play's interest in the biopolitics of care, as she argues that Denmark's "watch" is first a function of the sovereign body that bears responsibility for securing the kingdom's well-being at night. Her argument thus implicitly affirms the paradigm of sovereign vigilance ascribed to the *rex exsomnis*. But by the end of the play, she suggests, the "best watch" is recognized as that which the self—the implication is, any disciplined and caring self—exercises over its own bodily life. The paradigmatic center of constant and vigilant care is relocated from the sovereign body to the bodies of his subjects, and this becomes the optimum method of securing sleep among sovereign, subjects, and kingdom alike. Totaro thus draws our attention to the play's imagined transposition of the burdens of care from the center of the King's Two Bodies to the denizens of Denmark, as if the pastoral grid established by the King's care is preserved while the singular eye that watches over and sustains it is shut—only to be reawakened as a many-eyed Argus that anticipates the modern state. Yet if Shakespeare imagines this newfound vision of the care for sleeping life in the positive terms that Totaro ascribes to him, it seems strange that Denmark's prince only finds peaceful security in the final sleep of death, and that Denmark is then given over to Fortinbras, who is heir to a foreign throne that annexes Hamlet's kingdom. If *Hamlet* places the King's sleep at the core of Denmark's crisis of sovereignty, it remains difficult to see how exactly the play constitutes a Shakespearean affirmation of political or ontological certainty in its imagined redistributions of the burdens of care and watchful governance from the sovereign to his subjects.

Keeping these points close, I would like to turn to the ghost's narrative, where the sleeping King Hamlet's body natural and its poisoning by Claudius figure forms of gross carnality and rankness that resonate with de Grazia's assessment of royal pathology yet also suggest that the living dialectic between the bodies of sovereign and state is mutually affecting. The condition of poisoned sleep constitutes an unnatural amplification of the king's physical life that slides easily into his death, and moreover complicates the metaphysical transmission of the body politic to Prince Hamlet—Denmark's ideal successor in a patrilineal scheme of power. De Grazia's account of the disruption to patrilineal succession turns our attention to the forgotten link between land and identity at the heart of the play, which she argues constitutes the source of the sovereign authority of which Prince Hamlet is robbed. Like de Grazia, I am interested in the play's imagined relationship between sovereignty and physical environment, though my approach to these concerns is as cosmological and ecological as it is geographical. The King's retreat into his garden is a drawing inward of body natural and political territory alike, into a secure and holy domain of sleep. Claudius intrudes upon this space as a means of wresting the body politic from him, but the sovereign's sleep implies more than just a careless suspension of the king's conscious defenses. King Hamlet's sleeping condition also exposes both the common, physical reality of his body natural and the fleshly history of sin written into his soul. The ghost's narrative thus retroactively constructs an image of the sovereign body natural as a physical entity that coextends with its living humoral environment within an ecology of sovereign care: the king sleeps in a sanctified garden, meant to protect the sovereign's rest and preserve his attachment to the kingdom even during his temporary lapse into carelessness.

Yet the humoral flows of the sovereign's blood—opened up to its fecund surroundings and to the volatility of physical mixtures—expose a form of physical life that Claudius's poison takes hold of and destroys. This double truth makes the sovereign's sleep an equivocal event that oscillates between poles of carelessness and care, vulnerability and restoration, and sanctity and pollution. King Hamlet's sleep is a simultaneously biopolitical and political-theological event, during which a disruption to the fundamental care for physical life is also an occasion for political crisis. As Shakespeare's audience, we are asked to rethink the terms by which the early modern sovereign watches over the lives of his subjects and himself, even if the play refuses to provide us with easy answers. When Hamlet first encounters his father's ghost, he is told that

> Sleeping within my orchard,
> My custom always of the afternoon,
> Upon my secure hour thy uncle stole
> With juice of cursed hebona in a vial,

> And in the porches of my ears did pour
> The leperous distillment, whose effect
> Holds such an enmity with blood of man
> That swift as quicksilver it courses through
> The natural gates and alleys of the body,
> And with sudden vigor it doth posset
> And curd, like eager droppings into milk,
> The thin and wholesome blood. So did it mine,
> And a most instant tetter barked about
> Most lazarlike with vile and loathsome crust
> All my smooth body.
> Thus was I, sleeping, by a brother's hand
> Of life, of crown, of queen at once dispatched.
> (1.5.59–75)[36]

The ghost calls the king's sleeping hour "secure" because it is the time of day in which the king retreats from life as a king, withdrawing into a cocoon of protection that is *sine cura*. The scene should be one of idyllic removal from the cares of state, to a place that keeps the king safe from worry and treachery alike. Such associations between sleep, security, and pastoral retreat are familiar tropes in works like Sidney's *Arcadia*, in which a movement away from the world of politics and war dovetails with romantic idealizations of slumber and lethargy as escape.[37] The ghost's tale is also consistent with Ovidian and Senecan associations of sleep with the virtue of self-renewal and its Stoic figuration as a "care-charmer" that gives solace to weary minds and anxiously exhausted nerves.[38] The life of his body natural waxes while the mystical influence of the body politic wanes, as the king's sleep restores physical life in the manner common to humans and animals alike. But while these valences of sovereign sleep assume its natural and customary character, the ghost repeatedly insists that the murder is "most foul, strange, and unnatural," and thus imparts to it a radical evil—an evil whose perverse influence *Hamlet* suggests is in rather close proximity to the sacredness of sovereignty, and to the sanctified sleep of the king.

Just before Hamlet meets his father's ghost, the prince laments the nightly carousing and excessive drinking of the Danes at court. This inclination, he tells Horatio, is endemic to the souls of the Danish nation, and Claudius's indulgent drinking grossly exacerbates it. Hamlet muses that the new king should be sleeping, but he "doth wake tonight and takes his rouse" (1.4.8). And when Horatio asks his prince if such behavior is "custom," Hamlet admits as much, though he rues the implications: "Ay, marry, is't, / But to my mind, though I am native here / And to the manner born, it is a custom / More honored in the breach than the observance" (1.4.14–16). Prince Hamlet's words anticipate the ghost's story by figuring his uncle as an inversion of his father: Claudius indulges in a "custom" that keeps him and his subjects drunkenly awake into the early hours of the night, while King Hamlet's sleep is a "custom in the afternoon" that replenishes his health; also, Hamlet describes this flaw of Danish custom as a "vicious mole of nature" that burrows through the soul and storms the forts of reason, which anticipates his comparison of the king's ghost to an "old mole" burrowing through the earth under Hamlet's feet—the same "mole" whose influence leads the prince to affectations of madness in his plot for revenge. The mole of nature in Denmark's subjects, the prince imagines, takes over their "general censure" like a totalizing "corruption / From that particular fault," and so "the dram of evil / Doth all the noble substance often dout, / To his own scandal" (1.4.24–38). The shared imagery between Hamlet's descriptions of Claudius and the ghost's narrative of sovereign sleep suggests that villainy and corruption bear a substantial affinity with the humoral circulations of sleeping bodies, and are even drawn to the sacred life encrypted in the body natural of the king.

Such connections are further elaborated through Hamlet's descriptions of custom and the peculiarly spreading agency he attributes to evil. The "mole" of corruption is a natural presence in the Danish character, but this tendency threatens to grow and swell disproportionately, becoming a custom whose indulgence might overdetermine the ontological bearing of the Danish king and subjects alike. The "noble substance" falls victim to a "dram of evil": the process Prince Hamlet imagines looks ahead to the ghost's description of the sacredness attending King Hamlet's life in sleep, which then falls victim to the dram of poison that Claudius pours into his ear. The trajectories of corruption in these two cases move, however, through slightly different vectors. The Danish flaw is a seed of corruption that is already present, and it unfolds to take over its host. The poison, meanwhile, introduces a foreign agent through the king's ear that seethes through his blood and colonizes his body. Yet in both instances, we see a physical substance subtly corrupted and turned to fulfill a latent and wicked potential. Holiness and evil alike seem to preserve their particular qualities even as they are thoroughly blended within the environment and with each other, in keeping with the Stoic theory of physical mixtures and the seething volatility that permeates cosmic life. As Thomas G. Rosenmeyer notes in his discussion of *krasis* and Senecan drama, physical mixtures involve a thorough blending of bodies—such as life and death—that permeate the entire cosmos, yet "in this integration the two merged identities or substances are preserved *as* identities."[39] *Hamlet*'s Senecan vision of the decrepit state begins with a meditation upon the treacherously thin boundary between what is noble, sacred, and holy in the humoral environment and what is rank, accursed, and evil—imagining these qualities to emerge, somewhat unpredictably, from the indeterminate physical mixtures of life that circulate through and among all creatures. The ghost's story thus indicates that sovereign sleep, much like the drunken and "heavy-headed revel" of the Danes, risks indulging a mixture by which sacred life all too easily becomes accursed. Yet it is not simply the inability of the sovereign to maintain watchful, vigilant care that marks his sleep as an indulgent lapse in kingliness and a loss of sacred identity; it is rather the transformative powers of Claudius's poison, an active instrument of Senecan villainy mixed into the sanctified environment of the sleeping king, that brings about these consequences.

Part of the poison's efficacy seems due to the simple fact that during the king's sleep, his physical life becomes more vulnerable. In multiple terms the ghost casts the king's body natural as a miniature fortress or city whose defenses are suspended, its conduits of circulation open to hostile takeover—the poison enters through the "porches of my ears" and "courses through / The natural gates and alleys of the body." The distillment of "cursed hebona" that Claudius employs is a phrase used by both Marlowe and Shakespeare, but first coined by Gower, whose verse "hebenus, that slepy tre" in turn paraphrases a passage from Book 11 of Ovid's *Metamorphoses*. The line "hebenus, that slepy tre" refers not to "a tree having a soporific juice, but simply ebony (Latin *ebenus*), the wood used by the God of Sleep in the walls of his chamber."[40] Claudius's poison is an essential distillation of the wood that encases the chamber of Somnus, and his wicked alchemy infuses and corrupts the king's sleeping life. "So did it mine": the effects of the poison take hold between two bookends to the ghost's narrative, "Sleeping within my orchard" and "Thus was I, sleeping," further demarcating the event of sleep within the ecology of sovereign care.

The poison's substantial affinities with sleep, and with the humoral flows of the king's body natural in repose, seem in fact to purge the sovereign body of its sacred life. When the king's body releases slowly into what should be a brief and Edenic return to primordial life in recovery, Claudius's intrusion disrupts and violates that sanctified space by turning it rank. Hamlet is robbed "of life, of crown, of queen" as the poison saturates his sleeping body, and each of these three claims constitutes a distinct aspect of sovereign selfhood. But while "crown" and "queen" point clearly enough to the king's roles as head of state and head of the royal family, the term "life" constitutes a third identity that seems less explicitly tied to the purview of kingship per se. While presenting two distinct visions of the king's persona, the ghost's tale does not neatly split the king's life into separate domains. Rather, the ghost's tale demarcates a single form of life tied to the sovereign body natural, life that should remain sacred but which Claudius's treason pollutes and evacuates. So while the sovereign's bare or merely physical life is brought to the surface for Claudius to take, the presence of sacred life is occluded, as if the "cursed hebona" both transforms and removes it from the king's humoral circulation while hastening his bodily death.

Such sudden death is one of the worst medieval nightmares: "The horror is not only the fact of his murder, at the hands of his treacherous brother, but also the precise circumstances of that murder, in his sleep, comfortable and secure."[41] Thus Stephen Greenblatt connects the ghost's story to Hamlet's hesitation to kill Claudius while he prays, noting that Hamlet "remembers that Claudius took his father 'grossly, full of bread, / With all his crimes broad blown, as flush as May.'" Here, Hamlet worries that Claudius's blood may have been purged and cleansed by this confession, whereas the ghost has told him that his father's blood was in a state of extreme impurity, bound up with the repercussions of fleshly sin as well as the thickening effects of the poison. The controversies over Holy Communion and its claims to physically constitute a community of shared blood and body through Christ seem to haunt the ghost's tale of King Hamlet's death, much as they haunted Elizabeth's attempt to balance such religious controversies during her reign.[42] Moreover, these allusions coincide with the ghost's narrative precisely because they trace a shift from the smooth ideality and purity of abstraction into a condition of bodily life as such, which first swells into relief and is then annihilated by poison. In this sense, the ghost describes a crypto-theological effect taking hold of King Hamlet's body natural, through which the buried theological histories of sin and fleshly indiscretion resurface in the flow of sovereign blood and hold immediate consequence for the sacred life of the king and the state for which he cares.

In the ghost's words, the poison works to "posset" and "curd" the otherwise "smooth" body of the king. As an index to royal identity that is both physical and ideal, blood is the most crucial humor affecting the tenuous unity of bodies natural and politic—especially the common blood between father and son that patrilineal succession prioritizes, and which helps to constitute the "symbolics of blood" underwriting sovereign power in pre-biopolitical states.[43] Blood both contains and transfers sovereign legitimacy; it is a shared current that the ghost says runs "thin and wholesome," encrypting the line of the king. But the poison turns this sacred ideality of blood into a foul and unnatural counterimage, ruining the smoothness of sovereign sanguinity. The point here is twofold: blood can serve a similar sort of ideological function as does the body politic because it encodes monarchical continuity, tracing the family bloodline as a pure, uninterrupted flow. But blood is also a physical substance shared by all humans, and it resists idealization or abstraction because of this common status as well as its capacities to coagulate, thicken, and scab when exposed to air. Hence, blood equally recalls the materially recalcitrant qualities of the body natural. The poison that thickens, possets, and curds the king's blood while he sleeps arrests the recuperative flows of King Hamlet's bodily humors, extracting and transforming the animating substance of his physical life while also bringing out his flesh's history of impure transgressions.

But the ghost also describes his blood as if it were milk, "like eager droppings" that "posset" and "curd," and this attributes a maternal source to the sovereign's bodily life. Being overfull of blood, bread, or milk likewise recalls the quality of gluttonous sin that Prince Hamlet ascribes to his mother Gertrude's appetite for his father: "She would hang on him / As if increase in appetite had grown / By what it fed on" (1.2.143–145). Such poisonous thickening of the king's blood thus overcodes it as fleshly and feminine, further problematizing the ideal scheme of patrilineal succession. While the political crisis that follows the king's murder indicates a failed or imperfect transition of sovereign power—a power invested by the metaphysical continuity of the body politic—the flip side of that coin insists that the sacred life of sovereignty is in fact more precariously grounded in the physical life of the sovereign body natural, and even in the humoral substance and environmental mixtures that sustain it. In other words, Shakespeare imagines the infirmities of the king's body natural not only to compromise sovereign vigilance but also to weaken or corrupt the majesty of the body politic. And this seems possible precisely because the ground of sovereign power and its ecology of cares depend at least as much upon the king's physical corpus as they do upon a metaphysical form of sacred life or an image of kingly *dignitas*.

To clarify, I am not arguing that Shakespeare articulates a clear and novel theory of sovereign continuity grounded in bodily constitution and thereby entirely rejects the thought that kingship might entail a holy or sacred presence. But Shakespeare's depiction of sovereign sleep does tease out a certain conceptual aporia in the King's Two Bodies doctrine, since the physical realities and infirmities of sleep directly compromise the sacredness of the king's life and his claim upon it. And this results in a somewhat heretical image of sovereignty in *Hamlet*: it is an elusively fluid yet corporeal presence that is subject to physical contingencies, strange mixtures, and volatile transformations, and as such it cannot be securely grounded in theological or juridico-political abstractions. The physical ties between the sleeping body of King Hamlet, his son, and the body politic itself map a biopolitical crisis of state that enfolds bodily life, ontological presence, and political authority at once.

With the ghost's sinister description, Shakespeare also reveals his philosophical interest in the ill-fated passions and seething material mixtures explored in depth by Senecan tragedy. Gilles Deleuze calls attention to some underappreciated conceptual links between Senecan thought and Elizabethan tragedy in *The Logic of Sense*, asking, "What is the unity between Stoic thought and this tragic thought which stages for the first time beings devoted to evil, prefiguring thereby with such precision Elizabethan theater?"[44] For Deleuze, this unity is found in Seneca's powerful depictions of nature's physical mixtures as a "black depth wherein everything is permitted. . . . Everywhere poisonous mixtures seethe in the depth of the body; abominable necromancies, incests, and feedings are elaborated."[45] Corporeal mixtures circulate as a kind of throbbing material unconscious, and the blending of bodies in the cosmic whole is so thorough that no mixture can be considered better or worse than another. Yet in their capacity to alter bodies, these seething passions engender a second incorporeal order of difference—which Deleuze views as the domain of sense—that climbs to the surface of physical life to transvalue the structures of value and meaning that determine social and symbolic life. Deleuze's reading of Stoicism and Senecan drama thus provides some helpful coordinates for understanding not only Shakespeare's Stoic depictions of the flux of physical life in *Hamlet* but also the play's interest in the linguistic and temporal paradoxes that arise from the causal nexus of physical bodies like "dialectical attributes."[46] That is the phrase Deleuze uses to describe the ideas that spread over corporeal surfaces in the form of incorporeal *lekta*, or the "sayables" that are necessary components of Stoic ontology. On one side, there are unconscious physical movements, or passions-bodies that act as causes to other bodies in accordance with Stoic physics and the web of causation. Along the other side, there are incorporeals that spread across the surfaces of physical being, constituting an ideal order of meaning, or a sense-event that moves temporally forward and backward at once. And this strange temporality, the movement of bodily becoming in Denmark's body politic, bears the ghostly signature of the king's death in sleep—a phantasm that traverses the body of the kingdom and its rightful heir irrespective of linear time's unfolding.

Along such lines, the king's death-in-sleep is an event that clearly alters the sense of many structures or series organizing symbolic life in the kingdom of Denmark—for instance, the sense of family relations understood by the terms father, son, mother, and uncle; or the sense of the body that is Denmark, as in body natural, body politic, the King's Two Bodies, and so forth. The sense-event that takes place in Gertrude's closet manifests in bodily symptoms that refract King Hamlet's death-in-sleep through the surface of his son's own body. If the phantasm of the ghost's second visitation gives rise to an incorporeal *lekton*, then Gertrude enunciates it when she asks her son,

Alas, how is't with you,
That you do bend your eye on vacancy,
And with th'incorporal air hold discourse?
Forth at your eyes your spirits wildly peep,
And as the sleeping soldiers in th'alarm
Your bedded hair like life in excrements
Start up and stand an end.
(3.4.112–118)

Gertrude's vision links Prince Hamlet to Denmark's body politic by imagining a common state of interrupted sleep—the hairs on his head stir from their "bedded" repose, like so many soldiers of the state violently pulled from slumber to rigid attention by a sudden alarm. The second visitation of his father's ghost thus renders the surface of Prince Hamlet's body as a refraction of his father's body natural at the time of his murder: sleeping soundly, he is suddenly and violently wrested from that gentle state, his body subjected to a harsh awakening that rises up "like life in excrements." Like the sleeping body natural of the king, Prince Hamlet's body registers a vision—routed through the gaze of his mother, but "sayable" as an event—of incensed and turbulent passions rising to the surface. Yet it is also a phantasmatic aftereffect of the sovereign father's death-in-sleep, a fractured image that manifests and replays the death of King Hamlet through the body of Denmark's heir, as he holds discourse with the incorporeal air.

Perhaps this is why Gertrude's description of the Prince's appearance mirrors the conditional state that the ghost earlier tells Prince Hamlet *could* be produced if he were to describe the perils of his purgatorial surroundings, a tale whose "lightest word"

Would harrow up thy soul, freeze thy young blood,
Make thy two eyes like stars start from their spheres,
Thy knotted and combined locks to part,
And each particular hair to stand an end
Like quills upon the fearful porpentine.
(1.5.9–20)

These serial associations are both corporeal and incorporeal, and they bind Prince Hamlet's body and its sensations to the body of his father's sovereign sleep. Yet the play also problematizes a reading that aims to explain or disentangle the sense of these moments by appealing to the site of the king's murder as a clear origin from which these effects simply unfold in linear time. That is because King Hamlet's death is not simply a retroactive narrative delivered by the ghost but must itself be a fictional fantasy or phantasm, for how could the sleeping King Hamlet, if he truly was asleep, actually know that he was being poisoned by his treasonous brother, know that his body was being polluted by the "cursed hebona," and know that he was dying in exactly the manner so vividly described by the ghost? Most assuredly, the king died. But the matter of the sovereign's sleep grossly complicates the origins of the phantasm that traverses the various bodies of the play. It is as if the conceptual aporia that sleep presents for the theory of the King's Two Bodies, the altering of the case that is the sovereign body natural, is both an impasse and a site of genesis for a phantasm-event of the ghost's unreal narrative as well its incorporeal presence across the play.

Meanwhile, if there is a proposition that captures this sense-event in the play, a good candidate appears when Rosencrantz and Guildenstern confront the prince and ask him where they might find Polonius's body. Hamlet responds, "The body is with the king but the king is not with the body" (4.2.25–26). Hamlet's seemingly paradoxical proposition has a sense that responds to the problems posed by the king's death-in-sleep and by the conceptual aporia whose effects I have been mapping throughout the play. When the king sleeps, he is both with and not with the body, and he is both caring and not caring for the life of the state. This is because sleep throws him deeper into the body natural's physical mixtures, allowing him unconsciously to care for that form of life while also separating him from the king's vigilant care for the body politic. Or, Hamlet means that as prince he is the rightful king who lacks the body politic, but he carries Polonius's body as a comically macabre supplement. The point here is that none of these explanations sufficiently capture the sense of the prince's paradox, in accordance with Deleuze's contention that while the phantasm is neither said nor signified, it "does not exist outside of a proposition which is at least possible, even if this proposition has all of the characteristics of a paradox or nonsense."[47] The scene posits the prince as both mad and not mad, his speech nonsensical yet pregnant with meaning. It remains to be seen if and how Hamlet might find his way, like the Herculean Stoic sage in Deleuze's reading of Senecan drama, to a position of mastery over this phantasmatic event and the paradoxical temporality of becoming that it evinces.

At the opening of act 5, scene 2, Hamlet relates to Horatio his own fantastic narrative of an escape from death, due in no small part to the fighting in his heart "that would not let [him] sleep" (5.2.5). Hamlet of course reasons that because this moment of insomnia led him to discover the warrant for his head, it was a form of "rashness" whose end was shaped by divinity, and therefore seems to have conferred a political-theological guarantee of sovereign right upon the prince's head. But his appeal, I think, rather encourages us to see the story he tells Horatio as Hamlet's sovereign fantasy, which is also a return of the phantasm transformed: through insomnia, he rises to the surface of his physical being and counteractualizes the event of his father's death by mastering the bodily mixtures of sleep. Hamlet's insomnia erects a body of sovereign vigilance whose posture is modeled on the *rex exsomnis* and which resists the psychosomatic forces of dissolution that played a hand in usurping his father from the throne. And Horatio would seem to confirm this view when, after the prince informs him of Rosencrantz and Guildenstern's fate, the "antique Roman" responds, "Why, what a king is this!" (5.2.61). If we understand "this" to denote the prince rather than Claudius, then Horatio's remark puts Hamlet squarely in the place of the king. The prince's transformed habit of sleepless watch has spurred him to take on the mantle of sovereign power, and to order a decision on the life of his childhood friends. Hamlet's delusion both cures and sickens, in that he has transformed himself into the heroic bearer of sovereignty—"This is I, Hamlet the Dane" (5.1.46–47) as he attests at Ophelia's funeral—but for the prince to say this is to counteractualize the event-phantasm that also lays a path toward his fateful death.

That is because for Prince Hamlet to take on the mantle of sovereignty in Denmark, he must also imagine himself as a version of his Herculean father, prepared to accept the "fate" that "cries out / And makes each petty artery in this body / As hardy as the Nemean lion's nerve" (1.4.81–83). But what exactly does the prince mean by this early allusion to Seneca's Stoic hero and to the impenetrable animal skin that was draped over his body? Hamlet may be imagining himself as the mythically steely lion that is slain by Hercules, a fantasy that makes him into the willing victim of a sovereign decision on life handed down by his father. Or Hamlet could be metonymically imagining himself as Hercules, who wore the lion's skin as a second body protectively draped over the surface of his own physical body. In that case, the prince has effectively reversed the sense of his earlier claim that Claudius is "no more like my father / Than I to Hercules" (1.2.152–153), which would likewise entail a patricidal implication. Insofar as these crosscurrents of identification emerge from the Herculean figure of two mythically powerful bodies made into one, they would seem to point to the unresolved difficulties of sovereign embodiment presented by the King's Two Bodies and, more particularly, the monarch's watch over an ecology of care that is made doubtful by the event of sovereign slumber. The risk of sovereign sleep is precisely what Prince Hamlet appears to resist through his commitment and return to an antiquated model of sovereign vigilance and his eminently willing exercise of the decision to take the lives of Rosencrantz and Guildenstern in order to preserve his own. But with Prince Hamlet's untimely death and the transfer of the kingdom to Fortinbras, Shakespeare clearly draws our attention to the ultimate failure of the prince's gestures as a sufficient means of securing the ground of sovereignty and the health of the kingdom. Rather than the sovereign decision on life, *Hamlet* emphasizes the grounding force of the sovereign's physical life, made all the more apparent by its sudden absence.

We have seen the many ways that the play connects the figure of the sleeping sovereign and his violent death to the psychosomatic life of his son and, indeed, the life of Denmark's body politic. Claudius's "cursed hebona" alters the holiness of sovereign sleep by infusing the king's bodily life and its sanctified environs with a corrupting presence, and by this means he seems both to draw out and annihilate the physical life of the king. This sudden exposure and killing of the king's physical life in sleep generates a gap, an emptiness that submerges the king's sacred life and blocks his unworthy successor from its investiture, while manifesting across the play as an incorporeal phantasm that traverses the bodies of the prince and the kingdom. And while Prince Hamlet attempts to remedy this ghostly ailment by recovering his claim to sovereignty and restoring the kingdom of Denmark, his reliance on an outmoded model of sovereign authority ultimately places him in limbo. He is unable to look past the horizon of the King's Two Bodies and the sovereign power over life through threat of death, and so the prince stumbles just as a new path seems to appear. He remains stuck in a vigilant "interim" that he rightly claims as his own. Both he and the kingdom of Denmark lack an apparatus of sovereign care more adequately positioned within the emerging sphere of a political *oikonomia*, where the art of governing physical and moral life is untethered to the political theology of the King's Two Bodies.

Macbeth's Care

As in *Hamlet*, the crisis of sovereignty in *Macbeth* stems from the untimely death of a sleeping king. But Macbeth's insomnia more emphatically punctuates the self-annihilating consequences of a treasonous assault on sovereign sleep. The place of sleep in *Macbeth* thus elaborates on several key premises of *Hamlet*, as Macbeth finds himself guilty of having "murdered sleep" itself—which is how the disembodied voice of judgment names his transgression (2.2.41). If sleep can be murdered, then the play suggests it is a body with a strange life of its own, a body whose mixed attributes include a holy valence in the case of sovereign sleep. Macbeth's aggression against that body results in a punishing state of insomnia, which tyrannizes Macbeth's supposedly sovereign body and corresponds directly to the loss of political authority that culminates in his death. Macbeth is denied sleep, and moreover denied the investiture of sacred life that ostensibly secures sovereign power. His situation thus affirms an intimacy between holiness and sovereign sleep that is grounded in the physical restoration of the body natural, while it also underscores the heinous character of Macbeth's actions. The guilt of Duncan's murder then takes on the substantial character of a bodily humor that fuses with Macbeth's own physical life, becoming an insistent presence that surges and swells like "multitudinous seas" stained red with blood (2.2.66).

Killing the king in his sleep also aligns Macbeth with Scotland's barbaric, bloody past, and with the popular English image of Scotland as a primitive polity from which James Stuart sought to sever himself, even as he promoted the idea of a union between the kingdoms. Shakespeare uses the horrors of hallucinatory insomnia in Macbeth to connect him with James I and his struggles with sleep, as if to underscore the perilous task of managing England's body politic as it demands the reconstruction of its legitimating political doctrine. And Shakespeare uses a certain term in the play that captures a sense of the impossible desire to break cleanly with the past even as it clings to the present, a word that speaks to the conceptual enigmas posed by the King's Two Bodies doctrine: "cleave" embodied the same contradictory meanings for Shakespeare as it does in modern usage, signifying both a splitting apart and a clinging together.[48] And the King's Two Bodies is of course a cleft—a union of disjunction, upon which rests the well-being of the state and the authority of its sovereign. Moreover, the form of the cleft speaks to a most basic experience of sleep, in that sleep divides an otherwise continuous stream of waking consciousness in life by seeming to plunge the soul's mindful presence into a temporary void. But when insomnia denies the embodied soul access to the replenishing virtues of slumber, the soul is fractured and dislocated by hallucinatory effects of the sort that characterize Macbeth's short-lived experience as king. In *Tamburlaine*, Mycetes even uses the term cleave to encapsulate the very condition of kingliness and the many threats undoing it faces: "For Kings are clouts that every man shoots at, / Our crown the pin that thousands seek to cleave."[49] Christopher Marlowe's lines apply to Macbeth in two respects, since initially he seeks to cleave the crown from its rightful bearer, but he soon becomes a king whose capacity to manage the cleft defining kingship radically erodes.

In fact, *The Tragedy of Macbeth* appropriately represents Macbeth as a being who is both divided and embodies a vicious capacity to divide. Early on, Macbeth slices through lines of troops and individual bodies on the battlefield, and the wounded sergeant tells King Duncan that while at first the battle stood doubtful, "As two spent swimmers, that do cling together / And choke their art" (1.2.8–9), Macbeth single-handedly turned the tide, and "like valor's minion carved out his passage" (1.2.19). The sergeant goes on to tell how Macbeth, cutting through the field, arrived face to face with the rebel Macdonwald, "unseamed him from the nave to th'chops, / And fixed his head upon our battlements" (1.2.22–23). But when he is not on the battlefield, Macbeth's powers of division seem to run in the reverse direction, and only foreground a self-splitting that portends his inadequacy for the role of king. For instance, when Ross delivers news to Macbeth that he shall inherit Cawdor's title, that message carries with it an encryption of the weird sisters' second prognostication: the unspoken but latent confirmation that Macbeth will become Scotland's sovereign, will soon take upon himself the altered case of kingship and the crown that thousands are bent to cleave. Yet upon the delivery of Ross's news, Macbeth describes its effect in terms that nearly replicate Gertrude's description of Hamlet's appearance upon the second visitation of his father's ghost:

> Two truths are told,
> As happy prologues to the swelling act
> Of the imperial theme.—I thank you, gentlemen.—
> [*Aside*] This supernatural soliciting
> Cannot be ill, cannot be good. If ill,
> Why hath it given me earnest of success,
> Commencing in a truth? I am Thane of Cawdor:
> If good, why do I yield to that suggestion
> Whose horrid image doth unfix my hair
> And make my seated heart knock at my ribs,
> Against the use of nature? Present fears
> Are less than horrible imaginings.
> My thought, whose murder yet is but fantastical,
> Shakes so my single state of man that function
> Is smothered in surmise, and nothing is
> But what is not.
> (1.3.127–142)

Macbeth attributes his shaken condition to the heaviness of "Two truths," and the unspoken implication that he will be king. But he cannot imagine the truth of this event unless it involves the murder of King Duncan, which is consistent with Macbeth's assumption that titular authority must change hands through acts of war and physical aggression. And Banquo remarks upon this state of rapture by likening it to an altered case that doesn't quite fit, foreshadowing Macbeth's ill-suited role as king: "New honors come upon him, / Like our strange garments, cleave not to their mold / But with the aid of use" (1.3.144–146). These new titles appear not to cleave properly to the body inheriting them; rather than investing Macbeth's "single state of man" with an honor that balances metaphysical and physical ontologies in one formation, the phantasmatic image of "surmise" reduces ontology itself to an incorporeal shudder. Macbeth's own imagining of the wound that will cleave King Duncan from his life and his crown so disturbs him that he feels it extinguish his very sense of being.

Other signs point to this metaphysical determination of Macbeth's fate, and return us to the volatile power of obscure corporeal mixtures that, as in *Hamlet*, limn the sovereign's violent death in sleep while engendering transformative surface effects which alter the sense of things. Lady Macbeth, for instance, questions her husband's capacity to go through with killing King Duncan by associating Macbeth with corporeal feminine tendencies—he is "too full o'th'milk of human kindness" (1.5.18)—while figuring herself as a bulwark to Duncan's murder by embodying the masculine fortitude her husband lacks: "Hie thee hither, / That I may pour my spirits in thine ear, / And chastise with the valor of my tongue / All that impedes thee from the golden round" (1.5.26–29). The poisonous "spirits" of her tongue recall the poison Claudius pours into King Hamlet's ear, but Lady Macbeth's speech seems to wall in and lull to sleep Macbeth's conscience, encouraging him to kill King Duncan. Her words both call upon and manifest spirits that infuse humoral substance, which Lady Macbeth identifies with acts of making and unmaking alike: in this case, being too full of the "milk of human kindness" is to be unable to make one's self into a king, just as the overstuffed milkiness of King Hamlet's poisoned blood prevents Prince Hamlet's accession to sovereignty. But Lady Macbeth also looks to the surrounding night with the aim of perverting the natural good that governs nature, an art of occult *oikonomia* that calls upon the eldritch flows of darkness to thicken her blood against remorse, and to cloak the murder of the king while honing the couple's evil intention:

> Come, you spirits
> That tend on mortal thoughts, unsex me here,
> And fill me, from the crown to the toe, top-full
> Of direst cruelty! Make thick my blood,
> Stop up th'access and passage to remorse,
> That no compunctious visitings of nature
> Shake my fell purpose, nor keep peace between
> Th'effect and it! Come to my woman's breasts,

And take my milk for gall, you murd'ring ministers,
Wherever in your sightless substances
You wait on nature's mischief! Come, thick night,
And pall thee in the dunnest smoke of hell,
That my keen knife see not the wound it makes,
Nor heaven peep through the blanket of the dark,
To cry "Hold, hold!"
(1.5.41–55)

Lady Macbeth's lines summon forces to steel her to the deed of murder. But because she also calls upon these agents as a way of blocking out or isolating her from the flows of "remorse," we should pause over her exact meaning. On the one hand, she looks to the circulating substances of nocturnal life to reshape her and to sharpen her purpose; yet she also aims to separate or cleave from those elemental passions any tinge of remorse, any "compunctious visitings" of morality that might give her pause. Like all good Senecan villains, she looks to pervert the physical mixtures of the cosmos to achieve her fell end, drawing out nocturnal agents of "nature's mischief" that have the metamorphic power to alter holy and sacred forms of life. By manipulating the subtle line that divides holy from accursed, sacred from bare, Lady Macbeth occludes the presence of the sacred within herself, her vision of the king, and even in the air that surrounds his sleep.

Echoes here of the ghost's speech as it describes the dread ecology of King Hamlet's death in sleep can confer new sense upon Claudius's treachery. Moreover, such overlap between *Hamlet* and *Macbeth* might be read as instances of literary cleaving in which language, the form of mental impressions, and aspects of critical events from one play cling to the other. Unlike King Hamlet's ghost, however, Lady Macbeth embraces the volatile physical mixtures of thickening and transformation associated with night and the humoral environs of sleep. She actively seeks these accursed, "sightless substances" as agents to whet her purpose and her knife's edge, while weaving a fabric of darkness dipped in the "dunnest smoke of hell" to obscure the image of murder. These are the swirling spirits from which bodily humors take on shaping temperaments, and at night they pool into thick and foggy deposits of melancholy, lethargy, and forgetfulness. Polluted sleep and the radical forms of undoing that the play imagines thus imply spaces of ungendered chaos, sodomitical ruptures of rebellion and self-destruction first alluded to as the "multiplying villainies of nature / [that] swarm upon" Macdonwald and his forces (1.2.11–12).

Banquo, meanwhile, speaks to the ideal sanctity of sovereign sleep when he and King Duncan first arrive at Inverness:

Duncan: This castle hath a pleasant seat; the air
Nimbly and sweetly recommends itself
Unto our gentle senses.
Banquo: This guest of summer,
The temple-haunting martlet, does approve
By his loved mansionry that the heaven's breath
Smells wooingly here. No jutty, frieze,
Buttress, nor coign of vantage, but this bird
Hath made his pendent bed and procreant cradle.
Where they most breed and haunt, I have observed
The air is delicate.
(1.6.1–10)

Banquo gives an image of Inverness as it ought to be: a safe haven in which the king can open himself to the recuperative virtues of sleep, breathing air that is "delicate" and refreshing rather than thickened with evil intention. Duncan and Banquo alike recall King Hamlet's allusions to sleep in his orchard as a pastoral escape from the cares and strains of waking life, a relished removal from the public eye that renews the sovereign's body natural by caring for its physical life. And just as King Hamlet's blood is ideally "thin and wholesome," the air enfolding and infusing the sovereign's sleep at Inverness should be unpolluted and pure. The comparison thus underscores the atrocity of their action—an assault on sovereign sleep that saturates the surrounding darkness with Lady and Lord Macbeth's evil will.

The opportunity to kill Duncan while he sleeps also gives the couple a tantalizing vision of the perfect crime: they decide that culpability can be easily plastered onto the chamberlains sleeping near the "sticking-place," and thus the ambitious pair will avoid any implication of culpability:

Macbeth: If we should fail?
Lady Macbeth: We fail?
But screw your courage to the sticking-place,
And we'll not fail. When Duncan is asleep—
Whereto the rather shall his day's hard journey
Soundly invite him—his two chamberlains
Will I with wine and wassail so convince,
That memory, the warder of the brain,
Shall be a fume, and the receipt of reason
A limbeck only: when in swinish sleep
Their drenched natures lie as in a death,
What cannot you and I perform upon

Th'unguarded Duncan, what not put upon
His spongy officers, who shall bear the guilt
Of our great quell?
(1.7.59–72)

Lady Macbeth's wassail will transform the slumber of Duncan's servants into a "swinish sleep" that erases their memory, altering the "receipt of reason" into nothing but an empty "limbeck." It is an image of the brute, animal aspect of physical life succumbing to its most basic need, as if the sleeping human soul temporarily descends from the lofty heights of reason to feed from the earthly trough. But it also appears that the receptive, spongy powers of the brain's ward are not simply lost or suspended. Rather, these qualities are relocated to the body's surface, such that the inside becomes the outside through a transformative process of cosmic-humoral flux. The officers' sleeping bodies thus serve as sponges to which the guilt of the murder will stick, just as their shirts and daggers shall be stained with the king's blood, and just as Duncan's thickening physical life rises to the surface of his sleeping body. By summoning spirits of malcontent and violent nature, Lady Macbeth and her lord have crafted a kind of artisanal evil, a wicked alchemy that perverts the sanctified substances coursing through the living environment, thereby isolating the physical life of the sovereign only to annihilate it.

Immediately upon killing the sovereign, however, Macbeth is visited by a voice that condemns his act not as an act of homicide but rather a somewhat stranger and more severe metaphysical violation that murders sleep itself:

MACBETH: Methought I heard a voice cry "Sleep no more!
Macbeth does murder sleep"—the innocent sleep,
Sleep that knits up the raveled sleave of care,
The death of each day's life, sore labor's bath,
Balm of hurt minds, great nature's second course,
Chief nourisher in life's feast—
LADY MACBETH: What do you mean?
MACBETH: Still it cried "Sleep no more!" to all the house:
"Glamis hath murdered sleep, and therefore Cawdor
Shall sleep no more: Macbeth shall sleep no more."
(2.2.34–42)

Innocent sleep, Macbeth muses, is a rejuvenating bath, a psychic balm, and a nourishing virtue—a form of unconscious, somatic care that alleviates the cares of waking life. It represents what Richard Strier aptly describes as a "benign" force of nature in the play, which accords with Julia Lupton's elegant formulation that "in these images of repair, sleep winds a tunnel of comforting darkness around the self-abandoning consciousness of the sleeper."[50] At the same time, Macbeth's praise of sleep also represents it as a form of death that ends "each day's life," and so the strange nature of sleep seems divided against itself. Accordingly, the voice Macbeth hears splits his judgment in two: it is *Glamis* who murders sleep, but *Cawdor* who shall sleep no more. Macbeth's identity is again cloven, this time between the title he once held as the thane of Glamis, looking backward to a time before the play, and the title conferred upon him by King Duncan—the thane of Cawdor, who looks ahead to be king, but in becoming so shall never sleep again. And by being divided from the sanctified, life-sustaining properties of sleep, Macbeth's fate comes to taste humorously of a most bitter physical mixture. He embodies divided selfhood in so many respects save the one he most desires: the cleft of sovereignty that successfully binds natural and politic bodies into a single formation. It is fitting retribution for a man who has attacked the King's Two Bodies in its most fragile state of exposure, using sleep's wedge as a killing tool. Macbeth's doom is to be denied the sleep that renews physical life and magisterial presence, in a series of paranoid and debilitating bouts with sleeplessness that consume his conscience. Macbeth is forced to watch events unfold beyond his control, spiraling into hallucinatory paranoia while he "lack[s] the season of all natures, sleep" (3.5.142). While Lady Macbeth's evil summonings pollute the sacredness of Duncan's sleep and facilitate his death, her nefarious incantations also help to isolate Macbeth from the solace of sovereign sleep, and to divide him from the sacred life of sovereignty.

Macbeth's act of aggression and its punishment furthermore suggest that he adheres to an Elizabethan stereotype of antiquated Scottish barbarity, and that he imagines sovereign authority to be decided by acts of violent usurpation. When visited by Banquo's ghost, Macbeth laments the fact that his theft of Duncan's throne has seemingly rendered his claim to power illegitimate, and he displays a kind of nostalgia for an outmoded theory of sovereignty and its principle of investiture:

MACBETH: Blood hath been shed ere now, i'th'olden time,
Ere humane statute purged the gentle weal;
Ay, and since too, murders have been performed
Too terrible for the ear. The times has been
That, when the brains were out, the man would die,
And there an end; but now they rise again,

> With twenty mortal murders on their crowns,
> And push us from our stools. This is more strange
> Than such a murder is.
> (3.5.76–82)

Macbeth recalls a time when the continuity of the state and its legitimating force were not located in the body of the sovereign—when the spilling of royal blood was both an instance of raw aggression and a decisive transfer of the right to rule rather than a crime against the polity with a spectral afterlife. A time "when the brains were out, [and] the man would die, / And there an end" suggests a time when killing a man meant he was truly dead and gone, and one risked neither the haunting guilt nor ghostly visitations that now cripple Macbeth. But his phrasing also reckons the end result of physical conflict as the legitimating factor of political authority, giving the usurping victor right of rule based on strength and the capacity to take power.[51] Macbeth's remembrance of a time when pure force determined the course of political power implies that his position as monarch of Scotland both clings to an absent, antiquated tradition and is immediately cut off from any imagined future of kingship.[52] That verdict may obliquely connect Macbeth with King James through their battles with insomnia, even though the play's official stance is one that separates the two and ties James to the line of Stuart sovereignty through Banquo—a line which is itself a fiction originated by Stuart genealogists in an attempt to mythologize the Stuart claim to the Scottish throne.[53]

In other words, Macbeth imagines the grounding force of blood and physical life in much simpler terms than does the play, since the latter indicates that sovereign blood encrypts a presence that is always more than physical life, yet always bound to it. Shakespeare draws our attention not only to Macbeth's antiquated view of political right but also to the biopolitical uncertainty characterizing the playwright's own world as it grappled with rapid transformations in theories of sovereign legitimacy and the art of government. The metaphysical stain that neither Macbeth nor Lady Macbeth can flush from their souls thus further affirms Macbeth's outmoded faith in a symbolics of blood as the grounding basis of sovereignty. Hence, only too late does Macbeth come to the Senecan realization that not even "great Neptune's ocean" can "wash this blood" clean from his hand: "No, this my hand will rather / The multitudinous seas incarnadine, / Making the green one red" (2.2.63–66). Robert Miola links Macbeth's bloody language here to the John Studley translation of Seneca's *Hercules Oetaeus*.[54] This surging Stoic body of guilt clings to Macbeth's embodied soul, a swelling presence of psychosomatic anxiety that keeps him from sleep. He anticipates such a fate immediately after killing Duncan, though only by mistakenly believing he can purge any sense of guilty paranoia from the routines that sustain his physical life:

> But let the frame of things disjoint, both the worlds suffer,
> Ere we will eat our meal in fear, and sleep
> In the affliction of these terrible dreams
> That shake us nightly. Better be with the dead,
> Whom we, to gain our peace, have sent to peace,
> Than on the torture of the mind to lie
> In restless ecstasy. Duncan is in his grave;
> After life's fitful fever he sleeps well.
> (3.2.17–24)

The "fitful fever" of life will of course become Macbeth's defining burden, as waking cares consume him and prevent the most basic forms of nourishment (food and sleep) that might restore him.

Lady Macbeth, meanwhile, anxiously rehearses the event of Duncan's murder in her sleep, as an unconscious actor replaying her sin. In a sense, these characters form a cleft of opposing extremes: insomniac visions and sleepwalking trauma. They pervert sleep's nature by turning it against itself, as when Lady Macbeth's servant describes her sleepwalking fits to the doctor: "Since his Majesty went into the field, I have seen her rise from her bed, throw her nightgown upon her, unlock her closet, take forth paper, fold it, write upon't, read it, afterwards seal it, and again return to bed; yet all this while in a most fast sleep" (5.1.4–9). And of course, walking, talking, reading, and writing while one sleeps are, like the murderous violation of sleep's sanctity, marked as most unnatural: "A great perturbation in nature, to receive at once the benefit of sleep and do the effects of watching!" (5.1.10–12). Meanwhile, Macbeth watches while sorely missing the effects of sleep—he is enthralled by the visitation of Banquo's ghost, by the series of three apparitions that fixate his gaze in the witches' haunt, and later by the phantasmatic procession of Banquo's heirs. Ultimately, Macduff confirms the latent truth of all these insomniac visions, and seems to Macbeth to speak with a tongue that cleaves his spirit:

> MACDUFF: Despair thy charm,
> And let the angel whom thou still hast served
> Tell thee, Macduff was from his mother's womb
> Untimely ripped.
> MACBETH: Accursed be that tongue that tells me so,
> For it hath cowed my better part of man!
> And be these juggling fiends no more believed,

That palter with us in a double sense;
That keep the word of promise to our ear,
And break it to our hope.
(5.8.13–22)

Macbeth sees, too late, that he is undone by the double sense of cloven tongues, and his words align the prognostications of the weird sisters with the wicked thoughts earlier whispered into his ear by Lady Macbeth. The operations of the cleft work to undo the false king; Macbeth can be nothing more than a cloven mockery of kingship itself, isolated from both the waking presence and the sleeping life of sovereignty, in all its doubled dimensions.

Lear's Fury

From the threatening scene of polluted sovereign sleep in *Hamlet* to the humoral alchemy that facilitates *Macbeth*'s killing of the king, Shakespeare dramatizes the perils of monarchical slumber through a cosmological lens crafted from the materials of Senecan tragedy and its philosophical grounding in Stoicism. The king's care for the body politic is submerged in the unconscious physical mixtures of sleep, which Shakespeare figures as a biopolitical threat arising from a moment of sovereign carelessness that is as inevitable as the day's turning into night. In *King Lear,* Shakespeare pursues a related yet distinct line of thought, exploring the consequences of a commitment to sovereign vigilance that is grounded in a political theology of care of the sort endorsed by James I of England. Lear suffers from an affective surplus of care whose storm-like gathering in his embodied soul is a direct consequence of his decision to unburden himself of the demands of the body politic while retaining the pomp and circumstance of rule. His commitment to monarchical vigilance harmfully carries over into his postsovereign life, and as a ruler who never learned the art of self-care, Lear is woefully unprepared for the abdication he announces at the opening of the play. Lear's inattention to self and *oikos* is figured by his insomniac drive and refusal to sleep over the first four acts of the play, where Shakespeare draws on the Stoic principle that ethics is deeply imbricated with physics in depicting Lear's failure to attend to his body's most basic need for sleep—a concrete need to restore the physical basis and vital foundation of life in caring for the self. This point is in keeping with the play's indebtedness to *Hercules Furens*, whose protagonist, like Lear, suffers from exhaustion due to the overwhelming labors that are placed upon him. Lear's rage and insomnia-driven nomadism may result in less spectacularly violent outcomes, but his psychosomatic turbulence and its filial consequences are nonetheless inspired by Seneca's depiction of Hercules, as both Gordon Braden and Robert Miola have shown.[55]

But Shakespeare's tragedy also reflects upon the trials of self-care in its Christian dimensions by taking up the idea of care as a pastoral attitude of unyielding devotion, which in turn serves as a model for the sovereign's vigilant care for the King's Two Bodies. In this way, the play's depictions of care resonate with Foucault's insight that the resurrection of Stoic ethics and the problem of self-governance intersect in the early modern period with the spiritual discipline of the Christian pastorate and its highly developed techniques of care.[56] *King Lear* participates in the histories of governance and care that Foucault's late lectures elaborate by mounting a critical response to the synthesis of pastoral power and sovereignty that characterizes early modern political theology in its emphasis on vigilant care. Recall that for James I, the body politic and the crown that represents its investiture are rife with "thornie cares" that not only remind the sovereign of his simultaneously political and spiritual duty but also perturb and vex him so effectively as to rescind the comforting release of sleep. While James's text postdates Shakespeare's final play by several years, the image of restless kingly care that it endorses was quite familiar to Shakespeare and subjected to the playwright's critical assessment in a number of histories and tragedies, as Garrett Sullivan Jr. has convincingly shown.[57] I argue here that the virtue of Lear's sleep is to provide a simultaneously ethical and physiological benefit—a Stoic form of unconscious self-care—that eventually cures him of the psychosomatic disarray brought on by his hypervigilant sovereign hangover. Shakespeare thus uses the event of Lear's sleep to highlight an inevitable failure of the "pastoral monarch": namely, his inability to sustain the vigilant devotion and zeal demanded by both the logic of pastoral care and the political theology of the King's Two Bodies.

In the case of *King Lear*, the problem of the sovereign's care comes into focus quite early in the play, through the bodily gestures and affective comportment that mark Lear as a weary king in decline who seeks a release from political obligation. Lear's exhaustion stems directly from the "cares and business" of state that he is so intent to "shake" from his being (1.1.39), yet his weariness remains as a physical fact that persistently determines his moody and irascible ways in the world even after he has divided and relinquished his kingdom. In fact, his separation from rule seems only to augment the melodrama of his care, leading to increasingly disruptive fits of anger, cosmic fury, and an eventual madness—all of which imply that because Lear's sovereign care now lacks a clear and distinct object, it swells and twists into a spiraling tornado of self-harm that draws energy from his ongoing attachment to the vigilant posture of the *rex exsomnis*. "Go tell the Duke and's wife I'd speak with them," Lear barks from outside of Cornwall's house,

> Now, presently! Bid them come forth and hear me,
> Or at their chamber door I'll beat the drum
> Till it cry sleep to death.
> (2.4.115–117).

As his retinue and lines of affective investment steadily shrink, Lear's attachment to vigilance and his surplus of care become increasingly dangerous. The Fool anticipates this problem when he tells Lear, "Thou wast a pretty fellow when thou hadst no need to care for her frowning. Now thou art an O without a figure" (1.4.186–188). In other words, Lear's identity as sovereign guaranteed an outlet for his care, even as it demanded an ever-increasing amount of devotion to the state that resulted in both a lack of self-care and a willful inattention to his family. The Fool's comment thus underscores the division between the affairs of the *oikos* and the political cares that previously defined Lear in his sovereign identity, but which can no longer serve as a sustaining outlet for his devotion. But it also points, anachronistically, to the emerging seventeenth-century art of government that looked to paternal *oikonomia* as a new paradigm for political rule.

As the action unfolds and Lear finds himself wandering the wilderness, his travails consistently point to Regan's claim in act 1 that her father "hath ever but slenderly known himself" (1.1.298–299). Regan figures as slenderness of self-knowledge what the Fool jestingly suggests remains in the form of an "O" at the core of Lear's postsovereign self. Having devoted himself both to the obligations of kingship and to the image of himself as a mighty monarch, Lear never cultivated the knowledge that, in the Socratic and Stoic traditions, lays the necessary foundation of self-care in the form of virtue. And this foundational lack steadily derails his psychosomatic well-being, leading to a radical exposure to the elemental forces and physical mixtures of the cosmos. It is not until Lear's second period of sleep in act 4, scene 7, that his sanity is fully restored. Before that moment, however, we need only look to Lear's time on the heath to see that his period of physical exposure begins slowly to reveal to him the issue of his misguided care and the foundational lack that he embodies. At first, he looks to the surrounding elements and physical environment for a kind of corroboration of both his children's betrayal and his ensuing rage, still embodying the hypervigilant posture of the sovereign:

> Rumble thy bellyful. Spit fire. Spout, rain.
> Nor rain, wind, thunder, fire are my daughters.

> I tax not you, you elements, with unkindness.
> I never gave you kingdom, called you children;
> You owe me no subscription.
> (3.2.14–18)

Lear at once absolves his cosmological milieu from the sort of filial obligation he demands of his children, yet at the same time imagines the "servile ministers" of the environment to be colluding with his "two pernicious daughters" (3.2.21–22) by worsening his already distempered and passionate state. Lear wants both to disavow the relevance of the physical cosmos to his weighty affairs, and to see it bend toward him in recognition of his superior suffering and loss, as he is "more sinned against than sinning" (3.2.60).

Slowly, however, he comes to see that the cosmos demands its own measure of attention and care. The physical environment subjects Lear to the passionate flux and tempestuous reality of life, demanding an acknowledgment of the fragile vulnerability at the heart of embodied life. This process lays bare the truth that care necessarily entails a mutual self-exposure that mortal beings share:

> O, I have ta'en
> Too little care of this! Take physic, pomp;
> Expose thyself to feel what wretches feel,
> That thou mayst shake the superflux to them
> And show the heavens more just.
> (3.4.34–38)

Lear's use of the word "physic" is telling here, since it marks the extent to which the cure he envisions rests in knowledge of physis, or the physical cosmos that is, in the Stoic tradition, synonymous with self-knowledge. Unhae Park Langis describes the physic Lear needs as a form of healing guided by an awareness of "kinship with other beings" and just interaction with the natural world alike.[58] As we have seen throughout this book, Stoic physicalism affirms such insight, giving ontological priority to bodily mixtures such that ethical knowledge is knowledge of how bodies move and are moved by the physical web of causes that spreads across the organic, living whole of the cosmos. Lear's turn toward philosophy in act 3—embodied for Lear in Edgar's disguised identity as an impoverished riddler who embraces exposure and vulnerability—points to a dawning recognition of his need for such knowledge and its place in ancient Greek thought: "First let me talk with this philosopher . . . I'll talk a word with this same learned Theban" (3.4.152–155); "Noble philosopher, your company. . . . Come, good Athenian" (3.4.172–182). Shakespeare transposes the porch of the ancient Stoics into Poor Tom's hovel, where the former sovereign begins the process of self-transformation essential to ancient virtue ethics.

Yet Lear appears to shrink from the immediate implications of this philosophical turn, and instead backslides into the more familiar *habitus* of an enraged king whose desire to punish insubordination is now clothed in mock-juridical garb. If, as Kantorowicz argues, the figure of the *rex exsomnis* originates from the idea of the sovereign as the living embodiment of the law that never sleeps (*lex animata*), then Lear's insomniac frenzy in the mock trial scene appears to align him with that historical conjunction of sovereignty and juridical power.[59] Yet as the mock trial begins, Edgar offers a rhyme that seems both to implicate Lear in the failure of a pastoral watch and to call him out in his helplessness, as he is no longer capable of embodying the norm of sovereign vigilance and the commanding presence of the King's Two Bodies:

> Sleepest or wakest thou, jolly shepherd?
> Thy sheep be in the corn;
> And for one blast of thy minikin mouth
> Thy sheep shall take no harm.
> (3.6.41–44)

Nothing, of course, has proven more futile leading up to this moment than the blasts from Lear's "minikin mouth," so Edgar's cryptic rhyme lambasts Lear's self-righteous mockery of justice just as it reveals the folly of his attachment to the burdensome cares of sovereign vigilance.

When Lear finally assents to Kent's biddings—"Now, good my lord, lie here and rest awhile" (3.6.81)—his sleep releases him temporarily from the insomnia-fueled madness and tyranny of cares that consume him. Kent hopes that this moment will cure the former sovereign, even as he acknowledges the difficulty of that task:

> Oppressèd nature sleeps.
> This rest might yet have balmed thy broken sinews,
> Which, if convenience will not allow,
> Stand in hard cure.
> (3.6.96–99)

Kent's language here echoes Jasper Heywood's 1561 translation of Seneca's depiction of the sleeping Hercules, and the choral prayer that accompanies it:

> Keepe him fast bounde with heavy sleepe opprest,
> Let slomber deepe his Limmes untamed bynde,

Nor soner leave his unright raginge breaste
Then former mynde his course agayne may fynd.[60]

But there is more behind the Senecan resonances of Kent's prayer than the sort of verbal echoes of humanistic imitation that have long been seen as the central mark of Senecan drama upon early modern tragedy. The cure that Kent hopes for is a virtue and benefit to the embodied soul that the Stoics align with the *cura regentis*, whose movements sustain the organic, living whole that is the cosmos. Yet this restorative power is not granted until Lear's second sleep, and only fleetingly. For when Cordelia asks if any manner of "man's wisdom" might restore her father's "bereaved sense" (4.4.8–9), the gentleman beside her assures Lear's daughter that

There is means, madam.
Our foster nurse of nature is repose,
The which he lacks. That to provoke in him
Are many simples operative, whose power
Will close the eye of anguish.
(4.4.11–15)

Cordelia's hopeful response and prayer align her with the knowledge of the Stoic sage, whose divination guides action that is deeply attuned to the motions of the cosmos and to the secret virtues of its physical mixtures:

All blessed secrets,
All you unpublished virtues of the earth,
Spring with my tears; be aidant and remediate
In the good man's distress. Seek, seek for him,
Lest his ungoverned rage dissolve the life
That wants the means to lead it.
(4.4.15–20)

Cordelia wants for her father what the sage commands: a grasp of the motions of the physical cosmos that comes through the balanced judgment of a virtuous hêgemonikon, the ruling power that leads life through the active principle of the pneuma. Her use of the word "dissolve" further aligns her with the early modern poetic revival of Stoic physics, but, perhaps more remarkably, aligns the threat of vital dissolution with Lear's rage rather than his sleep.[61] Cordelia's vision of somnolence is thus striking in contrast to the scenes of humoral volatility and corruption that limn sovereign sleep in *Hamlet* and *Macbeth*, as well as the image of Lady Macbeth's occult manipulations of her humoral and environmental surrounds. Cordelia rather inhabits the posture of the Stoic sage, as Kent describes her upon receiving his letters. Although "now and then an ample tear trilled down / Her delicate cheek," she nonetheless remained "queen / Over her passion, who, most rebel-like, / Sought to be king o'er her" (4.3.12–14). Just as Seneca's wise man feels his troubles yet does not allow them to master him, Cordelia feels and rightly acknowledges the physical impulse of sadness that acts as a bodily cause to her tears, while maintaining the body of virtue and her proper orientation toward care of self and others.

If Cordelia plays the role of the Stoic sage, her tent becomes a restorative nursery that returns Lear to the vital foundations of his oikeiôsis. This recovery comes through the "heaviness of sleep" (4.7.23) and the restorative power that Cordelia brings as crucial therapy to his postsovereign, psychosomatic ailments of care. Sleep provides a release from the madness of sovereign care and places the monarch into contact with the unconscious yet purposive motions of the healing cosmos. It is a temporary shelter for vulnerable life, one that briefly yet poignantly renews the circle of care between Cordelia and her father, only to see it shattered upon their reentry to the world. As Sheiba Kaufman argues, the virtues of care flash briefly into sight but suddenly withdraw. "Ethical possibility," she writes, "often hinging on a form of care through hospitality and solidarity with others, is muted, lost, or forgotten."[62] Shakespeare's tragic Stoic cosmos remains turbulent to the end, despite Lear's ardent desire to release his cares and relinquish himself to rest under the watchful care of his daughter: "I loved her most, and thought to set my rest / On her kind nursery" (1.1.123–124). Yet Lear can only truly and completely turn away from his old manner of sovereign embodiment when he sleeps because that is the only condition of the body natural that entirely captures and suspends the sovereign's conscious will and active engagement with the body politic. The king's care remains, even though he has ostensibly rid himself of the burdens of managing the body politic and the thorny cares of state.

While Lear's central problem may seem to be his desire to retain the privileges and trappings of kingship after having relinquished the responsibilities of state, I have argued that Lear's physical body in fact retains the excess of cares that medieval and early modern political theology views as both an affective burden and a necessary attribute of sovereign embodiment. And as the play reveals, Lear lacks the proper object upon which to focus his care because he is unprepared to turn toward himself. Shakespeare ties Lear's fate to the care of the self that is at the heart of Stoic virtue ethics, suggesting Lear has been a king who takes too little care of those things that nurture and sustain his life in its creaturely capacities and domestic relations. Like all of Shakespeare's sovereigns, Lear has endured a commitment to political vigilance and monarchical duty that inevitably draws him away from forms of care necessary to flourishing as a human. His early decision to "disclaim all my paternal care" (1.1.114) for Cordelia attempts to sever a mutually beneficial relationship of domestic care that he instead ought to be cultivating, especially in light of his previous history of neglect.

By grounding Lear's fleeting moment of renewal in the "unpublished virtues" of an earthy sleep, Shakespeare takes up the key biopolitical conundrum that sleep presents for the care of the early modern self and its relations with others: to sleep is to care for the bodily life that sustains waking attention, but only insofar as sleep abandons the form of wakefulness that promotes ethical and spiritual care. The playwright introduces this problem to the early modern synthesis of sovereign vigilance and pastoral watch exemplified by the Stuart monarchy, rejecting the political-theological grounding of sovereign power in metaphysical abstraction. He instead draws attention to the newly emerging governmentality and its organizing paradigm of a political *oikonomia*, one that is based upon a cosmological-scientific form of knowledge and which entails a new ethics of care. The care for physical life begins to take on new meaning in a world where sovereignty is slowly shedding the mantle of political theology. In its emphasis upon the restorative virtues of sleep, Shakespeare's tragedy attributes a deep value to the king's physical life and its self-restorative capacities, minus its political-theological trappings. As Richard Halpern has argued, the play routes history and the assignation of value through the body, drawing our attention to "gestural manifestations of value" that "substitute for the production of social value."[63] Along such lines, I suggest that the king's sleep lays bare an emergent form of value even as it vexes the norms of kingly vigilance which, for political theology, necessarily define sovereign care.

Shakespeare's Somnolent Biopolitics

Shakespeare's tragic framings of sovereign sleep as both a political-theological emergency and a vital recovery of the monarch's physical life, I have argued, constitute biopolitical reflections on the vexations of sovereign care—especially as they pertain to the formation and deformations of the King's Two Bodies and the presumption of the sovereign's devotion to continual vigilance. We are now in a better position to assess the playwright's depictions of sovereign sleep and insomnia in light of the influential accounts of biopower and sovereignty developed by both Foucault and Agamben. Agamben of course builds upon and departs from Foucault's genealogy of biopolitics in significant ways, so it is worth reviewing some of the essential aspects of Foucault's account that hold special relevance for Shakespearean drama. The French thinker argues that biopolitics emerges precisely in the wake of an early modern shift from the sovereign power to take life to the newfound governmental art of a political *oikonomia*, which begins to cohere fully around the imperative to make live and the concept of population management during the eighteenth century. So while biopolitics proper does not enter the historical scene until well after Shakespeare's lifetime, as Foucault argues, its foundations were beginning to appear by the end of the sixteenth century, when explorations in governance sought to mediate between a juridico-legal notion of sovereignty and a model of paternalistic household management belonging to *oikonomia*. This meant that the emerging "art of government was caught," Foucault explains, "between an excessively large, abstract, and rigid framework of sovereignty on the one hand, and, on the other, a model of the family that was too narrow, weak, and insubstantial. . . . With the household and the father on the one hand, and the state and sovereignty on the other, the art of government could not find its own dimension."[64] But as Foucault also remarks, the government of the family was essential to the historical development of biopower, insofar as it provided some key features: "A power immanent to society (the father being part of the family), a power over 'things' rather than territory, a power with multiple finalities all of which concern the well-being, happiness, and wealth of the family, a peaceful, vigilant power."[65] In other words, Foucault's genealogy of biopower and biopolitics establishes a crucial role for the model of vigilant, paternal care whose presence I have been tracking in Shakespeare's tragic figurations of sovereign sleep and the King's Two Bodies, not to mention James I's attempts to articulate a model of kingly care grounded in the synthesis of pastoral vigilance and sovereignty.

Unlike Foucault, Agamben views sovereignty as a transcendent *dispositif* that is legible in political philosophy at least since the Greeks. The Italian philosopher argues that the production of a biopolitical body is in fact "the original activity of sovereign power," and with this claim he has established a genealogy and conceptual schematic for critical investigations of biopower and sovereignty that has shaped much recent scholarship on early modern literature.[66] No doubt part of Agamben's rapid and widespread adoption by early modernists can be explained by the fact that his theory of biopolitics and the structure of the sovereign exception suggest that biopolitics is in effect the residual product of any and all political operations that reveal the paradox of sovereign power's inclusionary exclusion. For Agamben, seemingly any historical or contemporary instance where biological life can be ascertained in a relation of subordinate dependence to ethical and political norms would be a biopolitical operation, because such a situation manifests, even if in a degraded form, the same exceptional structure that is the mark of sovereignty and its principle of legitimation by decision.

What, then, does Agamben have to say about the King's Two Bodies and its biopolitical significance? For Agamben, the body of the sovereign contains two forms of life, sacred and bare, that are enigmatically tied to a single body: the king does not have two bodies, but rather two *lives* that are bound together by a single corpus. The status of the sovereign's life thus reflects a complementary opposition to the life of the *homo sacer*—the contradictory figure of Roman law who can be killed but not sacrificed:

> Here the structural analogy between the sovereign exception and *sacratio* shows its full sense. At the two extreme limits of the order, the sovereign and *homo sacer* present two symmetrical figures that have the same structure and are correlative: the sovereign is the one with respect to whom all men are potentially *homines sacri*, and *homo sacer* is the one with respect to whom all men act as sovereigns.[67]

Agamben goes on to revise Kantorowicz's claim that the metaphysical body politic grounds the continuity of the state by arguing that "at the moment of the sovereign's death, it is the sacred life grounding sovereign authority that invests the person of the sovereign's successor."[68] This form of sacred life is passed from the body of one sovereign to the next, not in the form of a metaphysical or political body that infuses the body natural of the monarch but rather as the capacity to designate life that can be killed but not sacrificed—to identify the *homo sacer* potentially encrypted as bare life in the body of every subject. For Agamben, the significance of the sacred life that underpins the King's Two Bodies is precisely the biopolitical power to exclude biological life from inclusion in the political order, or from any normative significance whatsoever.

As we have seen, Shakespeare's depictions of a sovereign's death in sleep do not reflect the neat, structural symmetries between bare and sacred life that Agamben's account of sovereign power presumes. Rather, he seems to imagine forms of life in the sovereign body natural being strikingly metamorphosed, repositioned, and even evacuated as a consequence of the volatile physical mixtures that determine the event of sovereign sleep. Hence, in both *Hamlet* and *Macbeth*, while the immediate successor to the throne appears to kill the bare life of the sleeping sovereign, he is clearly not invested with the form of sacred life that, in Agamben's account, conditions sovereign power and assures its continuity. When King Hamlet and King Duncan are killed in their sleep, the terms of sovereignty's double exclusion are inverted. In their altered case, the sleeping kings' bodies may seem to manifest the quality of bare life that defines the *homo sacer* in its capacity to be killed outside of law, but the sacred life bound to them can neither be killed nor taken on by Claudius or Macbeth. Likewise, the sleeping sovereign body is incapable of decision per se, while Claudius and Macbeth appear to exercise a sovereign decision to designate and kill bare life—though neither of them is sovereign when they commit that act.

Shakespeare thus attributes to the physical life of the sovereign something more than simply the conjunction of sacred and bare life that Agamben theorizes constitutes the secret core of the King's Two Bodies. If there is a biopolitical significance to the playwright's depictions of sovereign sleep, then it is in its departure from some of Agamben's key presumptions. On the one hand, the unconscious force of sovereign sleep in Shakespearean tragedy has the power to undo the knot that holds together the King's Two Bodies. Holy and accursed, sanctified and bare, the sovereign body in sleep not only betrays the antitheses of doubled life that it encrypts—it also opens the sleeping body to the volatile humoral flows and cosmological forces animating living substance at large. The radical potential of sleep is both to amplify and to undo the fragile underpinnings of life that infuse the King's Two Bodies—to pull the physical life of the sovereign to the surface, and thus to facilitate its being taken. *Hamlet* and *Macbeth* suggest that this killing of the sovereign in sleep creates, as it were, an exception to the exception.

Yet the truly biopolitical significance of Shakespeare's thinking is perhaps most readily discerned in *King Lear*, where the physical life restored by Lear's postsovereign slumber gives us the faintest outline of an emerging biopower that is not yet captured by the technical grasp of a new art of government. Lear's sleep manifests a form of life that eludes the apparatus of sovereign seizure and its exertion of power through the threat of death. His sleep is no longer marked as a power of death—as it is in Christian political theology—but rather as a power of life, an immanent biological normativity whose impulse is to care for and sustain the physical life of the sovereign.[69] This power and its historical form of appearance are precursors to the form of state-based biopower that Foucault conceives as the widespread "administration" and "calculated management" of life. It is, in a sense, a necessary step toward that end, though one that is subtly and curiously embodied in a condition of restorative stasis and recovery that for Shakespeare constitutes a vitalist riposte to the sovereign seizure of life. If the political *oikonomia* that will develop into government as biopolitics does not fully emerge until the eighteenth century, then the nourishing virtues of sleep and the physical life they sustain in *King*

Lear are not exactly instances of "distributing the living in the domain of value and utility" but rather of what Foucault identifies as life's immanent power, the ontological precedent to biopolitical control which "constantly escapes" strategic attempts to master it.[70] And in Shakespeare's world, what occasion could better illustrate life's power to alter and escape the techniques of vigilant care than the event of sovereign sleep?

Chapter 4

"Watching to Banish Care"

Sleep and Insomnia in *The Faerie Queene*

This chapter investigates the roles of sleep and insomnia in books 1 and 4 of *The Faerie Queene*, in light of Edmund Spenser's wide-ranging philosophical and theological interests in the fraught connections between physical embodiment and ethical care.[1] While most of my discussion is devoted to Spenser's allegory of holiness, I conclude with a reading of book 4's depiction of Sir Scudamor's insomnia in the House of Care. Spenser's earlier handling of the nocturnal ventures of Redcrosse knight, which revolve around the hero's struggles with both sleep and sleeplessness, elucidate book 4's allegory of Care as a haggard blacksmith whose minions labor deep into the night. I argue that in book 1, Spenser develops a model of ethical care between Redcrosse and Una that reveals affinities with Stoic thought, while taking aim at some fundamental suppositions that guide Renaissance humanist and Christian political-theological commitments to vigilant care and militant spiritual fortitude. Meanwhile, in book 4, Spenser's turn toward forms of life and affiliation not buttressed by political theology emerges more clearly in his personification of Care as the headmaster to a team of hammering blacksmiths. The ongoing nocturnal labors of these entities figure Scudamor's insomnia as a harmful amplification of waking cares that prevents him from accessing the vital powers of self-recovery and restoration found in sleep.

Sleep is represented as a cold and deathly affair in the opening pages of Spenser's epic, and his allegory of holiness uses these common early modern associations to suggest that somnolence is perilous for Redcrosse knight. The fall of sleep brings a period of psychosomatic dissolution during which the self loses its capacities to think and to act in a willed manner, thereby annulling the foundations of humanist care and attention that we have seen endorsed by key figures of Renaissance humanism.[2] Sleep reduces the human to a state of physiological and spiritual precariousness that appears to be less than life yet more than death. As night arrives in the first canto of book 1, for instance, Archimago leads Redcrosse, Una, and the Dwarf "vnto their lodgings," and the company is described as being "drownd in deadly sleepe," whereupon the sorcerer begins to work his "mighty charmes, to trouble sleepy mindes" (1.1.36). It would therefore seem reasonable to claim, as both Northrop Frye and Deborah Shuger have, that the dark liquidity of sleep vexes Redcrosse knight as well as the author's Reformed political theology in book 1.[3] For Frye, Spenser's poem projects an "uneasy political feeling that the price of authority is eternal vigilance" and so sleep "is one of the three divisions of the lowest world, the other two being death and hell."[4] Meanwhile, Shuger aligns Redcrosse's slumber with a patristic tradition that distrusts sleep's compromising effects on the impassioned human soul. Yet no one has confirmed or challenged such claims through a focused reading of both sleep and sleeplessness in Spenser's Legend of Holiness, which requires us to unfold the overlapping theological, ethical, and physiological meaning of these events.[5]

Contemporary readers might well expect the poet to treat Redcrosse's sleep in explicitly Pauline terms, since the author's letter asserts that the hero's arms are modeled on the "armor of a Christian man specified by Saint Paul" in his epistle to the Ephesians.[6] But as Daryl Gless has pointed out, this letter to Raleigh was either omitted from or inconspicuously "buried" within early editions of the poem both during and well after Spenser's lifetime.[7] It was not until the eighteenth century that readers of Spenser's epic would have encountered his explicit reference to the armor of Ephesians in prefatory form. Despite this fact, I believe that Redcrosse's struggles with sleep and sleeplessness in the early cantos serve well enough to alert readers at all familiar with the New Testament to the armor's Pauline valences. Paul's epistles constantly use sleep to figure spiritual carelessness or a lapse in vigilance that compromises faith and makes believers vulnerable to assaults by the devil.[8] In Romans 13, for instance, Paul describes the body of the Christian community experiencing an awakening and illumination that leaves behind the old life of sin; in Ephesians 5, the apostle likewise urges Christians to "haue no fellowship with ye unfruteful workes of darkenes . . . for it is light that maketh all things manifest. Wherefore he saith, Awake thou that slepest, & stand up from the dead, & Christ shal giue thee light" (11–14).[9] For Paul, sleep symbolizes a spiritual backsliding into darkness and sin, against which Christians must struggle daily. And it is this Pauline perspective that I would like to situate against Spenser's images of sleep and sleeplessness in book 1.

I argue that Redcrosse's sleep is at best a temporary and minor threat to his spiritual fortitude—not nearly as calamitous as readers have presumed it to be. In fact, Spenser treats the hero's lack of sleep as a greater threat to his well-being and his spiritual virtue because it derails Redcrosse's concern for his unique obligations as the patron of holiness. Insofar as the hero's insomnia constitutes a failure to attend to his basic bodily need to sleep, it marks a notable and paradoxical aspect of the early modern care of the self: to sleep means to relax one's conscious guard against the forces of darkness and sin, but not to sleep means to refuse a crucial form of physiological and spiritual recovery that temporarily lifts the burden of worldly cares. For Redcrosse in particular, insomnia represents an undue pathological vigilance that blocks sleep's unique form of unconscious self-care. Spenser thus brings Redcrosse's physiological necessity for sleep and for phenomenal self-renewal into direct conflict with a stark approximation of Pauline ideals of unwavering spiritual vigilance and Christian militancy. The poem moreover suggests that Redcrosse embodies holiness even while he sleeps, and this situation resists the Pauline logic that for Christians, the body's essential role is to serve as an active instrument promoting God's will.[10] Spenser's allegory of holiness suggests, contra such paradigms, that human beings are radically unable to arise from spiritual slumber and to remain constantly vigilant. Our bodies are simply incapable of wearing God's holy armor at all times, or of continually being armed and ready to do what the Lord requires of us in confronting the "workes of darkenes."

It's no secret that Paul has been in vogue for Shakespeare criticism and for early modern literary studies at large, just as he is within a certain strand of contemporary continental thought. Recent and valuable work by a host of critics—including Julia Lupton, Graham Hammill, Ken Jackson, Gregory Kneidel, Catherine Winiarski, and Jonathan Gil Harris—has considered Paul's multivalent influence on Renaissance writers in sanguine terms.[11] This view of Paul's legacy equally characterizes (and in several instances, flows directly from) the recuperative spirit of work on the apostle by Alain Badiou, Giorgio Agamben, Slavoj Žižek, and others.[12] In various ways, early modern literary studies have revisited the Pauline corpus, using his religious poetics of mixed temporality and mixed bodies as mixed communities to propose a more tolerant, politically ingenious, presciently liberal, radical, or even multicultural Paul who remains crucially relevant to the politics of our world. The discussion ahead, however, both shares and charts Spenser's skepticism toward a Pauline vision of the militant Christian. My argument reads the allegorical thrust of book 1 as a commentary on some limitations to the apostle's zealous political-theological standards—especially as perceived and disseminated by Renaissance humanists such as Erasmus, as well as Reformation theologians including Martin Luther and John Calvin.[13] Certainly, Paul's writings provide essential elements of Reformed theology in early modern England, and it would be foolish to argue otherwise.[14] But the story of Redcrosse knight and Una nonetheless suggests that Pauline theology as well as his typological mode of allegory are not only insufficient for understanding the tasks of holy life, but can in fact threaten its pursuit.

I argue that in lieu of the militant and individualizing spiritual fortitude advocated by Paul's exhortations and many of his Reformation inheritors, book 1 develops a paradigm of mutual care between Redcrosse and Una that is inspired by Stoic ethics and its doctrine of oikeiôsis. While Spenser's representations of Redcrosse's rage, restorative slumber, and physical suffering explicitly invoke Seneca's tragic depictions of Hercules, the poet also constructs a Stoic vision of care as mutual fulfillment and the natural outcome of oikeiôsis—a process which begins as an immanent attachment to and care for the self in its corporeal constitution but grows to include other beings as life develops on its natural path toward virtue. Along such lines, while Spenser draws our attention to the ethical and physiological benefit of sleep for Redcrosse knight in particular, the vulnerability of nocturnal life also lays bare a fundamental human need for other humans. Through their experiences of sleep and insomnia, both Una and Redcrosse are subjected to moments of psychosomatic peril, insufficiency, or lack that demand the other's caring presence. Spenser's figurations of sleep and insomnia in book 1 thus enfold several meanings of care, locating the self amid a contradictory set of concerns for the physical body, the passionate soul, and the spirit alike.

For Spenser, care is an existential condition of worry, anxiety, and sorrowful constraint that determines waking life. In this sense, care is a burden that can envelop and even consume the self, and insomnia appears to exacerbate these damaging effects. But Spenser also shows that care can be a holy virtue and a good that alleviates such burdens when it is suitably given to others, echoing Seneca's claim that for human beings, care is that which perfects the good.[15] Both Redcrosse and Una are bound to the world and to each other through these dispositional tendencies. Book 1 depicts forms of care that they extend uniquely to each other—as solicitude, concern, and affective investment—which enliven the self and constitute a fulfilling bond between the two. But in the case of Redcrosse knight, book 1 complicates this reciprocal wholeness of mutual care through the urgency of the hero's need to sleep, which acts as an ethical counterweight and necessarily, if temporarily, removes him from the concerns of waking life. Redcrosse's sleep becomes an unconscious form of self-care that prepares him to face the world anew—it is an immanently restorative power housed in his physical body, which allows the hero to return to the waking cares placed upon him by Una and by his allegorical duty to embody the virtue of holiness.

Redcrosse Knight's (W)holiness

My readers will no doubt recall the essential implications of Paul's figural link between sleep and the flesh, a link whose afterlife this book has tracked in the work of Christian theologians from Cassian and Augustine to Luther and Calvin.[16] While the physical body is indispensable to Paul's soteriology, his references to sleep are primarily deployed as allegorical figurations of spiritual carelessness and vulnerability to sin rather than as instances of physiological harm or risk. Hence, in 2 Thessalonians 5:2, Paul warns the faithful to be vigilant, because "the day of the Lord shal come, euen as a thefe in the night." He goes on to characterize believers as "children of light, and the children of the day: we are not of the night nether of darkenes. Therefore let vs not slepe as do others, but le vs watch and be sober."[17] And being vigilant, sober, and in the light is typically equated with wearing the armor of faith that God provides, which keeps believers not only from having "fellowship with the unfruteful workes of darkenes" but also girds the faithful "euen to reproue them" (Ephesians 5:11). Likewise, Paul's letter to the Romans describes God's once chosen people as being misled from God's love because "their foolish heart was full of darkenes" (Romans 1:21), and so he urges, "It is now time that we shulde arise from slepe: for now is our saluation nerer, then when we beleued it. The night is past, & the day is at hand: let us therefore cast away the workes of darkenes, and let vs put on the armour of light, So that we walke honestly, as in the day: not in glotonie, and dronkennes, neither in chambering and wantonness, nor in strife and enuying" (Romans 13:10–13). Though this Pauline perspective implies that the inevitability of spiritual struggle might be likened to the inevitability of sleep, Paul's epistles nonetheless construct a normative ideal of constant, vigilant faith that forgoes the "workes of darkenes" and defies spiritual slumber.

Meanwhile, both patristic and early modern theologians develop Paul's doctrine of the flesh and his allegorical figurations of sleep to suggest that the physical experience of sleep actually aggravates the fleshly body, or the condition of depravity that defines the fallen human being. In book 8 of *Confes-*

sions, Augustine represents fleshly life as a soporific force that occludes a clear-sighted devotion to God:

> The burden of the world weighed me down with a sweet drowsiness such as commonly occurs during sleep. The thoughts with which I meditated about you were like the efforts of those who would like to get up but are overcome by deep sleep and sink back again. No one wants to be asleep all the time, and the sane judgment of everyone judges it better to be awake. Yet often a man defers shaking off sleep when his limbs are heavy with slumber.[18]

Extending Paul's political-theological emphasis on vigilant spiritual care, Augustine goes on to lament the "still live images of acts" of his carnal nature that "attack" while he sleeps. "While I am awake they have no force," he writes, "but in sleep they not only arouse pleasure but even elicit consent . . . how great a difference between myself at the time when I am asleep and myself when I return to the waking state."[19] Augustine's worries over sleep's capacity to suspend the conscious will and rational defenses of the human soul form a bridge from Paul's figural uses of sleep to early modern entanglements of both spiritual and corporeal aspects of slumber, many of which look to ancient philosophical discourses on sleep even as they reinforce the political-theological wisdom that sleep is a risky and perilous experience for Christians. For such thinkers, the fleshly depravity of sleep constitutes a moment of problematic inwardness, in that Christians who are asleep are temporarily removed from the ability to care for themselves and for others in their spiritual community. And as we have seen, both Martin Luther and John Calvin extend Paul's allegorical handling of sleep in ways that underscore the apostle's militaristic commitment to vigilant devotion and wakefulness in spiritual life, as exemplified in Luther's assurance that "the Apostle desires that Christians should take care of their bodies in such a way that no evil desires are nurtured thereby. . . . We should not destroy the body, but crucify its vices or evil passions."[20]

Likewise, in Erasmus's paradigmatic text on Christian militancy, *Enchiridion Militis Christiani*, the Dutch humanist argues that Christians are beset on all sides by supernatural foes who ruthlessly seek their destruction. Under such circumstances, Christians must resist the human tendency to slide into spiritual carelessness, and strengthen the shields that protect them in their faith:

> It is a meruaylous thing to beholde, how without care and circumspection we lyue, how ydelly we slepe now vpon the one syde and now vpon the other whan without ceasying we are beseged with so great a nombre

> of armed vices sought and hunted for with so great craft inuaded dayly with so great lyeng awayt. Behold ouer thy heed wicked deuyls that neuer slepe but kepe watche for our destruction armed against vs with a thousand deceits with a thousand craftes of noysances whiche enforce from on high to wounde our myndes with wepons brenning and dipped in deedly poison, than the which wepons neyther Hercules nor Cephalus had euer a surer darte except they be receyued with the sure and impenetrable shelde of faith.[21]

For Erasmus, care is the thread linking his vision of Renaissance humanist ethics to Pauline theology through a shared conviction that Christians must resist the natural inclination toward careless living. Instead, they ought to strengthen their shields of faith through vigilant spiritual care, keeping their "wepons . . . alway redy at hand, leest thyne so subtyle an enemy shuld take the sleper and vnarmed."[22] In comparing the darts shot by our demonic enemies to those of Hercules, Erasmus alludes to the poison of the Lernean hydra in which Hercules dipped his arrows—the same venom that soaked the tunic ultimately responsible for the hero's own death. Perhaps Erasmus intends a buried implication that the arrows of our devilish foes can likewise be turned against them, so long as they are met by a sufficiently well-girded soul. Or the Herculean metaphor may aim to suggest that without proper care, our soul's inherent capacities for virtue can be weaponized and turned against us, becoming a poison of self-harm that consumes our innermost being. At any rate, the end point of his mythological allusion is clear: the fiends' arrows are sure to be even more devastating than those of Hercules, unless we take sufficient care to buttress our "impenetrable shelde of faith" against them.

Spenser undoubtedly responds to these familiar political-theological and humanist associations of sleep with ethical and spiritual carelessness, and the affiliations he imagines between Redcrosse knight and Hercules may well be informed by Erasmian invocations of the Stoic hero. But Spenser's attention to the perils of insomnia in book 1 also deserves some contextualization—especially given Erasmus's claim that spiritual foes keep constant "watche for our destruction." As William Tyndale's translation of Erasmus's text suggests, the term "watche" is the proper opposite to sleep in Spenser's world, and it connotes vigilant care and wakefulness alike. Henry Cockeram's *The English dictionarie; or, An interpreter of hard English words* (1623) contains the first English version of the word "insomnia" in print, which Cockeram defines as "watching, want of power to sleepe," suggesting that sleeplessness could mark a specific lack or inability—a "want of power"—on the part of the early modern self.[23] Rebecca Totaro has also shown that during the period, "watch" evoked a history of civil vigilance and protection in medieval towns against the vulnerability occasioned by nightfall, as well as a sense of constant spiritual care for one's soul.[24] Just as early modern sleep paradoxically mortifies the self in order to restore it, watch can reflect both the presence of vigilant care and a lack of the ability to sleep.[25] While it seems entirely plausible to read Redcrosse's sleeplessness as a sign of spiritual fortitude along such lines—and thus an echo of familiar paradigms of Renaissance humanist care and political theology—I argue instead that the hero's insomnia constitutes a pathological version of watch. Spenser uses it to evoke misguided forms of vigilant care, incorporating Senecan depictions of Herculean rage and the refusal to sleep, as well as the Stoic view of sleep as a vital power of physiological and ethical restoration that attunes the corporeal soul's ruling principle to the rational motions of the cosmos. For Redcrosse, sleep is a therapy of bodily recovery and a crucial form of self-care; it offers him a temporary respite from the anguish of waking cares while renewing the physical life that serves as a material foundation to his being. Redcrosse's refusal to sleep thus constitutes a harmful and overly vigilant attunement of his sensing soul, which harms him in his obligations to care not only for himself but also Una.

Thus far, my characterizations of Spenser's relationship to Pauline political theology and the humanist legacies of sleep may raise a few eyebrows. Isn't Spenser's commitment to Pauline thought clear in *The Faerie Queene*, and especially so in book 1? After all, Redcrosse knight's armor is explicitly modeled on the armor of the militant Christian soldier that Paul describes in Ephesians 5, and Paul's writings served as a principal basis for the ongoing negotiations between spiritual and political life in Reformation England.[26] Yet if Spenser's Protestant allegory is unabashedly Pauline, or, as some have claimed, even Calvinist in its leanings, it shouldn't be difficult to find an ever-vigilant, unsleeping hero who embodies such ideals of Christian holiness. In fact, we can find one with ease in book 1. Only that figure isn't Redcrosse knight—actually, it isn't a person at all, but the lion that follows and protects Una in Redcrosse's initial absence. The lion is the only creature in book 1 that—as Spenser explicitly tells us—never sleeps. It instead guards Una tirelessly as they wander the wild: "Still when she slept, he kept both watch and ward, / And when she wakt, he waited diligent, / With humble seruice to her will prepard" (1.3.9). When Una and her protector seek shelter in Abessa's cabin, the lion protects her through the night, keeping watch "at her feet" (1.3.15) in an image that contrasts with elements of the earlier scene of Redcrosse's slumber in Archimago's cabin during which a dream spirit places itself "vpon his hardy head" (1.1.47) to play its wicked games. I will return to that image and discuss it at length, but first I want to develop a more substantial reading of Redcrosse knight's temporary creaturely substitute, which in turn clarifies his struggles with sleep and sleeplessness in both the first and second cantos.

Initially, Una and the lion seem to be a good fit; but there are plenty of clues that this coupling is less than ideal, the most obvious being the lion's violent death at the hands of Sansloy. But there is also the lion's horrific dismembering of the thief Kirkrapine, which Una must hear since Spenser tells us that she is wide-awake all night in the cabin, and

> In stead of rest, she does lament, and weepe
> For the late losse of her deare loued knight
> And sighes, and grones, and euermore does steepe
> Her tender brest in bitter teares all night
> All night she thinks too long, and often lookes for light.
> (1.3.15)

Una's lamentations keep her from sleep, and so must make her a witness to the lion's mutilation of Kirkrapine, though she casually exits the cabin the next morning. We may not expect to see such embittered weeping and then indifference from an allegory of truth, unity, and Christian edification, but then again, Spenser's poem would hardly be of interest if its devices were so cut and dried. The exact terms of Una's relationship with the lion are helpful here. Harry Berger Jr. calls the lion "inadequate for being too adequate"—a direct comment on the fantastical nature of the lion's sleepless watch. Berger argues that the lion "measures the distance between an ideal of protectorship and the more complicated demands Una and Redcrosse have been shown to place on each other."[27] In the context of literary romance, the lion cannot live up to the role Redcrosse knight plays as Una's partner in love and chivalry.

But there is more at work in Spenser's depiction of the lion, I think. The lion's being exaggerates a key tension that animates and antagonizes Redcrosse knight's character, which is the tension between basic physiological necessity and constant spiritual vigilance as figured by extremes of sleep and insomnia. The lion combines superhuman wakefulness with a form of inhumanly pure physis that calls attention to Redcrosse knight's absence, both by exaggerating this facet of the hero's allegorical core and by revealing the lion's inability to stand in for the absent knight. And insofar as the lion only protects Una because she captures and transforms his animal affections, she temporarily gives to the creature's humoral temperament what appears to be a more humanlike disposition. When the lion first encounters Una, he sees her as just another meal and wants to devour "her tender corse." But upon coming closer, he is enthralled by her appearance, "And with the sight amazd, forgat his furious forse" (1.3.5). The lion then begins to kiss her feet and lick her hands, and

Una is overwhelmed: "Her hart gan melt in great compassion, / And drizzling teares did shed for pure affection" (1.3.6). Una adds to the lion an affective and perceptual capacity that it could not maintain without her, allowing the beast to visualize her as something more than a physical body to be devoured. This radical shift in temperament and perception then provides the foundation of their sympathetic moment. In other words, Una's care draws out and positively transforms the creature's natural capacities in ways that it alone cannot achieve—a gesture that resembles the biopolitical sharpening of creaturely potential that Julia Lupton reads brilliantly as "animal husbandry" in Shakespearean contexts.[28] But the transformation that Spenser attributes to the lion here suggests that part of its allegorical duty is to call attention to the mutual demands and capacities for care uniquely reciprocated between Una and Redcrosse—demands that only they can fulfill for each other. For while the lion at first appears to embody a cross-species form of care enlivened by the affective bonds between heroine and beast, it is in the end a coupling that Una clearly dominates, and which is doomed.

Una does not attend to the lion's needs or capacities in ways that benefit the creature, but rather astonishes and transforms its animal disposition such that Una secures her own immediate needs for protection and companionship. The scene can thus be read as an instance of animal oikeiôsis that has been modified by Una's influence toward ends that benefit her instrumentally but are limited in their reach, and so the process cannot amount to a truly virtuous harmony. Explanations for this creaturely limitation can be found in Stoic writings on ethics and animal life from Cicero's *On Moral Ends* and Seneca's *Ethical Letters*, in which both Roman thinkers give accounts of the ancient Greek Stoic concept of oikeiôsis, or *conciliatio* in its Latin rendering. These texts are the likeliest sources for Spenser's engagement with Stoic ethics, and in particular its theory of the ever-widening circles of care that a living being is naturally disposed to develop over the course of its life. The Stoics consider oikeiôsis to begin at birth, and they attribute it to all forms of animal life, including humans. As the Stoic Cato informs Cicero, his interlocutor, "Every animal, as soon as it is born (this is where one should start), is concerned with itself, and takes care to preserve itself."[29] Oikeiôsis is thus grounded in the immediacy of sensation by which animals grasp themselves in their constitution as living beings. This fundamental sensation is a baseline effect of the tension or *tonos* generated by the pneuma, the active power that directs every animal soul to spread throughout the physical structure of its body. However, the capacities of any given body depend upon the particular degree to which the pneuma infuses it and determines its ruling principle, or hêgemonikon. In the case of human beings this ruling principle consists of rational cognition that is structured by concepts; for nonhuman animal life, this ruling principle is capable of forming cognitive representations of the world and of responding accordingly, but not upon the basis of conceptually structured thought.[30] As Seneca explains, "As each animal is attached to its own preservation, it both seeks out what will be beneficial and avoids what will be harmful. Impulses toward useful things are natural, aversions to their opposites are also natural."[31] So while life and oikeiôsis are rational processes in the broadest sense, not all life that the pneuma directs is itself capable of conceptually ordered, rational understanding. And in order to care for life in accordance with the Stoic definition of human virtue as the embodiment of reason, a given body must be capable of exercising such rational understanding.

While Spenser's depiction of the lion seems at first to suggest that Una and the lion belong mutually within the sphere of each other's developing oikeiôsis, or proper circle of care, the poet quietly withdraws this possibility in favor of emphasizing the lion's inadequacy, and in doing so he follows the Stoic insight that virtuous care between human beings is grounded in an affective disposition of rational sympathy that only they can fulfill.[32] While the creature may be capable of bringing an instrumental mode of assistance to Una, and one that even generates a display of compassion, their connection is not grounded in the virtue of mutual care such as that which underwrites the union between Redcrosse and Una. She herself remarks upon the lion's insufficiency even as she tames him, describing the dissolution of his "hungry rage, which late / Him prickt, in pittie of my sad estate" (1.3.7). The comparison to Redcrosse here is all too obvious, since Una's use of "prickt" recalls the opening line of canto 1—"A Gentle Knight was pricking on the plaine." And Una immediately qualifies her point of comparison by ruing Redcrosse's absence, and describing him as her own lost lion: "But he my Lyon, and my noble Lord/ How does he find in cruell hart to hate / Her that him lou'd, and euer most adord, / As the God of my life? why hath he me abhord?" (1.3.7). Una's "sorrowfull constraint" seemingly provokes a flash of human sympathy in the lion, but Spenser's terms indicate that this outburst is due to Una's ability to amaze and dominate the creature. For whatever compassion or affection she extends to it, the lion's relation to Una remains routed through its utter captivation: "The kingly beast vpon her gazing stood; / With pittie calmd downe fell his angry mood" (1.3.8).

Insofar as Una squelches the lion's anger, she attends therapeutically to a choleric physiological disposition not unlike the one that leads Redcrosse into Error's den and which later encourages him to abandon Una in Archimago's cabin. But the immediate issue here, as in all of Una's adventures with the lion, is that the beast simply cannot stand in for Redcrosse, who is the only partner capable of fulfilling the terms of mutual trust and care that both characters require. So while the lion guards her tirelessly when they take shelter in the cabin of "blind devotion," Una continues to lament because her current protector cannot replace Redcrosse. The lion may try, and Una may even want him to stand in for the knight, but this burden is too much for the beast. Although the lion's sleeplessness at first seems a boon, it eventually shows the creature to be an oversimplified reconciliation of creaturely passion and devoted protection, whose vigilance is an empty virtue. And this reductive framing of a complex ethic of care soon gives way to an allegory whose fate the poem determines unkindly, when Sansloy kills the lion. This episode foregrounds the knight's martial puissance as a combination of brute force and shrewd intellect that further emphasizes the lion's limited capacity to protect and serve as Una's companion without the powers of rational understanding. Sansloy is "strong, and of so mightie corse, / As euer wielded speare in warlike hand, / And feates of armes did wisely vnderstand" (1.3.42).[33] Meanwhile, Una's sorrow remains as an affective binding or emotional "constraint" upon her being—which is to say, a shackling of cares that only Redcrosse can break.

While her sleepless night during Una's adventures with the lion calls out the limitations of her affective pairing with the creature, it is worth noting that Una only experiences her relative loss of faith in Redcrosse after he abandons her in Archimago's cabin. And Redcrosse's separation from Una at this moment is a direct consequence of his nocturnal struggles in cantos 1 and 2, as he slides across extremes of deep sleep, passionate dreaming, and frenzied insomnia. When Archimago's "fit false dream" troubles Redcrosse's sleep at the end of the first canto, the spirit's neoclassical *katabasis* and summoning of the dream from the Cave of Morpheus allegorize the hero's sleep in psychomachic terms. And Redcrosse's responses to this dream episode, but especially to Archimago's illusions once the hero is awake, lead directly to the most egregious ethical failure of book 1, which is the knight's ill-fated decision to abandon Una.

When Archimago's messenger spirit first comes to the gates of Morpheus's house, it finds that "wakefull dogges before them farre do lye, / Watching to banish Care their enemy, / Who oft is wont to trouble gentle sleepe" (1.1.40). The image strategically splits care into two forms: a certain "care for" is implied on the part of the watchful, vigilant dogs protecting Morpheus, but worrisome "Care" is also the thing they wish to guard against, in preserving the god's state of perpetual slumber. Yet Archimago's messenger slips nimbly by these canine guardians, easily evading their zealous vigil, and the spirit manages to roust Morpheus's "lumpish head" (1.1.43) from its narcoleptic posture. Since the scene also anticipates core elements of the lion's guard over Una—a beastly yet devoted stand-in for Redcrosse knight, ostensibly guarding her sleep—it deserves further thought. The mistake that readers are perhaps encouraged to think they see at this moment is Redcrosse's falling asleep in Archimago's cabin, which suggests a lapse in watchful vigilance and care for Una. This would be allegorized by Morpheus, whose sleepy head is "deuoide of carefull carke" (1.1.44) and seems to prefigure Redcrosse's own sleeping condition, since we are told two stanzas later that when "that idle dreame was to him brought," Archimago commands it to go to that "Elfin knight" who "slept soundly void of euill thought" (1.1.46). "Carke" is a synonym for burden or care, but I think Spenser's doubling also means to play on Morpheus's "carke" as "carcass," both in its early modern meaning of "the living body considered in its material nature" and in its suggestion of being a corpse.[34] These connotations are also consistent with Hellenistic and biblical uses (Paul included) of the word *soma* to describe bodies that are enslaved, nearing death, or materially burdensome.[35] But insofar as Morpheus is an allegory of unadulterated sleep, even if his posture literalizes the heavy sluggishness of sleep, it lacks both the weight of worldly cares and the matter of physiological necessity.

The same cannot be said for Redcrosse's body, which requires sleep as a fundamental form of care for his embodied self, and this fact unsettles Spenser's immediate comparison between the two figures. I think the mistake that Spenser truly means to suggest at this moment, on the part of Redcrosse, is the false notion that he could ever entirely "banish Care"—understood both as the demands of care placed upon him in waking life and as care for his bodily life through the recovery and renewal of a good night's rest. But devotion to the one seemingly entails abandoning the other, so Redcrosse's sleep brings into focus a puzzling facet of his earthbound being: How to reconcile these contradictory demands of care, which are split along the lines of his sleeping and waking forms of life? This conundrum returns during Redcrosse's visit to the house of Pride with Spenser's depiction of Idleness, "the nourse of sin" who carries an unread prayer book and blindly leads Lucifera's train: "For of deuotion he had little care, / Still drownd in sleepe, and most of his days ded" (1.4.19). Being "drownd in sleepe" reminds readers of the description of Redcrosse and company under Archimago's roof. But Spenser also writes that "from worldly cares himself he did esloyne," so the issue is not simply that Idleness sleeps and therefore fails in his spiritual devotion, but rather that he sleeps as a means of evading all cares of the world, which are not solely theological in nature. Both Idleness and Morpheus offer impossible allegories of a total escape from care; unlike these figures, Redcrosse demands a form of physiological, therapeutic care that only sleep provides, and which allows him to return to the world's struggles anew. These pictures of sleep and sin thus confront Redcrosse as hypertrophic images of his own layered refusals of care, which enfold contradictory demands of his spiritual, physical, and amatory life.

Moreover, because the initial description of Redcrosse's sleep in canto 1 tells readers that he is "void" of evil thought rather than of "careful carke," his physiological condition in sleep plays foil to Morpheus in another key respect: Redcrosse is at this moment nothing but a sleeping carcass, or a body that seems to lack any spiritual sense or instrumental function. There are some strange and potentially confusing ideas that appear to be at work in Spenser's description, and they suggest that he may be grappling with Aristotle's account of the sleeping human soul and its biological as well as ethical significance. In book 1 of the *Nicomachean Ethics*, Aristotle claims with respect to virtue that "it is possible for the disposition to be present and yet to produce nothing good, as for example in the case of the person who is asleep, or in some other way rendered inactive."[36] In Aristotle's ethical system, the nutritive function of the soul is "by nature devoid of any share in human excellence" and can only actualize the potential to grow and decay that is common to all forms of life. A sleeping human therefore enters a temporary condition of inability to actualize what makes it human. The sleeping human embodies a state of lack-in-being, though for Aristotle this lack simply denotes certain faculties being present only in their potential, nonactualized forms. Putting it somewhat differently, in *The Generation of Animals* Aristotle calls sleep "a border-land between living and non-living" insofar as "a person who is asleep would appear to be neither completely non-existent nor completely existent."[37]

Spenser's phrase "void of euill thought" thus suggests at least two loosely Aristotelian interpretations of the hero's sleeping condition: Redcrosse sleeps soundly because he has no thought of harm coming to him, or he sleeps soundly with no evil thought present in his mind—his soul, suspended in a deep and dreamless sleep, is emptied of its mindful content and rests secure in its vegetative state. According to the second reading, Spenser's hero has been plunged into the void of sleep, but remains untroubled because no evil thought lurks therein. And yet, insofar as Redcrosse is "void" of evil thought, Spenser subtly opens a figural fault in what first seems to be an untainted condition of sleep. In other words, that which appears to be nothing but a lack of fault in Redcrosse's sleeping being becomes the very opening or "fault" into which Archimago's pagan dream deftly steps, in order to "abuse his fantasy" (1.2.46).

In theological terms, the void attributed to Redcrosse's sleep may mean that Spenser is also thinking of Augustine's concept of evil as absence or privation, a matter of distance from God. If sleep deprives the human of reason, it temporarily suspends the only means of accessing permanent and intelligible truths of God's universe. Hence, sleep is evil, a lack-in-being that eliminates our potential to be the ideal whole represented by a singular, thinking body whose will is actively turned toward God. If Spenser does mean to summon this Augustinian tradition, then the ambiguous valences of Redcrosse's sleep in the opening cantos essentially fuse an Aristotelian ontology of the sleeping soul with an Augustinian anthropology of the fallen human. But Aristotle's model requires a bit of work on Spenser's part, since Aristotle also views sleep as a process that actualizes the fundamental good toward which the nutritive function of the soul naturally inclines.[38] To understand sleep as a mode of lack or privation that is also evil contradicts the simple fact of sleep's recuperative power as an actualized good. It moreover suggests that an unwilled and unintentional function of life could be inherently sinful—an idea that is decidedly un-Aristotelian in its presumption of fallen life. For Aristotle, the exercise of a natural function like that of the vegetative soul in no way entails an ethical or ontological fault.[39]

A further appeal to Augustinian theology may clarify matters here, and help to explain how Redcrosse's sleep could at once signify a condition of privation and an actualized good, with respect to Spenser's own ethical and ontological thinking. In his tractates on the gospel of John, Augustine describes the origin of the Christian church and its sacraments as coming, quite literally, from a hole in the crucified body of Jesus, as if the wound opened in Christ's side repairs the chasmic gulf between God and humankind. John 19:34 tells of Christ's death on the cross, and of a soldier whose spear pierces the side of his body, opening a wound. Augustine connects this moment with Genesis 2:21–22, when God draws Adam's rib from a hole in his side while he sleeps in order to create Eve: "Here the second Adam, his head bowed, slept on the cross in order that from there might be found for him a wife—that one who flowed from the side of the One sleeping. O death from which the dead live again! What is cleaner than this blood? What is more healthful than this wound?"[40] In further describing this wound, Augustine writes "*Vigilanti verbo euangelista usus est* [the evangelist uses a wide-awake word]" to signify Christ's being wounded during the sleep of death. The word Augustine notes is *aperire*, which he argues means to "open up" rather than simply to pierce or to cut, and so Augustine claims that John's use of *aperire* is quite intentional, meaning to point to the fact that "the door of life was thrown open from which the mystical rites [*sacramenta*] of the Church flowed, without which one does not enter into the life which is true life."[41] In other words, Augustine reads Christ's incarnated sleep of death as a holy sleep that saves us from the privation of sin and mortality by turning lack into plenitude. A series of biblical events, from Adam's wound to the door of Noah's ark to the pierced body of Christ, structure Augustine's typological series through a mystical form of Christian emptiness, a lack that moves through the biblical ages and culminates in the birth of the true church, unleashing the abundant flow of the holy sacrament that John describes.

Like the John of Augustine's reading, Spenser himself uses a "wide-awake word," in the form of a pun that speaks to the challenges of constant vigilance and the lack-in-being that badgers Redcrosse knight. Critics have long recognized that Spenser's allegory plays on an idea of wholeness as holiness in book 1, though the homophonic depth of this pun has been underexplored.[42] The English word holy is derived from the Old English term *hal*, which can mean whole, uninjured, healthy, safe, or complete, and each of these meanings seems pertinent to the trials of Redcrosse knight and the stumbling blocks that mar his marriage to Una.[43] The critical consensus has been that Spenser's wholeness/holiness pun reflects a dyadic truth of Redcrosse's virtuous task: to live a holy life is to live a life that is part of the whole, united with Una and with the holy Christian church.[44] I do not want to dispute that basic claim but rather to modify it by suggesting that Spenser's pun also tends to undermine whatever possibilities of unity or wholeness it projects. This notion is already part of the pun itself, since the idea of a hole or a gap semantically inhabits and empties both wholeness and holiness of their harmonious, positively reinforcing meanings.[45] Spenser's pun may be connected to the Geneva Bible's translation of Ephesians 6, where Paul twice describes God's suit of armor as a "whole" that completes the Christian soldier's preparedness to battle the works of darkness:[46] "Put on the whole armour of God, that ye may be able to stand against the assauts of the deuil. For we wrestle not against flesh and blood, but against principalities, against powers, *and* against the worldly gouernors, *the princes* of the darkenes of this worlde, against spiritual wickedness, *which are* in the hie places. For this cause take vnto you the whole armour of God."[47] If Spenser modeled his hero's arms on this passage, the poet nonetheless reworks its implications to deepen his own allegory. When Redcrosse sleeps in Archimago's cabin, he removes his shield and armor, and so the hero's fleshly and physical forms of life come into sharper focus precisely because he is temporarily stripped of his Pauline markings and their attendant allegorical duties. In other words, he appears to be less than the ideal whole represented by Paul's militant Christian because he has relinquished the burden of a constant, watchful vigilance associated with the armor of God. So while Redcrosse knight may enjoy an allegorical "de-vicing" when wearing his Pauline arms, when he removes these trappings at night he is deprived of the power they signify. The hero's sleep thus calls attention to the limitations of vigilance—not to mention of being a successfully Pauline hero—but I also want to argue that it implies that Redcrosse embodies holiness even while his sleep subjects him to an apparent lack-in-being.

What I mean is that sleep's mortifying power and its emptying effects on Redcrosse knight's earthly body loosely connect him with Augustine's image of Christ, whose sleep of death and pierced side enigmatically opened the door to life. Christ threw himself into the ungodly void of death, or into the lack-in-being introduced by humanity's fall, in order to fill that void with the endless plenitude of his Godly life. Of course only Christ could ever embody such an enigma, so only Christ could mystically transform the sleep of death into a sacramental abundance. Spenser's Redcrosse may be bound to a life of *imitatio Christi* in the Pauline tradition, but as a Protestant allegory of holiness, his character also more decisively emphasizes the privation of his earthly life from Godly perfection as well as the bodily demand to care for that life in its mortal and physiological forms through sleep. The comparison with Christ is thus a graded analogy: just as the incarnate Christ died, descended into Hell, and rose triumphant, Redcrosse descends into sleep, recovers, and returns to the Faerie world to renew his quest. An ideal of constant spiritual vigilance is simply not possible for the hero of book 1, and this insufficiency is likewise marked by the ceaseless nature of the tasks assigned to him, even though he is the patron of true holiness. Redcrosse knight has a (w)hole complex, and try as he might to master it, his earthly being can never quite find its whole or holy completion within the allegorical world he traverses.[48]

While Spenser's Aristotelian and Augustinian figurations of sleep are meant to call attention to Redcrosse's insufficiencies in the early cantos of book 1, I would argue the poem goes on to develop other possibilities concerning both the source of the hero's virtue and the security of his physical attachment to it. For the question of what might make the hero whole or complete in his being is also a matter of understanding his natural constitution, or the physical basis of his oikeiôsis and its proper circles of inclusion. And it is clear that for Redcrosse knight, sleep must be included within this sphere of ethical consideration, though that means that he must remove his armor and thereby relinquish both his vigilant disposition and its external support. At the same time, Redrcosse must not leave Una's side, because she is *oikeion*, or an essential and proper part of the holiness that he seeks to sustain in waking life through the developing process of his oikeiôsis.[49] That is not to say that Una, or anything else for that matter, could entirely cure Redcrosse's allegorical condition of a lack-in-being. But it does mean that the two require each other's presence, and that they are obligated to measures of mutual care that fill the forms of being in which the other is lacking. On the one hand, Redcrosse's tendency to constantly "dis-pair" from Una indicates just how challenging

Spenser finds the task of holding together such an ideal whole that binds love, faith, and Christian fellowship in an impassioned yet difficult unity; yet on the other, the patron of true holiness embodies that virtue in the oikeiôsis that naturally binds him to himself, and which carries on securely even in his deepest moments of slumber.

A Pathological Watch

If we now return—perhaps better armed—to the scene of Redcrosse's sleep in canto 1, we can see that Spenser lays early ground for these ideas by indicating that Redcrosse's errors are the result of misrecognizing what is proper to his ethical life and to the circle of care that defines it. When the dream sits upon Redcrosse's head and begins its assault, Redcrosse's heart is "bathed in wanton bliss and wicked ioy" (1.1.47). It seems that the dark and liquid elemental forces of Morpheus's pagan spirit have unleashed a negative baptism of sexual licentiousness, threatening to wash away the inscription of God's law and whatever claim to holiness the hero might make.[50] But the stanza goes on to tell us "that *nigh* his manly hart did melt away," so the dream does not in fact manage to dissolve Redcrosse's spiritual fortitude or to erase the mark of "true holiness" that allegorically defines him. The hero has removed his armor, yet the spiritual shield that protects his heart seems to be working all the same—so long as he remains asleep. For while the dream spirit is not entirely successful in its intentions, it does manage to stir Redcrosse's passion in a way that carries over into his waking life. As the hero begins to experience the dream, he begins to worry, and "in this great passion of vnwonted lust, / Or wonted feare of doing ought amiss, / He started vp, as seeming to mistrust, / Some secret ill, or hidden foe of his" (1.1.49). The spirit does not succeed in separating him from Una, however—that comes later, as the hero battles insomnia.

This reading of the dream episode qualifies Shuger's account, which claims that the hero's melting heart is a sign that he is having a wet dream.[51] That seems right, and Shuger's reminder of the sexual nature of this struggle is a valuable rejoinder to the many readings that blithely evacuate concerns of the body and the erotic from Redcrosse's quest.[52] But Shuger concludes that insofar as Redcrosse has had a wet dream, he has involuntarily sinned, and so the dream has essentially achieved its purpose. For Shuger this episode confirms Spenser's Christian pedigree, placing him in a line that begins with Paul's claim in Romans 18 that "to wil is present with me: but I finde no means to performe that which is good," runs into Augustine's fear of the "unruly member" in *Confessions*, and goes on to determine both Luther's and Calvin's soteriologies of fleshly life born into sin. Shuger also cites book 10 of the *Confessions* as a likely source for Spenser's image of the hero's melting heart. Yet her argument that Redcrosse has in fact sinned cannot be the case, since Spenser clearly tells us that he awakens before "doing ought amiss," and it isn't the experience of the dream itself but rather its aftereffect upon the hero's awakening that severs Redcrosse from Una. This division and its exact cause demand scrutiny—especially since the supposedly relevant passage from the *Confessions* claims that "false visions" trump the faithful Christian's will only when that will is compromised by sleep.

While Archimago's lustful dream does aggravate and stir Redcrosse from his repose, the hero's fear and ensuing actions suggest that the real danger of this moment lies with Redcrosse's powers to think and to judge the impulse of his perceptions—which is to say, the ability to make mistakes regarding the cares and obligations of his waking life. When he does wake up, a spirit disguised as Una suddenly appears at his side, offering him a kiss. Though his anger rises at her maidenly indiscretion, "He stayed his hand, and gan himselfe aduise / To proue his sense, and tempt her faigned truth" (1.1.50). Here, Redcrosse manages to check his emotion, and to weigh and measure the presentation before him. He suspends his initial impulse toward judgment in favor of ascertaining the truth of the spirit's words and appearance. She goes on to accuse the knight of a cold indifference: "Die is my dew: yet rew my wretched state / You, whom my hard auenging destinie / Hath made iudge of my life or death indifferently" (1.1.51). This accusation dovetails with the spirit's suggestion, two stanzas later, that Redcrosse's sleep constitutes an ethical failure insofar as it literalizes his lack of care for Una, and she contrasts it with her own insomnia and feelings of amatory alienation: "Loue of your selfe, she said, and deare constraint / Lets me not sleepe, but wast the wearie night / In secret anguish and vnpittied plaint, / Whiles you in careless sleepe are drowned quight" (1.1.53). These charges essentially reverse the terms that actually and legitimately bind Redcrosse to Una. Their fidelity is not grounded in pity, though the spirit contends that Redcrosse should pity her unrequited love. Nor is it the case that his sleep constitutes an ethical lapse because it betrays Redcrosse's lack of care, or even that it shows him to be an indifferent "iudge" to Una's emotions, which the spirit describes in absolutist terms. Redcrosse falls for this trick, however, and during a moment of insomnia after the false Una departs, he first begins to doubt the true Una. He finds himself lying awake, "Much grieuv'd to think that gentle dame so light, / For whose defence he was to shed his blood" (1.1.55). Spenser's play on "light" and Redcrosse's doubt of his willingness to shed blood for Una may recall Paul's images of the armor of God from Ephesians but also his claim that husbands must be ready to give themselves for their wives just as Christ gave himself for the sake of the Church (Ephesians 5:22–30). Yet the poet has already indicated that Archimago's powers cannot transform the core of a faithful, sleeping heart, and so Redcrosse is wrong to put stock in the spirit's deceitful claim that "careless sleepe" has drowned his concern for Una, or in the implication that this apparent lack of care is a sign of ethical and allegorical failure. For when Redcrosse actually manages to fall back asleep, the dream renews its assault yet finds its "labour all was vaine" (1.1.55), and the spirit dolefully returns to Archimago to report this failure.

Hence, Archimago must reshape the two spirits summoned from Morpheus to suit his purpose more fittingly in the second canto:

> Eftsoones he tooke that miscreated faire,
> And that false other Spright, on whom he spred
> A seeming body of the subtile aire,
> Like a young Squire, in loues and lusty-hed.
> His wanton dayes that eyer loosely led,
> Without regard of armes and dreaded fight:
> Those two he tooke, and in a secret bed,
> Couered with darknesse and misdeeming night,
> Them both together laid, to ioy in vaine delight.
> (1.2.3)

Archimago spreads over the body of the dream a second body of "subtile aire," and this act perversely recasts the suit of Pauline armor that Una provides to her hero, as we are told in the letter to Raleigh. It makes sense that on the one hand Redcrosse struggles with this insubstantial miscreation, "Couered with darkness and misdeeming night," while on the other, there are very substantial and fleshly consequences to said trickery. When Archimago wakes Redcrosse and shows him the two spirits that he has remade, Redcrosse's "furious ire" (1.2.5) erupts and he nearly slays them both, risking a Herculean scene of domestic annihilation.[53] But Archimago keeps the knight at bay, and Redcrosse then tries unsuccessfully to return to sleep:

> Returning to his bed in torment great,
> And bitter anguish of his guiltie sight,
> He could not rest, but did his stout heart eat,
> And wast his inward gall with deepe despight,
> Yrkesome of life, and too long lingring night.
> At last faire *Hesperus* in highest skie
> Had spent his lampe, & brought forth dawning light,

> Then vp he rose, and clad him hastily;
> The Dwarfe him brought his steed: so both away do fly.
> (1.2.6)

Redcrosse's "anguish" becomes an agent of insomniac self-cannibalization, a twist of the flesh that gnaws at "his stout heart"—a heart that should remain faithful to Una and to God's law of faithful love, since the heart is the site of its spiritual inscription.[54] Instead, Redcrosse's sleepless heart becomes both the target and the engine of a spiteful force of self-consumption, and the failure to care for his basic bodily need to sleep only augments his lack of trust and faith in Una. Insofar as the heart is the physiological location of the soul's hêgemonikon or ruling principle, the scene indicates that Redcrosse's insomnia is in fact responsible for self-dissolving effects that readers have previously associated with the hero's sleep, and in this regard his insomnia resembles the harmful fatigue that thwarts Seneca's protagonist in *Hercules Furens*. The "guiltie sight" lingers traumatically in his sleepless mind, extending its influence to the point that Redcrosse breaks his bond with Una and flees her company—just as this form of pathological vigilance gnaws at the physical foundation of his oikeiôsis, it undoes the bonds that sustain his broader circle of care. While the phrase "guiltie sight" seems ambiguously to split responsibility for this moment between Archimago and Redcrosse, I want to argue that Spenser ultimately places the guilt squarely on the hero's shoulders—obviously, not because of the sight itself but because of Redcrosse's particular response to it.

At this moment Redcrosse lacks care, both in the sense of giving his bodily demands their due and as a careful evaluation of the state of affairs presented to him by Archimago, especially since these concern his partner in love and faith. But by the same token, one might also say that Redcrosse cares too much, since his insomniac isolation feeds this unhealthy perceptual investment, or an overly vigilant form of watch directed toward Archimago's empty illusion and its phantasmatic afterlife. When confronted by this trick, rather than give Una the benefit of his faith, Redcrosse assumes the worst and flies away—with both the dwarf and the armor that she initially brought and offered as a token of faith and trust in her hero. Sleep may be an apt metaphor for the lapse of martial or spiritual vigilance, but Spenser also suggests that his use of that metaphor is a ploy, and thereby encourages us not to fear the bodily transformation that resembles death and bereaves us of waking sense—a fear which seems to contribute to Redcrosse's mistaken sense of guilt and to his insomniac vigilance, both of which damage his health, his quest, and his bond with Una.

Redcrosse's insomnia, then, also plays upon the idea of emptiness that lurks in Spenser's punning semantics. While the hero's sleep seems to open a meta-physiological void or absence into which the dream lasciviously slides, his problematic relationship with (w)holes more pressingly extends into Redcrosse's waking life—when holes of doubt become sources of self-consuming spite and fear, which further compromise his perception and lead him to abandon both his partner and his obligations of care. The dream spirit plays a part in this process: the fantasy it abuses refers to an important capacity of the hêgemonikon of Redcrosse's soul, which has been agitated and shaken by his experience of the dream. But this state of agitation is precisely the Stoic definition of a passion—not an alien presence in the embodied soul or a moment of animal desire that has become problematically ascendant among the soul's divided functions, but rather a harmful shock that perverts the soul's natural orientation toward virtue. Seneca reflects this Stoic conviction in cognitive monism when he informs Lucilius that "reason and passion, as I said, don't have separate and distinct dwelling places but are the mind's transformation to a better and worse condition."[55] And clearly, it is Redcrosse's insomniac fit, derived from this psychosomatic agitation, that triggers his ill-advised act of judgment—or in Stoic terms, his mistaken assent—and then causes him to split from Una. This is because Archimago's trickery works best when Redcrosse is awake and subject to his own mistaken perceptual judgments, for which he does not take care or ethical responsibility. Spenser's depiction of the hero's insomnia suggests that being overly vigilant and attuned to misguided perceptions is much more perilous than the inward turn of sleep. For Redcrosse, insomnia more adequately mirrors his being unduly attached to misleading worldly cares and forms of passionate, fleshly strife that injure the self.

Hence, after this initial scene of Redcrosse's sleeplessness, Spenser continues to tie moments of nocturnal vigilance to forms of fiery self-consumption and mistaken heroism. Redcrosse's trip to the House of Pride, for instance, entails a suspect moment of insomnia at the beginning of canto 5, which makes it clear that Redcrosse bears the onus of responsibility for the series of ethical mishaps surrounding his and Una's bouts with sleepless isolation. The evening before his match with Sansjoy, Redcrosse falls prey to a watchful, fiery passion as he broods on an image of chivalric victory:

> The noble hart, that harbours vertuous thought,
> And is with child of glorious great intent,
> Can neuer rest, vntill it forth have brought
> Th'eternall brood of glorie excellent:
> Such restlesse passion did all night torment
> The flaming corage of that Faery knight,
> Deuising, how that doughtie turnament

> With greatest honour he atchieuen might;
> Still did he wake, and still did watch for dawning light.
> (1.5.1)

Redcrosse's "noble hart" is full of "virtuous thought" that keeps him awake and watching, as he imagines "glorie excellent" to come. We may feel tempted to read this scene in positive terms, as if his brooding both protects Redcrosse and sets the stage for his martial victory. But that would be overlooking the fact that Spenser only dangles this bit of heroic and spiritual orthodoxy before his readers after having already undermined its truth-value through another scene of insomnia in the previous canto.

There, we were left under the cover of night in the House of Pride, with the entire court having succumbed to Morpheus's "leaden mace"—except, that is, for Duessa and Sansjoy. Duessa arises "from her resting place" and comes to Sansjoy's room, where she finds Sansjoy hell-bent on the next day's fight, "broad awake" and "in troublous fit, / Forecasting, how his foe he might annoy" (1.4.45). Granted, one could argue that Redcrosse's insomnia is somehow better than Sansjoy's, since it protects him from an exposed and careless slumber during his night in the house of pride. If so, Spenser would intend this scene as a counterimage to Redcrosse's virtuous lack of sleep. But we should perhaps linger on Spenser's use of the word "Deuising" to describe Redcrosse's plotting, which returns us to the description of his poem's method in the letter to Raleigh: delivering "good discipline . . . clowdily enwrapped in allegorical deuises" (16). Here, "deuising" suggests that Redcrosse wrongfully invests his passionate care in an idea of martial honor that ultimately means nothing—he is simply wrapping up an empty present, as we shall see through events that soon take place on the battlefield. More than an image of heroism, Redcrosse's watchful, nocturnal brooding recalls the infestation of a "guiltie sight" that provokes his insomnia in canto 2, and which feeds an unhealthy form of passionate consumption.[56]

And so, the poem has done much to prepare us to view the scene of Redcrosse's fervent, insomniac watch in canto 5 as a lack of sleep that is also an ethical lapse, because it constitutes a refusal to care for the embodied earthly life that constitutes the basis of his ethical attachment to himself and to Una. When the battle finally takes place, Duessa begs Redcrosse to spare Sansjoy's life, but the hero displays a rabid desire for vengeance which only extends the choleric passion nourished by Redcrosse's insomnia: "Not all so satisfied, with greedie eye / He sought all round about, his thirstie blade / To bath in bloud of faithless enemy; / Who all that while lay hid in secret shade" (1.5.15). Duessa's "secret shade" abruptly falls over her lover and shields him from Redcrosse's piercing eye, whose fiery watch has burned through the night and into the day's military struggle. These interwoven episodes of insomnia, fiery consumption, and misguided confrontation form a series across cantos 1, 4, and 5, in which the poetics of sleep, insomnia, and care point unfavorably to Redcrosse and to Una. Both are guilty of succumbing, though in different ways and perhaps with different degrees of accountability, to a mutual loss of faith resembling Duessa's shallow infidelity and Sansjoy's "troublous fit [of] Forecasting." In other words, heroine and hero alike have abandoned their common pursuit of the whole that only they can inhabit, because both have misdirected their care toward unfitting others outside the circle that properly belongs to their oikeiôsis.

The "Cruell Cace"

When Spenser figures sleep and insomnia as moments of precarious nocturnal isolation, he imagines the self to be vulnerable and lacking in two respects—either psychically disarmed by the loss of reason and waking sense, or exposed to the corrosive effects of insomnia and unable to creep under the protective shroud of slumber. Both states seem to deprive the self of a necessary good, so obviously these extremes imply a conundrum of embodied life that occupies Spenser throughout book 1: Sleep is frightening, but so is insomnia, and we must inevitably fall into the troubling void of sleep because it is a fundamental need of embodied life. In seeking to accommodate this conundrum to the model of ethical life and virtue embodied by Redcrosse knight, Spenser develops a structure of mutual care between the hero and heroine of book 1. The poet's interweaving of sleep and sleeplessness with shifting affections, both false and true, slowly but methodically constructs this ethical paradigm by showing that couplings of Redcrosse and Una with other characters always fail to embody the forms of care that they give to and require from each other.

Not long after the two are first reunited through the efforts of Arthur, Redcrosse faces his most harrowing encounter with "Despayre" personified. He is tempted by the villain's promise of an "eternall rest," or a chance to lay his "soule to sleepe in quiet graue" (1.9.40) and thereby relinquish his life's cumbersome tasks—which is to say, Redcrosse's greatest temptation is that of utterly forsaking his cares in a permanent sleep that falsely promises to release him from all worry and concern. Despair's seductive claim that "Death is the end of woes" then opens yet another psychosomatic fault in Redcrosse, as the fiend's speech pierces and tunnels "through his heart. . . . And in his conscience made a secret breach" (1.9.48). Una's partner nearly succumbs to the temptation of abandoning care; it is only her hand that stays the dagger angling toward his throat, as she chastises him: "Why shouldst thou then despeire, that chosen art? / . . . Arise, Sir knight arise, and leaue this cursed place" (1.9.53). So while the canto's opening quatrain tells readers they will see that "Sir Treuisan flies from Despayre, / Whom Redcrosse knight withstands" (1.1.9), this gives us only a partial glimpse of the truth that actually arrives, since Redcrosse does not exactly stand up to Despair or manage to conquer the fear that Sir Trevisan could not. To say that Redcrosse "withstands" Despair is true only in the sense that by standing with Una that feat is made possible—both in the instance of this encounter and more broadly in Redcrosse knight's struggles with his innate tendency to succumb to dis-pairing influences.

Such stubbornly self-divisive energy dogs the hero of book 1, remaining a part of his being despite the many procedures of correction to which he is eventually subjected in the House of Holiness. While the psychomachic register of the sprite's descent in canto 1 figures the cave of Morpheus as a cavernous emptiness in Redcrosse's soul, and Despair's seductive rhetoric likewise strikes a fault in the hero's conscience, the disciplining purge that attempts to reshape him in canto 10 is applied to his physical body and supposedly leaves "no one corrupted iot" (1.10.26). This course of therapy would seem to have erased any minuscule amount of lingering sin, and thus to have effectively restored Redcrosse's spiritual being by way of bodily physic, discipline, and purgation.[57] Yet the stanza that follows this line tacks on another allegorical Christian figure whose aim to evacuate sin only adds to Redcrosse's regimen—"And bitter *Penance* with an yron whip, / Was wont him once to dispel euery day" (1.10.27). Redcrosse's convalescence does not, indeed cannot purify him in any complete sense, because his contrition is never enough. Not unlike the purging whip of Penance, Redcrosse's sleep must bind and "dispel" his body each and every day, as part of a ceaseless cycle that regenerates his life through mortifying and constraining effects. And much like his unconscious sleeping body, the "corrupted iot" may be reduced to a minimum of expression, but it can never be eliminated—Redcrosse's physical body and the care it requires will always remain part of his earthly tasks because his body is the vital engine that sustains his life and binds him to Una. And this binding to Una entails caring for his worldly partner, as Contemplation reminds him when Redcrosse longs not to "turn againe / Backe to the world, whose ioyes so fruitlesse are." Contemplation simply responds, "That may not be (said he) ne maist thou yit / Forgo that royall maides bequeathed care" (1.11.63).

If Redcrosse's necessity to sleep suggests that the care of the self remains essential to pursuits of holy truth, then Spenser grounds that point in the unconscious demands of Redcrosse's physical body and its immanent capacities for restoration. He parts ways with Augustinian and other Platonic legacies by resisting a notion of truth as an idealized, singular abstraction, or as a transcendent escape from bodily encumbrance and the world of sensation and strife. Spenser surely entertains these philosophical propositions, but he ultimately refuses to endorse them.[58] Book 1 rather suggests that tasks of thinking and living are entangled material processes; the paths to be taken involve defeat, rest, and beginning anew with the corporeal struggles of flesh and blood that must sustain us, even as they subject us to agonies of privation and passion. And this emphasis on the physicality of human struggle as life seeks both to sustain itself and to flourish indicates Spenser's indebtedness to Stoic physicalism and its ethical foundations—including the fact that while humans are attached to themselves by virtue of their simultaneously physical and rational natures, they must grow and properly develop this natural orientation toward reason by sensing and caring for the changing constitution that carries them across the various stages of a life cycle. As Seneca argues, "Although each thing's constitution changes, it is attached to its constitution in the same way. My natural attachment is not to the boy or the youth or the mature man but to myself."[59]

Thus far I have argued that Spenser's depictions of sleep underscore its vital role in the recovery of Redcrosse's physical life, and that the hero's insomnia constitutes a much greater threat to his embodied being. Drawing insight from both the Stoic theory of oikeiôsis and Seneca's depictions of Hercules, Spenser shows insomnia to erode the physical foundation and beginning point of Redcrosse's ethical life, thereby threatening to annul the basis of his care for both himself and Una. Meanwhile—and perhaps somewhat unexpectedly—we have seen that the hero's sleep does nothing to dissolve his natural connection to the virtue of holiness, despite the many humanist and political-theological associations of sleep with spiritual carelessness and an ethical lapse in vigilance. If I am right in arguing these points, along with the claim that sleep in no way impairs the physical basis or security of Redcrosse knight's oikeiôsis, then the significance of the hero's Pauline armor and its connections to virtue must be rethought. I want to suggest that Redcrosse's most effective and properly congenital weapon is not the Pauline armor that Una gives him, but rather the holiness that is constitutionally part of his being, and to which he preserves an ongoing attachment even while he sleeps. In this sense, the Pauline armor is not *oikeion*; it is neither part of Redcrosse's self-constitution, nor should it be included in the circle of his care as a necessary component of virtue. It may be a practical means to an end in the world of battling monsters and standing for a visible Christian allegory, but the armor is not essential to his properly virtuous and holy being, and it can in fact work against him.

Spenser truly drives this point home in his depiction of Redcrosse battling the dragon in canto 11, when the hero is roasted alive in his armor. The scene is explicitly modeled on elements from Ovid's and Seneca's gruesome accounts of Hercules's death, both of which depict the hero's demise as a process of physical disintegration that undoes the natural constitution binding him to himself—in other words, the primary attachment of oikeiôsis that marks the beginning point of ethical life. Hercules faces untold pain when the tunic soaked in the blood of the centaur Nessus is given to him by his wife, Deinara. It bursts into flames and begins to melt into Hercules's skin, penetrating even into the marrow of his bones. The story is very much in keeping with the Stoic theory of *sumpatheia*, according to which all bodies are connected by a causal web of tension that spreads across a cosmos of highly volatile physical mixtures.[60] Ovid describes the poison taking hold of Hercules as a "force of that evil" that "grew warm . . . released by the flames" of his altar and "flowed into the body of Hercules" (9.161–163). Hence, the poison's ability to destroy Hercules derives from a physical chain of causality, moving from the venom of the Lernean Hydra in which Hercules had earlier dipped his arrows, to the centaur's blood as it poured forth from the wound caused by the arrow's piercing his flesh, and on to the tunic soaked in Nessus's blood that Hercules unwittingly places upon his body. When Hercules attempts to pull the poisoned tunic from his burning skin, it only complicates his suffering:

> He tries without delay to tear away the death-bearing cloak:
> But where it is pulled, it pulls away his skin, a disgusting thing to tell,
> And either sticks to his limbs when he tries in vain to tear it away
> Or else exposes his lacerated limbs and enormous bones.
> The gore itself hisses like a plate glowing with heat when dipped into
> A frigid lake and boils with the poison's heat.
> The greedy flames consume his vital parts without restraint
> And from his body flows dark blue sweat;
> His roasting sinews sizzle and as the invisible plague liquefies
> His marrow, he raises his open hands to the stars.
> (9.166–175)

Ovid's vivid description is implicitly Stoic in its emphasis on the physical web of causes that determines Hercules's poisoning and its self-dissolving effects. In his own account of Hercules's demise, Seneca extends the Stoic hero's gruesome suffering across two entire acts of *Hercules Oetaeus*. As in Ovid's poem, atmospheric heat from the flames of Hercules's sacrificial altar activates the poisoned tunic, suggesting that both poets conceive a causal corporeal chain through which sympathetic energies of fire and passionate anger consume

Hercules at the core. Seneca's hero imagines this fiery passion as a ghoulish menagerie of animal life that infests his physical body, and drains his vitality through an overwhelming orchestra of pain:

> Ah, what scorpion inside me, what crab torn from the torrid zone and embedded in me scorches my vitals? Once capable of taking in air, my hollow lungs as they inhale now strain the dry tissue; my liver burns, its gall dried up, and the smoldering heat has driven off all my blood. The fiendish thing first consumed my skin, and from there made its way into my body; the scourge wasted my flanks, the bane completely devoured my limbs; it drained all the marrow from my bones, and is lodged in their hollows. The bones themselves cannot stay firm, they pull apart as the joints rupture, lose their mass and dissolve. My huge body has become insufficient, the Herculean limbs are not enough for this scourge. Oh how great is the bane that I acknowledge as vast! Oh terrible fiend! (3.1218–1232)

As the poisonous mixture seethes through Hercules's body, its unity dissolves into a figural swarm of animal life that he imagines pinching, tearing, and stabbing its way throughout his innermost recesses. The hero's organs collapse and melt, and his bones are emptied of their life-sustaining marrow; Seneca thus underscores the extreme slackening and dissipation of physical tension that constitutes the foundation of Hercules's own self-attachment, or oikeiôsis.[61]

Both Ovid and Seneca provide Spenser with distinctive, if somewhat ghastly, figurations of Hercules's death that are grounded in the ethical and cosmological foundations of Stoic thought. Moreover, the poisoned tunic can be read as a kind of harmful inversion of the other bodily surface for which Hercules is known—the skin of the Nemean lion that he wears as a protective shield for his own physical body. And Spenser seems to be thinking of such reversibility in his comparison of Redcrosse knight to Hercules in canto 11, which foregrounds the suddenly harmful and self-disintegrating effects of the hero's armor during his battle against the dragon. Redcrosse knight's first fall is precipitated by a great "flake of fire" that bursts from the monster's maw and superheats the metal shell that covers him. The Pauline armor then sears his body and causes pain so intense "that he could not endure so cruell cace, / But thought his armes to leaue, and helmet to vnlace" (1.11.26). The next stanza compares the hero's suffering to the scene of Hercules's gruesome death:

> Not that great Champion of the antique world,
> Whom famous Poetes verse so much doth vaunt,
> And hath for twelue huge labours high extold,

So many furies and sharpe fits did haunt,
When him the poysoned garment did enchaunt
With *Centaures* bloud, and bloudie verses charm'd,
As did this knight twelue thousand dolours daunt,
Whom fyrie steele now burnt, that earst him arm'd,
That erst him goodly arm'd, now most of all him harm'd.
(1.11.27)

The dragon fire has transformed the armor—both a token of Una's love and a sign of the hero's entry into the Pauline community—into a harmful physical body of "fyrie steele" that merges with and consumes the hero's own natural body. This transformation from instrumentally assisting to actively harming Redcrosse's physical life means that the armor does not, indeed cannot, belong within the sphere of Redrosse's oikeiôsis, even if it sometimes serves him. The distinction here is an important Stoic distinction between what is good or virtuous and therefore beneficial, and what is simply to be preferred or selected but remains indifferent concerning the question of virtue. As we have seen, Redcrosse's virtue is housed within the core of his physical life, in its autopoietic capacities for self-restoration and in the preservation of his attachment to holiness even when the hero sleeps. Spenser's comparison of Redcrosse with Hercules first indicates the poet's debt to Stoic ethics and its theory of oikeiôsis in his own construction of virtue, but also constitutes an instance of literary and theological one-upmanship insofar as it claims that Redcrosse's suffering is even greater than the "furies and sharpe fits" endured by the mighty Hercules.

There is yet another way in which Redcrosse succeeds where Hercules fails: Spenser's hero falls into a form of death-as-sleep that renews his physical life, whereas Seneca's stalwart Stoic burns himself upon a funeral pyre and forever extinguishes his mortal being. Immediately after Redcrosse falls prey to the dragon fire, Spenser gives us a wryly Senecan description of the knight, scorched and longing for death like Hercules struggling to escape from his own skin: "Faint, wearie, sore, emboyled, grieued, brent / With heat, toyle, wounds, armes, smart, & inward fire / That neuer man such mischiefes did tormente; / Death better were, death did he oft desire" (1.11.28). Redcrosse does indeed find death, though Spenser describes it as a form of sanctified and restorative sleep that is protected not only by the virtue of holiness that he embodies but also by the caring presence of his partner, Una. Hence, she watches and prays as he fights the dragon and twice sleeps the sleep of death and is twice reborn, which mark her as being capable of the lionlike vigilance that Redcrosse lacks.

Both times that he falls, "All night she watcht, ne once adowne would lay" (1.11.32). Only Una can give Redcrosse the care he needs, and only Una's caring presence can watch over his sleep in its physical and spiritual senses. While he retains his natural attachment to holiness in slumber, Redcrosse's temporary removal from waking cares is secured through the presence of Una, who belongs within his circle of oikeiôsis and whose own oikeôsis likewise includes Redcrosse knight when he is bound to his sleeping condition.

Yet while book 1 develops a structure of mutual care between Redcrosse knight and Una, which only they can inhabit and make whole, no final moment of allegorical wholeness ever quite arrives for this holy couple.[62] As Spenser's readers, we are left with an image of ethical care that resists universality in its particular configuration of the perils and demands of love, and which is also recalcitrant to an ideal of unwavering heroic vigilance—be it Frye's notion of political authority at the cost of perpetual vigilance, or Paul's model of unyielding spiritual care and Christian militancy. Spenser's view of the early modern legacies of Pauline theology runs slightly askew to the foremost Reformed perspectives of his world; his exposure of such fault lines also gives reason to pause over the contemporary renewal of enthusiasm for Paul in early modern studies and critical thought. But it also requires us to reassess Spenser's relationship to ancient ethics, and in particular the features of Stoic cosmology and ethics that ground that system in the life and causal priority of physical bodies as they endlessly mix and interact in often unexpected ways.

Along such lines, I have argued that Redcrosse's physical and fleshly embodiment both demands contravening forms of care and presupposes an incomplete condition that no suit of armor, nor any mortal pairing, can sufficiently cover, contain, or fill—because without this lack-in-being he cannot serve as an emblem of true holiness. Life's ruptures will always undermine the pursuit of holiness and the desire to become whole. For this reason, we must look to mutual trust in care, which Spenser finds to be a necessary and holy virtue, despite its apparent paradoxes. Even the marriage covenant between Redcrosse and Una, which unites the hero with his partner in love and faith, is subjected to a narrative force and obligation to the Queen that dis-pairs and again separates the two. For Spenser, the terms of care between persons bear much in common with those binding the holy Church and its bodily members: they are fragile and incomplete, always under threat and always in the process of being constituted anew. Book 1 thus refuses to acknowledge the completion of Redcrosse's pursuits or an end to his contradictory obligations of care. To leave the quest—and question—of embodying holiness open, after all, is the only answer that Spenser's poem provides.

The House of Care

Spenser's depictions of sleep and insomnia in book 1 ultimately constitute skeptical responses to the valorization of vigilance shared by Christian political theology and Renaissance humanism. But in the later books of his epic, the poet's interests in physical life and the restorative powers of sleep are framed in more secular terms, as is evident in the trials of Sir Scudamor and in particular his visit to the House of Care in canto 5. In typical Spenserian fashion, it is somewhat unclear whether the discord that seizes Scudamor and leads to his travails in the House of Care is the direct result of Ate's slanderous account of Amoret's infidelity with Britomart, or if we should trace its origins even further back in the poem. Such a reading would return us to the conclusion of book 3, and to Spenser's emendation of the original ending of the 1590 edition of the poem. In that version, after Britomart rescues Amoret from Busirane, book 3 concludes with an image of Scudamor and Amoret reunited in a gushy embrace that melts their senses and gives the impression that the two have fused into one: "Had ye them seene, ye would haue surely thought, / That they had been that faire *Hermaphrodite*. . . . So seemd those two, as growne together quite" (3.12.46a). If, as William Oram argues, "the heroes of book 3 attempt to achieve a fruitful social relationship, a loving harmony of dissimilar selves," then the 1590 ending to book 3 seems to threaten its own core premise.[63] The harmony between persons that Spenser suggests is necessary to friendship and social benefit cannot occur without some separation, of course, since harmonious relations between entities imply that those entities are to some extent autonomous. Spenser goes on to represent the work that consumes the denizens of the House of Care as the forging of "yron wedges" that "carefull minds inuade" (4.5.35), perhaps suggesting that the wedge of care is what first drives Scudamor and Amoret asunder, becoming the engine of production to the poem's ongoing narrative. Spenser's allegory of friendship thus begins with a poetic revision that quite literally splits the 1590 union of Amoret and Scudamor. The revised book 3 concludes with a scene of Scudamor's downtrodden spirit and ruined hopes at the gates of Busirane's castle, where "his expectation to despaire did turne, / Misdeeming sure that her those flames did burne" (3.12.45). Britomart of course successfully rescues Amoret and returns safely from the perils of Busirane's palace, but Scudamor has already fallen victim to his dread and abandoned the scene, taking Amoret's nurse Glauce with him.

It is possible that we are meant to read the fires of Care's forge as Scudamor's internalization of the dreadful flames that envelope Busirane's palace, to which Ate's accusations serve as a slanderous bellows—Scudamor's lack of faith, first in Britomart's rescue effort and second in both Britomart and Amoret's fidelity, results in an enflamed heart and physical distemper that erupts in the first canto and continues to smolder across book 4, illustrating both the virtuous potential of the physical body as well as its susceptibility to affective extremes. As Giulio Pertile has argued, Spenser's allegory is driven in the early books by moments that foreground the unconscious biological and somatic processes of private life, over and above the perceptual or intellective experience of characters (Guyon's swoon in book 2 is one key example). It is precisely when deadening the senses and temporarily freezing the activity of the hero's "vital spirits," he suggests, that the poem's allegorical figuration turns to the invisible motions of embodied life and their role in promoting or dismantling virtue.[64]

Something similar is at work in the case of Scudamor's psychosomatic inflammation and symptomatic bout of insomnia, though its poetic rendering as a form of heightened sensorial captivation and furious activity among workers in the forge suggests that in book 4 we are moving toward a greater concern with the social repercussions of virtue in its more public incarnations—and the notion that pursuing public virtue and heroism can overexert and exhaust the self.[65] That is not to say that Spenser's interest in the physiological foundation and vital processes of life does not continue in book 4. Clearly it does, as in his initial description of Ate, whose nature is nothing but the drive to sever and unseat both private and public forms of integrity. Spenser connects this drive with the realms "below" that harbor "damned sprights":

> Her name was *Ate*, mother of debate,
> And all dissention, which doth dayly grow,
> Amongst fraile men, that many a publike state
> And many a priuate ofte doth overthrow.
> Her false *Duessa* who full well did know,
> To be most fit to trouble noble knights,
> Which hunt for honor, raised from below,
> Out of the dwellings of the damned sprights,
> Where she in darknes wastes her cursed daies & nights.
> (4.1.19)

"Dissention" is a term worth lingering on, in that it implies a severing or separation that divides the root *sens* against itself. Ate's divisive power is a kind of negative virtue, which topples mighty men and empires alike. Spenser seems to attribute her capacity to do so to her dark and obscure origins. In fact, I would suggest that Spenser's slightly imprecise diction intentionally conflates the "noble knights" who hunt for honor with Ate's origins "from below," suggesting that the "damned sprights" are those excitable animal spirits attributed in early modern moral psychology and medical science to the physiological life of that "rational animal" also known as the human.[66] The obscure depths of the human body and its interwoven physiological and spiritual processes were objects of great philosophical, theological, and scientific concern in Spenser's world, even if these vital spirits were also ultimately an invisible power that eluded the empirical senses. In the case of Spenser's "noble knights, / Which hunt for honor," the risk seems to be that they may unearth something invisible yet "damned" that lurks within their own psychosomatic being. A further implication would be that Ate potentially dwells in the dark and personal depths of all humankind, waiting to be stirred from her slumber.

Whether or not Ate's influence over Scudamor begins before her official appearance in canto 1, he keeps the fires of jealousy smoldering inside him over the course of book 4, since the House of Care takes physical form as a blacksmith's forge in canto 5. When Scudamor first approaches Care's ramshackle cottage with Glauce, the two hear hammering from inside that alerts them to the fact that "some blacksmith dwelt in that desert ground" (4.5.33). Spenser's figurations of Scudamor's care as a vital fire that animates his body yet risks being hijacked and bellowed into full-blown wrath and fury make the blacksmith's forge and its master, Care, an ideal allegorical scene of personification. When Glauce and Scudamor step into Care's workshop, they

> found the goodman selfe,
> Full busily vnto his worke ybent;
> Who was to weet a wretched wearish elfe,
> With hollow eyes and rawbone cheeks forspent,
> As if he had in prison long bene pent:
> Full blacke and griesely did his face appeare,
> Besmeared with smoke that nigh his eye-sight blent;
> With rugged beard, and hoarie shagged heare,
> The which he neuer wont to combe, or comely sheare.
> (4.5.34)

The immediate description of Care as a "goodman selfe," whose devotion to his work is so complete that Spenser figures it as an active bending, suggests that Scudamor's practice of self-care is likewise painfully strained, if not entirely bent off course. What ought to be a natural ethical orientation toward the good, one that flourishes with the proper care of his soul, has instead become a source of crippling and self-consuming consternation. Care's physical appearance marks the extent to which Scudamor's care is eating away at his vitality rather than preserving it. At the same time, the vaguely ascetic markers—Care looks as if he has been wasting away in a prison cell, "pent" up much like monks doing deep penance in isolation from the world—simultaneously indicate Scudamor's failed *askesis* and his undue devotion to the jealous "smart" that consumes him. The blacksmith Care has been fully dedicated to his work, as is evident not only from his unkempt hair and beard but also his soot-stained skin and compromised eyesight. But these details also indicate that Care's diligent attention to his forge has, somewhat paradoxically, given rise to a form of carelessness and inattention to his own bodily life and physical appearance, just as Scudamor has imperiled his life by cultivating an unhealthy attachment to jealousy that stems from Ate's falsehood.

Scudamor's initial impression of Care soon gives way to a view of Care's six minions, "About the Andvile standing euermore, / With huge great hammers, that did neuer rest / From heaping stroakes, which theron soused sore" (4.5.36). John Steadman was the first to recognize that Spenser's image of these "sixe stronge groomes" and their discordant hammering creatively reshapes the legend of Pythagoras's discovery of the science of harmony. According to the tale, Pythagoras serendipitously uncovered the secret while walking by a blacksmith's forge and hearing the harmonic resonance of differently sized hammers striking the anvils. "Transformed into a figure of discord," Steadman argues, "the Pythagorean forge becomes an image of Scudamor's alienation from Amoret and Britomart through Ate's slanders. It is a broken harmony, the emblem of a broken friendship."[67] That seems true enough, but I would also argue that the alienation depicted in this scene involves a form of personal discord as self-estrangement, which stems from Ate's nefarious influence on Scudamor's physical life and its vital processes as much as his social relations with others. For Spenser, these enterprises are intimately connected, and the life of the personal body both shapes and is shaped by its social situation and the forms of care demanded of it.[68] His Stoic vision of Care suggests that it is both a burdensome obligation and a source of the world's sadness, but also a vital relation of benefit and support between living beings, one which they can turn back upon themselves by cultivating the capacity for virtue that defines them. Thus Cicero asserts that the "mental anguish . . . which often must be felt on a friend's account, has no more power to banish friendship from life than it has to cause us to reject virtue because virtue entails certain cares and annoyances [*curas et molestias*]."[69] Readers have long cited Cicero's essay on friendship as an important source for Spenser in book 4, but they have not fully appreciated the ways that Spenser draws on and responds to Cicero—and indeed the broader tradition of the Stoic ethics of care—by further emphasizing the need to care for the vital processes of life that are grounded in material and finite embodiment, which he places in direct tension with traditional obligations of the ethical and spiritual care of souls. Here as in book 1,

Spenser's human finds obligations across various forms of life and care that orient the self toward the world and toward its own physical capacities as a living, sensing, and thinking being.

Appropriately, then, Scudamor first encounters his care as a personification in the figure of the blacksmith, who then splits into the six grooms who labor together under his watch, forming a scene of collective union-in-division. On the one hand, the sound of their hammers, "Like belles in greatnesse orderly succeed[ing]," produces an effect of rising sonic amplification by way of an ordered progression. But the poet also remarks upon the fact that the grooms' order is disordered by the fact that they are all six strapping, "strong groomes, but one then other more; / For by degrees they all were disagreed" (4.5.36). The physical differences are visible in both their bodies and the size of the hammers they bear, as well as the discordant racket they make "from heaping strokes, which thereon soused sore," but their laboring energies find unity in the overall effect of an amplification or excess that characterizes their work: "That he which was the last, the first did far exceede" (4.5.36).

But what exactly is that work? Based on the following stanza, it looks as if the excess produced by the laboring smiths serves only to inflate the status and appearance of Care itself. Care no longer appears as a "wretched wearish elfe" with sunken cheeks, but has been subdivided into minions who grow increasingly larger, until the last in line "like a monstrous Gyant seem'd in sight . . . So dreadfully did he the anduile beat, / That seem'd to dust he shortly would it driue: / So huge his hammer and so fierce his heat, / That sem'd a rocke of Diamond it could riue, / And rend a sunder quite, if he thereto list striue" (4.5.37). Since we have already been told that the work of Care's forge is the production of "yron wedges" of "vnquiet thoughts, that carefull minds inuade" (4.5.35), Care's inflated being and the concomitant increase in power both to divide and augment should be read as figurations of Scudamor's care, in its propensity to swell and increase simply by virtue of the belabored attention he bestows on it. This is why Scudamor, on stepping farther into the cabin, finds himself immediately drawn into the visual spectacle of the work performed by Care and his minions:

> Sir *Scudamor* there entring, much admired
> The manner of their worke and wearie paine;
> And hauing long beheld, at last enquired
> The cause and end thereof: but all in vaine;
> For they for nought would from their worke refraine,
> Ne let his speeches come vnto their eare.

And eke the breathfull bellowes blew amaine,
Like to the Northern winde, that none could heare:
Those *Pensifnesse* did moue; and *Sighes* the bellows weare.
(4.5.38)

Scudamor's care has been transfigured into an incessant work of "wearie paine" that is nonetheless entirely captivating. His vision of the laboring smiths elicits an admiration and curiosity that leads him to enquire the "cause and end" of their work, but the smiths remain silent, their attention fully consumed by the work they perform. Devoted to the singular task of hammering away at Care's anvils, the workers' heightened focus and productivity conduce solely to the generation of more care. More precisely, the poet's allegorical figuration of Scudamor's care as a scene of nocturnal production imagines a surplus of care being garnished for the benefit of Care, the master blacksmith, and at the direct expense of Scudamor's vital capacity to restore his bodily life through sleep—a capacity personified by the disordered union of the laboring grooms, who do not work for themselves but instead for the sake of Care itself. Such a reading implies that both Scudamor and the workers of the forge, who present to him an allegorical rendering of his own vital powers in disarray, are working to produce an endless supply of care that only increases the power and allegorical being of the master to which they are enthralled. Scudamor's inability to perceive the "cause and end" to this diligent work of the blacksmiths also perfectly captures the futility of a heart and mind so obsessed with a particular affective burden—in this case, jealous care—that it enters a new zone of careless inattention to the world and its demands, including even the most basic of bodily needs. Hence, when he perceives that care's workers will not heed his queries, Scudamor lays "his wearie limbs" (4.5.39) upon the floor, hoping to restore his vital powers through sleep. Instead, he finds himself craving a release that will not come:

There lay Sir *Scudamor* longing while expecting,
When gentle sleep his heauie eyes would close;
Oft chaunging sides, and oft new place electing,
Where better seem'd he mote himselfe repose;
And oft in wrath he thence againe vprose;
And oft in wrath in layd him downe againe,
But wheresoeuer he did himselfe dispose
He by no meanes could wished ease obtaine:
So euery place sem'd painefull, and ech changing vaine.
(4.5.40)

Scudamor's psychosomatic inflammation persists, and once again grows into a state of wrath. The visual and sonic stimulation provided by the spectacle of care's workers looks at once to be the result and driving force behind his fury. Scudamor's insomnia is simultaneously the cause and effect of an enflamed care that involves both his bodily sensations and his psychic faculties. The discordant note first stuck by Ate has now escalated into a chorus of hammers whose "sound his senses did molest," while "the bellowes noyse distrurb'd his quiet rest, / Ne suffred sleepe to settle in his brest" (4.5.41). Adding yet more fuel to the fire, the surrounding wildlife join in the fun, as "dogs did barke and howle / About the house, at sent of stranger guest: / And now the crowing Cocke, and now the Owle / Lowde shriking him afflicted to the very sowle" (4.5.41). Scudamor's sensorial agitation seizes and tortures his animal life, a point which Spenser slyly underscores by making Scudamor's environmental surroundings teem with animal activity that mirrors the endless productions of Care's forge. In other words, Care exposes Scudamor's oikeiôsis to a nefarious form of capture, in turn blocking him from the benefit of restorative sleep that naturally belongs to him and which he desperately needs.

The excessive and self-erasing nature of Scuadmor's care is further indicated by its figuration as the ongoing "smart" of his wounded heart, a pain that continues even beyond the scene of hammering and focused production by Care's team of blacksmiths. Care, the "wicked carle the maister Smith," sneakily nips Scudamor's flesh with a "paire of redwhot yron tongs" just as he finally manages to fall asleep despite the racket of the workshop. Yet when the hero looks for the source of this aggravation, Care is nowhere to be found: "Yet looking round about him none could see; / Yet did the smart remaine, though he himselfe did flee" (4.5.44). Certainly, Care flees the scene, but Spenser's ambivalent pronouns also leave us with the feeling that this painful "smart" is so all-consuming that it causes Sir Scudamor's own sense of self to vanish as well. Spenser has already conceived the effects of this smarting wound as an erasure of the human self, which becomes clear when we read the painful smart of canto 5 in light of the smart that Scudamor experiences in the first canto, when he hears Ate's slanders against Amoret and Britomart. There, the hero's heart is pierced "with inward griefe, / As when in chace / The Parthian strikes a stag with shiuering dart, / The beast astonisht stands in middest of his smart" (4.1.49). The wound that Scudamor experiences in the earlier passage not only arrests his senses and leaves him in a state of shock; it also achieves these ends through a kind of animalization of his being that emphasizes his susceptibility to forces not entirely human, but which nevertheless animate him. The "smart" in both cantos 1 and 5 conveys a vital, animal power that undoes the fundamental ground of Scudamor's sense of self, and makes the sensation of suffering into a new basis of his ontological bearing. And it is precisely because Scudamor's life takes this form in the House of Care that the master smith and his minions are able to extract from it a surplus that feeds them in their productive efforts and allegorical being alike—all at the expense of Scudamor's ability to restore his bodily life through its immanent virtues of self-recovery.

As the vital benefit of sleep eludes the jealousy-stricken Scudamor, the poem reveals that the hero's amplification of a misguided notion of care is both a refusal to care for his physical life and an ethical failure, only exacerbating the fact that he has made a mess of his spiritual and ethical duties by falling prey to Ate's slanders. In this way, Scudamor's life is, like that of all Spenser's heroes, unavoidably attached to both the physical and spiritual demands of care. Indeed, the wedge of care's most fundamental work may be to antagonize and further divide forms of life that correlate in the early modern world to political theology and physis, thereby exposing a life that is nonsacred and merely living, yet capable of becoming an object of technical care. As ethical value in Spenser's world begins, ever so slowly, to separate itself from an exclusive attachment to the Christian theology of virtue, a new kind of value emerges, one that pertains to the physical life and vitality of the body and which has a place in premodern histories of biopower.[70] The poet's interest in insomnia and his depiction of it as a threat to psychosomatic integrity thus point to the material, unconscious processes of life and their centrality to the well-being of the laboring human—both of which make Spenser's epic poem an important site of discovery for the early modern world's mounting fascination with the vital power of living beings, and their approaching future as objects of scientific and biopolitical concern.

Chapter 5

"Inhabit Lax"

Insomniac Care and the Vital Virtue of Sleep in *Paradise Lost*

This chapter explores the ethics of care in John Milton's *Paradise Lost* through recurring images of sleep and wakefulness, which I argue constitute poetic adaptations of the Stoic theory of oikeiôsis. For Milton, like the Stoics, sleep is a therapy that restores life through contact with its rational and vitalistic foundations in a physically living cosmos. His poem's Christianization of central features of the ethical cosmology of Stoicism appears in its depictions of care as a heavenly virtue perfected by God's sleepless watch over His creation, echoed in turn by the angelic circle of care that bounds the garden of Eden while the first couple sleep, and given waking human shape through the harmonious activities that constitute the basis of Adam and Eve's domestic affiliation in their paradisal garden. Yet while Milton imagines care as a virtuous activity that cultivates what is near and dear to life, fallen care also appears in the poem: first in the guise of a malignant form of watch embodied by the insurgent Satan while the angelic host slumbers, and later as the postlapsarian burden of a susceptibility to the passions, which for Adam and Eve necessitates a reciprocal duty to care not only for themselves but also for each other's newly formed "anxious cares" (8.185).[1] Care in *Paradise Lost* synthesizes Stoic ethical insight with a Christian promise of the regenerative potential of life, and sleep is at the heart of Milton's physical conception of life's vital capacities for restoration and recovery both before and after the Fall.

Meanwhile, the poet fundamentally connects his vision of the origin of evil as a state of ontological privation to the condition of insomnia—an outgrowth of gnawing nocturnal care that causes Satan to awaken into a new form of life as a fallen creature. Satanic care, that is, gives rise to a deficient mode of individuation that breaks from the union of angelic slumber and the blissfully vitalist landscape of sleep in Heaven. This eruption of Satanic care as a malignant watch that stands apart from God comes to define demonic life throughout the poem. It is a tortured wakefulness that can never rest, immersed in a world of fallen cares first elaborated across the poem's opening books through the agonizing ecology and terms of embodiment in Hell. For Milton, insomnia thus figures the origin and alienating consequences of an evil whose influence eventually spreads into the first human couple's bower like a cosmic pestilence in Senecan tragedy. Yet sleep continues to hold the promise of contact with a regenerative power and eventual restoration through the seed that Eve carries and the care for life that she and Adam must learn to adopt beyond the boundaries of the garden. In this way, Milton's shifting representations of sleep and care not only syncretize Stoic philosophical and Christian perspectives but also ascribe a uniquely early modern biopolitical value to the vital processes of physical life and care. And in *Paradise Lost*, it is insomnia rather than sleep that threatens to corrupt such processes by dislodging life's natural attachment to virtue.[2]

The Stoic view of sleep as a benefit to the corporeal soul that restores the foundational tension of oikeiôsis, as I argue in chapter 2, appears in the figure of Herculean slumber at the center of Seneca's *Hercules Furens*—a volume that Milton knew well and quoted from while defending tyrannicide in *The Tenure of Kings and Magistrates*.[3] Adam's paradoxical description of sleep as a force that "with soft oppression seize[s]" (8.288) the first man soon after awakening into life also draws Milton's Adam into poetic resonance with Jasper Heywood's English rendering of Seneca's sleeping Hercules:

> Keepe him fast bounde with heavy sleepe opprest,
> Let slomber deepe his Limmes untamed bynde,
> Nor soner leave his unright raginge breaste
> Then former mynde his course agayne may fynd.[4]

We shall see that Adam, like Hercules, will demand the restorative therapy of sleep for his corporeal soul, though the terms of this demand differ strikingly in their pre- and postlapsarian incarnations. When Adam and Eve awaken after their first night of fallen slumber—during which a "dewy sleep / Oppressed them" (9.1044–1045)—Milton compares their transformed state to that of the "Herculean Samson . . . destitute and bare / Of all their virtue" (9.1060–1063).

Fusing Samson with Seneca's Hercules, Milton draws attention to the newly tragic conditions of life into which Adam and Eve awaken, now stripped of their natural capacities to flourish with virtuous ease in the garden. Such poignant scenes of slumber and awakening in *Paradise Lost* reveal the deep affiliation between Milton's conception of the natural impulse guiding life and care among God's creatures and the Stoic theory of oikeiôsis. From the vitalistic architecture of creation to the unfolding dialectics of care in Heaven and Hell and on Earth, Milton's epic is in closer dialogue with Stoic thought than we have recognized.

By aligning these aspects of *Paradise Lost* with principles of Stoicism, my aim is not to suggest that Milton was a thoroughgoing neo-Stoic—to discourage us from that notion, there is Christ's explicit condemnation of "the Stoic last in philosophical pride / By him called virtue" (4.300–301) among the parade of Greek philosophers in *Paradise Regained*. But in his rebuttal of Satan's suggestion that the son of God should seek worldly knowledge, Christ also recognizes the virtue of Socratic epistemic humility when he tells Satan that "the first and wisest of them all professed / To know this only, that he nothing knew" (4.293–294). The Son's genealogy of Greek thought is, much like the descent of humanity from Adam and Eve, a story of progressive degradation from which it is nonetheless possible to cull seeds of insight and wisdom, even as such moments always point further back to an architectonic truth grounded in the event of creation.[5] And that image is consistent with Milton's relationship to classical precedents in literature and philosophy more broadly: they constitute a pagan history from which he draws selectively and creatively. As Socrates and the Stoics following his lead asserted, the care of the self is the utmost task of philosophy, and it is central to Milton's view of ethical life as well—even if he thinks that the end of self-care risks being perverted by caring too selfishly and not spiritually enough for one's individual life and for what is rightly near and dear to it, including the well-being of others and the glorification of God. For Milton's Adam and Eve, attention to the physical conditions of life and virtue that they share with the natural world more broadly—both before and after their expulsion from Eden—are essential to these efforts. If Milton's epic evinces a vitalist cosmology that conceives of body, soul, and spirit as a material unity, then it is the Stoics, following Socrates, who provide the most coherent ancient model for such a thoroughgoing commitment to monism through their cosmological ethics of care.[6] While this chapter will develop these claims through its readings of sleep and sleeplessness in *Paradise Lost*, some further unpacking of Stoic thought in relation to the cosmological, ethical, and metaphysical principles most active in *Paradise Lost* is needed to prepare the way.

Stoicizing Milton

In a letter to Lucilius that addresses the Stoic conception of the good, Seneca explains: "Our school holds that what is good is a body, because what is good acts, and whatever acts is a body. What is good benefits; but in order for something to benefit, it has to act; if it acts, it is a body."[7] Cause is corporeal because only bodies exist in the Stoic cosmos, while the four incorporeal "somethings" of time, place, void, and sayables merely subsist among the web of bodies-as-causes that actively joins each part. All bodies are guided by a telos that arises from the influence of the pneuma—itself understood as the body of reason—that is thoroughly mixed with the denser corporeal matter of physical entities as it inherently seeks to accomplish the good. Seneca identifies this good with benefit, or that which is "helpful," because it promotes the flourishing of cosmic parts within the whole. For the Stoics, Zeus, or god as rational pneuma, engenders matter, gives material bodies their shape, and also causes sensing souls to form within certain types of material entities. The cosmos and all its parts thus participate in a unified psychosomatic process that is guided by the pneuma, the "designing fire" that forms a hierarchy of bodies whose capacities move from cohesion (*hexis*) to organic nature (physis) to perceptive soul (psyche) to reason (logos).[8] In the vitalistic cosmology of Stoicism, matter is inherently valuable because it is formed and guided by this natural telos as an expression of godly agency and cosmic rationality. Even at the most fundamental stage of pneuma acting to form matter into a body, it bestows a benefit that establishes, as it were, the simultaneously physical and metaphysical foundation of virtue. And as we have seen in earlier discussions of Stoic physicalism and the school's theory of bodily mixtures, the total blending (*krasis*) of matter and pneuma—the respectively passive and active principles of physical bodies—means that each bodily part of the cosmos, no matter how small, is thoroughly imbued with pneuma.[9]

While Milton's materialism has been a topic of criticism and intellectual controversies over *Paradise Lost* for over half a century, hardly any of the prominent discussions consider it in light of Stoic precedents.[10] One of the only readers to acknowledge Milton's debt to Stoicism, A. S. P. Woodhouse, notes that the Stoics "recognized a single substance which in its passive mode or aspect was matter, and in its active, reason or, as the Stoics did not scruple to call it, God."[11] For Woodhouse, the Stoic connection with Milton's thought is perhaps most salient in a shared emphasis upon the "creative activity of God" within matter. Milton would no doubt balk at making God entirely synonymous with the active principle of reason that permeates the physical cosmos—his God is more mysterious and less knowable, after all, than any single sense conveyed by such a philosophical proposition. Yet his conception of spirit as a manifestation of God's activity that is thoroughly mixed with the passivity of matter and endows it with a natural telos does show, as Woodhouse recognized, a deep affinity with conceptions of the cosmos attributed by Diogenes Laertius to Zeno and his Stoic followers, which also inform Seneca's claim that the good is corporeal.[12] God, or Zeus, has "many different names" in accordance with his various manifestations as substance, reason, and fate. The Stoic vision of cosmic creation posits god as both the original entity and as an immanently creative, ongoing presence in matter: "In the beginning, then, being by himself, god turned all of substance through air into water; and just as the sperm is contained in the seminal fluid, so god, being the seminal principle of the universe, remains in the moist substance and adapts matter to himself for the generation of the things to come."[13] Like Milton's conception of the original matter formed by God and out of which the cosmos is created, the Stoics understand matter to be implanted with seeds of all future genesis by virtue of the rational pneuma as the active principle of life that sustains the whole. For this reason, they also describe god as "a living being, immortal, rational, perfect in happiness, immune to anything bad, exercising forethought for the cosmos and all it contains."[14] God's perfect care is infused as an active principle throughout the cosmic whole, working within each of its living and material parts to actualize the good.

The locus classicus for discussions of Milton's own conception of living matter in *Paradise Lost* is the explanation Raphael gives to Adam in book 5 of the hierarchy of beings, in which the affable angel describes a distinctively vitalistic teleology grounded in Stoic principles. He informs Adam that "all things" are composed of "one first matter all" (5.470–472) seeking an ultimate end: to return to union with God, thereby completing its circular passage through the body of creation. So long as any manifestation of this substance is "not depraved from good" it will eventually "up to Him return" (5.470–471), participating in a unifying cosmic process of benefit that cycles through the animate parts of the living whole:

> So from the root
> Spring lighter the green stalk, from thence the leaves
> More airy, last the bright consummate flower
> Spirits odorous breathes: flow'rs and their fruit,
> Man's nourishment, by gradual scale sublimed
> To vital spirits aspire, to animal,
> To intellectual, give both life and sense,
> Fancy and understanding, whence the soul

Reason receives, and reason is her being,
Discursive or intuitive: discourse
Is oftest yours, the latter most is ours,
Differing but in degree, of kind the same.
(5.479–490)

From the basic capacities of cohesion and growth to vital, animal, and intellectual virtues of psychosomatic life, matter and vital spirits are thoroughly mixed within each creature as it strives to return to God. Not only do creatures with a capacity to exercise discursive reason aim at the good; so too do those entities whose participation in reason involves only the physical processes of cohesion and growth. Stella P. Revard describes Raphael's "plea for the creaturely community" as a lesson whose principles are implicitly Stoic: the "functioning of the parts of the plant may be likened to the functioning of the universe, having been infused in its creation by vital living force or goodness. . . . By emphasizing the oneness of living creation, sustained in good by God, Raphael has instructed Adam of the danger when a part of that creation chooses separate or 'private good' for itself in violation of the good for the continuing whole."[15]

Milton's matter is thus endowed with a living telos that Raphael later describes as a "vital virtue" and "vital warmth" (7.236), infused by the "Spirit of God" (7.235) and active in each part of the whole of living creation. Such matter is inherently norm-positing in its activity as an efficacious substance released from God, through which He creates the cosmos and by which acts of creation continue to unfold in time across the "scale of nature" (5.509) that Adam is taught to recognize. For Milton, matter is a virtue in several senses. It is good because it was made by God; good because it bestows the benefit of being upon the creatures of God; and finally, good because it contains all future goods of creation in the form of a repository, or what Milton calls a "seed bank" in his discussion of creation in book 1, chapter 7 of *Christian Doctrine*.[16] In an earlier chapter from *Christian Doctrine*, Milton also describes the power of the Holy Spirit that infuses matter as an active virtue: "At another time [it means] the father's power and virtue, especially that divine breath [*afflatum*] which creates and fosters all things: in the way many interpreters, both ancient and more recent, understand that verse Gen. 1:2: *the spirit of God brooded*. There, however, the son seems rather to be understood, through whom the father is so often said to have created all things."[17] Matter and spirit are virtues in tandem, associated respectively with what Milton calls passive and active principles of creation.[18] Like the Stoic understanding of matter and pneuma, Milton's matter and spirit are polar tendencies or expressions of each other that run along the continuum of a single substance.[19]

For this reason, Milton's vital matter mixes or blends completely—though to various degrees of efficacy—both spiritual and corporeal capacities within each created entity in a manner akin to the Stoic theory of *krasis*, or total blending. In his description of angelic corporeality, Willian Kerrigan remarks that when Milton's angels have sex, they "mix totally [and are] exempt from the law that two bodies cannot inhabit the same space, which binds only dense and 'exclusive' corporeality."[20] This is also the argument made by the Stoics with respect to *krasis*, and it is key to their explanation of how bodily matter is thoroughly mixed with the corporeal human soul, or passive matter with active pneuma in living creatures and indeed all entities.[21] Kerrigan's basic point holds true not only for angelic bodies extended in space but also for the corporeal and spiritual capacities that inhere within the matter God uses to create all bodies in Milton's cosmos. Angels perfect the virtues of spiritual matter because "total they mix, Union of Pure with Pure / Desiring; nor restrain'd conveyance need / As Flesh to mix with Flesh, or Soul with Soul" (8.627–629). Human bodies are less perfect relative to angelic bodies because they are constrained by the greater degree of corporeal expression inherent to their material natures. But the matter out of which they are created is nonetheless also a mixture of the spiritual and corporeal expressions of a single substance—as is the case for any given body in the cosmos despite its position along the scale of life that is described by Raphael. There is no substance dualism dividing spirit from matter in *Paradise Lost*, but rather a complete blending of active and passive principles, or spiritual and corporeal dispositions whose relative degrees of presence within a given body determine the capacities that organize the natural hierarchy of bodies in the living cosmos. And while receiving these truths requires looking to biblical scripture—or in Adam's case, listening attentively to God's messenger—it also involves empirically grasping the order that appears to human beings through the natural world we inhabit and which God has created with purpose: "Surely all the world's contents, made in orderly beauty for some purpose and benefit, attest the pre-existence of some sovereign agent who in all these things set himself a purpose."[22] These core features of Milton's materialism—the thorough mixing of passive and active principles in a single substance, the spiritual vitality of all created matter, the understanding of the active principle as a spirit or breath, the generativity implanted within matter like a "seedbank," and perhaps most significantly, the living telos that guides bodies and orchestrates goodness as a form of benefit active among all parts of the living whole—find their closest philosophical kinship with ancient Stoicism.

From these principles of material genesis arise certain ethical considerations, for the Stoic school and for Milton alike. Because the pneuma is the inherent bodily cause of all matter, the Stoics argue it is also the active force guiding the first impulse of life as care. This impulse bestows an awareness to every animal of its own constitution as a living being, thereby affirming its oikeiôsis and establishing the first step of the process by which the living animal recognizes and makes a home for itself in the world.[23] Oikeiôsis becomes the virtuous path of flourishing, as human beings grow to become citizens of the cosmos, guided by reason to constitute and care for a community ruled by natural law. Katja Vogt describes this ideal cosmopolitan outcome as an eventual recognition that "one relates to everyone in the world as a fellow-inhabitant of the same 'home.'"[24] Through oikeiôsis, we affirm our capacities to flourish within our natural habitat, among other living and nonliving beings in their respective natures. In his *Art of Logic*, Milton offers a definition of habitus that accords with these Stoic insights regarding human life and its affirmative orientation toward the good. While Milton's discussion is primarily metaphysical, the ethical and the metaphysical converge in his definition of habitus as that which belongs to a subject "by its very nature" in the affirmative mode.[25] Just as oikeiôsis begins with the first impulse affirming life and then looks outward to develop broader circles of care appropriate to its flourishing, to live well in *Paradise Lost* is to care for one's natural ends as established by God, given immediately to the awareness of human beings and further developed through the proper use of reason. For humans, that includes the use of discursive reason to affirm one's habitus within the hierarchy of all created beings—a power that is based upon the vital spirit's infusion of the rational soul in a creaturely and physical body.[26] In other words, Milton's notion of creaturely habitus in *Paradise Lost* shares the teleological and naturalistic framework of Stoic oikeiôsis.

In addition to these normative principles, however, Milton shares with the Stoics an interest in the physical—indeed, physiological—causes of ethical mishaps and failures. The Stoics argue that the rational animal bears a distinctive susceptibility to perversion, through influences that can cause it to swerve from its natural orientation toward the good and deprive of it of its capacity to flourish. A "rational being is perverted," the Stoics claim, "due to the persuasiveness of external pursuits or sometimes to the influence of associates. For the starting-points of nature are never perverse."[27] A perversion is a turning that bends or twists nature from its proper course, an idea that will resonate with the coming argument as it tracks figures of perverse turning that mark Satan's distorting influence across the poem.[28] Milton's preferred term for these turns from the good is "privation," which is the larger point of concern in his discussion of habitus from *Art of Logic*. As he explains, while habitus is what belongs to an entity in its affirmative nature, privation is the negation thereof. Following Plutarch, Milton defines privation as a form of negation "by corruption and removal" of a given capacity, which prevents the actualization of a natural end.[29] And these principles can be squared with his poetic depiction of evil as the privation of goodness in *Paradise Lost*. In Milton's epic, Satan's turn from God represents the primal scene of a discordance that introduces nonentity to the cosmos, and which inaugurates his own vigilant commitment to a perversion of the angelic habitus that is proper to his and to all angelic being. Hence, Satan's all-consuming end is to bring cacophony from the harmony that would otherwise organize life in accordance with Godly reason. This is why he tells his fellow denizens in Hell that "our labor must be to pervert that end / And out of good still to find means of evil" (1.165). Satan, by turning from God, brings privation into the order of being. God of course mends this gap when he tells the Son, "I can repair / That detriment (if such it be to lose / Self-lost) and in a moment will create / Another world" (7.152–155). He then commands the angelic host, "Meanwhile inhabit lax, ye pow'rs of Heaven" (7.162). To "inhabit lax" encourages the angels to dilate their physical being and affirm their habitus—to relax, spread out, and occupy the space that has just been vacated by Satan's fall.[30] The physical and ontological slackness that God urges at this moment thus turns into a mode of fulfillment, as the heavenly host inhabits the newly increased elbow room in Heaven and fully restores the good to a space temporarily deprived of it.

Understood as a dilation or loosening of angelic being, "inhabit lax" also resonates with the psychosomatic slackness that for Stoic thinkers defines the condition of sleep. Sleep is a slackening of the fundamental tension that holds all bodies together and, according to various degrees of activity by the pneuma, causes both sensation and rational thought. The Stoics reportedly held that "sleep occurs when the sensory tension [*tonos aesthetikos*] is relaxed in the ruling part [hêgemonikon] of the soul."[31] While sleep is a beneficial slackening of the soul, the Stoics define an absolute slackening of the soul's perceptive tension as the natural death of the organism. Meanwhile, "They say that the passions are caused by variations of the breath [pneuma]." Such variations constitute discordance with the natural law of the cosmos, which for the Stoics manifests through harmonic motions of this same "vital breath" or pneuma. Hence, sleep's slackening effects bring true rest only to the soul that is ruled by reason and whose physical motions accord with the pneuma, as Seneca argues: "Real tranquility is the state reached by an unperverted mind when it is relaxed."[32] Perversion is a passion that distorts natural reason—a discordant and agitated turning of the corporeal soul that disturbs its inclination toward the good, and which can reverberate through sleeping and waking states alike.

If sleep slackens the ruling principle of the soul by loosening the psychosomatic tension that makes sensation, reason, and virtue possible, how should we understand this experience as it bears upon the care for life in Milton's epic? When Adam first succumbs to the "soft oppression" of sleep, he believes he is beginning to "dissolve" into his formerly "insensible" (8.288–291) state of nonexistence. On the one hand, Adam's description of sleep as self-dissolution would seem to suggest an approaching lack or loss of being, in keeping with a tradition elaborated by Christian writers from Paul to Augustine to Erasmus, all of whom figure sleep as a dangerous relaxation of vigilance and thus a threat to spiritual virtue. Yet Milton pursues the opposite line of thought: sleep is not privation, but rather the fulfillment of a relaxed habitus which he correlates with the inherent vitality and natural telos of God's creation, while insomnia is the privative that negates this habitus of creaturely life. Like the Stoics, Milton depicts sleep's slackness and regenerative powers as a simultaneously physiological and ethical benefit, and as an experience that preserves the minimal degree of tension or *tonos* necessary to establish a living being's proper attachment to itself—the first principle of life as care, and the basis of oikeiôsis. The poet uses these associations to figure insomnia as a perverse threat to the living creature, epitomized by Satan's break from God and from the organic cosmic whole represented as a slumbering vitalist unity in Heaven.

A Sublime Slackening

In Milton's prelapsarian cosmos, we should expect to find a vision of sleep untainted by the associations with fleshly regard and spiritual carelessness that are found in Pauline and Augustinian theology and elaborated variously by Renaissance commentators.[33] One possibility appears in book 4, where Adam describes "the timely dew of sleep / Now falling with soft slumberous weight" (4.614–615) upon the first couple's eyelids; likewise, Adam and Eve's nighttime prayer of adoration describes God's "goodness infinite both when we wake / And when we seek, as now, Thy gift of sleep" (4.734–735). Their description of sleep as a "gift" offering pleasant relief from daily toil recalls Piso's formulation of sleep in Cicero's *On Moral Ends* as both a "gift" and an "antidote" to labor, whose strangeness is offset by its therapeutic effects. Were it not for such restorative measures, Piso remarks, "We would think its existence contrary to nature, since it deprives us of sensation and the ability to act."[34] Yet Adam and Eve's prelapsarian slumbers are entirely absent of the sort of debilitating and unnatural effects that Cicero's work ascribes to sleep, as well as any theological associations with the strife of fleshliness or privation from the good. Even the toilsome experience of labor is absent in a garden where work, as David Simon observes, is "perfectly calibrated" so as not to make the body hurt.[35] For Adam and Eve, God's care is perpetually active as the guiding impulse of nourishing and sustaining activities. It extends through the cosmos even while His creatures sleep, thereby preserving the subtle motions of a cosmic oikeiôsis that directs their "pleasant labor" (4.625) by day and sustains the first human couple in their nocturnal bower. Sleep in Eden "merely typifies what will be experienced outside sleep," writes Michael Lieb, "rather than providing an escape from the oppressions of reality."[36] Work and rest alike are easy endeavors in Eden.

Still, the couple's security—to be without care in paradisal slumber—seems also to depend upon the watchful vigilance of the angels Ithuriel and Zephon, commanded by Gabriel to "leave unsearched no nook / But chiefly where those two fair creatures lodge / Now laid perhaps asleep secure of harm" (4.790–791). Their vigilant care proves well founded, since the angels immediately find Satan, crouching close to Eve's sleeping ear and plotting to infect her with "inspiring venom" (4.804). This episode and Eve's ensuing account of her dream in book 5 have been avidly discussed, with critics focusing primarily on the events that take place within the dream itself and how they might bear upon Eve's ethical culpability for the Fall.[37] What interests me here is not the content of Eve's dream—at least not yet—but the moral psychology of sleep that Adam uses to assuage her sense of unease upon awakening. He tells her that "Reason" is the "chief" faculty of her soul, which simply "retires / Into her private cell when nature rests" (5.100–109). If it is natural both to rest and to have the soul's rational capacities recede, then Adam's words reveal that for human beings the condition of sleep is at once a biological norm and a suspension of the normative capacities that define humans as beings who naturally exercise discursive reason—a form of reason whose back-and-forth motion resembles the ebb and flow of human life as it cycles naturally through periods of sleep and wakefulness. So while sleep occupies a holy place in God's creation, it is also a manifestation of humanity's relative imperfection and vulnerability—only God can be perfectly vigilant and constant in his care, while beings of a lesser nature inevitably fall under the shroud of slumber. If Adam and Eve's security in sleep depends in part upon the "strict watch" (4.562) of the angels, it is fair to say that their sleep is at least indirectly blemished by the fact of Satan's fall and the threat he represents to them—a threat that can only be imperfectly protected against by the angelic watch and the circle of vigilant care it forms in patrolling the circumference and interior of the garden.[38] This is why Uriel asserts that Gabriel's chief "care must be to find" (4.575) the fallen angel who has "ventured from the deep to raise new / Troubles" (4.574–575) that will come to haunt the slumbering Eve. For a truly untainted image of sleep—as well as an explanation of why human sleep is necessary as both a restorative benefit and a regenerative power of life—we must first look to another moment, which is Raphael's somewhat nostalgic description of angelic sleep in book 5.

In that passage, Raphael depicts sleep as a state of blessed ease in Heaven, brought on by evening exhalations from the throne of God:

> Now when ambrosial night with clouds exhaled
> From that high Mount of God (whence light and shade
> Spring both) the face of brightest Heav'n had changed
> To grateful twilight (for night comes not there
> In darker veil) and roseate dews disposed
> All but th'unsleeping eyes of God to rest,
> Wide over all the plain and wider far
> Than all the globous Earth in plain outspread
> (Such are the courts of God) th'angelic throng,
> Dispersed in bands and files, their camp extend
> By living streams among the trees of life,
> Pavilions numberless and sudden reared,
> Celestial tabernacles where they slept
> Fanned with cool winds, save those who in their course
> Melodious hymns about the sov'reign throne
> Alternate all night long.
> (5.648–657)

From God's holy exhalations to the streams and winds that cool Heaven's denizens—who are similarly "dispersed" across the plains—to the "melodious" vocalizations of air that honor the deity, the geographic expansiveness of Heaven and its circulations of water and air harmonize with sleep's affective release. As Lieb notes in his account of the poem's dialectics of creation, "God's mount takes on the characteristic of the mythopoeic mountain which is the source of life."[39] Along with cosmic exhalations of "ambrosial night," both light and shade emerge from and return to the mount, exhibiting a "pattern of cyclical return" that is both "creative and sustaining" of the angelic union with God.[40] The circle is of course the geometric figure used to describe the expanding path of oikeiôsis, which Milton imagines here as an immanently restorative spirit of Godly care in sleep. It expands outward to move through and encompass all things in Heaven, and eventually is drawn back into the holy mount just as cycles of inhalation and exhalation sustain a complex living organism. Milton's figuration of the physical vitality of Heaven thus aligns angelic rest with a connatural flow of life as it cycles through the vast openness of the plains and back to God's palatial dwelling. Even those angels who take turns to wake are in a kind of glorious trance, devoting their attention entirely to a musical harmonizing that coextends with God's total sovereignty over the ecopolitical unity of Heaven.[41]

By virtue of this harmonic unity, organic life in Heaven constitutes an aesthetic and political hierarchy through which the vital spirit actively flows, consonant with the Greek senses of organon as both a musical instrument and a tool used by an artisan.[42] God plays several roles in this passage: he is the player whose breath enlivens the instrument, the artisan who crafted it, and chief auditor of its holy diapason.[43] God made the bodies that coconstitute this single cosmic body, infusing them with the breath of life that moves through the bodies of the angels who sleep and through those who sing His praises, while "God's own ear / Listens delighted" (9.626–627). This immanent corporeal unity and its basis in the infusion and circulation of vital breath—which acts as the cause to the sensations that move through these interanimated bodies and to the pleasures which that activity generates—recall the ancient Stoic doctrine that the cosmos is Zeus's living body, infused with the pneuma of divine reason.[44] Yet in Milton's image of prelapsarian heavenly slumber, these elements combine to form a structure of care that makes sleep essential to angelic being. It is an aspect of the celestial habitus through which the community is deeply, even unconsciously imbricated with each other and with the holy, living landscape. In his account of Milton's political thought and its vitalist commitments, John Rogers suggests that the poet tends to some manner of "organizational discourse" or "language describing the systemic interaction of individual agents that political philosophy was obliged to share with natural philosophy."[45] If natural science and politics converge in this passage, it is important to note that their shared foundation is the cohesive vitality by which the slumbering heavenly organism maintains its proper degree of living tension and dwells in harmonious relaxation: the breath of spirit, or pneuma, that flows through, animates, and cares for the creaturely community. Sleep is a vital virtue that affirms this physical unity of divine creation. It deepens contact with the inherent goodness of living matter, and with God's sovereignty over and care for his creatures. Heavenly slumber thus lays bare the biopolitical organization of life and natural law in Milton's Heaven.

These evening transformations in Heaven occur just after the angels have danced and feasted in an earlier display of waking harmony with God's anointing of the Son, and so their sleep is also physiologically significant as a moment of postdigestive pleasure in heavenly twilight.[46] Yet curiously, Raphael informs Adam that both evening and morn take place in Heaven simply for the sake of "change delectable" rather than any decisive "need" (5.629). This seems to assign a unique value to the metabolic processes of life represented by eating and drinking, though the angel's phrase also subtly retracts the insinuation that those processes are necessary for reproducing and sustaining the life of heavenly bodies. The reasons given are rather aesthetic reasons: these motions take place for the sake of pleasing sensations of alteration that move through the bodies of Heaven, so that God may in turn sense and take pleasure in the subtle harmony that arises from such fluctuations, as the individual parts of the heavenly host relax the psychosomatic tension that individuates them and they increasingly meld into each other. This corporeal mixing of angelic bodies facilitates harmonic unity through a physical interpenetration among the angels and the immense living ecology of Heaven. Raphael's poetic description thus figures slumbering life in Heaven as a vitalistic physical process whose aesthetic pleasures shore up the ecopolitical unity of God's creation. While the angels do not need sleep to replenish their physical bodies in a manner akin to the needs of human bodies, sleep is nonetheless welcome as a mode of relaxed sensation and corporeal slackness during which the eyes and ears of God remain vigilant and take deep pleasure. Sleep thus confers upon the angelic organism the benefit of glorifying God by virtue of receiving His spirit in the form of psychosomatic creativity at rest.

If the slackening release of sleep is a loosening of angelic being that opens these creatures to a deeper union with God, it constitutes a mode of deindividuation akin to the unconstrained union of angelic sex.[47] And it is incorporation with this common body of sublime slackness that Lucifer resists by turning away from God to become the being of deprived wakefulness that is Satan. In the scene that Raphael describes, the vigilant isolation of sleeplessness actualizes Lucifer's deviance from God and his sovereign domain:

> But not so waked
> Satan (so call him now: his former name
> Is heard no more in Heav'n).
> (5.657–659)

Satan's wakefulness is a moment of psychosomatic tension that separates him from the slack habitus that is proper to Lucifer's angelic being as part of Heaven's slumbering community, and it therefore constitutes a decisive act of free will that introduces privation to the cosmos by turning from God. It is not until the approaching evening in Heaven that Lucifer's turn is fully realized, though his displeasure is at first referred to indirectly by Raphael's suggestion that "all seemed [pleased] but were not all" (5.617) with God's anointing of the Son. Lucifer still smarts from the wound of pride felt earlier in the day when God proclaimed the Son as His right hand, and warned that "him who disobeys / Me disobeys, breaks union, and that day, / Cast out from God and blessed vision, falls / Into utter darkness, deep engulfed" (5.611–614). Lucifer's pride is an affective vice (in more than one sense) keeping his eyes open and his mind constrained when he should be sleeping. When sleep closes the eyelids of the living being, it suspends the visual sensation most closely aligned with the sin of pride; pride, as Augustine remarks, is an "appetite for a perverse kind of elevation" that turns the mind toward an image of the self rather than resting it upon the foundation provided by God.[48] Milton captures this notion of selfishness in his description of Lucifer's envy upon seeing the Father anoint the Son: "Fraught / With envy against the Son of God that day," Lucifer "could not bear / Through pride that sight and thought himself impaired" (5.661–665). To be im-paired suggests that the turn from God is implicitly a turn toward the self, a harmful doubling that pairs the self with a vision of itself as an object of desire and glory, thereby losing sight of God. This sense of Satanic impairment upon seeing the Son anointed also plays linguistic counterpart to God's eventual "repair" of the detriment that is opened by Satan's turn, which takes the form of His creation of the Earth and its human inhabitants.

Milton's negative genesis of evil is thus embedded in the scene's ambivalent figurations of care in Heaven, divided between God's care for His slumbering vitalist creation and the antipathy to it that is nurtured by Lucifer's gnawing nocturnal care. For that reason, the moment gives us a Miltonic view of the origin of evil that is also the beginning of the care of the self. What I mean by this point will hopefully become clearer as my argument develops, but the underlying thought is that before Satan's insomniac individuation from the heavenly host, the "self" does not, strictly speaking, exist as an entity that solicits care. Indeed, the angelic organism rather denotes a kind of unity of life in intellect, sensation, and action whose physical immediacy to God makes the notion of a self and the ongoing project of self-care redundant.[49] This is presumably why the angels eat and sleep yet are not tasked to do so as part of a careful regimen necessary for the recovery of life and spiritual virtue. Their sleep is instead a function of the cyclical and physical motions of "change delectable" that please God and his creatures alike, establishing the circular pathway of His cosmic care for creation. Angel bodies have no need for an external power of cure or repair; the corporeal injuries occasioned by the war in Heaven, for instance, are merely fluctuations of "spirits that live throughout / Vital in every part" and remain incapable of receiving "in their liquid texture [any] mortal wound" (6.343–348). This thought sheds further light on the nature of the repair that God announces He will make to the rupture caused by Satan's turn: insofar as Satan's selfish ways are in themselves irreparable, the care that is born from his pride will endure for eternity. God's creative repair of that fault forms a being whose habitus naturally involves the care of the self as a virtuous end, thereby mending the depravity of selfishness that arises from Satan's sleepless break with the union of Godly Heaven. For these newly created beings, sleep is an essential power of restoration that renews contact with the divinity that shaped them into life. That is clear from Adam's first encounter with the "soft oppression" of sleep, which leads to a dream of revelation after which he awakens to find himself before God.

With Soft Oppression Seized

"How can immortal man 'return' to God? He need only feed the 'quick instinctive motion' and 'lively vigor' there from the beginning," writes William Kerrigan.[50] His point holds true for unfallen humankind's activities in waking life, which require above all else obedience to God and an understanding that by following their natural impulses toward right reason, the care that Adam and Eve take for themselves and for each other cannot lead them astray. The "quick instinctive motion" that Kerrigan mentions is part of Adam's narrative of awakening into life, which he relates to Raphael in book 8. While Kerrigan clarifies the long way back to God, it is also true that Adam returns to God, in another sense, almost immediately after his first awakening, when he falls asleep and meets his maker through a dream of revelation. But there are certain implications—first principles, even—to be derived from Adam's account of his original moment of wakefulness in Eden, which will clarify the meaning of Adam's sleep and its place in God's ongoing work of creation.

The desire to narrate this event, Adam tells Raphael, is social: "Desire with thee still longer to converse / Induced me" (8.252–253). It encourages him to poeticize his entry into the world despite the inherent difficulties of narrating such a first experience. As Adam proceeds, it becomes clear that part of Milton's task is to explain the first man's desire for sociability through an appeal to the natural impulses that first situate him within his ecological milieu, and which guide him toward an actualization of the bodily and rational capacities bestowed on him. And in doing so, Milton incorporates elements of the Stoic theory of oikeiôsis. Along with the classical discussions of oikeiôsis to be found in Diogenes Laertius, Seneca, and Stobaeus, an important early modern reference point for Milton was the 1631 *Prolegomena* to Hugo Grotius's *De Jure Belli Ac Pacis*. In the opening pages of this work, Grotius rejects the notion that human creatures are motivated exclusively by a natural instinct to seek their own private advantage over others, and he aligns his perspective with the first principle of the Stoic school:

> For man indeed, is a living body, but far more excellent than all others, and much more differing from the rest, than they do one from another; as may easily be demonstrated by many actions, which are proper only to mankind. Among which, this is one, that he greedily affects Society, that is, Community; yet not any but that which is peaceable, and according to the Model of his Understanding, Regular, with those of his own kind; which the Stoicks term *oikeiôsis*, Familiarity. Men, saith Chrysostom, with men have Society naturally; and why not, seeing that Beasts with Beasts have the same. And in another place he tells us, That nature hath instill'd into our minds the very seeds of Vertue.[51]

While in this passage Grotius underscores the social aspects of oikeiôsis that develop from the initial impulse of self-care, he later attributes this human appetite for society to "principles internal as to man" that have been implanted, like seeds of virtue, by God. This is why, he adds, "even that Law of Nature, whereof we have already treated, Whether it be that which springs from Society, or that which is of a larger extent, although it flow from principles internal as to man, yet may deservedly be ascribed unto God. Because it was originally his will, that such principles should be instilled unto us . . . Neither can we (say Chrysippus and the Stoicks) derive Justice from any Root than from Jove himself."[52] For Grotius, then, Stoic oikeiôsis provides a classical touchstone for his own theory of the natural inclination of humankind toward communally beneficial relations of care.[53] Moreover, he looks to incorporate those aspects of the Stoic tradition into his notion of "seeds of Vertue" as divinely implanted capacities to be developed in accordance with our natural agency and propensities for sociality.[54]

Through Adam's narrative of the first impulses of his experience of life, Milton alludes to Grotius's argument and to its Stoic foundations: the principle behind our natural desire for the social, which the Stoics identify with the first impulse of life, is the awareness that begins with life in a body and disposes us to care. As Adam tells Raphael:

> As new waked from soundest sleep
> Soft on the flow'ry herb I found me laid
> In balmy sweat which with his beams the sun
> Soon dried and on the reeking moisture fed.
> Straight toward heav'n my wond'ring eyes I turned
> And gazed a while the ample sky till raised
> By quick instinctive motion up I sprung
> As thitherward endeavoring and upright
> Stood on my feet.
> (8.253–261)

Adam's first sensation is the softness of the "flow'ry herb" on which he lay as it seems to meld with the dewy sweat of his skin, whose "reeking moisture" the sun feeds upon, thereby immediately situating Adam's body and its physiological processes within the vital cycle of created life as it is earlier described by Raphael, both in his "one first matter" speech and in his descriptions of angelic slumber. Adam awakens from this circuit of physical life, at least figuratively speaking, into an innate awareness of his bodily constitution that coextends with the word "soft." It is nicely poised between the simile he uses to compare his entry into living awareness with a coming out of sleep and his sense of finding himself placed on a bed of greenery by way of touch. Touch is that strange sensation which, as Aristotle notes, differs from other senses insofar as the organ that feels is also the medium of feeling.[55] It therefore plays a special role in affirming Adam's embodied constitution and his innate understanding of himself as a living, sensing creature embedded within the physical processes of creation. Seneca offers a relevant explanation of animal oikeiôsis and the initial awareness of human self-constitution as an inherent understanding of "constitution as such" rather than a "definition of understanding."[56] The human creature innately grasps its condition as a living being as the basis of its oikeiôsis, though early in life this "understanding of its own constitution is vague, rudimentary, and unclear," he observes. Yet it forms the essential foundation of our orientation toward self and world, and so begins the natural path of our development as rational animals. Adam of course awakens into a fully grown human condition, so we would expect at least some of his self-orienting perceptions to be fairly clear and distinct. Yet even as he recalls with some clarity the feeling of softness, he notes that it came to him through a sense of touch that remained indistinct with respect to its derivation. Is the softness the sense of Adam's own body, the grass underneath it, the thin veil of "balmy sweat" enveloping him, or does it denote sensations that move among all of these bodies as they participate in a softness generated out of the nested processes of life? While fuzzy and indistinct, these minute perceptions also form the material basis of Adam's innate understanding of his bodily constitution. They constitute the subtlest beginnings of the psychosomatic tension that initiates Adam's oikeiôsis as he awakens into the greater clarity of human cognition, and begins to care for those things that are near and dear to his life.

While Milton thus incorporates into Adam's first experience of life an important role for the fuzzy and indistinct perceptions of softness as they rise into a more finely attuned awareness, Adam's oikeiôsis also entails a natural movement outward and upward from the body—"Straight toward heavn my wond'ring eyes I turned"—that performs a meaningful reversal in the broader narrative of Godly creation. For while Adam's first sensation of himself as a living being affirms his physical connection and embeddedness within the vital processes of other bodies on Earth, his next sensorial impulse is immediately drawn, like the sweat being pulled out of his skin and evaporated by the Sun, up and toward the sky. As Kerrigan notes, it is as if the "physiological impulses of the body" (222) are themselves pointed toward Heaven, though Adam does not yet possess a full understanding of himself as a creature of God. The spirit that infuses his material body with life and care nonetheless guides Adam's sight in a manner that repairs Satan's perverse turning, insofar as his gaze immediately turns to Heaven and God: "Straight toward heav'n my wond'ring eyes I turned." This visual turn then tugs at the "quick instinctive motions" of body and limb, encouraging him to arise, as if Adam's "I" feeds off the skyward sight before his eyes, invigorating his bodily capacities for joyful motion and guiding them into an "upright" standing. Milton's turns of verse thus affirm the cyclical turnings of a vital landscape that includes Adam's body, enlivening and bringing him into an awareness of the rational impulses that move through him as they rise from subtle and fuzzy indistinctness to a clarity that draws him into an upright posture for the first time.[57]

These instinctive motions quickly lead Adam to look "about me round" (8.261) and further take in his natural surroundings. As this process unfolds, however, Milton continues to emphasize a kind of fuzziness mixed with moments of perceptual clarity. "About me round I saw / Hill, dale, and shady woods and sunny plains," Adam states, but this seeing is then strikingly, even awkwardly conjoined to an awareness of qualities more suited to hearing: "And liquid lapse of murmuring streams" (8.262–263) he continues. Likewise, Adam's heart overflows with "fragrance and with joy," as if its effusions are not only felt within but also smelled from without. Accentuating the simultaneous joyfulness and unthreatening confusion of Adam's fresh awakening, Milton affirms a pattern of perplexity that Regina Schwartz finds across numerous scenes of creation in *Paradise Lost*. As God's creatures oscillate "between epistemological confidence and uncertainty," they are led to a kind of reconciliation through the act of praise—an impulse that places a natural limit on knowledge while nonetheless encouraging an understanding of the natural world, which Schwartz also aligns with Stoic precedents.[58]

I would like to suggest that these initial moments of Adam's oscillating experience of creation spur Adam toward the sort of praise that Schwartz describes, yet in the form of a question that will then lead him directly into the experience of sleep. The first stirrings of this question appear when he turns his gaze from his surroundings and toward himself:

Myself I then perused and limb by limb
Surveyed and sometimes went and sometimes ran
With supple joints as lively vigor led.
But who I was, or where, or from what cause
Knew not.
(8.267–271)

As he quickly moves beyond an innate understanding of himself as a living and sensing being, Adam displays the greater clarity of a self-aware and wakeful "I," but only at the cost of becoming equally aware that he lacks knowledge of its ultimate cause. Likewise, as he begins to speak with words that seem not quite to belong to him yet are perfectly suited to their task of naming all that he sees, Adam is moved to ask "How came I thus?" while instinctively grasping

Not of myself: by some great Maker, then,
In goodness and in pow'r preeminent.
Tell me how I may know Him, how adore,
From whom I have that thus I move and live
And feel that I am happier than I know!
(8.277–282)

Though Adam recognizes himself to be a being created by a preeminently beneficial maker, and that innate understanding can be traced back to the first impulses of life bestowed upon him, there is nonetheless a limit to his natural understanding. It can only be through divine revelation that Adam comes to know securely who in fact his creator is, and how to praise him. For "no one can have a right perception of God with nature or reason as sole guide, without God's word or his messenger," as Milton writes in *Christian Doctrine*.[59] And sleep is the vehicle through which this revelation occurs, as if Milton means to insist upon the deep connection between sleep and Godly care that reveals the ongoing work of creation and repair. Sleep brings Adam to a fuller understanding of himself and his origins through the power of revelation, but it accomplishes this end through a psychosomatic slackening that is also an essential habitus of his being. It puts Adam into contact with the divine, or what the Stoics call the *cura regentis* that sustains and cares for the cosmos and all its living parts, allowing Adam to affirm his position within the whole through his praise of God.

Relating his memory of this first, eventful fall into sleep, Adam describes it as a power of release that returns him to the posture and affects that earlier constituted his awakening into life:

> While On a green shady bank profuse of flowers
> Pensive I sat me down. There gentle sleep
> First found me and with soft oppression seized
> My drows'd sense untroubled, though I thought
> I then was passing to my former state
> Insensible and forthwith to dissolve.
> (8.286–291)

Sleep's drowsy dissolution matches the environmental rhythms of gently flowing water that Adam discovers upon his first exploration of the world. Kristin Poole has shown that descriptions of bodily or phenomenological dissolution are a frequent trope in early modern poetry, and that the use of the word "dissolve" reveals a literary physics largely modeled on ancient Stoic cosmology.[60] Poole describes Stoic matter as a pneumatic continuum of constant transformations in which the human body participates, and so dissolving or melting affirms the sense in which material boundaries are both transitory and permeable for entities that live as parts within an organic whole. Her insight helps us to grasp why Adam's fall into sleep is felt—and retroactively described—in such an "untroubled" manner. Sleep signals a material transformation that Adam instinctually grasps as belonging to the vital cycles in which his embodied life participates, as was similarly evident to him upon his first awakening info life. Sleep's paradoxically gentle-yet-forceful arrival ends Adam's physical and metaphysical wandering by seizing yet peacefully dissolving the psychosomatic tension that situates him in the world.

On the one hand, this change to his being is not in itself threatening, since Adam's experience of it accords harmoniously with the ecological surroundings and material processes that, up to this moment, are all he knows. Yet a subtle irritant affects him in his experience of waking life, and his use of the word "pensive" points to the powers of intellection as the culprit. They stem directly from Adam's turn toward himself, which gives rise to a question that his creation is in fact meant to answer: What is this "I" with which I peruse myself, or from another angle, the self whose perceptive capacities rise to such a degree of clarity that they turn back upon their apparent source with such a curious and individuating gaze? Adam, that is, repeats Satan's selfish turn but with a difference, as sleep immediately releases him from the subtle worry prompted by this moment of unknowing intellection before it can rise to the passionate pitch of fallen care. Instead, sleep prepares Adam for a dream in which God leads him to his "mansion" in the "garden of bliss" (8.296–299). Upon being "stirred" by a sudden appetite to eat the fruit that appears to him in the dream, Adam awakens to find "all real as the dream / Had lively shadowed" (8.308–311). Interestingly, however, Adam tells Raphael that his first impulse on reawakening would have led him to begin anew his wandering, "had not He who was my guide / Up hither from among the trees appeared, / Presence Divine" (8.312–314). Adam's natural, lively impulse to wander would continue endlessly, moving from waking life to dream and back again, without the arresting presence of God. The result of the first man's sleep is thus a therapeutic and divine repairing of the subtle impulses of distress, as Adam returns to wakefulness in the garden but is now face-to-face with his creator, ready to be given secure knowledge as revelation of his origin and the boundaries of his being.

Adam again falls asleep during the extraction of his rib, but he identifies the cause of this second slumber to be the taxing nature of his sensorial and discursive encounter with God: "In that celestial colloquy sublime / As with an object that excels the sense, / Dazzled and spent, sunk down, and sought repair / Of sleep which instantly fell on me, called / By nature as in aid, and closed mine eyes" (8.455–459). Adam's being is less perfect than that of the angels, and so his sleep is a necessary form of physical and sensorial restoration by nature. But Adam's sleep here not only repairs his individual body in its capacities for sensation and discursive reason; it also creatively repairs the absence or gap that he tells God he feels without a companion to match his particular form of "social communication" (8.429), since his sleeping body provides the material for Eve's making out of a physical wound. Adam's care for himself is to be balanced by his care for Eve, which is also God's means of addressing the sense of unease that overtakes Adam when he turns to peruse the nature of his own body and wonders from what cause he "first drew air" (8.284). Eve will help Adam maintain a sufficient eye on God and a concern for the ends that are proper to his being as an "I," since their union in mutual care is a counterbalancing measure against the overly selfish turn that care can take for them both.

Adam is thus "overjoyed" upon awakening and seeing that Eve is real, and he speaks to the subtle chain of God's repair of Satan's turn by proclaiming, "This turn hath made amends" (8.491). Earlier, Eve describes her own awakening and ambivalent fall into Adam's embrace through a corporeal and affective tension that first causes her to turn from herself toward Adam, and which anticipates the first man's description of his first encounter with sleep, as if their pairing were itself a manner of soft yet necessary constraint to the care of each other: "With that thy gentle hand / Seized mine, I yielded" (4.488–489). Through His creation of Adam and Eve alike, God turns Satan's turn into works that mend the privation of selfishness by virtue of both the beneficial forms of care that sustain their mutual oikeiôsis and the daily labors that call for their secure nocturnal rest. As Adam explains, "God hath set / Labor and rest as day and night to men / Successive. . . . Other creatures all day long / Rove idle unemployed and less need rest. / Man hath his daily work of body or mind" (4.612–618). The vital role of sleep in both the physical process of Adam and Eve's creation and in their ongoing life together further confirms insomnia as the fundamental figure for selfishness and the privations of fallen care—a figure introduced to Milton's cosmos by Lucifer's insomniac turn into Satan.

To return to that scene and its deeper implications, Lucifer's sleepless separation from the slumbering angelic organism causes Satan to emerge in name and being as a creature who aims to deprive. It therefore marks the negative genesis of evil in Milton's cosmos. Critics have long discussed the scene of Heaven's twilight with respect to Lucifer's gathering of the rebellious angels in Heaven and the event of the Fall, but no one has made such an explicit connection between the origin of evil and Satan's insomnia—which is essential to grasping Milton's depictions of evil as privation both here and throughout the poem.[61] In the passage spoken by the voice of Raphael, Milton's line break falls between "waked" and "Satan (so call him now: his former name / Is heard no more in Heav'n)" (5.657–658). This poetic turning calls attention to Satan's insomnia because it is the precise moment at which his individual being appears as such, newly modulated by a will to perversion that turns endlessly from the good. Lucifer's insomniac soul is twisted and agitated, incapable of the beneficial relaxation that sleep affords through the harmonizing motions of divine care. His sleeplessness thus opens a gap that is doubly marked by the verse's turn and by the sudden absence of the name of Lucifer that will no longer be heard in the sensorium of Heaven. In this illicit wakefulness, Satan stands apart not only from the angels who sleep and sing in harmony with God but also from the flawless watch of the deity's perpetually unsleeping eyes.[62] Satan chooses to wake and to plot, while the rest of Heaven slumbers under the care of God, dwelling within the organic unity and oikeiôsis of His creation.

Yet Satan's insomnia is also compelling from a metaphysical perspective: it is the action in which the deprivation of sin first appears. Pushing off from Stephen Fallon's ingenious explanation of Milton's ontology of evil, if sin is understood as evil, it lacks substance, because sin is nothing more than a privation of goodness.[63] This position would seem to contradict Milton's account of habitus and privation in *Art of Logic* when he writes, "I would also not call sin a privation; because if this or that is a sin or a vice it is not a privation."[64] Yet as Fallon notes, Milton's point here is that the privation of goodness must inhere within a particular action as it veers from God. The action itself is something; yet insofar as it sinfully negates a telos otherwise aiming at a good, metaphysically speaking it is an instance of privation and therefore evil.[65] I would expand upon Fallon's point by noting that in his discussion of privatives, Milton also constructs a hierarchy of difference that ranks privatives first in a descending order of disagreement, followed by "adverse things," then "contradictories," and finally "relatives." Milton explains this hierarchy as follows: "Adverse things are indeed oppositely adverse, but not in such a way that they cannot be mingled; but privatives admit of no mixture, and privation is usually the removal and elimination, or at least deficiency, of *habitus*."[66] These remarks are helpful in situating Satan's insomnia, especially since Milton argues that the prefix "in" does not "always signify privation, but often an adverse *habitus*."[67] We might therefore be tempted to read Satan's insomnia as an instance of adverse habitus rather than deprivation. Yet I think that misses something essential to Milton's imaginative rendering of Satanic insomnia and its cosmic aftermath. Wakefulness is naturally part of the angelic habitus, as is sleep, and so it constitutes what Milton would call an adverse habitus with regard to sleep. After all, angels both sleep and wake by nature, and alternation between these states admits of mixture or in-between states, as we have already seen. Moreover, such alternation is pleasing to God and his creatures alike as the "change delectable" that is inherent to the vital processes of creation. Far from constituting evil, mixtures of adverse habitus seem necessary in engendering the aesthetic pleasures of Heaven and the cycles of life that affirm creation. But insomnia, which should be understood here as a deprivation of the natural habitus of sleep, is another matter. Satan's perverse watch perfectly figures the metaphysics and ontology of evil because his wakeful turning from God is the action through which a condition of deprivation suddenly appears in the guise of insomnia. It turns from the good embodied by the habitus of Godly sleep and constitutes a deficient mode of wakefulness as deprivation—rather than an adverse habitus—that figures the cosmic origin of evil.[68]

Through his deviant insomnia, Satan inaugurates a dialectic of mutual privation with Beelzebub, in antipathy to the good. Satan stirs his bedfellow Beelzebub by asking,

> Sleep'st thou, companion dear? What sleep can close
> Thy eyelids? And remember'st what decree
> Of yesterday so late hath passed the lips
> Of Heav'n's Almighty? Thou to me thy thoughts
> Wast wont, I mine to thee wast wont t'impart:
> Both waking we were one. How then can now
> Thy sleep dissent?
> (5.673–679)

Satan nefariously contrasts Beelzebub's sleep with the pair's earlier waking and sensing of an unspoken unity in opposition to God's anointing of the Son. His rhetorical strategy is that of a wounded lover, who deploys passion as a means of cultivating Beelzebub's favor.[69] Satan maintains that Beelzebub's slumber divides him from his "companion dear," and constitutes an infidelity through privation of the affective and sensorial bonds that unite them. By drawing his cohort into the orbit of his waking affections while the rest of Heaven slumbers, Satan subverts the structure of care that underpins angelic sleep. He accuses his bedfellow of no longer caring for him and for their union by virtue of sleep's "dissent"—a hissing etymological play on the severing of the sense that bound them to one another during the waking day. Satan's complaint thus perversely recasts the true betrayal being brought on by the false angel's speech, whose physical effects we are told "infused / Bad influence into th'unwary breast / Of his associate" (5.695–696). Milton's image of fiendish influence deploys early modern physiological associations of sleep with an airy fluidity that encourages ethical and spiritual slackness as well as sentient lapse. And just as the proper path of Stoic oikeiôsis can be corrupted by the perverse instruction of one's associates, Satan's influence in this passage is figured as a rerouting of the breath that inspires the organic unity of slumbering and singing angels, and which constitutes the natural starting point of their habitus. If evil is a privation or turning away from God and the angelic habitus of sleep, then here that turn is facilitated by sleep's slackening effects of pneumatic dispersion. Satan's wakefulness thus also constitutes an aspiration to the perfection of God's perpetual watch caused by Lucifer's prideful care, which in turn causes the emergence of Satan's name, as indicated by Milton's turn in verse and the sudden absence of Lucifer's being.[70]

By pivoting from beneficial slackness to malicious dissent, Satan's turn from God begins to grow a countercommunity of negative attachments and bad feelings—a community of fallen care that is more fully realized in the scene of demonic awakening in Hell, where the transformed bodies of Heaven's rebels are newly saturated by the agonies of endlessly waking cares. Appropriately, for the newly transformed Satan and those angels who choose to follow him, their natural capacity for goodness will now lie forever dormant. But before turning to that moment in Milton's poem, I want to linger on some of the key elements conspiring in Satan's turn from God; more particularly, his hissing influence and the act of dissent vis-à-vis my earlier claim that the fiend's insomnia emerges from a backdrop of unified organic life infused by the pneuma-like exhalations from God's holy mount. In *Christian Doctrine*, Milton argues that in the "sacred books" of scripture the "word Spirit" means "either the breath of life which we take in, or the vital or sensitive or rational faculty, or some action or affection belonging to them."[71] Milton's "ors" conjoin what is often held separate in ancient theories of the distinct forms of psyche defining plant, animal, and human life. This point has implications for understanding Milton's monism and his corporealist psychology of the human, since the soul and the body are not two distinct elements but rather a single unity that is the human, "a body or substance which is individual, animated, sensitive, and rational."[72] For Fallon, this passage reflects an "Aristotelian hylomorphism" according to which the soul is the form of the body. Yet he also observes that Milton's conviction that the rational soul is no different in kind from the other two categories into which Aristotle divides psyche—vegetative and sensitive—is at odds with the view espoused by "the great Christian Aristotelian Thomas Aquinas."[73] The difference between them is, I think, best explained by the influence of Stoic cosmology and its monism of substance, according to which all corporeal entities are caused by and composed of the same rational pneuma that distributes varying capacities of cohesion, growth, sense, and reason to the parts of the cosmos. Milton's affiliations with the Stoic theories of matter and pneuma as the vital force responsible for physical causation and creation thus become clearer, as they illuminate his conception of the vital, sensitive, and rational faculties that are functions of the same creative "breath of life" in its various capacities.[74] In that passage from *Christian Doctrine*, he goes on to describe the creation of Adam in Genesis as follows: "But that from that infused breath of life it was not something divine—part of the divine essence, as it were—that was imparted to man by God, but only something human, representing a fixed portion of divine virtue, you may learn most abundantly from other passages of Scripture. For he infused the breath of life even into the other animate creatures too."[75] Just as the Stoics argue the pneuma gives rise to matter and soul alike, Milton conceives of the life principle as a pneumatic power infusing organized bodies, which makes them variously capable of living, sensing, and reasoning for themselves; we should however note that Milton is at pains to clarify that this breath is not, strictly speaking, part of God's essence, nor is it to be understood as His actual breath. It is instead a potency given by God that is inherent to matter and the cause of free will in rational beings. This means that the life spirit can be deprived of its habitus, and that very possibility is what I argue is behind Milton's depiction of Satan's turn from the organic unity of heavenly sleep and his cultivation of a conspiratorial insomnia.

Accordingly, Satan's fall and his negative influence over a third of the angelic host anticipate the sensorial capture and pneumatology of sin in Milton's description of Eve's temptation by the serpent, which also emphasizes the play of an airy turning:

> Oft he bowed
> His turret crest and sleek enamelled neck,
> Fawning, and licked the ground wheron she trod.
> His gentle dumb expression turned at length
> The eye of Eve to mark his play. He, glad
> Of her attention gained, with serpent tongue
> Organic or impulse of vocal air
> His fraudulent temptation thus began.
> (9.528–531)

The turning seems at first to indicate a turn of the serpent's "gentle dumb expression" toward Eve, yet upon the verse's turn at "length" it becomes difficult to assign the previous line's action of turning solely to Satan. After all, Eve's eye itself turns—or is turned?—toward that gesture. The linearity of cause and effect is enfolded within a mutual turning of the serpent's body and Eve's eye, and the two gestures are themselves collapsed into the turning "length" of Milton's verse, whose movements mirror the spiraling corporeal folds of the serpent's body. Once Satan, inhabiting the serpent, has gladly captured Eve's visual attention, his tongue's influence begins its work of "organic or impulse of vocal air"—and Milton's metrical emphasis upon the syllabic "pulse" recreates the fiendish pulse of breath that nudges Eve's habitus along the path of perversion.[76]

This circular pneumatology of sin bears the same physiological and affective stamp of Satan's perverse watch and insomniac turn from God, even as it similarly collapses cause and effect into an occulted temporality in keeping with Milton's ontology of evil as privation. If evil began with an "impulse" to turn away, when exactly did that motion first occur? Here, too, Milton is likely thinking of Augustine's notion in *City of God* that "when the will relinquishes that which is superior to itself and turns to that which is inferior, it becomes evil not because that towards which it turns is evil, but because the turning itself is evil."[77] Satan's activity here and throughout the poem is a continually spiraling return of the turn from God, first figured as a sleepless dissent from the vital union of heavenly slumber. The scene of Satan's insomnia and its implication that the fiend perverts the harmonic processes of God's creation prepares us to see his influence across the poem as a discordant breath whose turning motions bring about further turnings toward selfishness, decay, and death. Hence, Sin's birth from Satan's head takes place during a "bold conspiracy" (2.751) or common breathing among Heaven's rebels, and Sin turns alluringly back toward Satan and captures his affections when he sees himself in her and acts on that impulse in the incestuous miscreation of Death: "Thyself in me thy perfect image viewing / Becam'st enamoured" (2.764–765).

While Satan's compulsive attraction to the image of himself that he sees in Sin derives from his original pride and perverse watchfulness, it also loosely resembles Eve's own propensity for visual captivation—a resemblance which has implications for his initially unsuccessful attempt to win Eve over in her sleep. As Eve relates the story of her own first awakening into life to Adam, she describes her earliest experience as one of visual captivation: "That day I oft remember when from sleep / I first awaked and found myself reposed / Under a shade on flow'rs, much wond'ring where / And what I was, whenever thither brought and how" (4.449–452). She is soon drawn to "look into the clear / Smooth lake" where she finds "answering looks / Of sympathy and love" so alluring she would have "fixed / Mine eyes till now and pined with vain desire" (4.458–466) were it not for God's intervening explanation that the creature Eve sees is herself. Milton clearly marks Eve's visual circuit here as one formed by "looks / Of sympathy and love" (4.465–466), so in that regard it is unlike Satan's prideful gaze of self-infatuation. But a tendency toward visual captivation is nonetheless present, and it returns when she later admits to Adam a certain reluctance to go to sleep at night. "But wherefore all night long shine these?" she asks; "For whom / This glorious sight when sleep hath shut all eyes?" (4.657–658). Adam goes on to reassure her that "Millions of spiritual creatures walk the earth / Unseen both when we wake and when we sleep" (4.677–678), providing more than ample praise for the glory of God's creation. Yet it would seem that Eve's proclivities for visual experience also inform Satan's strategy in his attempts to woo her. As she herself notes when describing her dream to Adam, the voice she heard encouraged her to resist sleep and wake instead by appealing to her visual sense:

> Now reigns full orbed the moon and with more pleasing light
> Shadowy sets off the face of things—in vain
> If none regard! Heav'n wakes with all his eyes
> Whom to behold but thee, Nature's desire,
> In whose sight all things joy with ravishment,
> Attracted by thy beauty still to gaze.
> (5.41–47)

The subtle yet decisive difference between the strange voice's directions and Eve's own wistful acknowledgment of the nocturnal glories of creation is that the former imagines all eyes being led to gaze back upon Eve herself. That is to say, Eve's relation of her dream confirms the Satanic aim delineated earlier, when Ithuriel and Zephon had found him "squat like a toad close at the ear" of the sleeping Eve. Milton describes the fiend's intention to "taint" with an

> inspiring venom . . . Th'animal spirits that from pure blood arise
> Like gentle breaths from rivers pure, thence raise
> At least distempered, discontented thoughts
> Vain hopes, vain aims, inordinate desires
> Blown up with high conceits engend'ring pride.
> (4.804–809)

Satan wants to inflate Eve's ego by infusing her soul with the venom of pride—a process that Milton imagines as a "dev'lish art" turning Eve's vital spirits from purity toward states of distemper and distortion, culminating in the sinful impulse of pride and a harmful turning toward the self. The circular pneumatology of sin thus displays clear traces of its origins in Satan's malignant watch during twilight in Heaven.

Such a manner of perverse influence even appears, somewhat paradoxically, to be working between Adam and Eve in the moment just before her fateful temptation occurs, when they debate Eve's proposal to "divide our labors" (9.214) and separate from each other. Eve's affect—"As one who loves and some unkindness meets" (9.271)—registers hurt at Adam's unwillingness to part, which Eve says implies a lack of "firmness" in her commitments to God and to Adam alike. Her spouse responds that Eve should not underestimate their enemy's "malice and false guile . . . [for] Subtle he needs must be who could seduce / Angels" (9.306–308). Adam's words unconsciously perform a subtle mimesis of the subtlety that he attributes to Satan, as he calls to readers' minds the scene of Beelzebub's seduction. His words take the shape of that moment, as the angel Raphael first related it to him:

> Nor think superfluous others' aid:
> I from the influence of thy looks receive
> Access in every virtue, in thy sight
> More wise, more watchful, stronger if need were
> Of outward strength while Shame, thou looking on
> (Shame to be overcome or overreached)
> Would utmost vigor raise and, raised, unite.
> Why shouldst not thou like sense within thee feel
> When I am present and thy trial choose

With me, best witness of thy virtue tried?
So spake domestic Adam in his care
And matrimonial love.
(9.308–319)

It is worth reading this passage alongside Satan's cultivation of antipathy toward God and his calling forth of a union in dissent with Beelzebub. By affirming an increase of watchfulness, wisdom, and strength from Eve's "influence," Adam both repeats Milton's key word for the negative detriment of Satan's fall and seemingly elaborates the extent of God's repair through the creation of the first couple and their matrimonial bond of interpersonal care. In other words, the passage further encourages my reading of their domestic affiliation, or oikeiôsis, and its affirmation as a site of regeneration that fixes the fault of Satan's perverse turn from the unity of slumbering care in Heaven. Adam becomes his best self, the self that cares most perfectly and virtuously, through attention to the care he takes while Eve is witness. Their domestic care, and Adam's participation in it, is the proper object of Eve's eye.

Or at least, that is what Adam would have Eve believe with his "superfluous" words. Perhaps the dissent between them already bears the taint of Satan's original turn from God and his perverse influence on Beelzebub, insofar as Adam's sense of shame at the idea of being outdone while Eve looks on is a spur that closely resembles the pride of selfishness.[78] Just as Satan accused his bedfellow of dissenting from the affective bonds of care uniting them, Adam charges Eve with not feeling a "like sense" of beneficial influence when he is present to her. But the care that Eve needs from Adam is not a showy display of how she makes him stronger, better, and more like God—those are of course Lucifer's selfish aspirations, and they seem to bear upon this moment too. By arguing against their separation for dubious and selfish reasons, Adam's mistaken care has a hand in Eve's fall. The better care is rather, as James Kuzner suggests, an affective union in shared vulnerability that also makes good on Adam and Eve's common claim to discursive reason, without presuming that the exercise of one capacity would mutually exclude the other.[79] These aspects of Adam and Eve's domestic care are part of their natural habitus, or in Stoic terms the oikeiôsis that is proper to them as rational creatures and which serves them in building their home in the world. It is appropriate that Adam describes the threat to this structure of care as a possible "swerve" from reason and natural teleology, resulting from the failure to keep "strictest watch" (9.359–363), though he too swerves from his responsibilities as a domestic partner to Eve when his care mimics Satan's perverse complaint to Beelzebub.

All Hell Is Awake

Adam's unconscious physical and linguistic mimicry returns us to the scene of original antipathy to God's care, which is inaugurated by Satan's perverse watch and expands into an ever-widening circle of inclusion among the angels who fall under his perverse influence. The first coconspirator to Satan's perversion and hissing dissent is his sleeping companion, Beelzebub, as I have already discussed. But the extent and consequences of their mutual turning is more fully realized by the infernal community of Milton's Hell. Turning to that scene in the first book of the poem, the demonic bodies of Hell are largely characterized by intersecting affects of astonishment and fatigue. Book 1 is a story of demonic awakening into endless restlessness, of the arrival into a world of feeling and thinking in a body whose "empyreal substance" is newly burdened by its baser mode of existence. The former angels are described as having denser, more oppressive bodies transformed by their fall. They are compared first to fallen leaves, then to uprooted plants, and finally to the "floating carcasses" (1.302–310) of Egyptian soldiers drowned in the Red Sea. This hierarchical movement from leaves to plants to soldiers' bodies seems to affirm the material continuity and reciprocity of all bodies, even these, in God's cosmos. Yet at the same time, the image captures the distraught and scattered condition of the fallen army, whose wretchedness is indexed to a newly Hellish physiology: "So thick bestrewn, / Abject and lost lay these, covering the flood, / Under amazement of their hideous change" (1.311–313). Their demonic awakening discloses a physical environment of intense suffering that grossly amplifies to the point of distorted pain the sensations of "lively vigor" that Adam describes upon first awakening into life. Satan's face physically reflects this newfound condition, where "deep scars of Thunder had intrencht, and care / Sat on his faded cheek" (1.600–602). Stephen Fallon reads the care on Satan's brow as evidence of an increasing loss of angelic "ductility," and a sign of the "advanced congealing" of Satan's animate body.[80] Fallon's insight also suggests that the weight of care increases along with the further materialization of living substance—in turn making the benefits of affective recovery and release from care afforded by sleep all the more alluring to denizens of Hell. In Milton's cosmos, the burden of living matter is synonymous with care, and we see the mutual intensification of both substances in book 1, even as demonic being is decisively removed from the vital benefit of sleep.

This is why the fallen angels' debate in book 2 concerns above all how best to manage the newfound weight and seemingly endless pain of fallen care. Satan begins this discussion by asserting that their newly acquired pain is in fact a kind of ethical and political boon to the rebel angels because it will serve them as the negative basis for a community of sufferers who all seek to minimize rather than accumulate shares in their newly inherited kingdom. Unlike the "happier state / In Heaven which follows dignity [and therefore] might draw / Envy from each inferior" (2.24–26), Hell's endless pain encourages none to seek a greater portion of this perverse value. And thus, Satan reasons, there will be no source of "strife" or "faction" but rather an "advantage then / To union and firm faith and firm accord, / More than can be in Heav'n" (2.31–37). He then asks his cohorts how best to respond to their lot. Moloch proposes perpetual war even at the risk of death, wanting to be equal in stature to God, and "rather than be less / Cared not to be at all. With that care lost / Went all his fear" (2.47–49). Better to rage and risk utter annihilation, Moloch argues, since they are already in the worst state possible. Even if God unleashes his "utmost ire," it will "quite consume us" and reduce the crew to nothing, thereby erasing their pain and ending what would otherwise be perpetual suffering. But Belial counsels against Moloch's strategy, arguing that the demons ought not risk destruction. "For who would lose, / Though full of pain, this intellectual being . . . To perish rather, swallowed up and lost / In the wide womb of uncreated night / Devoid of sense and motion?" (2.146–151). Belial thus recognizes the inherent value of intellectual activity and sensation, as well as what he falsely characterizes as the liberty to move about freely. He goes on to describe Moloch's misguided inclination as a death fantasy that the almighty will in no way bring about: God would never willingly end the punishment that he has decided must fit their crime. Instead, Belial suggests that the group might grow accustomed to their new domain, "And void of pain / This horror will grow mild, this darkness light . . . If we procure not to ourselves more woe" (2.219–225). The former angels just want to feel better, and Belial surmises they might transform their care into a more palatable form as they become habituated to the newly adverse mixtures of suffering. If anything, Belial guesses, their further meddling might only cause them more pain by stirring God's wrath yet again. He therefore counsels "ignoble ease and peaceful sloth" (2.226–228) rather than action. To this plan of slothful inaction resembling the laxity of sleep, Mammon responds with yet another scheme. "We can create and in what place so'er / Thrive under evil and work ease out of pain / Through labor and endurance" (2.260–262). Mammon guesses that through activity, not inaction, the troop might build a world to inhabit. In turn, he suggests, "Our torments also may in length of time / Become our elements, these piercing fires / As soft as now severe, our temper changed / Into their temper, which must needs remove / The sensible of pain" (2.274–278). There's a misguided trajectory to all these strategies as they move from Moloch's desire to actively clash with God's external power, to Belial's slothful "sit and do nothing," to Mammon's folding of power back upon self and environment in the form of labor that looks to create another world. Wrath, sloth, and pride are all apparent in these tactics, but in each case the desired outcome is a release from the ruin of "public care" (2.303) that we are told rests upon Beelzebub's brow and which discloses the affective core of Milton's infernal community.

Yet Moloch's, Belial's, and Mammon's doubtful articulations of an end to care—by utter negation of death, slothful metamorphosis of pain, or finally, through hard labor—all show that the demons' fate is simply to endure their torment without reprieve, to watch and feel the heightened tension of their care for an eternity without the slackening release of sleep. The benefit of sleep has been eliminated from the fallen angels' habitus, forcing them to embody and embrace the agony of perpetual activity. They have come to their senses only to realize that Hell is the waking nightmare of the illusory freedom for which they fought, constraining them to experience perverse manifestations of movement, feeling, and sensation without end. These "irksome hours" (2.526) take many forms: for some, a "Typhoean rage . . . [and] wild uproar" that Milton compares to the agony of Hercules who "felt th'envenomed robe and tore / Through pain up by the roots Thessalian pines" (2.539–544); for others, endless wakefulness is an occasion to exercise their "intellectual being" and, confirming Belial's sense of its value, temporarily lose themselves in "wand'ring mazes" of metaphysical pleasures that "with a pleasing sorcery could charm / Pain for a while, or anguish, and excite / Fallacious hope" (2.566–568). But even if the demons manage for a brief spell to tame their sense of pain by substituting a stronger affect for it, this is not the same as being released from their fallen care—that is a condition which only sleep could temporarily afford them, and which God has seen to fit to withdraw in his punishment for their disunion.

Another band of demons seems to realize this truth once Satan has departed, and they look to drink from the river of Lethe, "To lose / In sweet forgetfulness all pain and woe / All in one moment" (2.607–609). Yet they, too, are barred from this attempted release by Medusa's vigilant guard and by the fact that the water itself actively flies from their lips. Even the landscape of Milton's Hell serves as caretaker of the astonished and perpetual fatigue allotted to these newly transformed wanderers:

Thus roving on
In confused march forlorn th'advent'rous bands
With shudd'ring horror pale and eyes aghast
Viewed first their lamentable lot and found
No rest.
(2.614–618)

Perpetual pain, hypervigilant torment, and "eyes aghast" forever—as a perverse mimicry of God's eternal and uninterrupted watch, the sensorial environs of Hell render the demons "equal" to the almighty insofar as they, like him, are now incapable of sleep and must embody a constant care. It is a realm without rest, a hard oppression whose affective baseline is the steady psychosomatic tension of suffering. Reading back to these events of books 1 and 2 after hearing Raphael's account of the angel's holy slumber and God's perpetual watch in Heaven, we can see that Milton subtly figures damnation as an endless exclusion from the slackening release of sleep. Hell amplifies and extends to infinity, that is, the perversion of watch first constituted by Satan's turning away from the Godly community of sleepers in Heaven.

The Perverse Influence

Such images of demonic sleeplessness and endless psychosomatic tension resonate with the situation Adam and Eve face after their own fateful decision to eat from the tree of knowledge. Along with the cosmic shock expressed by Earth's wound and Nature's sigh, Eve's care is fundamentally perverted by her consumption of the fruit. She promises the tree that "henceforth my early care / Not without song each morning and due praise, / Shall tend thee" (9.799–801), which disrupts the cycle of daily prayer that each morning honors and reaffirms the first couple's recognition of their first awakening into life by the virtues of divine creation. Fallen care now comes to define life for humankind as Milton goes on to depict the swiftly ensuing consequences of their transgression in terms that closely resemble the sensational torment and affective shock experienced by Satan and company after their ejection from Heaven. This is especially evident when, after gorging herself on the forbidden fruit and delivering her misguided prayer, Eve approaches Adam to relay her story. Its effects are immediate:

> Adam, soon as he heard
> The fatal trespass done by Eve, amazed,
> Astonied stood and blank while horror chill
> Ran through his veins and all his joints relaxed.
> From his slack hand the garland wreathed for Eve
> Down dropped and all the faded roses shed.
> (9.890–893)

Milton's description suggests the recirculation of a fallen affect that mimics the astonished shock and amazement felt by the fallen angels upon first awakening in Hell. Yet this suspended animation also causes Adam to experience a physiological slackening, since "all his joints relaxed" and his "slack hand" drops the garland he has been making for Eve, a symbol of flourishing husbandry—by which I mean a symbol of Adam's nuptial care for Eve and of their mutual care for the garden that belongs to their oikeiôsis. I am somewhat unsure what to make of the fact that Adam's body at this moment seems to enfold sensorial shock and astonishment—a kind of perceptive tightening—with slackness. Perhaps Milton means to suggest that because Adam hasn't yet actually eaten the fruit, he is poised on the edge of his fall, and these mixed affects pull him in different directions at once. It is as if Adam's body unconsciously manifests, for one last time, the relaxing slackness of an unperverted mind whose foundation rests upon Godly care and proffers sleep under His watchful protection. Or, this psychosomatic relaxation could be a rippling echo and intensification of the "effeminate slackness" exhibited in his decision to let Eve wander, for which Michael will later rebuke him as the starting point of their Fall. The image also returns us to the Stoic theory of *tonos* as the natural foundation of physical vitality, sentience, and even reason, whose prelapsarian incarnations Adam is about to shed from his being. As Sharon Achinstein notes, Milton's description of Adam's astonishment is "represented as a momentary collapse of bodily vitality," so the relaxation of his joints anticipates the unleashing into human life of what the Stoics view as the total relaxation of all psychosomatic tension: death.[81]

Hence, once Adam actively chooses to follow Eve in eating the fruit, the two immediately copulate and fall into an unhealthy slumber that Milton describes as a "dewy sleep / [that] Oppressed them," both "grosser" and "bred of unkindly fumes" that threaten rather than restore their physical life (9.1044–1049). Just as the fallen angels' bodies take on a denser, grosser kind of material substance, Adam and Eve's postlapsarian sleeping bodies take on the simultaneously material and metaphysical weight of an adverse mixture that makes sleep into a dewier sort of oppression. Garrett Sullivan Jr. describes this shift to grosser sleep as a sign that Adam and Eve's physical embodiment has likewise shifted downward along the hierarchy of natural life and matter articulated by Raphael. As he writes, "Sleep not only plays a part in the human drama of the Fall, but in the broader ontological, concoctive, and vital drama outlined by Raphael."[82] This unrefreshing and grosser form of sleep is thus heavy with the form of care that burdens the soul, causing them to arise the next morning "as from unrest" (9.1052), even wearier than at the close of the previous day's events. And Milton's choice of a literary icon to figure their newly transformed and "darkened" state upon awakening is the "Herculean Samson":

> Each the other viewing
> Soon found their eyes how opened and their minds

How darkened. Innocence that as a veil
Had shadowed them from knowing ill was gone,
Just Confidence and Native Righteousness
And Honor from about them, naked left
To guilty Shame: he covered but his robe
Uncovered more. So rose the Danite strong,
Herculean Samson, from the harlet-lap
Of Philistean Dalilah and waked
Shorn of his strength, they destitute and bare
Of all their virtue.
(9.1059–1063)

Adam and Eve's sleep is no longer a perfectly pitched restoration of the body after its daily activities, so their awakening into fallen life confirms a newly weakened, bare, and stripped condition of being.[83] Scenes of human awakening prior to this moment have revealed the natural impulses of life and beneficial care first bestowed upon humankind by Godly creation to be perfected through the blissful daily activities of life in Eden. But here Milton incorporates Seneca's figure of the tragic Hercules awakening into anagnorisis after annihilating the life and sustaining relations of his *oikos*. Just as the biblical Samson's locks of power are shorn and the Senecan Hercules's weapons stripped while both heroes sleep, Milton's first couple are deprived of their natural virtues and capacities to flourish with ease during their unhealthy slumber. Samson's locks and Hercules's club find their Miltonic originals in the cosmic precedent of Eve's hair—a metonymy for the human "innocence that as a veil / Had shadowed them from knowing ill," and which the poet describes in book 4 as a "veil" of "unadorned golden tresses" (4.304–305) that affirms both the relational virtues of domestic care and the first couple's state "with native honor clad / In naked majesty" (4.289–290). The first couple's natural attachment to beneficial care is physiological at its foundation, and that virtue in its unfallen state is honed as an outgrowth of their corporeally created natures—natures which they now have irrevocably altered.

Thus, when the Fall alters the material processes of life in *Paradise Lost*, Adam and Eve find themselves subjected to a newly volatile physical mixture that blends psychosomatic weakness, passion, and of course death with the vitalistic principles of creation.[84] This fundamental transformation in the natural virtues of earthly physis causes them to lose their secure attachment to what Milton describes in his *Apology for Smectymnus* as the form of reason that "the Stoics . . . call the Hegemonicon . . . the common Mercury conducting without error those that give themselves obediently to be led accordingly."[85] Adam and Eve are now vulnerable to an emotional volatility that Milton figures as an irrevocable disruption to the harmonious psychosomatic integration with their ecological habitation and an attenuation of the soul's ruling principle:

> Not only tears
> Rained at their eyes but high winds worse within
> Began to rise, high passions—anger, hate,
> Mistrust, suspicion, discord—and shook sore
> Their inward state of mind, calm region once
> And full of peace, now tossed and turbulent:
> For Understanding ruled not and the Will
> Heard not her lore, both in subjection now
> To sensual Appetite who from beneath
> Usurping over sov'reign Reason claimed
> Superior sway. From thus distempered breast
> Adam estranged in look and altered style
> Speech intermitted thus to Eve renewed.
> (9.1121–1133)

The discordant cosmic motions of the Fall move through their corporeal souls and transform the relations of care between them. It is, as Milton writes, an "estranged" and "altered" relationality that veers from the natural telos guiding life and care, becoming instead an echo of the fallen care that first appears with Satan's insomniac swerve from the sleeping unity of Heaven. It now takes shape as endless, "fruitless hours" of "mutual accusation" (9.1187–1188) in speech that rehearses in human form the drama of dissent and perverse influence by which Satan first implicates Beelzebub, and which continues in scenes of endlessly frustrated activity in Hell.

These echoes of fallen care in speech soon take cosmic shape as a pestilence of deprivation that preys upon fallen life when Sin appears in Paradise, "Once actual, now in body, and to dwell / Habitual habitant; behind her *Death* / Close following pace for pace" (10.585–589). Described as "dogs of Hell" and "wasteful furies" by God, both Sin and Death arrive to dwell as deprivations in the habitus of bodily life. Milton's description of the infernal couple evokes familiarly Senecan allegories of passion as an ecological disease that circulates through the volatile bodily mixtures of the cosmos, as does his elaboration of the Sun's response to this spread of sin: "At that tasted fruit / The sun as from Thyéstean banquet turned / His course intended" (10.687–689), while the "changes in the heav'ns, though slow, produced / Like change on sea and land, sideral blast, / Vapor and mist and exhalation hot, / Corrupt and pestilent" (10.692–695). The cosmic turning that marks Sin's entrance into the body of creation becomes the corrupt counterpart to the holy exhalations from God's mount in book 5. Given the close proximity of sin and insomnia first articulated by Satan's fall, it is no surprise that as this pestilent deprivation spreads, we also come to find Adam sitting in "gloomiest shade" and falling into a "troubled sea of passion tossed" (10.718) that wracks his soul with newfound cares. His despair soon turns to a fit of insomnia within the transformed nocturnal environs of the garden:

> Thus Adam to himself lamented loud
> Through the still night, not now as ere Man fell,
> Wholesome and cool and mild, but with black air
> Accompanied, with damps and dreadful gloom
> Which to his evil conscience represented
> All things with double terror.
> (10.845–850)

The Fall has transformed Adam's cosmological surroundings as well as his affective and physiological disposition, throwing him into afflictions of despair and insomnia—the archetypal condition of deprivation that marked Satan's break with Godly goodness. Gloom, chill, and darkness now dominate the night, and this material environment folds into Adam's nocturnal conscience of despair. The emphasis upon his isolation—lamenting loudly "to himself" while the surrounding night is unresponsively black and still—simultaneously underscores Adam's insomnia as a form of selfishness, by which his perverted mind doubles back on itself to augment its ambient sense of terror. Thus, when Eve approaches him with "soft words," seeking to attend therapeutically to his "fierce passion" (10.865), Adam responds by cursing her and refusing her gestures of matrimonial care.

Eve's insistent care for Adam, however, becomes the changed foundation of their domestic affiliation. For despite Adam's retreat into selfish, insomniac isolation, Eve takes on the posture of the suppliant, soliciting from him an awareness of their shared plight and a reminder that Adam is no fortress unto himself. Her prostration, which repeats in supplicatory form the physical lowering of sleep, becomes a crucial scene of repair to the care between them which then makes possible a new standing for each other.[86] "But rise," Adam encourages her, "let us no more contend, nor blame / Each other, blamed enough elsewhere, but strive / In offices of love how we may light'n / Each others burden in our share of woe" (10.958–961). While God's "timely care" (10.1057) has retreated from the garden, and its absence is felt in Adam and Eve's sudden inability to sleep and their ensuing dialogue of despair, Eve's supplication amid the transformed conditions of care nonetheless points the way toward renewal. As Adam indicates, the burdens of fallen care now appear as objects of the supportive domestic care that will give shape to the first couple's transformed oikeiôsis: they must learn to care for each other's care in their burdensome "share of woe."

A Regenerative Oikeiôsis and the Biopolitics of Care

The first couple will of course be rescued from eternal death by the sacrifice of the Son, but Milton makes it clear that they will no longer sleep the pure sleep or work the easy form of labor that dwelling in the garden once afforded them. Adam speaks unwittingly to this prelapsarian bliss and the shape of its loss in book 8, when he praises the "sweet of life from which / God hath bid dwell far off all anxious cares / And not molest us, unless we ourselves / Seek them with wand'ring thoughts and notions vain" (8.184–187). Adam and Eve were meant to care for the bower and the garden in which they dwelled, and for each other, but not for those things that God marked as beyond their being and thus inappropriate to their oikeiôsis—most centrally, of course, the Tree of Knowledge and all the anxious cares the consumption of its fruit brought into the compass of their affections. Thus when the angel Michael arrives to eject them from Eden, he proclaims, "To remove thee I am come / And send thee from the garden forth to till / The ground from whence thou wast taken, fitter soil" (11.261–262). Adam and Eve must now turn to agrarian toil and hard labor in the earth, leaving behind the effortless abundance that grows in the garden. But in a sense, Michael's words also mean that the ground they must now work is the ground of earth that forms the material self, by caring for their newly burdened bodies and all the unruly feelings and cares that accompany this hardened form of life. And in such a state, their only respite will come from a sleep whose regenerative powers have diminished in the face of these increased burdens of care.

Hence, Adam's response to the fate pronounced by Michael again reproduces the astonishment and sensorial constraint of the fallen angels in book 1, as well as his initial response to Eve's transgression: "For Adam at the news / Heart-strook with chilling gripe of sorrow stood / That all his senses bound" (11.263–265). This chilling suspension of sense binds Adam to the sorrow that flickers among the cold fires of Hell, and to the compulsory sensations of shock and pain that distinctively animate and constrain fallen care. In other words, the affective afterlife of Satan's fall reverberates through Eden, and its perverse influence will doggedly follow Adam and Eve into the uncertain life that awaits them in a world of anxious cares and fitful sleep. Just before this moment, we are privy to a conversation between God and his watchful guard showing that angelic care, too, has been transformed as a consequence of the Fall. It is no longer a form of beneficial protection embodied by the celestial creatures when they watch over sleep in Eden. The angels instead take a posture of vigilance "more wakeful" than that of Argus Panoptes, guarding against the first couple's return to the garden. In doing so, their care will preserve those "pure immortal elements" that must by God's natural law purge the "unharmonious mixture foul" (11.50–51) that Adam and Eve now embody. Newly blended with the malnourishment of the fruit, their corporeal souls are permanently tainted by the discordant signature of Satan's perverse influence. And yet here, too, God shall provide an antidote in the form a new physical mixture that promises repair: He commands Michael to reveal this promise to Adam, and to "intermix / My covenant in the woman's seed renewed" (11.115–116). Mortal life blends sin and grace in their transformed bodies and in all the human bodies that will follow, such that God's promise remains as a vital element thoroughly mixed with the decay of death. This mixture of sin and grace now defines the creaturely life of the body and demands a new sort of biopolitical care. The mortal body must be attended to in the physiological and vital impulses that precariously sustain it, but Adam and Eve must also care for the degenerative effects of sin that inhere within and weigh upon them as so many physiological and ethical burdens of care.

These and other lessons must be learned both in waking discourse and through revelation in sleep. But while Eve's eyes are drenched so that she falls asleep at the foot of the hill, Michael applies drops that bring Adam into a trance conducive to prophetic clarity to be delivered on the ascent. The scene thus repeats while repairing the structure of harmoniously slumbering care and watchfulness in Heaven, with Eve playing the part of the angelic organism at rest and Adam in a wakeful trance, both partaking in the power of a regenerative and revelatory somnolence. But Eve's sleep is significant too insofar as the seed of restoration she carries is itself a slumbering yet vital presence in her corporeal being, one whose transmission is essential to the process of God's cosmic repair. Because this presence sleeps, it cannot yet be actualized in the mortal conditions of waking life—such is not possible for the transformed habitus of a life deprived by sin yet which nonetheless contains the sleeping seed of its salvation. The poem appropriately concludes with a scene of renewed awakening that affirms a Christian oikeiôsis in which domestic affiliation and care are newly burdensome endeavors yet also cultivate a "seed to come" (12.600) that promises full restoration upon the day of its eventual awakening. Thus, upon her own awakening from a sleep that is once again restorative and regenerative, Eve remarks:

> God is also in sleep and dreams advise
> Which he hath sent propitious, some great good
> Presaging, since with sorrow and heart's distress
> Wearied I fell asleep. But now lead on . . .
> By me the promised seed shall all restore.
> (12.609–623)

As Joshua R. Held argues, Eve speaks as a lover in this passage, offering Adam a sonnet in blank verse that mitigates their mutual loss of Eden by affirming the "couple's regained unity" and assuring him of the "Promis'd seed" of restoration she contains within.[87] Eve's affirmation of domestic care and this future promise yet again repairs the breach opened in Heaven by Satan's gnawing, insomniac care, which had been further extended by Eve's transgression. But it is important that she speaks this sonnet immediately upon awakening from a slumber that restores rather than further corrupts her changed physiology, thereby corroborating the slumbering yet ultimately regenerating power of the redemptive seed that lives within her. The moment also repairs the earlier scene of her awakening into the distempered state of the "Herculean Samson," restoring sleep itself by reaffirming its place in the habitus of human life and in the ongoing poetics of Godly creation and care. Thus, when Michael explains to Adam that caritas will become the paradigm of Christian virtue and soul "of all the rest" (12.585), while Eve reminds him that "God is also in sleep" (12.611), Adam's visionary, vertical ascent and Eve's holy, horizontal posture form a crux suggesting the shape of God's grace to come will involve both the active labors of Christian charity and the restorative powers of a somnolence that works in mysterious and even revelatory ways—including the illuminations of the "sovereign vital lamp" (3.22) that Milton himself feels, and the actions of the holy Muse that visits his "slumbers nightly" (7.29) to guide him safely through the perils of composing his Christian epic.[88]

In an oft-cited passage from *Areopagitica*, Milton describes the reality of fallen life as a thoroughgoing mixture that demands our most careful attention: "Good and evil we know in the field of this World grow up together almost inseparably; and the knowledge of good is so involv'd and interwoven with the knowledge of evill, and so many cunning resemblances hardly to be discern'd, that those confused seeds which were impos'd on *Pscyhe* as an incessant labor to cull out and sort asunder, were not more intermixt."[89] With so many "cunning resemblances" between good and evil, fallen life is like the "confused" heap of seeds that Venus thrust upon Psyche and demanded she sort as punishment for her erotic transgressions with Cupid. The despair-inducing, "incessant labor" of sifting good from bad, of caring properly for care amid the thoroughly turbulent mixtures of a fallen cosmos, is a burden familiar to Milton in both its Renaissance humanist and classically Stoic forms. In *Paradise Lost*, he gives us a poetic myth of its origins with Satan's insomniac care and its depriving influence as it circulates through God's creation and comes to inhabit the physical foundations of human life and its attachment to virtue. The early books' vision of life that flourishes naturally according to reason becomes a form of life that can only approach the virtues of flourishing imperfectly, and through the expenditures of toilsome care whose perverse apotheosis is the deprivation of insomnia. Yet despite the introduction of such fallen care to the cosmos, Milton's vision of a Christian grace to come also preserves a distinctive, even sacred role for sleep. He lends a special value to the unconsciously restorative and regenerative motions that care for life through a vital process that is curiously untethered to the voluntary will or intentionality of human consciousness, and which acknowledges the ongoing work of regenerative creation and subtle repair that ultimately belongs to God. Thus, as the circle of angelic care—now protecting the garden with "dreadful faces" and "fiery arms" (12.644)—thrusts Adam and Eve beyond its circumference, it is holy rest which takes pride of place in the first couple's newfound orientation: "The world was all before them, where to choose / Their place of rest, and Providence their guide" (12.646–647).

Coda

A Vital Rationality

This book has shown how changes in attention to sleep during the early modern period register both the waning force of political theologies of vigilant care and a mounting interest in the subtle physiology of corporeal life. Through the protagonist's dramatic encounters with sleep and insomnia at the center of Jasper Heywood's translation of Seneca's *Hercules Furens*, and in Shakespeare's tragic depictions of the physical life of sleeping sovereigns, we have seen a Stoic-inspired emphasis on transformative physical mixtures that seem to threaten the stability of ethical and political norms central to the care for embodied life. Yet despite entertaining these associations, both Heywood and Shakespeare find within the subtle physiology of sleep a form of restorative solace and renewal whose cosmological implications thwart long-standing philosophical, political-theological, and humanist wisdom aligning sleep with ethical and spiritual carelessness. From these dramatic scenes of sleep and insomnia—and their place in a lesser-known literary tradition of the somnolent Hercules—we moved to Spenser's and Milton's epic poetry to consider the close-knit relationship that both writers imagine between sleep and the ethics of care. Spenser's conceptions of the holy virtues of sleep and the ethics of watchful care determine the relationship between Redcrosse and Una and constitute an early modern variant of Stoic oikeiôsis—so, too, does Milton's notion of the means by which Adam and Eve actualize the virtues of their own domestic affiliation, as well as the recovery and consolidation of their physical life through sleep both before and after the Fall. Yet Milton's poem also represents a kind of paradigmatic realization of this book's central line of argument, in that it conceives the origin of cosmic evil as a pernicious lack that does not emerge through the physical transformations of sleep, but rather in the form of a gnawing, nocturnal care that prevents the salutary slackness of sleep and leads Satan to experience an archetypal moment of insomnia.

The story that *Vital Strife* has told thus places sleep and insomnia at the center of a significant transformation in the care for early modern life that is most visible through the political-theological, ethical, and scientific-cosmological registers of early modern corporeality. Care shapes and forms human life at its core, an idea that is present among various schools of ancient ethical thought but which is most pronounced among the Stoics, who construct a complex ethics of waking care yet also attribute a distinctive form of therapy to the corporeal soul's relaxation in rest. The Stoics thus play a central part in the early modern literary fascination with the paradoxes of care that define sleep and insomnia. In these final pages, I turn to two prominent seventeenth-century philosophers whose perspectives on the nature of corporeal life and care are best seen through the lens of sleep and its neo-Stoic resonances: René Descartes and Margaret Cavendish. The juxtaposition of these thinkers not only shows that sleep plays a central role in what each considers to be their major contributions to the domain of philosophy but also how in the case of Cavendish her systematic picture of nature as a living, rational whole appropriates Stoic principles in order to reject the Cartesian view of sleep as a space of confusion and uncertainty.

For Descartes, sleep is an epistemological and ethical dead end. It induces forms of confused thought and perception that can only lead us away from the clarity that confirms truths about the natural world, including the nature of corporeality. As he writes in the *Meditations on First Philosophy*, "Bodies are not strictly perceived by the senses or the faculty of imagination but by the intellect alone," and this awareness "derives not from their being touched or seen but from their being understood."[1] An intellect that understands is one that perceives clearly and distinctly. It is an intellect that knows the essence of things by maintaining a vigilant watch over itself while eschewing the inherently confusing sense perceptions that impair human understanding—an intellect that manifests care through constant attention to its own wakeful activity. Descartes thus establishes a basis for trust in the powers of the intellect insofar as it is fully alert, capable of discerning the nature of living bodies and—in the case of human beings—both the nature and the right use of the minds that inhabit them. For Descartes, of course, corporeality is in no way inherently disposed toward self-knowledge or care; it is simply the nature of *res extensa* to take a physical shape while lacking any inherent psychic capacity. Sensation is a mechanical effect of springlike motions in the body that direct the mind to form an idea, but the body is not in itself capable of such perceptual or intellectual activity. At the same time, Descartes does think that sensation is more or less reliable as a conduit of information about the environmental milieu that surrounds us and can either help or harm our efforts at well-being. In the sixth and final *Meditation*, he argues that even though bodily sensations are "confused modes of thinking" that result from the "intermingling of mind with the body," it is nonetheless evident that nature provides sensation for a purpose, which is "to inform the mind of what is beneficial or harmful for the composite of which the mind is a part; and to this extent they are sufficiently clear and distinct."[2] And in the concluding paragraph of the work, Descartes reveals the centrality of sleep to his account when he asserts that "I know that in matters regarding the well-being of the body, all my senses report the truth much more frequently than not. . . . This applies especially to the principal reason for doubt, namely my inability to distinguish between being asleep and being awake. For I now notice that there is a vast difference between the two, in that dreams are never linked by memory with all the other actions of life as waking experiences are."[3]

There are two points to be drawn from this Cartesian framework as they bear upon this book's animating concerns and its final juxtaposition of Descartes with Cavendish. The first is that Descartes's God has taken significant care in designing the mechanisms of nature such that bodily sensations serve this fairly reliable role, even though they are simply mechanical functions. God's careful design supplants the sort of teleological care that Cavendish, following the Stoics, conceives as an immanent feature of rational and sensitive matter in the cosmic whole. The second point is that for Descartes, unlike Cavendish, a certain continuity of waking perceptions disclosed to the intellect—when combined with the consolidating powers of memory—ultimately resolves the doubt about the distinction between sleep and wakefulness that motivates his entire inquiry. Physical nature does not itself sense, think, or care, but God's engineering allows us to establish the grounds of a new epistemology of waking vigilance in the care for clear and distinct ideas, which in turn rescues us from the skepticism of sleep. Like a range of thinkers before him from the ancient world to the early modern—including Plato, St. Paul, Augustine, and Erasmus—Descartes draws vigilance and virtue into a symbiotic relationship, though he transposes that coupling from its more familiar domains of spirituality and ethics into a primarily epistemological register by arguing that knowledge belongs solely to the intellect and its capacity to ascertain the essences of things by way of his new procedure. Sleep is still a threat, though more so to intellectual than bodily or spiritual integrity, and vigilant care is the guiding principle for a properly attentive intellect if it hopes to touch upon the true nature of things.[4] Meanwhile, the body's ultimate role is to sustain that process through its mechanical actions. As Steven Shapin notes, Descartes's musings on the body led him to a newfound fascination with longevity, and to the notion that ethics and medicine should serve essentially the same function, which is to promote scientific knowledge that prolongs our corporeal existence.[5] From one vantage, then, Descartes's thought epitomizes the early modern valuation of physical life that this book has tracked through images of sleep and insomnia by positing the extension of corporeal life as the anchoring value guiding medical science; but in another sense he departs from it by removing the sleeping body from any active participation in rationality or sense-making while valorizing the relation of an attentive mind to its own wakeful activity as the foundation of a new epistemology.

Cavendish, meanwhile, positions her views of sleep and corporeal activity in *Observations upon Experimental Philosophy* as a rebuttal to the central features of this Cartesian framework, in turn revealing the Stoic underpinning of her late philosophies of matter, sensation, and reason. More specifically, Cavendish radicalizes the Stoic view of nature as a living, rational whole by creatively reimagining the school's doctrines of oikeiôsis and ethical care. While the Stoics understand oikeiôsis to be an attribute limited to human and nonhuman animal life, Cavendish extends its central features to all forms of matter. Drawing on Thomas Stanley's account of Chrysippus and the "first appetite" of living creatures in *The History of Philosophy* (1656), she attributes an oikeiôsis-like disposition to each and every particle of matter within the living, rational whole of nature. Everything is made of a thorough "commixture" of rational, perceptive, and self-moving capacities that Cavendish argues are distributed throughout each and every part of the cosmos. Matter is familiar and dear to itself, inherently comprehending and caring for its own constitution as a way of belonging to the living cosmic whole. And for those bodies that experience sleep and wakefulness as naturally shifting conditions of their life, such foundational activities continue even during the deepest moments of slumber.

In the final chapter of her *Observations upon Experimental Philosophy*, Cavendish mentions her admiration for ancient philosophers and offers a series of detailed responses to doctrines associated with various figures and schools of ancient thought: Thales, Plato, Pythagoras, Epicurus, Aristotle, and a final section devoted to ideas culled from the Skeptics, Cyrenaics, and Academics.[6] Cavendish engages these thinkers not simply to illustrate her understanding of their distinctive positions but, more to the point, so as to clarify how her own thought differs from theirs, and thus provide her readers with "more intelligible and clear" opinions concerning "the truth in natural philosophy."[7] Given the argument I have pursued over the course of *Vital Strife*, what is most striking about Cavendish's survey of ancient thought is the conspicuous absence of the Stoics. But as Eileen O'Neill surmises in her introduction to the *Observations*, it's likely that Cavendish avoided mentioning the school precisely because of its deep affinities with her own conceptions of nature, vitality, and matter, which might have made her vulnerable to charges of unoriginality among uncharitable and mostly male philosophers. And such worries would not be unfounded: Henry More had already written to Anne Conway in response to some of Cavendish's earlier work, saying that the Duchess of Newcastle was likely "secure from anyone giving her the trouble of a reply."[8] To be clear, by placing aspects of Cavendish's thought in dialogue with ancient Stoicism, my aim is in no way to suggest that her tactically obscured relationship to the school makes her unoriginal. Rather, I think Cavendish elaborates in a radical and sophisticated manner the school's view of nature as a living, rational whole by creatively reimagining its doctrine of oikeiôsis.[9]

Cavendish would have found a wellspring of material on Stoicism when reading Stanley's *History of Philosophy*, the work that she mentions as a key source for her survey of the ancients at the end of her *Observations*. Stanley's volume collects over seven hundred pages of translated material from Diogenes Laertius's *Lives*, various works by Cicero, and other Latin and Greek fragments outlining principles of the ancient schools. The following passage appears at the beginning of chapter 3, "Of First Natural Appetite," in part 8 of Stanley's book, which is devoted to the Stoics:

> The first appetite of a living creature is to preserve itself, this being from the beginning proper to it by nature, as *Chrysippus* in his first Book of Ends, who affirms that the care [of] our selves, and the consciousness thereof, is the first property of all living Creatures. For, Nature producing a living creature, intended either to alienate it from it self, or to commend it unto its own care; but the first is not likely; it followeth therefore, that Nature commendeth to every thing the preservation of itself, whereby it repulseth whatsoever is hurtful, and pursuieth what is convenient.[10]

Here, Stanley's translation of Diogenes Laertius relates—without explicitly naming—the Stoic theory of oikeiôsis. He uses the language of care to articulate the nascent inclination that constitutes a foundational awareness of and concern for embodied life, and which he identifies, following Chrysippus, as the "first property of all living Creatures." Nature could not do otherwise, for to produce a living creature whose principal end was self-alienation makes no sense. Instead, creaturely life emerges from an embodied constitution that is immediately and persistently disposed to care for itself, and to seek out those things "convenient" to its flourishing while rejecting whatever is harmful to it.

Cavendish radically extends these and other features of living creatures into the material fabric of the cosmos itself in her *Observations*. Arguing that nature is an organic whole, "a self-moving, and consequently a self-living and self-knowing infinite body, divisible into infinite parts,"[11] she goes on to assert that both sensation and reason belong to all matter, and that these capacities serve as the necessary ground of any bodily action, motion, or causal change.[12] Just as the Stoics developed their theory of cosmic sympathy across all parts of the whole through an appeal to the notion of *krasis*, or total blending, Cavendish asserts that all matter is a thorough "commixture" of rational, sensitive, and gross kinds.[13] As she writes, "Nature is an infinite composition of rational, sensitive and inanimate matter; which although they do constitute but one body, because of their close and inseparable conjunction and commixture; nevertheless, they are several parts, (for one part is not another part) and therefore every part or particle of nature, consisting of the same commixture, cannot be single or indivisible."[14] For Cavendish, the blending of these three kinds of matter within each part is so thorough that any single part, no matter how small, is bound to contain them all.

If all matter senses and thinks to infinity within a single cosmic whole, how are we to understand the parts of nature and their individual actions as such? The Stoics ascribe an active principle of primary causation to the pneuma that infuses particular bodies and gives them a share of autonomy, though it is the same stuff as that which moves through all bodies situated within the web of causation that spreads across the universe. In the case of living creatures, the tensional motion of the pneuma grounds an innate understanding of their own constitution and serves as the basis of animal oikeiôsis. But Cavendish contends that every particular part of nature's infinite body—not simply animal bodies—is endowed with such an understanding of itself within its proper bounds, which in turn guides its actions based on the place it occupies within the whole:

> As infinite nature has an infinite self-motion and self-knowledge; so every part and particle has a particular and finite self-motion and self-knowledge, by which it knows itself, and its own actions, and perceives also other parts and actions; which latter is properly called perception; not as if there were two different principles of knowledge in every particular creature or part of nature; but they are two different acts of one

> and the same interior and inherent self-knowledge, which is a part of nature's infinite self-knowledge.[15]

Knowledge and perception, reason and sensation: these are "two different acts of one and the same interior and inherent self-knowledge" of matter, and these capacities are distributed across all material parts of nature. Nature encounters and comes to know itself through the rational sense shared among each of its parts, and this process describes the unified reality of nature's ongoing and "infinite self-understanding."

It is for this reason, as Cavendish goes on to argue, that she must reject the common view among philosophers that sleep is "a privation of the act of sense."[16] Sensation is rather an activity that continues, as she insists,

> without any rest. Neither do I think the senses can be lockt up in sleep; for, if they be self-moving, they cannot be shut up; it being as impossible to deprive self-motion of acting, as to destroy its nature; but if they have no self-motion, they need no locking up at all, because it would be their nature to rest, as being moveless. In short, sense being self-motion, can neither rest nor cease; for what they call cessation, is nothing else but an alteration of corporeal self-motion: and thus cessation will require as much a self-moving agent, as all other actions of nature.[17]

Sensation is unceasing in Cavendish's cosmos, even when bodies sleep, for all bodily activities are caused by the inherent and continuous agency of matter. While philosophers have long argued that sleep suspends perception and reason alike, for Cavendish it is nothing more than an "alteration" of the "corporeal self-motion" that she understands to be the principal cause that animates all matter. Just as the Stoics argue that sleep is simply a relaxing of the perceptive tension that constitutes bodily life, Cavendish sees sleep as merely a subtle shift in the corporeal figurative motions of sense and reason that are synonymous with causation. While a particular body's agency may ebb and flow with sleep, it is neither completely dissolved nor entirely "lockt up," insofar as that body continues sensing its place and exercising its inherent capacities for self-motion as an affirmation of its oikeiôsis-like belonging to the whole.

Margaret Cavendish thus elaborates a strikingly neo-Stoic conception of sleeping life and its teleological orientations in sharp contrast to René Descartes's notion of sleep as a domain of confusion and uncertainty. Descartes's crisp distinction between the operations of the careful intellect and the doubt-inducing space of sleep both draws on the long-standing connection between vigilance and virtue that *Vital Strife* has tracked from ancient to early modern worlds and reformulates it as the epistemological anchor and principal value of a new approach to knowledge and nature. The Cartesian body, meanwhile, concomitantly becomes the site of a new kind of ethical value that esteems those purely physical operations which ought to be promoted and extended for the sake of sustaining rational life as it strives to understand the world it encounters. This account is not to render judgment against Descartes about the consequences of his systematic picture of corporeality and rationality for our own world, but rather to show how that picture transposes core features of the relationship between sleep and ethical care that occupied poets and philosophers for centuries before him. Meanwhile, Cavendish offers another vision of such relations through her own account of corporeality and cosmic reason, which in turn rejects central elements of the system introduced by Descartes. The ancient Stoics articulate principles that are essential to her systematic picture of nature as rational, living whole, and to her notion of sleep as an activity during which the subtle figurative motions of corporeal matter continue to affirm a particular body's way of belonging to the cosmos. Sleep participates in a form of reason that reveals the latter's broader role in organizing and sustaining Cavendish's vitalist cosmos. Yet as I hope *Vital Strife* has shown, the Stoics and their distinctive view of sleep not only inform this picture but also hold an extraordinary—if underappreciated—place in broader histories of sleep and ethical care well beyond the early modern encounter between Descartes and Cavendish. It is a history worth reactivating, given our propensities for distraction, forgetting, and carelessness—even if, as the Stoics also remind us, we find ourselves at home in these and other forms of sleeping life, from time to time.

Notes

Introduction

1. Seneca, letter 121.17 (c. 65 AD). Seneca, *Letters on Ethics*, trans. Margaret Graver and A. A. Long (Chicago: University of Chicago Press, 2015), 487.

2. Several critics have noted that the English word "care" is etymologically derived from the old English *caru* or *caeru*, yet closely resembles the Latin *cura* both in form and meaning. While the *OED* asserts that the English "care" is in "no way related to the Latin *cura*," for early modern writers both the Latin and Old English etymologies converged in the English word "care" and its many ethically meaningful senses, which ranged from worry, grief, anxiety, and distress, to attentive concern, solicitude, nurture, and even love. On early modern confusion regarding the etymologies of "care," see Richard Hillyer, *Divided between Carelessness and Care: A Cultural History* (New York: Palgrave Macmillan, 2013), 21–36; Jeff Dolven, *Take Care* (New York: Cabinet Books, 2017), 27 and 53–54; and Sheiba Kian Kaufman, "Care," in *Entertaining the Idea: Shakespeare, Performance, and Philosophy*, ed. Lowell Gallagher, James Kearney, and Julia Reinhard Lupton (Toronto: University of Toronto Press, 2020), 115–131. On early modern care as a form of love that can also entail distress, see Joshua Scodel, *Excess and the Mean in Early Modern English Literature* (Princeton, NJ: Princeton University Press, 2002), 28–29.

3. The passage is spoken by Piso, Cicero's spokesman for the positions of his teacher, Antiochus of Ascalon in Cicero, *On Ends* 5.57, trans. H. Rackham, *Loeb Classical Library* 40 (Cambridge, MA: Harvard University Press, 1914), 459.

4. Erasmus, *Enchridion Militis Christiani: An English Version*, ed. Anne M. O'Donnell (Oxford: Oxford University Press, 1981), 32.

5. For an illuminating account of carelessness as an emotional and epistemological catalyst to early modern scientific understanding, see David Carroll Simon, *Light Without Heat: The Observational Mood from Bacon to Milton* (Ithaca, NY: Cornell University Press, 2018).

6. Gordon Teskey distinguishes between a classical Roman ideology of human life as "existence in the world" and a Christian ideology of human life as "existence in time," a difference made apparent by St. Paul's epistles and his allegorical figurations of sleep as death, which subordinate the mortal constraints of bodily life to the promise of an eternal life after death. See *Allegory and Violence* (Ithaca, NY: Cornell University Press, 1996), 51. On sleep and the Pauline epistles, see my discussion in chapter 1, under the section "Body, Flesh, Vigilance: Pastoral Care and the Political Theology of Sleep."

7. Rolf Soellner argues that early modern English writers took part in a widespread "*Hercules Furens* convention" that drew upon Seneca's play as well as other classical literary and philosophical sources associating Hercules with madness and melancholy, including Euripides's *Herakles* and Pseudo-Aristotle's *Problemata*. He also notes that Erasmus of Rotterdam's *Adages* refers to the *Herculanus morbus* and ascribes its cause to the hero's excessive labors and constant threats of Juno. See Rolf Soellner, "The Madness of Hercules and the Elizabethans," *Comparative Literature* 10, no. 4 (1958): 309–324.

8. On the history of the watch as a medieval form of urban security, and its role in *Hamlet*, see Rebecca Totaro, "Securing Sleep in *Hamlet*," *SEL Studies in English Literature 1500–1900* 50, no. 2 (Spring 2010): 407–426.

9. Refer to the entries for *insomnia* and *sleepless* in the *OED*.

10. Graham Hammill, *The Mosaic Constitution: Political Theology and Imagination from Machiavelli to Milton* (Chicago: University of Chicago Press, 2012), 3.

11. Margaret Cavendish, *Philosophical Fancies* (London: J. Martin and J. Allestrye, 1653), 12.

12. Margaret Cavendish, *Philosophical and Physical Opinions* (London: J. Martin and J. Allestrye, 1655), 30.

13. I am thinking in particular of Victoria Kahn's *The Future of Illusion: Political Theology and Early Modern Texts* (Chicago: University of Chicago Press, 2014) and its crystal-clear elaboration of a secular strand in early modern thought that rejects the illusions of political theology and places newfound value on the human capacity for metaphor and poetic creativity, stripped of any connection to divine transcendence or a supernatural origin.

14. John Rogers, *The Matter of Revolution: Science, Poetry, and Politics in the Age of Milton* (Ithaca, NY: Cornell University Press, 1996). For Rogers, "Vitalism . . . secured into the fabric of the physical world a general scheme of individual agency and decentralized organization that we can identify as protoliberalism" (12). By banishing at once the centralizing logic of Puritan providentialism and Royalist mechanism, Rogers argues, English vitalism opened a path to the liberal subject of modernity and clarified the concept of self-determining agency upon which it rests. My own argument suggests the extent to which Stoic vitalism and early modern literary adaptations of its core principles conceive the human as a self that is materially part of a whole, and whose autonomy is most clearly discerned upon recognizing its interconnections with others and with a broader living cosmos that is guided by an organizing and active principle of reason. Such a conception of rational selfhood discloses an ethics of care at odds with a protoliberalist notion of autonomy as a strictly bounded individualism, and instead articulates a vision of self-autonomy as a steadily dialectical negotiation with the motions of physical life that sustain each part of the cosmic whole.

15. See Emile Brehier, *The History of Philosophy: The Hellenistic and Roman Age* (Chicago: University of Chicago Press, 1971), 33, for the claim that Stoics developed a "vital cosmology." In making this point I am offering an addendum to Rogers's intellectual historical argument that attributes the foundations of English vitalist thought to Paracelsian philosophy. Rogers describes Paracelsus's doctrine of nature as a kind of materialist animism whose principles are entirely consistent with Stoic thought: "a truly bodily plenum that incorporated all that had been known as psyche and soul into the natural world of moving bodies," and which reintroduced "figures of reason

and sentience into the sphere of material processes" (10). As my discussion of Stoic cosmology across the introduction and chapters 1 and 2 will illustrate, these positions are thoroughly worked out and systematized by the ancient Stoics, and they deeply inform the literary and philosophical works of the Roman Stoic Seneca.

16. Key works comprising this Lucretian episode include Jonathan Goldberg, *The Seeds of Things: Theorizing Sexuality and Materiality in Renaissance Representations* (New York: Fordham University Press, 2009); Gerrard Passanante, *The Lucretian Renaissance: Philology and the Afterlife of Tradition* (Chicago: University of Chicago Press, 2011); David Norbrook, Stephen Harrison, and Phillip Hardie, eds., *Lucretius and the Early Modern* (London: Oxford University Press, 2015); and Ada Palmer, *Reading Lucretius in the Renaissance* (Cambridge, MA: Harvard University Press, 2014). The surge of critical interest in Lucretius's Epicurean poem has also led to scholarship tracking Epicurean atomist thinking beyond the early modern period and into modernity, including Amanda Jo Goldstein's *Sweet Science: Romantic Materialism and the New Logics of Life* (Chicago: University of Chicago Press, 2017), and Liza Blake and Jacques Lezra, eds., *Lucretius and Modernity* (London: Palgrave Macmillan, 2016).

17. Christopher Brooke's insightful history of Stoicism and political thought describes Stoic oikeiôsis as a "building block in the Stoics' fundamental argument *against* the Epicureans," who argued that pleasure is the first natural impulse of animal life and therefore its guiding principle. See *Philosophic Pride: Stoicism and Political Thought From Lipsius to Rousseau* (Princeton, NJ: Princeton University Press, 2012), 49. Wayne Martin also characterizes oikeiôsis as a theory developed in direct opposition to Epicurean principles in his essay "Stoic Transcendentalism and the Doctrine of *Oikeiôsis*," in *The Transcendental Turn*, ed. Gardner and Grist (Oxford: Oxford University Press, 2015), 342–368. These accounts are in part based on a passage in Diogenes Laertius describing oikeiôsis as follows: "They [the Stoics] say that an animal's first impulse is to preserve itself, because nature from the start makes the animal attached to itself . . . for in this way it repels what is harmful and pursues what is appropriate. What some people [Epicureans] say, namely that the primary impulse of animals has pleasure as its object, the Stoics claim is false. For they say that pleasure, if it is actually felt, is a by-product that arises only after nature, by itself, has sought and found what is suitable to the animal's constitution; it is in this way that animals frolic and plants bloom." Diogenes Laertius, *Lives of the Eminent Philosophers*, ed. James Miller, trans. Pamela Mensch (Oxford: Oxford University Press, 2018), 7.85–86, 343–344. On the theory of oikeiôsis as arising from fundamentally biological and medical considerations of organic life and assimilation, see Roberto Radice, *Oikeiôsis: ricerche sul fondamento del pensiero Stoico e sulla sua genesi* (Milan: Vita e Pensiero, 2000), 263–312.

18. Gail Kern Paster's *The Body Embarrassed: Drama and the Disciplines of Shame in Early Modern England* (Ithaca, NY: Cornell University Press, 1993) and *Humoring the Body: Emotions and the Shakespearean Stage* (Chicago: University of Chicago Press, 2004) represent one pole of recent approaches to corporeality and selfhood in early modern literary studies, which emphasizes the carnivalesque unruliness and unpredictability of bodily humors that escape efforts of self-control. Meanwhile, Michael Schoenfeldt's *Bodies and Selves in Early Modern England* (Cambridge: Cambridge University Press, 1999) stands at the other pole, drawing attention to early modern physiologies of digestion as enabling sites of disciplined yet empowering self-governance. For a shrewdly Nietzschean

argument regarding the affirmative power of the passions in early modern literature, and a critique of the so-called new humoralism advanced by Paster, Schoenfeldt, and others, see Richard Strier, *The Unrepentant Renaissance: From Petrarch to Shakespeare to Milton* (Chicago: University of Chicago Press, 2011).

19. Andrew Boorde, *A Compendyous Regyment or a Dyetary of Healthe* (London: Wyllyam Powell, 1567), 30.

20. Boorde, *A Compendyous Regyment*, 30–31.

21. William Vaughan, *Approved Directions for Health, Both Naturall and Artificial* (London, 1612), 58.

22. As Blanchard writes, "Seventeenth century physicians even recommended a 'sleep cure' for madness based on the period of unconsciousness experienced by Hercules before he regained his sanity. Such a period of oblivion they reasoned allowed the black bile that had ascended from the stomach to the brain to be breathed out." *Hercules: Scenes from a Heroic Life* (London: Granta: 2005), 60.

23. Vaughan, *Approved Directions for Health*, 60.

24. Sasha Handley, *Sleep in Early Modern England* (New Haven, CT: Yale University Press, 2016), 40.

25. See Foucault's claim that an "affirmation of the body" on the part of the bourgeoisie in turn "converted the blue blood of the nobles into a sound organism and a healthy sexuality." Michel Foucault, *The History of Sexuality, Volume 1: An Introduction* (New York: Vintage Books, 1990), 126.

26. Michel Foucault, *Security, Territory, Population: Lectures at the College de France, 1977–1978*, ed. Arnold Davidson, trans. Graham Burchell (New York: Palgrave Macmillan, 2007), 127.

27. Michel Foucault, *The History of Sexuality*, 143.

28. In this sense, my perspective on early modern sleep is amenable to the notion of an "affirmative biopolitics" articulated by a range of thinkers who elucidate the political capacities of natural life. Roberto Esposito's essay, "Community, Immunity, Biopolitics," *Angelekai* 18, no. 3 (2013): 83–90, provides a succinct account of his immunitarian theory and its relationship to the possibility of an affirmative biopolitics, which Esposito explores in greater detail in his trilogy, *Communitas* (Stanford, CA: Stanford University Press, 2009), *Bios* (Minneapolis: University of Minnesota Press, 2008), and *Immunitas* (Cambridge, UK: Polity, 2011). Perhaps closer in conceptual kin to my account of the normativity of early modern sleep, however, is Miguel Vatter's *The Republic of the Living: Biopolitics and the Critique of Civil Society* (New York: Fordham University Press, 2014). Vatter's account of civil society and biopolitics draws on a diverse range of republican political thinkers—including Machiavelli, Hegel, Marx, Spinoza, and Arendt—in arguing for a synthesis of natality and normativity. Vatter explores this dyadic relation as a site of resistance to the "normalization brought about by the government of life" and an affirmative biopolitics that reveals the "inner continuity between republican rule of law and commune-ist organization envisaged by the critics of civil society from Hegel and Marx through Arendt and Foucault" (Vatter 6).

29. Jen Rust's impressive review essay, "Political Theology and Shakespeare Studies," *Literature Compass* 6, no. 1 (2009): 175–190, provides a thorough accounting of early criticism (up to 2008) in early modern studies that makes use of Agamben's biopolitical theorization of the sovereign exception. More recent work that deploys Agam-

ben's conceptual schema linking biopolitics and sovereignty to states of exception includes Julia Lupton, *Thinking with Shakespeare: Essays on Politics and Life* (Chicago: University of Chicago Press, 2011); Julia Lupton and Graham Hammill, eds. *Political Theology and Early Modernity* (Chicago: University of Chicago Press, 2012); Daniel Cadman, "'The very nerves of state': Biopolitics and Sovereignty in Shakespeare's Vienna," in *Lectures de Measure for Measure de William Shakespeare*, ed. Delphine Lemonnier-Trexier and Guillame Winter (Rennes, FR: Presses Universitaires de Rennes, 2012); Daniel Juan Gil, *Shakespeare's Anti-politics: Sovereign Power and the Life of the Flesh* (New York: Palgrave Macmillan, 2013); Nichole Miller, *Violence and Grace: Exceptional Life between Shakespeare and Modernity* (Evanston, IL: Northwestern University Press, 2014); and Timothy A. Turner, "Othello on the Rack," *Journal for Early Modern Cultural Studies* 15, no. 3 (2015):102–136.

30. Giorgio Agamben, *Homo Sacer: Sovereign Power and Bare Life*, trans. Daniel Heller-Roazen (Stanford, CA: Stanford University Press, 1998), 140.

31. See Juila Reinhard Lupton, *Thinking with Shakespeare: Essays on Politics and Life* (Chicago: University of Chicago Press, 2011) and Garret Sullivan Jr., *Sleep, Romance, and Human Embodiment: Vitality from Spenser to Milton* (Cambridge: Cambridge University Press, 2012). In his account of sleeping life in early modernity, Sullivan argues that the inclusion of the Aristotelian nutritive soul in the life of humankind does not, for premodern writers at least, adhere to the conceptual caesurae that define Agamben's biopolitical machine and therefore guide his interpretation of Aristotle.

32. Lupton, *Thinking with Shakespeare*, 31.

33. Giorgio Agamben, *The Use of Bodies*, trans. Adam Kotsko (Stanford, CA: Stanford University Press, 2016), xx. Jonathan Crary has furthered our understanding of the biopolitics of sleeping life under late capitalism, and along with Eric Santner shows that in a contemporary world of incessant, "24/7" activity and "economic busyness," sleep has become something like a final horizon to the apparatuses that capture and direct life toward constant if somewhat mind-numbing forms of activity. See Crary, *24/7: Late Capitalism and the Ends of Sleep* (London: Verso, 2013) and Santner, *The Weight of All Flesh: On the Subject-Matter of Political Economy* (Oxford: Oxford University Press, 2015). There is a precapitalist history to the modern conditions that Crary and Santner diagnose, which *Vital Strife* helps to articulate.

34. Georges Canguilhem, *A Vital Rationalist: Selected Writings from Georges Canguilhem*, ed. François Delaporte (Brooklyn, NY: Zone Books, 1994), 68.

35. Georges Canguilhem, *The Normal and the Pathological* (Brooklyn, NY: Zone Books, 1989), 126. This norm-positing capacity and its philosophical significance are not entirely synonymous with the concept of normativity elaborated by Michel Foucault. Foucault argues that the sociological and institutional codification of the norm is an extended historical event, giving rise to societies in which a dynamic web of power organizes social reproduction through the statistical assessment of medicalized persons and populations, aiming at an overall process of normalization. (See his College de France Lecture Series, in particular *Security, Territory, Population*, 56–57 and 63.) For Canguilhem, however, the "normal" state that medical therapeutics aims at is determined by the sick individual and their responsiveness to "dreaded states or behaviors" that constitute pathological norms. Social norms and the ethical, political, or even medical elaboration of an ideal "normality" are seen as extensions of a fundamentally biological dynamism, which is itself an

inherently normative activity. Canguilhem's notion of normativity is thus broader and more supple than the concept of normativity that has been inherited from Foucault and which now dominates much literary criticism and critical theory—a concept that also drives the widespread aim among critics and theorists of all stripes to resist, subvert, queer, or deconstruct the so-called normative. This paradigm of antinormativity limits our understanding of human life insofar as that life seeks particular ends or makes judgments about how to live and act well, in part by extending a vital normativity that it shares with organic life at large. This is why Canguilhem conceives human *technē*, as do the Stoics, as the elaboration of a capacity that is fundamentally biological and inherently normative. Esposito offers his own view of some salient differences between Canguilhem and Foucault on the concept of the norm in relation to biological life in *Immunitas*, 141–144. For an illuminating discussion of normativity that underscores its centrality to ethics and notions of autonomy while remaining sensitive to the unique vexations presented by erotic life and sexuality, see Mark Miller, "Introduction: Chaucer and the Problem of Normativity," in *Philosophical Chaucer: Love, Sex, and Agency in the Canterbury Tales* (Cambridge: Cambridge University Press, 2004), 1–35. For a recent revaluation of the concept of normativity and its place in the entangled histories of scientific and ethical thought, see Lorraine Daston, *Against Nature* (Cambridge, MA: MIT Press, 2019).

36. Canguilhem, *The Normal and the Pathological*, 126–127.

37. Canguilhem, *The Normal and the Pathological*, 174.

38. Canguilhem, *The Normal and the Pathological*, 169.

39. Sebastian Rand argues that Canguilhem's contention, "strictly speaking, the norm does not exist," reveals his commitment to a Kantian notion of normativity as that which is grounded in a nonnatural and transcendent aspect of human life as rational activity. I do not share Rand's view of Canguilhem's thought in this regard, insofar as I understand the concept of organic normativity he develops in *The Normal and the Pathological* to derive from an immanently norm-establishing capacity that is ontologically prior to norm-following, a claim that Rand disputes. See Sebastian Rand, "Organism, Normativity, Plasticity: Canguilhem, Kant, Malabou," *Continental Philosophy Review* 44 (2011): 341–357.

40. Seneca, *Anger, Mercy, Revenge*, trans. Robert A. Kaster and Martha C. Nussbaum (Chicago: University of Chicago Press, 2010), 42.

41. Due to the fragmentary nature of the Stoic archive, some have argued that a reconstruction of Stoic ethical thought is difficult, if not impossible. This notion seems to have further merit in that there are apparent contradictions among texts that reproduce Stoic arguments but which are composed by philosophers who do not consider themselves to be members of the school—Cicero's *On Moral Ends*, which contains an important account of Stoic oikeiôsis, is a key example here. Nonetheless, there are numerous historians and philosophers whose work on ancient and classical thought aims at comprehensive reconstructions of core Stoic ethical doctrines, including books such as Katja Vogt's *Law, Reason, and the Cosmic City: Political Philosophy in the Early Stoa* (Oxford: Oxford University Press, 2007), Troels Engberg-Pedersen's *The Stoic Theory of Oikeiôsis: Moral Development and Social Interaction in Early Stoic Philosophy* (Aarhus, DK: Aarhus University Press, 1990), Margaret Graver's *Stoicism and Emotion* (Chicago: University of Chicago Press, 2007), and most recently Jacob Klein's stellar essay, "The Stoic Argument from *Oikeiôsis*," *Oxford Studies in Ancient Philosophy* 50 (2016): 143–200.

Klein begins from the first principle of oikeiôsis in providing a comprehensive account of Stoic ethics that responds convincingly to the major controversies and resolves many apparent inconsistencies across the archive.

42. Martin, "Stoic Transcendentalism and the Doctrine of *Oikeiôsis*," 345.

43. These translations of the term appear variously in Alexander J. Dressler, "Matter, Language, and Attachment in Seneca's Moral Epistles," (PhD diss., University of Washington, 2009), 64; Klein (2016); Martin in Gardner and Grist (2015); Vogt (2016); Engberg-Pedersen (1990), and Reinhardt Brandt, "Self-Consciousness and Self-Care: On the Tradition of Oikeiosis in the Modern Age," *Grotiana* 22/23 (2001/2002): 73–92.

44. See Hans Blumenberg, *Care Crosses the River* (Stanford, CA: Stanford University Press, 2010), 148.

45. Daniel Heller-Roazen, *The Inner Touch: Archaeology of a Sensation* (Brooklyn, NY: Zone Books, 2007), 114.

46. This is the view shared by Plato and Aristotle, as I show in chapter 1 under "Asleep in the *Polis*."

47. Diogenes Laertius, *Lives of the Eminent Philosophers*, trans. Pamela Mencsh (Oxford: Oxford University Press, 2018), 7.158, 367.

48. Ilaria Ramelli, ed., *Hierocles the Stoic: Elements of Ethics, Fragments and Excerpts*, trans. David Konstan (Atlanta: Society of Biblical Literature, 2009), 14–15.

49. Klein, "The Stoic Argument from *Oikeiôsis*," 174.

50. Klein, "The Stoic Argument from *Oikeiôsis*," 174.

51. Michel Foucault, *The Care of the Self: Volume 3 of the History of Sexuality*, trans. Robert Hurley (New York: Vintage Books, 1988), 42.

52. See my discussion in chapter 2 under "The Physics of Care."

53. Michel Foucault, *The Hermeneutics of the Subject: Lectures at the Collége de France, 1981–1982*, ed. Arnold Davidson, trans. Graham Burchell (New York: Palgrave Macmillan, 2005), 266.

54. Foucault, *Hermeneutics of the Subject*, 281–282.

55. Foucault, *Hermeneutics of the Subject*, 275.

56. Foucault, *Hermeneutics of the Subject*, 280.

57. Agamben, *Use of Bodies*, 54.

58. Agamben, *Use of Bodies*, 54.

59. Cited in Thomas G. Rosenmeyer, *Senecan Drama and Stoic Cosmology* (Berkeley: University of California Press, 1989), 41.

60. Johan C. Thom, *Cleanthes' Hymn to Zeus: Text, Translation, and Commentary* (Tübingen, DE: Mohr Siebeck, 2005), 9. The first Renaissance edition of the poem appeared in a 1568 collection edited by Fulvius Ursinus and printed in Antwerp.

61. Thom, *Cleanthes' Hymn to Zeus*, 40.

62. Soellner, "The Madness of Hercules and the Elizabethans," 309.

63. Gilles Deleuze and Felix Guattari, *What Is Philosophy?*, trans. Hugh Tomlinson and Graham Burchell (New York: Columbia University Press, 1994), 176.

64. Deleuze and Guattari, *What Is Philosophy?*, 175. On Deleuzian hyperrationalism, see Levi R. Bryant, *Difference and Givenness: Deleuze's Transcendental Empiricism and the Ontology of Immanence* (Evanston, IL: Northwestern University Press, 2008), 9–11.

65. Desiderius Erasmus, ed. Margaret Mann Phillips, *The "Adages" of Erasmus: A Study with Translations* (Cambridge: Cambridge University Press, 1964), 194. For more

on the many lives of Hercules in the Renaissance, see the introduction to chapter 2, footnote 3.

1. Heavy with Care

1. Desiderius Erasmus, *Praise of Folly* (New York: Penguin, 1978), 73.

2. On Folly's ties to a landscape whose plant life suggests Homeric amnesia and a sleeplike "forgetfulness of past wrongs" (29), see Jessica Wolfe, "Homer, Erasmus, and the Problem of Strife," in *Renaissance Papers*, ed. Thomas Hester and Christopher Cobb (Rochester, NY: Camden House, 2003), 1–32.

3. Michel Foucault, *History of Madness*, ed. Jean Khalfa, trans. Jonathan Murphy and Jean Khalfa (New York: Routledge, 2006), 23.

4. Foucault, *History of Madness*, 24.

5. Foucault, *History of Madness*, 24.

6. This English translation is numbered 90 in Charles H. Kahn, *The Art and Thought of Heraclitus: An Edition of the Fragments with Critical Commentary* (Cambridge: Cambridge University Press, 1979), 70. On this fragment's relevance to Heraclitus's claim in fragment 88 that "as the same thing there exists in us living and dead and the waking and the sleeping and young and old: for these things having changed round again are these ones," see G. S. Kirk, *Heraclitus: The Cosmic Fragments* (Cambridge: Cambridge University Press, 1954), 135–148.

7. On these various meanings and their punning effects, see M. Marcovich, *Heraclitus: Greek Text with a Short Commentary* (Merida: Los Andes University Press, 1967), 244–245.

8. Kahn, *The Art and Thought of Heraclitus*, 215.

9. Kirk, *Heraclitus*, 148.

10. Plato, *Phaedo* 65b, in *Plato: Complete Works*, ed. John M. Cooper (Indianapolis: Hackett Publishing, 1997), 56.

11. 498a–b. All references to *The Republic* are from Plato, *The Republic*, trans. R. E. Allen (New Haven, CT: Yale University Press, 2006).

12. The Form of the Good can be further explained as the power behind the "being known" of intelligible things; it causes both knowledge and truth, and for that reason it is more valuable than knowledge and truth alike.

13. See 1102b10 in Aristotle, *Nicomachean Ethics*, trans. Sarah Broadie and Christopher Rowe (Oxford: Oxford University Press, 2002), 110.

14. Aristotle, *Nicomachean Ethics*, 1099a1, 103.

15. Aristotle, *Nicomachean Ethics*, 1102b30, 110.

16. Aristotle, *Nicomachean Ethics*, 1147a12–14, 193.

17. Aristotle, *Eudemian Ethics*, trans. Michael Woods (Oxford: Oxford University Press, 1992), 1216a3–8, 5.

18. Aristotle, *Nicomachean Ethics*, 1157b5–10, 213.

19. Aristotle, *Nicomachean Ethics*, 1169b15, 236.

20. Aristotle, *Nicomachean Ethics*, 1170a15–20, 237.

21. These points to some extent anticipate Seneca's understanding of care as the means by which the good is perfected for human beings. Yet Aristotle's formulation does not suggest the ambivalences of *cura* that are so essential to the Stoic perspec-

tive, nor does it allow for the ongoing activity of care in sleep that the Stoic theory of oikeiôsis implies.

22. Sir Thomas Browne in *Religio Medici* explicitly criticizes Aristotle's essay in such terms:

> *Aristotle*, who hath written a singular Tract of Sleep, hath not methinks thoroughly defined it; nor yet *Galen*, though he seem to have corrected it; for those *Noctambuloes* and night-walkers, though in their sleep, do yet injoy the action of their senses; we must therefore say that there is something in us that is not in the jurisdiction of *Morpheus*; and that those abstracted and ecstatick souls do walk about in their own corps, as spirits with the bodies they assume; wherein they seem to hear, and feel, though indeed the Organs are destitute of sense, and their natures of those faculties that should inform them.

Sir Thomas Browne, *The Works of Sir Thomas Browne*, ed. Charles Sayle, vol. 1 (London: Grant Richards, 1904), 105.

23. Aristotle, *Parva Naturalia*, in *The Works of Aristotle*, vol. 3, ed. W. D. Ross (Oxford: Clarendon Press, 1931), 456b20, 372.

24. Aristotle, *Parva Naturalia*, 454b10, 366.

25. Aristotle, *Parva Naturalia*, 454b25, 366.

26. See for instance the philosopher's claim that a principle virtue of the nutritive soul is "a capacity of the sort which preserves the thing which has it, as the sort of thing it is" in Aristotle, *De Anima*, trans. Christopher Shields (Oxford: Oxford University Press, 2016), 416b15, 31.

27. Gilles Deleuze, *The Logic of Sense*, trans. Mark Lester (New York: Columbia University Press, 1990), 5.

28. See the stemma of Stoic ontology and accompanying discussion in A. A. Long and D. N. Sedley, *The Hellenistic Philosophers: Volume 1* (Cambridge: Cambridge University Press, 1987), 163.

29. D. J. T. Bailey, "The Structure of Stoic Metaphysics," in *Oxford Studies in Ancient Philosophy* 46 (Summer 2014): 253–309.

30. From Diogenes Laertius, *Lives of the Eminent Philosophers*, ed. James Miller, trans. Pamela Mensch (Oxford: Oxford University Press, 2018), 7.39–41, 329; also quoted in Long and Sedley, *The Hellenistic Philosophers*, 158. See also the fragment from Sextus Empiricus's work, *Against the Professors*: "Posidonius said he preferred to compare philosophy to a living being—physics to the blood and flesh, logic to the bones and sinews, and ethics to the soul." Quoted in Long and Sedley, *The Hellenistic Philosophers*, 159.

31. Laertius, *Lives of the Eminent Philosophers*, 7.86, 344.

32. Laertius, *Lives of the Eminent Philosophers*, 7.118, 353.

33. Laertius, *Lives of the Eminent Philosophers*, 7.158, 367.

34. Hierocles, *Hierocles the Stoic: Elements of Ethics, Fragments and Excerpts*, ed. Ilaria Ramelli, trans. David Konstan (Atlanta: Society of Biblical Literature, 2009), 11.

35. Hierocles, *Hierocles the Stoic*, 14.

36. Alexander J. Dressler, "Matter, Language, and Attachment in Seneca's Moral Epistles," PhD diss. (Seattle: University of Washington, 2009), 65.

37. Seneca, *Letters on Ethics*, trans. Margaret Graver and A. A. Long (Chicago: University of Chicago Press, 2015), 121.17, 487. Latin original in Seneca, trans. Richard M.

Gummere, *Epistles, Volume III: Epistles 93–124*, Loeb Classical Library 77 (Cambridge, MA: Harvard University Press, 1925), 406.

38. Daniel Heller-Roazen, *The Inner Touch: Archaeology of a Sensation* (Brooklyn, NY: Zone Books, 2007), 114.

39. Heller-Roazen, *The Inner Touch*, 114.

40. Seneca, *Letters on Ethics*, 56.6, 161.

41. Seneca, *Letters on Ethics*, 124.14, 500.

42. Seneca, *On Benefits*, trans. Miriam Griffin and Brad Inwood (Chicago: University of Chicago Press, 2011), 4.13.1–2, 93–94.

43. Quoted in Roberto Polito, "Sextus on Heraclitus on Sleep," in *Sleep*, ed. T. Wiedemann and K. Dowden (Bari: Levante, 2003), 53–70, 65.

44. Seneca, *Letters on Ethics*, 90.41, 334.

45. Bernard F. Batto, "The Sleeping God: An Ancient Near Eastern Motif of Divine Sovereignty," *Biblica* 68, no. 2 (1987): 153–177. Quotation from 156–157.

46. Batto, "The Sleeping God," 172.

47. "Hymns to Amun-Ra," lines 121–122, in Charles Dudley Warner, ed., *Library of World's Best Literature: An Anthology in Thirty Volumes* (New York: Warner Library Co., 1917).

48. Michel Foucault, *Security, Territory, Population: Lectures at the Collège de France, 1977–1978*, ed. Arnold Davidson, trans. Graham Burchell (New York: Palgrave Macmillan, 2007), 127.

49. 2 Thessalonians 5:5–6 (King James Version).

50. John A. T. Robinson, *The Body: A Study in Pauline Theology* (Chicago: Allenson, 1952), 28.

51. Robinson, *The Body*, 28.

52. Robinson, *The Body*, 30.

53. David Brakke, *Demons and the Making of the Monk: Spiritual Combat in Early Christianity* (Cambridge, MA: Harvard University Press, 2006), 85.

54. See Brakke, *Demons and the Making of the Monk*, 79–85.

55. From *Bohairic Life of Pachomius 10*, quoted in Brakke, *Demons and the Making of the Monk*, 84.

56. Brakke, *Demons and the Making of the Monk*, 87–94.

57. Translation of original Latin text with commentary is from Esther de Waal, *A Life-Giving Way: A Commentary on the Rule of St. Benedict* (Collegeville, MN: Liturgical Press, 1995), 102.

58. See the chapter on Benedict's work in Dom David Knowles, *The Monastic Order in England: A History of Its Development from the Times of St. Dunstant to the Fourth Latern Council* (Cambridge: Cambridge University Press, 1940), 3–30.

59. Homily 14 on 1 Timothy 8 in John Chrysostom, *The Homilies of S. John Chrysostom, Archbishop of Constantinople, on the Epistles of St. Paul the Apostle to Timothy, Titus, and Philemon* (Oxford: J. Parker, 1843), 122.

60. Gregory of Nyssa, "On the Making of Man," in *Dogmatic Treatises, Etc.*, ed. Phillip Schaff (New York: Christian Literature Publishing, 1892), 630.

61. On the parameters of this dilemma and its place in monastic techniques of self-care and transformation, see David Brakke, "The Problematization of Nocturnal Emissions in Early Christian Syria, Egypt, and Gaul," *Journal of Early Christian Studies* 3, no. 4 (1995): 419–460.

62. John Cassian, *The Conferences*, trans. Boniface Ramsey (New York: Paulist Press, 1997), 2.22.5.1, 766.

63. Augustine, *Confessions*, trans. Henry Chadwick (Oxford: Oxford University Press, 2008), xxx.41–42, 203.

64. See Richard Strier's essay, "Against the Rule of Reason: Praise of Passion from Petrarch to Luther to Shakespeare to Herbert," in Gail Kern Paster, Katherine Rowe, and Mary Floyd-Wilson, eds., *Reading the Early Modern Passions: Essays in the Cultural History of Emotions* (Philadelphia: University of Pennsylvania Press, 2004), 23–42.

65. Martin Luther, *Commentary on Romans*, trans. J. Theodore Muller (Grand Rapids, MI: Kregel Publications, 1976), 188–189.

66. Luther, *Commentary on Romans*, 189.

67. Luther, *Commentary on Romans*, 192.

68. John Calvin, *Commentaries*, ed. David Torrance and Thomas Torrance, vol. 8 (Grand Rapids, MI: Eerdmans, 1959–1972), 286–287.

69. John Calvin, *Commentaries*, ed. David Torrance and Thomas Torrance, vol. 11 (Grand Rapids, MI: Eerdmans, 1959–1972), 217.

70. Robinson, *The Body*, 81–83.

71. John Calvin, *Institutes of the Christian Religion*, trans. Henry Beveridge (Grand Rapids, MI: Eerdmans, 1989), 53.

72. Calvin, *Institutes of the Christian Religion*, 54.

73. Calvin, *Institutes of the Christian Religion*, 55.

74. John Calvin, "Psychopannychia," in *Selected Works of John Calvin: Tracts and Letters*, ed. Henry Beveridge and Jules Bonnet, 7 vols. (Edinburgh: Calvin Translation Society, 1851), 3:377–451, 390.

75. Erasmus, *Enchridion Militis Christiani: An English Version*, ed. Anne M. O'Donnell (Oxford: Oxford University Press, 1981), 33.

76. Erasmus, *Enchiridion*, 42.

77. Erasmus, *Enchiridion*, 136.

78. Richard Halpern, *The Poetics of Primitive Accumulation: English Renaissance Culture and the Genealogy of Capital* (Ithaca, NY: Cornell University Press, 1991), 29.

79. On the importance of the Magdalen School in early English humanism, see Daniel Wakelin, *Humanism, Reading, and English Literature 1430–1530* (Oxford: Oxford University Press, 2007), 1–3, 133–140.

80. William Nelson, ed., *A Fifteenth Century School Book: From a Manuscript in the British Museum (Ms. Arundel 249)*, (Oxford: Clarendon Press, 1956), 1–2.

81. Nelson, *A Fifteenth Century School Book*, 3–4.

82. Nelson, *A Fifteenth Century School Book*, 28.

83. See the discussions of Dametas's immoderate sleep in Sir Phillip Sidney's *Arcadia* and Falstaff's gluttonous sleep in *Henry IV, Part 1*, in Garrett Sullivan Jr., *Sleep, Romance, and Human Embodiment: Vitality from Spenser to Milton* (Cambridge: Cambridge University Press, 2012), 55, and 83, for the idea that immoderate sleep is both a harm to physical health and a form of spiritual corruption or sin.

84. See Lynn Enterline, *Shakespeare's Schoolroom: Rhetoric, Discipline, Emotion* (Philadelphia: University of Pennsylvania Press, 2012) and Rebecca Bushnell, *A Culture of Teaching: Early Modern Humanism in Theory and Practice* (Ithaca, NY: Cornell University

Press, 1996). Bushnell's argument is positioned, though somewhat vaguely, as an anti-Foucauldian polemic against new historicist accounts of classroom discipline as the foundation of humanist subject formation. While I am in sympathy with her claim that early modern humanist pedagogical practices ought not be conceptually reduced to a purely instrumentalizing model of disciplinary power, I think she misses the suppleness of Foucault's analysis of discipline, which critics such as Enterline and Halpern have more carefully considered within the context of early modern humanism. As Halpern argues, humanist discipline does not achieve its ends primarily through coercion and physical threats (though it sometimes depends on such strategies), but more strategically by shaping the energetic and imitative propensities of the child. See Halpern, *Poetics of Primitive Accumulation*, 19–60.

85. Enterline, *Shakespeare's Schoolroom*, 11.

86. Jeff Dolven, *Scenes of Instruction in Renaissance Romance* (Chicago: University of Chicago Press, 2007), 3.

87. Richard Mulcaster, *Mulcaster's Elementarie*, ed. E.T. Campagnac (London: Humphrey Milford for Oxford University Press, 1927), 27.

88. Mulcaster, *Elementarie*, 2

89. Mulcaster, *Elementarie*, 27.

90. Mulcaster, *Elementarie*, 257.

91. Jeff Dolven reads this passage as a sign of Mulcaster's faith in "the wise, attentive, preventative care of the humanists," a form of care that guards against peril and which he contrasts with images of solicitude and reparative care that respond therapeutically to the cares that are synonymous with sorrow and suffering in Spenser's *Faerie Queene*. For Dolven, Spenser's poetics of care departs from Mulcaster's humanist precepts by limning what Dolven calls a "symbiotic embrace" of care, or care as a dialectical process shuttling between poles of worry and recovery. When care is directed toward others by characters clearly marked as evil, it begins to dislodge itself from the structural axis of good and evil, cultivating an energy that disrupts the ethical architecture of the poem. See Dolven, "Besides Good and Evil," *SEL: Studies in English Literature 1500–1900* 57, no. 1 (Winter 2017): 1–22.

92. Mulcaster, *Elementarie*, 44.

93. Gur Zak, *Petrarch's Humanism and the Care of the Self* (Cambridge: Cambridge University Press, 2010).

94. It is of course worth noting that classical literature (Plutarch, in the case of sleeping Timotheus) provides Mulcaster with his exemplary figure for the sleeping potential of children and the ecologies of care that sustain and develop them, as well as the fact that his reliance on insights of Aristotelian virtue ethics draws upon and modifies explicitly—and with a more favorable attitude than thinkers such as Calvin—knowledge from pagan sources.

95. See Andrew Hadfield, *Edmund Spenser: A Life* (Oxford: Oxford University Press, 2012), 31, in reference to Mulcaster's stern disposition. On the place of love in Mulcaster's pedagogy and in humanist reforms more broadly, see Dolven, *Scenes of Instruction in Renaissance Romance*, 216–228.

96. Fuller, *Worthies*, 600, quoted in Hadfield, *Edmund Spenser*, 31.

97. Cicero, *On Moral Ends*, ed. Julia Annas (Cambridge: Cambridge University Press, 2001), 5.55, 136.

98. Aristotle, *Metaphysics*, trans. Richard Hope (New York: Columbia University Press, 1952), 1074b, 265.

99. Hans Blumenberg, *Care Crosses the River* (Stanford, CA: Stanford University Press, 2010), 147.

100. Blumenberg, *Care Crosses the River*, 150.

101. On the vigilant operations of the Cartesian intellect and the dubiety of sleep, see my discussion in the coda.

102. In what came to be known as the "Hercules at the Crossroads" motif in the Renaissance, the youthful Hercules is on his way to tend the cattle of his father, Amphitryon, when he encounters two women at a crossroads representing virtue and pleasure. He knowingly chooses the way of the former along with the life of hardship that this choice entails. Virtue is often represented in these neoclassical works as Athena, with her counterpart cast as Aphrodite. For a comprehensive list of Renaissance and early modern works depicting this theme, see the entry for "Choice of Heracles" in Jane Davidson Reid, *The Oxford Guide to Classical Mythology in the Arts, 1300–1990s* (Oxford: Oxford University Press, 1993), 527–530.

2. Hercules Asleep

1. While a number of compelling questions might arise concerning Heywood as literary translator, the argument I pursue in this chapter does not take up the issue of translation, nor does it engage in comparative work between Seneca's Latin and Heywood's English. My interest is in the philosophical—and more specifically, the intersecting cosmological and ethical—aspects of the play as they bear on its representations of sleep and insomnia. My analysis thus more or less holds true for Seneca's play as it does for Heywood's, though I elect to use Heywood's translation as my source text for a few reasons: it was the first English translation available to the writers at the heart of this book, and their representations of sleep, insomnia, and madness often contain verbal echoes of Heywood's play, while displaying affinities with its Stoic ecological thinking about material causation, volatile corporeal mixtures, and the proximity of physical life and ethical care.

2. All references to the play are from the modern reprint of the Thomas Newton collection, featuring an introduction by T. S. Eliot. Seneca, *Seneca: His Tenne Tragedies*, ed. Thomas Newton (New York: Alfred K. Knopf, 1927).

3. Two distinct traditions concerning Hercules took shape during the Renaissance. The dominant and more prolific of these two represents Hercules as a paradigm of virtue, reason, and fortitude, in turn aligning the hero both with Christ and with humanist accomplishments in ethical and intellectual forms of life. Alongside this virtuous vein runs a second current, drawing inspiration primarily from Seneca's *Hercules Furens*—but also the tragedy *Hercules Oetaeus* and Ovid's epic poem, *Metamorphoses*—which emphasizes the hero's susceptibility to madness, extreme violence, and tragedy. As Kathleen Riley notes, it was this second tradition that "held the greater literary potential and had arguably the greater creative impact," and so she connects the mad Hercules motif with characters such as Marlowe's Tamburlaine and Shakespeare's Macbeth, Coriolanus, and Antony. Yet while Riley, Rolf Soellner, Robert Miola, and Gordon Braden have all convincingly shown that the type of Hercules's madness proliferated among depictions of

rage and anger in early modern literature, no one has connected early modern scenes of restorative sleep to the figure of Herculean slumber at the core of Seneca's tragedy, which I argue often accompanies the more widely acknowledged depictions of fury. On the two major traditions of Hercules in the Renaissance, see Kathleen Riley, *The Reception and Performance of Euripides's* Herakles (Oxford: Oxford University Press, 2008), 92–116. On the legacies of Hercules among medieval Christian, Renaissance, and early modern writers, see Emma Stafford, *Herakles* (New York: Routledge, 2012), 201–225. On the *Hercules Furens* convention in early modern literature and its connection to Senecan drama in particular, see Gordon Braden, "Herakles and Hercules: Survival in Greek and Roman Tragedy (With a Coda on *King Lear*)," in *Theater and Society in the Classical World*, ed. Ruth Scodel (Ann Arbor: University of Michigan Press, 1993), 245–264; Robert Miola, *Shakespeare and Classical Tragedy: The Influence of Seneca* (Oxford: Oxford University Press, 1996), 122–174; and Rolf Soellner, "The Madness of Hercules and the Elizabethans," *Comparative Literature* 10, no. 4 (1958): 309–324.

4. For a thorough review of the critical landscape up to 1970, see Anna Lydia Motto and John R. Clark, "Senecan Tragedy: A Critique of Scholarly Trends," *Renaissance Drama* 6 (1973): 219–235.

5. T. S. Eliot's predecessors John Cunliffe and F. L. Lucas both argue for this view of Seneca's profound influence and importance for Elizabethan literature. See John William Cunliffe, *The Influence of Seneca on Elizabethan Tragedy* (London: Macmillan, 1893), and F. L. Lucas, *Seneca and Elizabethan Tragedy* (Cambridge: Cambridge University Press, 1922).

6. T. W. Baldwin's *William Shakespeare's Small Latine & Lesse Greeke* (Urbana: University of Illinois Press, 1944) is the classic study underscoring the influence of Terence, Ovid, and other Roman poets on Shakespearean drama while downplaying the Senecan influence. Howard Baker's *Induction to Tragedy* (Baton Rouge: Louisiana State University Press, 1939) argues that the native medieval tradition far outweighs Seneca's influence on Elizabethan tragedians, while G. K. Hunter's essay, "Seneca and the Elizabethans: A Case Study in 'Influence,'" *Shakespeare Survey* 20 (1967): 11–26, emphatically extends Baker's core claims. Catherine Belsey takes stock of these accounts in arguing for an Elizabethan synthesis of Senecan soliloquy with the dilemmas of conscience dramatized by English morality plays in "Senecan Vacillation and Elizabethan Deliberation: Influence or Confluence?," *Renaissance Drama, New Series, Vol. 6: Essays on Dramatic Antecedents* (1976): 65–88.

7. Gordon Braden, *Renaissance Tragedy and the Senecan Tradition: Anger's Privilege* (New Haven, CT: Yale University Press, 1985) and Robert S. Miola, *Shakespeare and Classical Tragedy: The Influence of Seneca* (Oxford: Oxford University Press, 1992).

8. Intellectual historical approaches to Stoicism and the political cultures of early modern England include Quentin Skinner, *Foundations of Modern Political Thought*, vols. 1 and 2 (Cambridge: Cambridge University Press, 1978), Richard Tuck, *Philosophy and Government 1572–1651* (Cambridge: Cambridge University Press, 1993), and Margo Todd, *Christian Humanism and the Puritan Social Order* (Cambridge: Cambridge University Press, 1987), all of which discuss the Renaissance revival of Stoicism and its influence upon humanist thought in such terms; more literary-historical accounts include Geoffrey Miles, *Shakespeare and the Constant Romans* (Oxford: Oxford University Press, 1996), Adriana Alice Norma McCrea, *Constant Minds: Political Virtue and the Lipsian Par-*

adigm in England, 1584–1650 (Toronto: University of Toronto Press, 1997), Reid Barbour, *English Epicures and Stoics* (Amherst: University of Massachusetts Press, 1998), and Andrew Shifflett, *Stoicism, Politics and Literature in the Age of Milton* (Cambridge: Cambridge University Press, 1998). See also Jessica Winston, "Seneca in Early Elizabethan England," *Renaissance Quarterly* 59, no. 1 (2006): 29–59, and Linda Woodbridge, "Resistance Theory Meets Drama: Tudor Seneca," *Renaissance Drama* 38 (2010): 115–139, for two accounts of the Elizabethan political implications of the English translations of Seneca's plays collected in the Newton edition. A uniquely cosmological account of Senecan tragedy whose arguments have deeply shaped this book's approach to Stoicism and early modern literature is Thomas Rosenmeyer's *Senecan Drama and Stoic Cosmology* (Berkeley: University of California Press, 1989). See also Braden's complimentary review of Rosenmeyer's book in *Comparative Literature* 45, no. 1 (1993): 66–68.

9. See Miles, *Shakespeare and the Constant Romans*, 9. Barbour's *English Epicures and Stoics* is noteworthy here for drawing attention to neo-Stoic notions of constancy and resolution that are also flexible and open to change. As Barbour notes, for some seventeenth-century writers adapting ethical models of constancy from Seneca and Marcus Aurelius, "resolve" also meant "dissolve" or "disintegrate," which suggested that exhibiting the virtue of constancy could sometimes mean being open to fluctuation, change, and development precisely for the sake of the good. See Barbour, *English Epicures and Stoics*, 114–118.

10. Among classicists, this argument has most recently found a home in Christopher Star's *The Empire of the Self: Self-Command and Political Speech in Seneca and Petronius* (Baltimore: Johns Hopkins University Press, 2012). C. A. J. Littlewood likewise argues in *Self-Representation and Illusion in Senecan Tragedy* (Oxford: Oxford University Press, 2004) that the Stoic sage often comes to resemble the "autonomy of a tyrant" by exerting absolute rule over "a world they construct and sustain for themselves" (8). Likewise, Charles Segal's *Interpreting Greek Tragedy: Myth, Poetry, Text* (Ithaca, NY: Cornell University Press, 1986) argues that the correlation between the protagonist's emotional state and the surrounding ecology is simply a rhetorical strategy in Senecan drama, a "grandiose version of the pathetic fallacy" (317) rather than an instance of Stoic *sumpatheia* grounded in the school's ancient cosmological principles.

11. For a similar argument concerning the aim of Stoic ethics, see Jonathan Dollimore's claim that Stoicism aims to "reconstitute one's sense of self by withdrawing from the social reality that has threatened it" in *Radical Tragedy: Religion, Ideology and Power in the Drama of Shakespeare and His Contemporaries* (Durham, NC: Duke University Press, 2003), 31.

12. Braden, *Renaissance Tragedy and the Senecan Tradition*, 21.

13. Braden, *Renaissance Tragedy and the Senecan Tradition*, 21.

14. Braden, *Renaissance Tragedy and the Senecan Tradition*, 3.

15. Katja Vogt, *Law, Reason, and the Cosmic City: Political Philosophy in the Early Stoa* (Oxford: Oxford University Press, 2008), 5.

16. See my discussions of Stoic oikeiôsis in the introduction under "Physiology, Normativity, and Biopower" and in chapter 1 under "The Body of Sleep: Stoic Slackness and the Tension of Care."

17. Seneca, *Letters on Ethics*, trans. Margaret Graver and A. A. Long (Chicago: University of Chicago Press, 2015), 9.3, 40.

18. Seneca, *Letters on Ethics*, 59.2, 172.

19. On the essential roles of affect and *eupatheia* in Stoic ethics, see Vogt, *Law, Reason, and the Cosmic City*, 5 and 105. See also Margaret Graever's illuminating discussion of *eupatheiai* in *Stoicism and Emotion* (Chicago: University of Chicago Press, 2007), including her insight that Stoic *eupatheiai* ought not be considered "flat" or "less intense" than typical human emotions, but rather as "corrected versions of human feelings . . . like the easy movements of a powerful athlete, forceful but without strain" (53).

20. Strikingly, Braden does mention care at the end of the first chapter of *Renaissance Tragedy and the Senecan Tradition*, but he views care as yet another expression of the Stoic self's theatricality, which serves as a basis for comparison between the Stoic sage and the good actor. As he relates the story of Seneca's suicide, Braden argues that Seneca faces his end committed not only to his suicide as a final act of self-control but also to the "care of his friends," insofar as his action bequeaths to them an enduring image of his life. For Braden, Seneca's care draws the philosopher outward but only because of the need for acknowledgment and admiration of his sage-like performance as a theatrical gesture. And this point leads Braden to offer an explanation for why Seneca wrote tragedies of such spectacular violence and passion: "The forces in which he deals devastate the outside world as other, only to restore it as audience" (27). In other words, the isolation of the sage in his self-assured security ultimately leads him to look for recognition of this accomplishment among his audience as viewers rather than fellow citizens of the cosmopolis.

21. See the discussion of Canguilhem and Stoicism in the introduction under "Physiology, Normativity, Biopower."

22. Gilles Deleuze's account of Stoic ethics emphasizes the sage's activity not only vis-à-vis the corporeal body of reason but also the incorporeal *lekta*, or "sayables," whose sense differs and detaches from the physical moorings of the representational image of virtue and its material enunciation. For Deleuze, the Stoic sage cognitively grasps and selects the action that affirms this evental site, bringing her will into harmony with the cosmos. The sage is a sort of logical craftsman who "sets up shop at the surface" where sensation and sense (meaning) form a Möbius-like topology and the *kalon* emerges as a membrane of assent. See Gilles Deleuze, *The Logic of Sense* (New York: Columbia University Press, 1990), 146.

23. The letter moves through discussions of Platonic and Aristotelian accounts of causality in order to reject them both, though Seneca's recapitulation of these doctrines sometimes misrepresents the positions. On the Stoics as the proper heirs of Socrates, see the introduction in A. G. Long, ed., *Plato and the Stoics* (Cambridge: Cambridge University Press, 2013), 1–10, and Vogt, *Law, Reason, and the Cosmic City*.

24. This Stoic god, as Ricardo Salles argues, "is providential and benevolent in that he purposively acts on the cosmos and cares for it." Ricardo Salles, ed., *God and Cosmos in Stoicism* (Oxford: Oxford University Press, 2009), 4.

25. Seneca, *Letters on Ethics*, 65.12, 187.

26. Salles, *God and Cosmos in Stoicism*, 9.

27. Susan Sauvé Meyer, "Chain of Causes: What Is Stoic Fate?," in Salles, *God and Cosmos in Stoicism*, 76.

28. Rosenmeyer, *Senecan Drama and Stoic Cosmology*, 100–101.

29. Rosenmeyer, *Senecan Drama and Stoic Cosmology*, 101–102.

30. Seneca, *Anger, Mercy, Revenge*, trans. Robert A. Kaster and Martha C. Nussbaum (Chicago: University of Chicago Press, 2010), 1.8.2, 21.

31. Seneca, *Anger, Mercy, Revenge*, 1.8.3, 21.

32. Rosenmeyer, *Senecan Drama and Stoic Cosmology*, 67.

33. Gareth Williams, *The Cosmic Viewpoint: A Study of Seneca's* Natural Questions (New York: Oxford University Press, 2012), 12.

34. Williams, *The Cosmic Viewpoint*, 92.

35. Deleuze, *Logic of Sense*, 131.

36. Seneca, *Anger, Mercy, Revenge*, 3.26.4, 85.

37. Rosenmeyer, *Senecan Drama and Stoic Cosmology*, 113.

38. Littlewood, *Self-Representation and Illusion in Senecan Tragedy*, 59.

39. Littlewood, *Self-Representation and Illusion in Senecan Tragedy*, 62.

40. On the idea of split causality and the Stoics, see Deleuze, *The Logic of Sense*, especially "Eighteenth Series of the Three Images of Philosophers," 127.

41. Deleuze, *The Logic of Sense*, 131–132.

42. Seneca, *Seneca: His Tenne Tragedies*, 16.

43. Seneca, *Seneca: His Tenne Tragedies*, 15.

44. Seneca, *Seneca: His Tenne Tragedies*, 13.

45. John G. Fitch, *Seneca's Hercules Furens: A Critical Text with Introduction and Commentary* (Ithaca, NY: Cornell University Press, 1987), 23.

46. Fitch, *Seneca's Hercules Furens*, 24.

47. Seneca, *Seneca: His Tenne Tragedies*, 11.

48. The translation appeared in 1560, roughly one year before his translation of *Hercules Furens*. See Winston's "Seneca in Early Elizabethan England" on the historical chronology of the translations collected in Newton's edition.

49. This exchange is reproduced in Peter Happe's essay, "The Restless Mind That Would Never Raging Leave: Jasper Heywood's *Theyestes*," *Medieval English Theater* 27 (2005): 16–33, on page 19.

50. Rosenmeyer, *Senecan Drama and Stoic Cosmology*, 74.

51. See Margarethe Billerbeck's entry for *Hercules Furens* in *Brill's Companion to Seneca: Philosopher and Dramatist*, ed. Andreas Heil and Gregor Damschen (Leiden: Brill 2013), 425–433.

52. Seneca, *Seneca: His Tenne Tragedies*, 12.

53. Seneca, *Seneca: His Tenne Tragedies*, 12.

54. On the weirdly compressed temporality of Juno's opening speech as a feature of Senecan drama more broadly, see Jo-Ann Shelton, "Problems of Time in Seneca's *Hercules Furens* and *Thyestes*," *California Studies in Classical Antiquity* 8 (1975): 257–269. On the Stoic conception of time as an incorporeal that necessarily couples two incommensurate "readings" of time as *Aion* and *Chronos*, which correspond to intensive and extensive measurements, see Deleuze, *Logic of Sense*, 61, 164, 168.

55. Priscilla Sakezles, "Aristotle and Chrysippus on the Physiology of Human Action," *The Society for Ancient Greek Philosophy Newsletter* (1996): 454, 6.

56. Seneca, *Seneca: His Tenne Tragedies*, 39.

57. The scene thus illustrates Michel Foucault's recognition that the connections among sleep, dietetics, and the care of the self appear "increasingly intertwined" in later Roman philosophy. See Michel Foucault, *The Hermeneutics of the Subject: Lectures*

at the Collège de France, 1981–1982, ed. Arnold Davidson, trans. Graham Burchell (New York: Palgrave Macmillan, 2005), 59.

58. Seneca, *Seneca: His Tenne Tragedies*, 39.

59. Seneca, *Seneca: His Tenne Tragedies*, 39.

60. This detail is attributed to Ptolemy Hephaestion's *New History* and collected by Photius in chapter 190 of his *Biblioteca*.

61. Sauvé Meyer, "Chain of Causes," 87.

62. Seneca, *Seneca: His Tenne Tragedies*, 41.

63. Seneca, *Seneca: His Tenne Tragedies*, 42.

64. Seneca, *Seneca: His Tenne Tragedies*, 42.

65. Seneca, *Seneca: His Tenne Tragedies*, 42–43.

66. Fitch, *Seneca's Hercules Furens*, 35.

67. Seneca, *Letters on Ethics*, 36.8–11, 116.

68. Seneca, *Seneca: His Tenne Tragedies*, 43–44.

69. Plutarch, *Moralia, Volume XII: Concerning the Face Which Appears in the Orb of the Moon. On the Principle of Cold. Whether Fire or Water Is More Useful. Whether Land or Sea Animals Are Cleverer. Beasts Are Rational. On the Eating of Flesh*, trans. Harold Cherniss, W. C. Helmbold, Loeb Classical Library 406 (Cambridge, MA: Harvard University Press, 1957), 367.

70. I use the phrase "cognitive-perceptual" to describe the animal's inherent grasping of its constitution based on the discussion of Stoic psychological monism and its significance to oikeiôsis in Jacob Klein's essay, "The Stoic Argument from *Oikeiôsis*," *Oxford Studies in Ancient Philosophy* 50 (2016): 143–200.

71. Hierocles, *Hierocles the Stoic: Elements of Ethics, Fragments and Excerpts*, ed. Ilaria Ramelli, trans. David Konstan (Atlanta: Society of Biblical Literature, 2009), 14–15.

72. Seneca, *Seneca: His Tenne Tragedies*, 44.

73. Seneca, *Seneca: His Tenne Tragedies*, 46.

74. Seneca, *Seneca: His Tenne Tragedies*, 47–48.

75. Seneca, *Seneca: His Tenne Tragedies*, 49.

76. Seneca, *Seneca: His Tenne Tragedies*, 49.

77. Seneca, *Seneca: His Tenne Tragedies*, 49.

78. Seneca, *Seneca: His Tenne Tragedies*, 51.

79. Seneca, *Seneca: His Tenne Tragedies*, 51.

80. Seneca, *Seneca: His Tenne Tragedies*, 51.

81. Rosenmeyer, *Senecan Drama and Stoic Cosmology*, 76.

3. "The Body Is with the King, but the King Is Not with the Body"

1. King James VI and I, *Political Writings*, ed. Johann P. Sommerville (Cambridge: Cambridge University Press, 1994), 239.

2. King James VI and I, *Political Writings*, 249.

3. See Ernst H. Kantorowicz, *The King's Two Bodies: A Study in Medieval Political Theology* (Princeton, NJ: Princeton University Press, 1997), 130–143, especially 130–1n131, 133–4n146, and 143n167.

4. As Foucault argues, "pastoral power is a power of care" which "initially manifests itself in its zeal, devotion, and endless application. . . . The shepherd is someone

who keeps watch . . . above all else in the sense of vigilance with regard to any possible misfortune." See Michel Foucault, *Security, Territory, Population: Lectures at the Collège de France, 1977–1978*, ed. Arnold Davidson, trans. Graham Burchell (New York: Palgrave Macmillan, 2007), 127. See also my discussion in chapter 1 under "Body, Flesh, Vigilance: Pastoral Care and the Political Theology of Sleep."

5. Foucault, *Security, Territory, Population*, 95.

6. *Representations* 106 (Spring 2009) features a special forum on *The King's Two Bodies* with essays by Stephen Greenblatt, Richard Halpern, Victoria Kahn, Bernhard Jussen, and Lorna Hutson. Work on Shakespeare and questions of sovereignty relative to biopolitics includes: Meredith Evans, "Rumor, the Breath of Kings, and the Body of Law in *2 Henry IV*," *Shakespeare Quarterly* 60, no. 1 (Spring 2009): 1–24; James Kuzner, "Unbuilding the City: *Coriolanus* and the Birth of Republican Rome," *Shakespeare Quarterly* 58, no. 2 (Summer 2007): 174–199; Ken Jackson, "'Is It God or the Sovereign Exception?': Giorgio Agamben's *Homo Sacer* and Shakespeare's *King John*," *Religion and Literature* (Autumn 2006): 85–100; Julia-Reinhard Lupton, *Citizen-Saints: Shakespeare and Political Theology* (Chicago: University of Chicago Press, 2005), *Thinking with Shakespeare: Essays on Politics and Life* (Chicago: University of Chicago Press, 2011), and *Shakespeare Dwelling: Designs for the Theater of Life* (Chicago: University of Chicago Press, 2018); Debora Kuller Shuger, *Political Theologies in Shakespeare's England: The Sacred and the State in* Measure for Measure (London: Palgrave Macmillan, 2001). See also Jenifer R. Rust's excellent review article "Political Theology and Shakespeare Studies" in *Literature Compass* 6, no. 1 (January 2009): 175–190. More recent work connecting Agamben's concepts of biopolitics and sovereignty with early modern literature includes Julia Lupton and Graham Hammill, eds. *Political Theology and Early Modernity* (Chicago: University of Chicago Press, 2012); Daniel Cadman, "'The Very Nerves of State': Biopolitics and Sovereignty in Shakespeare's Vienna," *Lectures de Measure for Measure de William Shakespeare*, ed. Delphine Lemonnier-Trexier and Guillame Winter (Rennes, FR: Presses Universitaires de Rennes, 2012); Daniel Juan Gil, *Shakespeare's Antipolitics: Sovereign Power and the Life of the Flesh* (New York: Palgrave Macmillan, 2013); Nichole Miller, *Violence and Grace: Exceptional Life between Shakespeare and Modernity* (Evanston, IL: Northwestern University Press, 2014); Timothy A. Turner, "Othello on the Rack," *Journal for Early Modern Cultural Studies* 15, no. 3 (2015): 102–136.

7. Stephen Orgel's claim that the "marvels of stagecraft . . . are the supreme expressions of Renaissance kingship" is a foundational example. See *The Illusion of Power: Political Theater in the English Renaissance* (Berkeley: University of California Press, 1975), 58.

8. Agamben's discussion of Kantorowicz is found in *Homo Sacer: Sovereign Power and Bare Life* (Stanford, CA: Stanford University Press, 1998), 91–103. On Schmitt and the State of Exception as paradigmatic, see *State of Exception* (Chicago: University of Chicago Press, 2005).

9. All Shakespeare references in this chapter are from William Shakespeare, *The Complete Pelican Shakespeare*, ed. Stephen Orgel and A. R. Braunmuller (New York: Penguin Books, 2002). The quotation is from *2 Henry IV*, 1080–1122.

10. See my discussion of this scene in chapter 4 under "The 'Cruel Cace.'"

11. Shakespeare, *The Tragedy of King Richard III*, 904–957.

12. Christopher Hibbert, *The Virgin Queen* (London: Viking, 1990), 231. According to the Stonyhurst manuscript "The relation of the Lady Southwell of late Q. death,

primo Aprilis, 1607," Elizabeth Southwell heard the queen say, "I am tied with a chaine of iron about my feet . . . I am tied, I am tied, and the case is altered with me" during Nottingham's visit. Quoted in Marie Axton, *The Queen's Two Bodies: Drama and the Elizabethan Succession* (London: Royal Historical Society, 1977), 30.

13. *Correspondence of King James VI of Scotland with Sir Robert Cecil and Others in England, During the Reign of Queen Elizabeth* (Westminster: J. B. Nichols and Sons for the Camden Society, 1861), 72.

14. Refer to the entry for "evil" in the *Oxford English Dictionary*.

15. *Correspondence of King James VI of Scotland*, 72.

16. On the cultural misogyny prevalent during Elizabeth's final years, see Steven Mullaney, "Mourning and Misogyny: *Hamlet*, *The Revenger's Tragedy*, and the Final Progress of Elizabeth I, 1600–1607," *Shakespeare Quarterly* 45, no. 2 (Summer 1994): 139–162.

17. In a provocative discussion of Plowden, Kantorowicz, and the phrase "the case is altered," Lorna Hutson maintains that its significance in Plowden and at large has more to do with an emerging sense of Tudor jurisprudence than with the bodies natural and politic that compose the King's Two Bodies. Hutson argues that Plowden and his contemporaries were responding to the increasing need for interpretive juridical action, aiming to shape a jurisprudence that could rule on cases in which the strict letter of the law did not apply, or in other words, instances of the legal exception construed through an Aristotelian model of *epieikeia*. While I find Hutson's argument compelling in both its archival ingenuity and its thorough readings of Plowden's *Reports*, she seems ultimately to regard the juridical sphere as the prime mover of the changing conception of the King's mystical body and its bearing upon the kind's body natural. Thus, in her reading of *Richard II*, she argues that Shakespeare employs "the idea of trial by battle, with its emphasis on the unity of word and body . . . not to represent the always already lost unity of the body politic and the body of the king, but to suggest an impasse in the judicial system" (186). See her chapter "Not the King's Two Bodies: Reading the 'Body Politic' in Shakespeare's *Henry IV*, Parts I and II," in *Rhetoric and Law in Early Modern Europe*, ed. Lorna Hutson and Victoria Kahn (New Haven: Yale University Press, 2001), 166–198. Hutson's emphasis upon the juridical sphere, however, risks isolating jurisprudence and theories of sovereignty from an analysis of the biopolitical dimensions of early modern sovereignty, which are points of emphasis for my account of Shakespearean tragedy.

18. Axton, *The Queen's Two Bodies*, 29. Although the earliest publication date of Jonson's play is 1609, Nashe's pamphlet dates back at least to 1597, when Jonson was imprisoned in the Marshalsea and Nashe had fled to Yarmouth after the performance of their seditious play *The Isle of Dogs*. See William Selin's introduction to Ben Jonson, *The Case Is Altered* (New Haven, CT: Yale University Press, 1917).

19. From Plowden's *Reports* quoted in Axton, *The Queen's Two Bodies*, 28.

20. Axton, *The Queen's Two Bodies*, 28.

21. Axton was writing in the 1970s, when this particular tract had only recently been discovered in manuscript form. It had therefore not been considered by Ernst Kantorowicz in his study of the King's Two Bodies. Axton views the tract as evidence that Plowden's theory was developed in direct response to the Tudor-Stuart succession crisis. See Axton, *The Queen's Two Bodies*, 18–25.

22. There are multiple references to Elizabeth's final days being characterized by a strangely meditative state, including sources that claim she actively refused to sleep,

and others indicating that she was a victim of extreme insomnia, sitting upon a pile of cushions while staring blankly into space and sucking intermittently on her finger (from which her coronation ring had been removed by filing, since it had grown into her skin). In the roughly three to four hours immediately before her death, however, she apparently fell into bed and moved in and out of consciousness until her final breath. See Hibbert, *The Virgin Queen*, 258–260; *Correspondence of King James VI of Scotland*, li–liii; and Caroline Levine, *The Heart and Stomach of a King: Elizabeth I and the Politics of Sex and Power* (Philadelphia: University of Pennsylvania Press, 1994), 168.

23. See G. P. V. Akrigg, ed., *Letters of King James VI and I* (Berkeley: University of California Press, 1984), 13, for references to de Mayarne's memoir and James's many health problems, especially insomnia. See also Mayarne's manuscript note on the health of James I, reproduced in the original Latin in Norman Moore, MD, *The History of the Study of Medicine in the British Isles* (Oxford: The Clarendon Press, 1908), 164.

24. The mutuality of James I's political authority and the court masque, especially those penned by Ben Jonson, is well documented. So are Elizabeth's attachments to theater and her enjoyment of elaborate, lengthy performance. On James I and the masque, the essential work is Stephen Orgel, *The Illusion of Power* (Berkeley: University of California Press, 1975); see also Jonathan Goldberg, *James I and the Politics of Literature* (Baltimore: Johns Hopkins University Press, 1983). On Elizabeth, see historical biographies such as Levine, *The Heart and Stomach of a King*, and Hibbert, *The Virgin Queen*. For an account of Elizabeth and the politics of theater, see Louis Montrose, *The Purpose of Playing: Shakespeare and the Cultural Politics of Elizabethan Theater* (Chicago: University of Chicago Press, 1996).

25. See the firsthand account of the king's visit to Oxford for three days' worth of plays performed in his honor during which he fell asleep from apparent boredom and distaste in Henry Paul, *The Royal Play of Macbeth* (New York: Macmillan, 1950), 22.

26. King James himself seems to have shared with Shakespeare, and indeed, with the literary landscape at large, a personal interest in sleep's mysterious and potentially troubling effects. In April 1605, King James entertained a visitor to court by the name of Richard Haydocke, a physician trained at Oxford and living in Salisbury. Arthur Wilson's *History of England*, penned in 1653, recounts Haydocke's visit as follows:

> In the beginning of James's reign Richard Haydock of New Colledg in Oxford, practised Physick in the day, and Preached in the night in his Bed. His Practice came by his Profession, and his Preaching (as he pretended) by Revelation: For he would take a Text in his sleep, and deliver a good Sermon upon it, and though his Auditory were willing to silence him, by pulling, haling, and pinching, yet would he pertinaciously persist to the end, and sleep still.

While Wilson's account comes a half century after the fact, Frederick Hard has found multiple references to Haydocke in other works including John Stow's *Annals* (1615), Sir Richard Baker's *A Chronicle of the Kings of England* (1643), and letters from various aristocrats, all of which indicate that the case was familiar to members of James's court and to those in its immediate environs. Because of his interest and professed background in assessing instances of supernatural activity and "spiritual revelation," James brought Haydocke to London and sat up observing him sleep for two consecutive nights, hoping to see this strange phenomenon of automatic preaching take place. After these observations, the king contemplated the matter for nearly three weeks before finally deciding that Haydocke was a fraud, at which point he confronted the physician and obtained a confession. James then granted him clemency, provided that Haydocke make a full and public confession of his deceitful crimes. See Fredrick Hard, "Richard Haydocke and Alexander Browne: Two Half-Forgotten Writers on the Art of Painting," *PMLA* 55, no. 3 (September 1940): 727–741, for the above quotation from Wilson. For a recent account of these events, see chapter 1 in Carole Levin's *Dreaming the English Renaissance: Politics and Desire in Court and Culture*. (New York: Palgrave Macmillan, 2008).

27. Significant biblical passages tying sleep to death often figure sleep as an anticipatory, earthly form of temporary death before the rebirth of eternal salvation at the hand of God. Examples include Psalms 3:5, Psalms 13:3, Psalms 121:3–4, Proverbs 4: 14–16, Proverbs 19:15, John 11:14, and 1 Corinthians 15:20. In terms of literary representations, Sir Philip Sidney, for instance, names sleep the "Brother of quiet death" in *Astrophil and Stella* as well as the *Arcadia* ("And so of all sides they went to recommend themselves to the elder brother of death"), and Robert Southwell's *St. Peter's Complaint* calls "Sleepe, deathes allye: oblivion of tears." For these and further Elizabethan poetic references tying sleep to death, as well as classical precedents ranging from Homer to Seneca, see Jean Robertson, "Macbeth on Sleep," *Notes and Queries* 14 (1967): 139–141. A striking Jacobean dramatic example of the close proximity between sleep and death is found in John Webster's *The Duchess of Malfi*, and is discussed at length in chapter 5 of Garret Sullivan Jr.'s *Memory and Forgetting in English Renaissance Drama: Shakespeare, Marlowe, Webster* (Cambridge: Cambridge University Press, 2005).

28. Kantorowicz, *The King's Two Bodies*, 27.

29. Kantorowicz, *The King's Two Bodies*, 16.

30. Kantorowicz, *The King's Two Bodies*, 24 and 19.

31. From Plowden's *Reports*, quoted in Kantorowicz, *The King's Two Bodies*, 13.

32. Kantorowicz, *The King's Two Bodies*, 25.

33. Margreta de Grazia, Hamlet *without Hamlet* (Cambridge: Cambridge University Press, 2007), 30.

34. Rebecca Totaro, "Securing Sleep in *Hamlet*," *SEL* 50, no. 2 (Spring 2010): 407–426.

35. Totaro, "Securing Sleep," 421.

36. Shakespeare, *Hamlet*, ed. Orgel and Braunmuller, 1337–1391.

37. On this point in relationship to politics and the passions, see Garret Sullivan's essay "Romance, Sleep, and the Passions in Sir Phillip Sidney's *The Old Arcadia*," *ELH* 74 (2007):,735–757.

38. For a series of contemporary poetic and dramatic references to sleep in its more idyllic senses, see Albert S. Cook, "The Elizabethan Invocations to Sleep," *Modern Language Notes* 4, no. 8 (December 1889): 229–231. Cook locates the phrase "care-charmer" describing sleep in works from Samuel Daniel, Bartholomew Griffin, and Beaumont and Fletcher, and shows that multiple Elizabethan references to sleep and its figurations can be traced to Seneca and Ovid, in particular Book 11 of Ovid's *Metamorpohses*.

39. Thomas G. Rosenmeyer, *Senecan Drama and Stoic Cosmology* (Berkeley: University of California Press, 1989), 115.

40. Henry Bradley, "Cursed Hebenon (Or 'Hebona')," *The Modern Language Review* 15, no. 1 (January 1920): 85–87.

41. Stephen Greenblatt, *Hamlet in Purgatory* (Princeton, NJ: Princeton University Press, 2001), 231.

42. Refer to the 1559 Book of Common Prayer, which attempted to balance competing ideas of the sacrament and the doctrine of transubstantiation. See Diarmaid MacCulloch, *The Later Reformation in England, 1547–1603* (New York: Palgrave, 1990), 26–27.

43. Michel Foucault, *The History of Sexuality: Volume 1: An Introduction* (New York: Vintage Books, 1990), 148.

44. Gilles Deleuze, *The Logic of Sense*, trans. Mark Lester (New York: Columbia University Press, 1990), 131.

45. Deleuze, *The Logic of Sense*, 131.

46. Deleuze, *The Logic of Sense*, 5.

47. Deleuze, *The Logic of Sense*, 214.

48. Refer to the entry for "cleave" in the *OED*. Also, see Sigmund Freud's essay "The Antithetical Meaning of Primal Words" in *Complete Works Vol. XI*, ed. James Strachey (London: Hogarth Press, 1910), 155–161. Freud compares the double, antithetical senses of words to the combinatory process of dreams, which indicates "a particular preference for combining contraries into a unity or for representing them as one and the same thing" (155). His discussion takes examples from Egyptian, Arabic, and Indo-Germanic languages and includes both the English "cleave" and the Latin *sacratio*.

49. Christopher Marlowe, *Tamburlaine*, in *The Complete Works of Christopher Marlowe*, ed. Fredson Bowers, vol. 1 (Cambridge: Cambridge University Press, 1973), 2.4.8–9.

50. Richard Strier, *The Unrepentant Renaissance: From Petrarch to Shakespeare to Milton* (Chicago: University of Chicago Press, 2011), 139, and Julia Reinhard Lupton, *Shakespeare Dwelling: Designs for the Theater of Life* (Chicago: University of Chicago Press, 2018), 95.

51. Macbeth's understanding of sovereignty appears to constitute an instance of the despotic form of "a commonwealth by *acquisition*" rather than a "political commonwealth, or commonwealth by *institution*," according to Hobbes. This is the "natural force" route of attaining sovereignty that Hobbes says takes place by act of "conquest, or victory in war," but the transference of sovereignty actually takes place not as an effect of the *victory* itself but through the *consent* of the vanquished. Macbeth's act of conquest in sleep elides the possibility of a vanquished Duncan conferring consent, so Shakespeare both anticipates and problematizes this facet of the Hobbesian theory of sovereignty. See Thomas Hobbes, *Leviathan* (Oxford: Oxford University Press, 1996), chaps. 17–20.

52. The associations between outmoded barbarity and Scottish royalty were rampant in Elizabethan London. As Geoffrey Bullough notes, "That some Englishmen not only disliked the Scots but regarded Scottish history as a chronicle of violence was shown in the 1606 Parliament, when Sir Christopher Piggot . . . rose in the House during a discussion on 23 February about the Union of the two countries." Piggot, according to a contemporary account, delivered a caustic "invective against the Scots and Scottish nation; using words of scandal and obloquy, ill beseeming such an audience, and not pertinent to the matter in hand." In particular, Piggot's speech was controversial because it claimed that the Scottish nation "had not suffered above two kings to die in their beds [i.e., sleeping peacefully and dying of natural causes], these 200 years. Our king hath hardly escaped them; they have attempted him." Upon referring directly

to the Gowrie conspiracy that had plotted against James's life and, more broadly, to the widespread opinion that Scottish kings were highly subject to the violent tendencies of murderous revolt that their countrymen exemplified, Piggot was arrested and detained in the Tower of London, banned from ever serving in Parliament again. See Geoffrey Bullough, *Narrative and Dramatic Sources of Shakespeare*, vol. 7 (London: Routledge and Kegan Paul, 1973), 428–429.

53. The fabricated Stuart genealogy is one that James I endorsed, and it is found in Holinshed's *Chronicles*. This fact makes it difficult, if not impossible, to determine if Shakespeare had any knowledge of its historical accuracy. Holinshed's error reproduces an error from his primary source, William Harrison's English translation of John Bellenden's *Croniklis of Scotland with the cosmography and dyscription thairof, 1535*. The *Croniklis* of Bellenden "are themselves a translation into the Scots vernacular from Hector Boece's Latin *Scotorum Historiae, 1526*, which in its turn drew on various still earlier sources," including John Fordun's Latin *Scotichronicon* and Andrew of Wyntoun's *The Orygynale Cronykil*. See Arthur Melville Clark, *Murder under Trust: Or, The Topical Macbeth and other Jacobean Matters* (Edinburgh: Scottish Academic Press, 1981), 12–14.

54. Macbeth's language at this moment very likely draws from John Studley's translation of Seneca's *Hercules Oetaeus*. See Robert Miola, *Shakespeare and Classical Tragedy* (Oxford: Oxford University Press, 1992), 92–121.

55. See Gordon Braden, "*Herakles* and *Hercules*: Survival in Greek and Roman Tragedy (with a Coda on *King Lear*)," in *Theater and Society in the Ancient World*, ed. Ruth Scodel (Ann Arbor: University of Michigan Press, 1993), and Robert Miola, *Shakespeare and Classical Tragedy: The Influence of Seneca* (Oxford: Oxford University Press, 1992), 143–174. Miola argues that Shakespeare's *Othello* likewise draws on Seneca's tragedy in its tragic structure and depictions of Othello's mounting rage in "Othello Furens," *Shakespeare Quarterly* 41, no. 1 (1990): 49–64.

56. As Foucault argues, "the general problem of 'government' suddenly breaks out in the sixteenth century" across multiple domains, including the "government of oneself. The sixteenth century return to Stoicism revolves around this reactualization of the problem of how to govern oneself." Michel Foucault, *Security, Territory, Population*, 88.

57. I am thinking not only of *Hamlet* and *Macbeth* but also the depictions of sovereign weariness in the *Henriad*, which Garrett Sullivan illuminates in *Sleep, Romance, and Human Embodiment: Vitality from Spenser to Milton* (Cambridge: Cambridge University Press, 2012), 72–96.

58. Unhae Park Langis, "Humankindness / *King Lear* and the Suffering, Wisdom, and Compassion within Buddhist Interbeing," in *Literature and the Religious Experience*, ed. Matthew Smith and Caleb Spencer (London: Palgrave Macmillan, 2021). Two helpful accounts of such connections in Stoic ethics and physics are Thomas G. Rosenmeyer, *Senecan Drama and Stoic Cosmology* (Berkeley: University of California Press, 1989), and Brad Inwood, "Why Physics?," in *God and Cosmos in Stoicism*, ed. Ricardo Salles (London: Oxford University Press, 2009).

59. See Kantorowicz, *The King's Two Bodies*, 130–143, esp. 130–1n131, 133–4n146, and 143n167.

60. See my full discussion of Heywood's translation of Seneca's *Hercules Furens* in chapter 2.

61. See Kristin Poole's account of poetic dissolution and the Stoic resonances of the term in "'My Hand Would Dissolve, or Seem to Melt': Poetic Dissolution and Stoic Cosmology," in *Geographies of Embodiment in Early Modern England*, ed. Garrett Sullivan Jr. and Mary Floyd-Wilson (Oxford: Oxford University Press, 2020), 152–156.

62. Sheiba Kian Kaufman, "Care," in *Entertaining the Idea: Shakespeare, Performance, and Philosophy*, ed. Lowell Gallagher, James Kearney, and Julia Reinhard Lupton (Toronto: University of Toronto Press, 2020), 115–131.

63. Richard Halpern, *The Poetics of Primitive Accumulation: English Renaissance Culture and the Genealogy of Capital* (Ithaca, NY: Cornell University Press, 1991), 218.

64. Foucault, *Security, Territory, Population*, 103.

65. Foucault, *Security, Territory, Population*, 103.

66. Agamben, *Homo Sacer*, 6.

67. Agamben, *Homo Sacer*, 85.

68. Agamben, *Homo Sacer*, 101.

69. See Foucault's claim that "the old power of death that symbolized sovereign power was now carefully supplanted by the administration of bodies and the calculated management of life." *History of Sexuality*, 139–140.

70. Foucault, *History of Sexuality*, 143–144.

4. "Watching to Banish Care"

1. In *The Pain of Reformation* (New York: Fordham University Press, 2012), Joe Campana draws attention to an ethics of vulnerability at the heart of Spenser's epic poem. His view finds support among other critics such as James Kuzner in *Open Subjects: English Renaissance Republicans, Modern Selfhoods, and the Virtue of Vulnerability* (Edinburgh: Edinburgh University Press, 2011) and Giulio Pertile in *Feeling Faint: Affect and Consciousness in the Renaissance* (Evanston: Northwestern University Press, 2019), who share Campana's interest in moments when the pursuit of virtue and its ostensible grounding in sensorial and intellective firmness gives way to valuable experiences of psychosomatic vulnerability, dissolution, or disorientation. This chapter contributes to these emerging conversations on Spenserian vulnerability through its emphasis on the vulnerable condition of sleep as a crucially restorative form of ethical care in *The Faerie Queene*.

2. This includes Desiderius Erasmus and Richard Mulcaster, Spenser's own schoolmaster. See my discussion of Renaissance humanist care in chapter 1 under "English Humanist Ecologies of Care."

3. See Deborah Shuger, "'Gums of Glutinous Heat' and the Stream of Consciousness: The Theology of Milton's *Maske*," *Representations* 60 (Autumn 1997): 1–21.

4. See Northrop Frye, *Fables of Identity: Studies in Poetic Mythology* (New York: Harcourt, Brace, & World, 1963), 73, and Michael Dolzani, ed., *Northrop Frye's Notebooks on Renaissance Literature*, in *Collected Works of Northrop Frye* (Toronto: University of Toronto Press, 2006), 20:12, 17–18, for references to Spenser's supposed irrational fear of sleep.

5. Garrett Sullivan Jr. argues that sleep challenges the moral physiology of temperance pursued by the hero Guyon in book 2 of *The Faerie Queene*. Sullivan's account fits with Frye's claim that Spenser's Protestant epic displays an overarching distrust of sleep, though it seems to me worth thinking about the respective virtues allegorized by Redcrossse and Guyon in terms of their differing relationships to sleep and sleeplessness. See

Sullivan's pathbreaking *Sleep, Romance, and Human Embodiment: Vitality from Spenser to Milton* (Cambridge: Cambridge University Press, 2012), chap. 1. See also the discussion of Guyon's sleep by Sullivan and Mary Floyd-Wilson in their introduction to *Environment and Embodiment in Early Modern England* (London: Palgrave Macmillan, 2007), 1–13.

6. Edmund Spenser, *The Faerie Queene*, ed. Thomas P. Roche (New York: Penguin, 1987), 41.

7. Darryl Gless, *Interpretation and Theology in Spenser* (Cambridge: Cambridge University Press, 2004), 48–49.

8. Romans 13, 1 Corinthians 11, Ephesians 5, and 1 Thessalonians 5 provide Pauline images of sleep that figure spiritual laxity, sin, backsliding, and loss of faith. See the extended discussion of Pauline political theology, sleep, and pastoral care in chapter 1.

9. Biblical quotations are from *The Geneva Bible: A Facsimile of the 1560 Edition* (Madison: University of Wisconsin Press, 1969).

10. On this point, see Robert H. Gundry, *Soma in Biblical Theology* (Cambridge: Cambridge University Press, 1976), especially 195–197.

11. See Julia Reinhard Lupton, *Citizen-Saints: Shakespeare and Political Theology* (Chicago: University of Chicago Press, 2005); Ken Jackson, "'All the World to Nothing': *Richard III*, Badiou, and Pauline Subjectivity," *Shakespeare* 1 (June 2005): 29–52; Graham Hammill and Julia Reinhard Lupton, "Sovereigns, Citizens, and Saints: Political Theology and Renaissance Literature," and Catherine Winiarski, "Adultery, Idolatry, and the Subject of Monotheism," in the special issue of *Religion and Literature* 38, no. 3 (Autumn 2006); Gregory Kneidel, *Rethinking the Turn to Religion in Early Modern English Literature: The Poetics of All Believers* (Basingstoke, UK: Palgrave Macmillan, 2008); and Jonathan Gil Harris, *Untimely Matters in the Time of Shakespeare* (Philadelphia: University of Pennsylvania Press, 2009).

12. These reflections are commonly saturated with a sense of optimism regarding the histories and futures of Pauline thought. Philosophical accounts include Giorgio Agamben, *The Time That Remains* (Stanford, CA: Stanford University Press, 2005); Alain Badiou, *St Paul: The Foundation of Universalism* (Stanford, CA: Stanford University Press, 1997); and Slavoj Žižek, *The Puppet and the Dwarf* (Cambridge, MA: MIT Press, 2003) and *The Monstrosity of Christ: Paradox or Dialectic* (Cambridge, MA: MIT Press, 2009). Julia Lupton charts the influence of these and other accounts among critics of early modern literature in "The Pauline Renaissance: A Shakespearean Reassessment," *The European Legacy* 15 (2010): 215–220.

13. My reading of Pauline theology derives in part from Nietzsche's *The Antichrist* as well as the argument of Gilles and Fanny Deleuze in their essay "Nietzsche and St. Paul, Lawrence and John of Patmos," in *Essays Critical and Clinical*, ed. Dan Smith (London: Verso, 1998), 36–52. Much of that essay elaborates D. H. Lawrence's reading of the Apocalypse and his interest in an aristocratic image of Christ, whose doctrine of love preached individual refinement and care of the self over a collective political-theological orientation. Deleuze contrasts Lawrence's notion of Christ with Paul's doctrine of an infinite indebtedness to God, which Deleuze cites (by way of Nietzsche) as the structuring ecclesiastical principle of Christianity. As far as I know, this essay has not yet been considered among the recent discussions of Pauline thought and early modern political theology.

14. On the crucial relationship between Pauline scripture and the claims, ideologies, and interpretive practices of English reformers, see John Coolidge's study *The Pauline Renaissance in England: Puritanism and the Bible* (Oxford: Clarendon Press, 1970).

15. Warren T. Reich identifies the duality of *cura* in the ancient Roman world with, on the one hand, Virgil's depiction of "vengeful Cares" (*ultrices Curae*) at the entrance to the Underworld in book 6 of the *Aeneid*, and on the other, Seneca's claim that "in humans, the good is perfected by care (*cura*)." Quoted in Reich, "History of the Notion of Care," *Encyclopedia of Bioethics* (New York: Macmillan, 1995), 319–331. On competing notions and etymologies of care in early modern England, see also my discussion in the introduction.

16. See chapter 1 under "Body, Flesh, Vigilance: Pastoral Care and the Political Theology of Sleep."

17. 2 Thessalonians 5:5–6.

18. Augustine, *Confessions*, trans. Henry Chadwick (Oxford: Oxford University Press, 2008), 8.5.12, 141.

19. Augustine, *Confessions*, 10.30.41, 203.

20. Martin Luther, *Commentary on Romans*, trans. J. Theodore Muller (Grand Rapids, MI: Kregel Publications, 1976), 192. For more on Luther's and Calvin's readings of Pauline vigilance, see chapter 1 under "Body, Flesh, Vigilance: Pastoral Care and the Political Theology of Sleep."

21. Erasmus, *Enchiridion Militis Christiani: An English Translation*, ed. Anne M. O'Donnell (Oxford: Oxford University Press, 1981), 33.

22. Erasmus, *Enchiridion Militis Christiani*, 42.

23. See the entries for "insomnia" and "sleepless" in the *OED*.

24. See Rebecca Totaro, "Securing Sleep in *Hamlet*," *SEL* 50 (Spring 2010): 407–426.

25. On nocturnal watch as a form of vigilant political care, which Shakespeare uses to expose monarchical fantasies of "perpetual wakefulness," see Sullivan Jr.'s discussion of the *Henriad* in chapter 3 of *Sleep, Romance, and Human Embodiment*.

26. See Coolidge, *The Pauline Renaissance*, and Diarmaid MacCulloch, *The Later Reformation in England, 1547–1603* (New York: Palgrave, 2001), 71–73, 75–76, and 136.

27. Harry Berger Jr., "Sexual and Religious Politics in Book 1 of Spenser's *Faerie Queene*," *English Literary Renaissance* 34, no. 2 (2004): 201–242, 223.

28. Julia Reinhard Lupton, *Thinking with Shakespeare: Essays on Politics and Life* (Chicago: University of Chicago Press, 2011), 25–67.

29. Cicero, *On Moral Ends*, ed. Julia Annas, trans. Raphael Woolf (Cambridge: Cambridge University Press, 2001), 70.

30. Jacob Klein, "The Stoic Argument from *Oikeiôsis*," *Oxford Studies in Ancient Philosophy* 50 (2016): 143–200, 184–186.

31. Seneca, *Letters on Ethics*, trans. Margaret Graver and A. A. Long (Chicago: University of Chicago Press, 2015), 121.21, 488.

32. On the Stoic ethical aim of cultivating the right "affective and relational disposition" as the necessary ground to virtuous action, see Katja Vogt, *Law, Reason, and the Cosmic City: Political Philosophy in the Early Stoa* (Oxford: Oxford University Press, 2007), 5.

33. The lion's death recalls Gordon Teskey's claim that in an allegory, death is the closure of being in its capacity to become; when allegories die they fulfill and complete

whatever allegorical sense they are meant to have. See his essay, "Death in an Allegory," in *Imagining Death in Spenser and Milton*, ed. Elizabeth J. Bellamy, Patrick Cheney, and Michael Schoenfeldt (London: Palgrave Macmillan, 2003), 65–77.

34. This is the second and now obsolete definition given for "carcass" in the *Oxford English Dictionary*.

35. Gundry, *Soma in Biblical Theology*, 6–13.

36. Aristotle, *Nicomachean Ethics*, trans. Sarah Broadie and Christopher Rowe (Oxford: Oxford University Press, 2002), 1099a1, 103.

37. Quoted in Cynthia A. Freeland, "Aristotle on Bodies, Matter, and Potentiality," in *Philosophical Issues in Aristotle's Biology*, ed. Allan Gotthelf and James G. Lennox (Cambridge: Cambridge University Press, 1987), 392–407.

38. See Aristotle's claim that there is a form of excellence actualized by the sleeping soul, in *Nicomachean Ethics*, 1102b1–1102b5, 109.

39. This point is consistent with Aristotle's extended discussions of excellence and the function of the human soul in book 1 of *Nicomachean Ethics*, where he argues that there are different kinds of excellence in which the human soul participates under various conditions, even if the proper function of the human soul is to actualize "complete excellence." See especially sections 1.7–1.9 (1097a15–1100a5) and 1.13 (1102a5–1103a10).

40. Augustine, *Tractates on the Gospel of John 112–124*, trans. John W. Rettig (Washington, DC: Catholic University of America Press), 51.

41. Augustine, *Tractates on the Gospel of John 112–124*, 50. The citation of Augustine's original is from *Corpus Christianorvm, Series Latina XXXVI: Sancti Avrelii Avgvstini* (Turnholt, BE: Typographi Brepols Editores Pontificii, 1954), 661.

42. Mention of the whole/holy pun in critical commentary on book 1 includes Harry Berger Jr., "The Spenserian Dynamics," *SEL: Studies in English Literature* 8 (1968): 1–18; James Nohrnberg, *The Analogy of the Faerie Queene* (Princeton, NJ: Princeton University Press, 1976), 279; Douglas Brooks-Davies under the entry for "*The Faerie Queene*, Book 1" in A. C. Hamilton, ed., *The Spenser Encyclopedia* (Toronto: University of Toronto Press, 1990), 259–263; and Maureen Quilligan, *The Language of Allegory: Defining the Genre* (Ithaca, NY: Cornell University Press, 1979), 40. With her comments in *Incest and Agency in Elizabeth's England* (Philadelphia: University of Pennsylvania Press, 2005), Quilligan stirred up a minor debate over the phrase "perfect hole" that describes Amoret's wound at the conclusion of book 3. Quilligan doesn't mention Jonathan Goldberg's discussion of the pun in *Endlesse Worke: Spenser and the Structures of Discourse* (Baltimore: Johns Hopkins University Press, 1981), 3. Ken Hieatt attacks Quilligan's reading, and the debate among these three critics is summarized and given fresh meaning by Lauren Silberman in "'Perfect Hole': Spenser and Greek Romance," *Spenser Studies* 23 (2008): 283–291. I am inclined to agree with Silberman's account of the pun on Amoret's wound, as well as her suggestion that the scene probably alludes to Achilles Tatius's pun on the Greek term ὁλόκλερον (*holókleron*), meaning "entire" or "complete in all its parts," in his romance *Clitophon and Leucippe*. But neither Silberman nor any of the critics she responds to in this context address the whole/holy pun in book 1, and no critic has understood it to include any sense of "hole" as emptiness in the legend of Redcrosse knight and Una.

43. See the entry for "whole" in the *Oxford English Dictionary*.

44. See "*The Faerie Queene*, Book 1" and also Quilligan, *Language of Allegory*, 33–37.

45. David Lee Miller approximates this claim when he argues that a logic of negation informs Spenser's neo-Platonic representations of ideal completion, but Miller never explicitly calls out the pun, nor does he align this force of negation with either Redcrosse's bodily presence or Spenser's ontology of the virtue of holiness. See "Spenser's Poetics: The Poem's Two Bodies," *PMLA* 101 (1986): 170–185.

46. Paul's original text uses the Greek term *πανοπλιαν*, or panoply.

47. *The Geneva Bible: A Facsimile of the 1560 Edition* (Madison: University of Wisconsin Press, 1969).

48. My reading of the "hole" in Spenser's pun owes something to the concept of holey space developed by Gilles Deleuze and Felix Guattari in *A Thousand Plateaus: Capitalism and Schizophrenia* (Minneapolis: University of Minnesota Press, 1987). But Spenser's pun suggests that his vision of physical vitality departs from their immanently plenist view of the cosmos. Redcrosse's mortal being rather presents a vision of immanent decay in sinful, fleshly life—a kind of paradoxically negative vitalism—closer to Reza Negarastani's imaginative variation and "demonization" of Deleuze and Guattari's concept. See Reza Negarastani, *Cyclonopedia: Complicity with Anonymous Materials* (Melbourne: re.press, 2008).

49. On various terms containing the ancient Greek root *oikos* that are relevant to an understanding of Stoic *oikeiôsis*, including *oikeion*, see Klein, "The Stoic Argument from *Oikeiosis*," 150.

50. For a clear account of distinctions between the strictly Calvinist and Reformed Anglican views of baptism, and Spenser's handling of these differences in book 1, see William H. Marshall, "Calvin, Spenser, and the Major Sacraments," *Modern Language Notes* 74, no. 2 (1959): 97–101.

51. See Shuger, "'Gums of Glutinous Heat,'" 6–7.

52. Jonathan Goldberg critiques many of these readings in *The Seeds of Things: Theorizing Sexuality and Materiality in Renaissance Representations* (New York: Fordham University Press, 2009), chap. 3.

53. The hero's furor at this moment thus constitutes an instance of the widespread Elizabethan "*Hercules furens* convention" that Rolf Soellner has tracked in literary, philosophical, and medical discussions from antiquity to the early modern period. See Soellner, "The Madness of Hercules and the Elizabethans," *Comparative Literature* 10, no. 4 (1958): 309–324.

54. See Romans 1:15, 21–28. On the metaphysical, juridical, and political implications of Paul's relocation of the Jewish law of circumcision to the law of faith inscribed upon the heart, see Giorgio Agamben, *The Time That Remains: A Commentary on the Letter to the Romans* (Stanford: Stanford University Press, 2005).

55. Seneca, *Anger, Mercy, Revenge*, trans. Robert A. Kaster and Martha C. Nussbaum (Chicago: University of Chicago Press, 2010), 1.8.3, 21.

56. At this moment Redcrosse also resembles Duessa, when she frivolously tells Sansjoy that she is "Ioyous, to see his ymage in mine eye," meaning she covets the reflection of her dead lover, Sansfoy, and sees his image in his brother's face—a fact which only makes her new allegiance to Sansjoy all the more heinous.

57. Concerning Spenser's (and more generally, early modern Protestantism's) oscillation between forms of spiritual and bodily cure that fold into one another, see Beth Quitslund, "Despair and the Composition of the Self," *Spenser Studies* 17 (2003): 91–106.

I am convinced by Quitslund's analysis in this respect, but I part ways with her claim that after his visit to the House of Holiness, Redcrosse is completely "cured" of the psychosomatic ailment personified by Despair. I understand the point of this episode to be that such a cure is impossible, so long as Redcrosse knight remains bound to his earthly body.

58. My point here is not to suggest that Spenser is or is not a "Platonist" but rather that his poem directs energies toward what Nietzsche identified as the task of overturning Platonism—a task that Gilles Deleuze argues actually begins within Platonic thinking. See his discussion of the "paradoxes of pure becoming," which betray a buried dualism of copies and simulacra in Platonic thought, in Gilles Deleuze, *The Logic of Sense*, trans. Constantin V. Boundas (New York: Columbia University Press, 1990), 1–4.

59. Seneca, *Letters on Ethics*, 121.16, 487.

60. On the corporeal causal chain of Stoic physics and cosmology, see my discussion of Jasper Heywood's translation of Seneca's *Hercules Furens* in chapter 2 under "*Krasis* and *Ira*."

61. Deleuze attributes to the Stoics a "discovery of passions-bodies and of the infernal mixtures which they organize or submit to," which he sees as key features of both Senecan tragedy and Elizabethan theater. But his interpretation of what is essential to this Stoic perspective holds equally true for the Ovidian vision of Hercules's death as it does for Seneca's: "The poisoned tunics begin their deadly work by burning into the skin and by devouring the surface. The deadly work then reaches more deeply, in a trajectory which goes from the pierced body to the fragmented body, *membra discerpta*. Everywhere poisonous mixtures seethe in the depth of the body; abominable necromancies, incests, and feedings are elaborated." See Deleuze, *The Logic of Sense*, 131.

62. There's a Heideggerian feel to this situation, though I don't want to overemphasize it given the theological underpinnings of book 1 that seemingly steer Spenser away from a notion of selfhood radically determined by finitude. But in chapter 6 of the first division of *Being and Time*, Heidegger offers a compelling footnote on how he came to identify *care* as the Being of Dasein, by way of thinking through Aristotle and Augustine: "The way in which 'care' is viewed in the foregoing existential analytic of Dasein, is one which has grown upon the author in connection with his attempts to Interpret the Augustinian (i.e., Helleno-Christian) anthropology with regard to the foundational principles reached in the ontology of Aristotle." Martin Heidegger, *Being and Time*, trans. John Macquarrie and Edward Robinson (New York: Harper Perennial, 1962), 492. I take Spenser's interests in an Augustinian idea of fallen humanity (or "thrownness" as a dispersion of the created self after sin enters the world), and in Aristotelian and Stoic ontologies of the human being, as providing philosophical grounds resembling those of Heidegger's investigation.

63. William A. Oram, "Spenserian Paralysis," *SEL Studies in English Literature 1500–1900* 41, no. 1 (2001): 49–70, 57.

64. See Giulio Pertile, "'And All His Sences Stound': The Physiology of Stupefaction in Spenser's *Faerie Queene*," *English Literary Renaissance* 44, no. 3 (2014): 420–451, especially 428–430.

65. See Oram, "Spenserian Paralysis," 56, for the claim that we are moving into slightly more secular concerns in the later books.

66. As Richard Sugg describes the pervasive "spiritual physiology" of the early modern period, "Spirits could move back and forth with surprising ease between the material and the immaterial, the mental and the physical sides of human life." Richard

Sugg, *The Smoke of the Soul: Medicine, Physiology and Religion in Early Modern England* (New York: Palgrave Macmillan, 2013), 47.

67. John M. Steadman, "The 'Inharmonious Blacksmith': Spenser and the Pythagoras Legend," *PMLA* 79, no. 5 (1964): 664–665.

68. For an account of Spenser's legend of Friendship that emphasizes a dialectic between boundaries erected through disciplined self-control and a selfhood defined by its open vulnerability to the social, see James Kuzner, *Open Subjects: English Renaissance Republicans, Modern Selfhoods and the Virtue of Vulnerability* (Edinburgh: Edinburgh University Press, 2012).

69. Seneca claims that care perfects the human good in *Letters on Ethics*, 124.14, 500. The Cicero quotation is from *Cicero: On Old Age; On Friendship; On Divination*, trans. W. A. Falconer, Loeb Classical Library 154 (Cambridge, MA: Harvard University Press, 1923), 159–161.

70. Jeff Dolven arrives at a similar conclusion regarding the care for physical life in *The Faerie Queene* in "Besides Good and Evil," *SEL Studies in English Literature 1500–1900* 57, no. 1 (Winter 2017): 1–22.

5. "Inhabit Lax"

1. All references to the poem are from John Milton, ed. Gordon Teskey, *Paradise Lost: A Norton Critical Edition* (New York: Norton, 2005).

2. Here I am indebted to William Kerrigan's insight that "if astronomy for Milton was a science of intellectual curiosity, medicine was a science of personal crisis." William Kerrigan, *The Sacred Complex: On the Psychogenesis of* Paradise Lost (Cambridge, MA: Harvard University Press, 1983), 201.

3. See Jackson Campbell Boswell, *Milton's Library: A Catalog of the Remains of John Milton's Library and an Annotated Reconstruction of Milton's Library and Ancillary Readings* (New York: Garland Publishing, 1975), 221–222, for works by Seneca familiar to Milton. On *Hercules Furens* and book 1's depictions of Satan as a tyrannical monarch, see Martin Dzelzainis, "*Paradise Lost* II.4 and Seneca's *Hercules Furens*," *Notes and Queries* 45 (1998): 49–50. On Hercules as a recurring figure in Milton's poetry and prose, with particular attention to the issue of tyrannicide, see Stella P. Revard, "The Politics of Milton's Hercules," *Milton Studies* 32 (1996): 217–245.

4. Seneca, *Seneca: His Tenne Tragedies*, ed. Thomas Newton (New York: Alfred A. Knopf, 1927), 43–44.

5. Gordon Teskey aptly describes Milton as "a thinker of the *archē*, of the origin and 'governing principle'" in *Delirious Milton: The Fate of the Poet in Modernity* (Cambridge, MA: Harvard University Press, 2006), 6.

6. On the political ramifications of Milton's vision of a well-ordered, virtuous soul as both an ethical ideal and the basis for a republicanism rooted in the Socratic tradition, see Rachel Foxley, "'Due Libertie and Proportiond Equalitie': Milton, Democracy, and the Republican Tradition," *History of Political Thought* 34, no. 4 (2013): 614–638.

7. Seneca, *Letters on Ethics*, trans. Margaret Graver and A.A. Long (Chicago: University of Chicago Press, 2015), 117.2, 464.

8. Aetius, 1.7.33 (*SVF* 2.1027), in *The Hellenistic Philosophers*, ed. A. A. Long and D. N. Sedley, vol. 1 (Cambridge: Cambridge University Press, 1997), 274.

9. See my discussion of *krasis* in chapter 2.

10. The thought that Milton's cosmology and theory of matter might owe something to the Stoics was first developed in A. S. P. Woodhouse's seminal essay on Miltonic creation and the poet's conception of the relationship between God and matter. See A. S. P. Woodhouse, "Notes on Milton's Views on the Creation: The Initial Phases," *Philological Quarterly* 28, no. 1 (January 1949): 211–236. For relevant passages on Stoicism, see 219 and 222. More recently, D. Bentley Hart finds similarities between Milton's monism and that of the Stoics, arguing that the "oneness of the primary matter underlying the diversity of all its secondary manifestations" makes for a "continuity of substance between things and God" that is "nearer Stoic than neoplatonic monism" (22). Yet while Hart's provocative essay acknowledges these connections, it does not explore them any further. See D. Bentley Hart, "Matter, Monism, and Narrative: An Essay on the Metaphysics of *Paradise Lost*," *Milton Quarterly* 30, no. 1 (1996): 16–27. Meanwhile, in *"Matter of Glorious Trial": Spiritual and Material Substance in* Paradise Lost (New Haven, CT: Yale University Press, 2009), N. K. Sugimura suggests that Milton appealed to neo-Stoic thought and the doctrine of incorporeals in his attempt to figure Chaos and Night, and more broadly to "think through the problem of interstitial spaces" (250). Yet she mischaracterizes this supposed Stoic influence as a form of Senecan dualism (Seneca is rather, like all Stoics, a monist with respect to psychology and cosmology alike), which Sugimura argues is then routed and modified through the thought of Justus Lipsius. Other critics have explored Stoic influences on Milton's ethical thought through familiar themes of constancy and retreat into an inner paradise of virtue, but none have considered the theory of oikeiôsis or its connection with Stoic physics. See Andrew Shifflett's account of the Son in Milton's *Paradise Regained* in chapter 5 of *Stoicism, Politics and Literature in the Age of Milton: War and Peace Reconciled* (Cambridge: Cambridge University Press, 1998), and Joshua R. Held, "Eve's 'Paradise Within' in *Paradise Lost*: A Stoic Mind, a Love Sonnet, and a Good Conscience," *Studies in Philology* 114, no. 1 (2017): 171–196.

11. Woodhouse, "Notes on Milton's Views on the Creation," 222. On Milton's knowledge of Diogenes Laertius's *Lives of the Eminent Philosophers*, see Boswell, *Milton's Library*, 152.

12. According to Diogenes, the Stoics "hold that there are two principles of the universe: the active and the passive. The passive principle is unqualified substance, namely matter, while the active principle is the reasoning power in it, namely god. For the latter, being eternal, fabricates every single thing throughout the entirety of matter." See Diogenes Laertius, *Lives of the Eminent Philosophers*, trans. Pamela Mensch (Oxford: Oxford University Press, 2018), 7.134, 359.

13. Laertius, *Lives of the Eminent Philosophers*, 7.136, 360.

14. Laertius, *Lives of the Eminent Philosophers*, 7.147, 364.

15. Stella P. Revard, *The War in Heaven:* Paradise Lost *and the Tradition of Satan's Rebellion* (Ithaca: Cornell University Press, 1980), 54.

16. John Milton, *The Complete Works of John Milton. Volume VIII: De Doctrina Christiana Part 1*, ed. John K. Hale and J. Donald Cullington (Oxford: Oxford University Press, 2012), 293.

17. Milton, *De Doctrina Christiana*, 247.

18. As Milton writes in *De Doctrina Christiana*, "So it is clear that the world was established out of some kind of matter. For since 'activity' and 'passivity' are relational terms,

and since no agent can act outside itself unless there exists something to be acted upon, which doubtless is matter, it seems that God could not have created this world out of nothing—'could not,' not from any lack of power or omnipotence, but because there had to be something already in existence which by being acted upon might receive the almighty force of his efficacy. . . . That matter should always have existed outside God—although it is only a passive Principle, depends on God." Milton, *De Doctrina Christiana Part 1*, 289–291.

19. As Stephen Fallon has argued, spirit and matter are for Milton two modes of the same substance: "Spirit is rarefied matter, matter is dense spirit. All things, from insensate objects through souls, are manifestations of this one substance . . . [and] all corporeal substance is animate, self-active, and free." See *Milton among the Philosophers: Poetry and Materialism in Seventeenth-Century England* (Ithaca, NY: Cornell University Press, 1991), 81. Phillip J. Donnelly has contested Fallon's claim by suggesting that he fails to distinguish between categories of matter (*materia*) and body (*corpore*), which Donnelly argues are meaningful distinctions for Milton. See Phillip J. Donnelly, "'Matter' Versus Body: The Character of Milton's Monism," *Milton Quarterly* 33, no. 3 (1999): 79–85. To my mind, Donnelly's worry does not take into account two earlier essays on Milton's materialism and corporeality. First, John Reesing offers a clear-sighted account of corporeality as "a real and positive perfection eminently present in God" (167), and therefore always potentially present in the material substance or matter that he releases from himself to go about the work of creation. See Reesing, "The Materiality of God in Milton's De Doctrina Christiana," *The Harvard Theological Review* 50, no. 3 (1957): 159–174. Second, A. S. P. Woodhouse refers to Milton's claim in *Christian Doctrine* that even God's "divine virtue and efficiency" could not produce "bodies out of nothing . . . unless there had been some bodily power in the substance of God, since no one can give to another what he does not possess." As Woodhouse notes, "Among the inescapable implications which Milton does not seek to evade is the admission of an element of corporeality in the Deity" (Woodhouse, 222).

20. Kerrigan, *The Sacred Complex*, 212.

21. Hierocles, for instance, contends that "the soul is not enclosed in the body as in a bucket, like liquids surrounded by jars, but is wondrously blended and wholly intermingled, so that not even the least part of the mixture fails to have a share in either of them. . . . Thus, too, what pertains to shared affect [*sympatheia*] is total for both. For each shares the affects of the other, and neither is the soul heedless of bodily affects, nor is the body completely deaf to the torments of the soul." Hierocles, *Hierocles the Stoic: Elements of Ethics, Fragments and Excerpts*, ed. Ilaria Ramelli, trans. David Konstan (Atlanta: Society of Biblical Literature, 2009), 11.

22. Milton, *De Doctrina Christiana Part 1*, 26.

23. See also my discussion of Stoic oikeiôsis in the introduction. Milton's other likely classical sources for the theory of oikeiôsis, in addition to passages from Diogenes Laertius, would have included Cicero's *On Moral Ends*, 3.20–21, which describes the Good as a form of harmony or *homologia* of which the rational animal becomes aware as its oikeiôsis expands beyond its natural primary attachment to itself, and Seneca's letter 121. There are also extracts from Hierocles the Stoic's treatise, *Elements of Ethics*, which describe the circular pattern of oikeiôsis, that Milton would have found in the collection

of philosophical fragments by Stobaeus. And finally, Milton would have encountered a reference to oikeiôsis in the *Prolegomena* to Hugo Grotius's *De jure belli ac pacis*, in a passage which I discuss later.

24. See Katja Maria Vogt, "The Stoics on Virtue and Happiness," in *The Cambridge Companion to Ancient Ethics*, ed. Chris Bobonich (Cambridge: Cambridge University Press, 2017), 183–199. On oikeiôsis and teleology, see Troels Engberg-Pedersen, *The Stoic Theory of Oikeiôsis: Moral Development and Social Interaction in Early Stoic Philosophy* (Aarhus, DK: Aarhus University Press, 1990), especially 16–35. On oikeiôsis and the Stoic political theory of cosmic citizenship as being a rational animal and, more perfectly, living in accordance with natural law, see Katja Maria Vogt, *Law, Reason, and the Cosmic City: Political Philosophy in the Early Stoa* (Oxford: Oxford University Press, 2008), 99–110.

25. John Milton, *Complete Prose Works, Volume VIII: 1666–1682*, ed. Don M. Wolfe (New Haven, CT: Yale University Press, 1982), 267.

26. As both Arthur E. Barker and Diane McColley have argued, Milton views human life as a process of regeneration seeking continuity with the ways of God. For McColley this involves an "active response . . . according to the norm of right" (16), and this basic principle holds true both for prelapsarian and postlapsarian life. See Arthur Barker, "Structural and Doctrinal Pattern in Milton's Later Poems," in *Essays in English Literature from the Renaissance to the Victorian Age, Presented to A.S.P. Woodhouse*, ed. Millar MacLure and F. W. Watt (Toronto: University of Toronto Press, 1964), 189, and Diane Kelsey McColley, *Milton's Eve* (Urbana: University of Illinois Press, 1983), 16.

27. Diogenes Laertius, *Lives of Eminent Philosophers, Volume II: Books 6–10*, trans. R. D. Hicks, Loeb Classical Library 185 (Cambridge, MA: Harvard University Press, 1925), 7.89, 197.

28. Cognates of the English word "pervert" are often used to translate variants of Diogenes's original Greek term, *diastrephō*, which can also be rendered as "turn" or "distort." The Loeb edition and Perseus online both use "perverted," while the more recent Oxford translation uses "distorted." See Laertius, *Lives of the Eminent Philosophers*, 7.89, 344.

29. John Milton, *Complete Prose Works: Volume VIII*, ed. Maurice Kelley (New Haven, CT: Yale University Press, 1982), 267.

30. The phrase also echoes a passage from Cicero's treatise, *De Domo Sua*, which is pitched as the author's attempt to recover his Palatine Hill home from takeover by Clodius. Cicero's enemy had seized and transformed his property into a temple to *Libertas* while he was exiled from Rome, and Cicero describes his impious motivation to "live in an unhampered sumptuousness [*habitare laxe et magnifice*]" by uniting two estates. Cicero, *Pro Archia. Post Reditum in Senatu. Post Reditum ad Quirites. De Domo Sua. De Haruspicum Responsis. Pro Plancio*, trans. N. H. Watts, Loeb Classical Library 158 (Cambridge, MA: Harvard University Press, 1923), 115, 269.

31. Laertius, *Lives of the Eminent Philosophers*, 7.158, 367.

32. Seneca, *Epistles, Volume I: Epistles 1–65*, trans. Richard M. Gummere, Loeb Classical Library 75 (Cambridge, MA: Harvard University Press, 1917), 56.6–7, 377.

33. See my discussion of the Christian political theology of sleep in chapter 1 under "Body, Flesh, Vigilance: Pastoral Care and the Political Theology of Sleep."

34. Cicero, *On Moral Ends*, ed. Julia Annas (Cambridge: Cambridge University Press, 2001), 5.54, 136.

35. David Carroll Simon, *Light without Heat: The Observational Mood from Bacon to Milton* (Ithaca, NY: Cornell University Press, 2018), 170.

36. Michael Lieb, *The Dialectics of Creation: Patterns of Birth and Regeneration in* Paradise Lost (Amherst: University of Massachusetts Press, 1970), 66.

37. For a helpful recounting of these critical conversations, see Stephen Hequembourg's essay, "Milton's 'Unoriginal' Voice: Quotation Marks in *Paradise Lost*," *Modern Philology* 112, no. 1 (2014): 154–178.

38. As Gabriel commands the company of angels, "Uzziel, half these draw off and coast the south / With strictest watch, these other wheel the north! / Our circuit meets full west" (4.782–784).

39. Lieb, *The Dialectics of Creation*, 82.

40. Lieb, *The Dialectics of Creation*, 83.

41. This moment is anticipated from a narrative perspective by a passage in 4.257–266, where "murmuring waters" fall "disperst" across the landscape of the Garden and "vernal airs . . . attune / The trembling leaves." Birdsong, flowing water, circulating air, and thriving vegetation all exhibit a deeply connected unity of life and material substance. From a chronological-cosmic perspective, however, the later passage offers the vision of an earlier vitalist unity.

42. On the significance of these Greek meanings of organon to theories of the organism and life in modern biological sciences, see George Canguilhem's "Epistemology of Biology," in *A Vital Rationalist: Selected Writings from George Canguilhem*, ed. Francois Delaporte (New York: Zone Books, 2000), 81. On Milton's interest in *harmonia mundi* and his poetry as the "majestic culmination" of that tradition, see Regina M. Schwarz, *Remembering and Repeating: On Milton's Theology and Poetics* (Chicago: University of Chicago Press, 1993), 77.

43. A similar description of heavenly harmony and a discordant Fall appear in Milton's "At a Solemn Music":

> Disproportion'd sin
> Jarr'd against nature's chime, and with harsh din
> Broke the fair music that all creatures made
> To their great Lord, whose love their motion sway'd
> In perfect Diaposon, whilst they stood
> In first obedience and their state of good. (19–24)

44. On the Stoic god as a corporeal entity who acts upon matter from its interior, see Ricardo Salles's introduction in Ricardo Salles, ed., *God and Cosmos in Stoicism* (Oxford: Oxford University Press, 2009), 4–6. Milton's prelapsarian cosmology, as Gordon Teskey observes, "bears more than a casual resemblance" to the sort of pagan pantheism advanced by the Stoics, in which the cosmos is a living, physical being. See Gordon Teskey, *Delirious Milton: The Fate of the Poet in Modernity* (Cambridge, MA: Harvard University Press, 2006), 104.

45. John Rogers, *The Matter of Revolution: Science, Poetry, and Politics in the Age of Milton* (Ithaca, NY: Cornell University Press, 1996), 108.

46. On the centrality of physiology and gustatory practices to Milton's Christian ethics, see Michael Schoenfeldt, *Bodies and Selves in Early Modern England: Physiology and*

Inwardness in Spenser, Shakespeare, Herbert and Milton (Cambridge: Cambridge University Press, 1999), 131–168.

47. See Raphael's description of the angels' erotic union as "easier than air with air" in 8.620–629.

48. Augustine, *The City of God against the Pagans*, trans. R. W. Dyson (Cambridge: Cambridge University Press, 1998), 4.13, 608.

49. N. K. Sugimura makes a similar point in her analysis of a common angelic intellect, arguing that Satan's falling away from this perfection introduces a "highly individualized" form of cognition. See Sugimura, *Matter of Glorious Trial*, 192–193.

50. Kerrigan, *The Sacred Complex*, 222.

51. Hugo Grotius, *The most excellent Hugo Grotius, his three books treating of the rights of war and peace*, trans. William Evats (London: Printed by M. W. for Thomas Basset and Ralph Smith, 1682), iii.

52. Grotius, *The most excellent Hugo Grotius*, vi.

53. For accounts of Grotius and Stoic oikeiôsis that emphasize the interweaving of personal and social forms of care, see Christopher Brooke, *Philosophic Pride: Stoicism and Political Thought from Lipsius to Rousseau* (Princeton, NJ: Princeton University Press, 2012), 48–65, and Reinhardt Brandt, "Self-Consciousness and Self-Care: On the Tradition of Oikeiosis in the Modern Age," *Grotiana* 22/23 (2001/2002): 73–92.

54. Appropriately enough, Milton describes his first and only meeting with Grotius in Paris during his European tour as being driven by a social impulse, having deemed Grotius "a most learned man . . . whom I ardently desired to meet" in his *Second Defense of the English People*. See Stephen Orgel and Johnathan Goldberg, eds., *John Milton: A Critical Edition of the Major Works*, (Oxford: Oxford University Press, 1991), 321.

55. See Aristotle's discussion of touch in *De Anima* 2.11, where he argues that "we perceive the objects of touch not in virtue of having been affected by the medium but simultaneously with the medium," unlike objects of perception with respect to the other senses. Aristotle, *De Anima*, trans. Christopher Shields (Oxford: Clarendon Press, 2016), 423b–415, 46.

56. Seneca, *Letters on Ethics*, 121.12–13, 486.

57. For Adam and for Milton's readers, the moment captures what Deleuze and Guattari describe as the "standing up" of a work of art: Adam extracts a bloc of sensations from his lived experience to form a living, vibratory monument that is also Milton's poetic monument of the first impulses affirming life. Gilles Deleuze and Felix Guattari, *What Is Philosophy?* (New York: Columbia University Press, 1996), 163–164. See also my discussion of the sleeping Hercules as an "aesthetic monument" in the introduction under "Herculean Aesthetics."

58. Regina Schwartz, *Remembering and Repeating: On Milton's Theology and Poetics* (Chicago: University of Chicago Press, 1993), 49.

59. Milton, *De Doctrina Christiana Part 1*, 27.

60. Kristin Poole, "'My Hand Would Dissolve, or Seem to Melt': Poetic Dissolution and Stoic Cosmology," in *Geographies of Embodiment in Early Modern England*, ed. Garrett Sullivan Jr. and Mary Floyd-Wilson (Oxford: Oxford University Press, 2020), 152–176.

61. On Satan's free choice to separate himself from the whole by "refusing the rest of twilight," see Revard, *The War in Heaven*, 57. Patricia Parker similarly discusses the threshold state of heavenly twilight as a turning point for the Fall, connecting it with Eve's liminal status and the ambiguous signifier "eve-ning" in "Eve, Evening, and the Labor of Reading in *Paradise Lost*," *English Literary Renaissance* 9, no. 2 (Spring 1979): 319.342.

62. Milton's figure of unyielding perceptual vigilance calls up the political-theological associations of pastoral power and Godly care with sleepless devotion as deployed by James I in his image of the sovereign's "ever wakeriffe care" for the body politic. See my discussion of Shakespearean tragedy and the King's Two Bodies in chapter 3. Needless to say, that alignment reflects the Stuart absolutist ideology of sovereign power that Milton found abhorrent. Just as no mortal king could ever aspire to the perfection of an endless watch, Lucifer's less than perfect being requires sleep, even if he aspires to equal footing with the almighty.

63. Fallon, *Milton among the Philosophers*, 170–171.

64. Milton, *Complete Prose Works*, 268.

65. Milton makes a near identical point in his discussion of the Fall of humankind in *Christian Doctrine*: "It is called Actual, not because sin is properly an action—since in reality it is a privation—but because it is usually involved in an action. For every action is in itself good: its irregularity or deviation from the rule of law is alone properly evil. Hence the action itself is not the material out of which sin [is made], but simply and solely the underlying thing and *hyopkeimenon* in which [it exists]." Milton, *De Doctrina Christiana Part 1*, 425.

66. Milton, *Complete Prose Works*, 269.

67. Milton, *Complete Prose Works*, 268.

68. This metaphysical distinction between privatives and adversaries may also contribute to a clearer understanding of Milton's Chaos. Milton's description of Chaos as "adverse to life" has led some of his finest critics, including John Rogers and Regina Schwartz, to view its ontological and ethical status as a contradiction to Milton's vitalist monism. Yet if Chaos relates to life not as a privation but rather as an adverse habitus, the presence of Chaos can be accommodated within a vitalistic cosmos.

69. On the homoerotics of this scene, see Jonathan Goldberg, *The Seeds of Things: Theorizing Sexuality and Materiality in Renaissance Representations* (New York: Fordham University Press, 2009), 196–197. Satan's plea also recalls the false Una's claim that Redcrosse knight's sleep is a betrayal that severs him from his care for Una. See my discussion of the hero's insomnia in chapter 4 under "A Pathological Watch."

70. John Leonard argues that the point at which Satan's name "comes into being" is in God's warning to the Son of a rising foe (5.721). But this statement comes after the moment of Satan's insomnia in Heaven. Even if we are meant to understand God's comment as taking place simultaneously with Lucifer's sleepless watch, it is still the case that Milton clearly makes Lucifer's insomnia the event during which Satan's name first appears. See *Naming in Paradise: Milton and the Language of Adam and Eve* (Oxford: Oxford University Press, 1990), 93.

71. Milton, *De Doctrina Christiana Part 1*, 303.

72. Milton, *De Doctrina Christiana Part 1*, 303.

73. Fallon, *Milton among the Philosophers*, 99.

74. Fallon suggests that "Milton in his new materialist metaphysic [of the 1650s] has moved toward a pneumatic conception of the soul itself" (*Milton among the Philosophers*, 102), but he attributes this conception to an Aristotelian influence and compares Milton's view with passages from *Generation of Animals* that suggest the pneuma is a substance "more divine" than the physical elements, and that it mediates between body and soul. Yet here too, the apparent tensions or discrepancies between Aristotle and Milton are resolved by an appeal to the Stoic conception of pneuma as the primary cause of matter and life in a cosmology of substance monism.

75. Milton, *De Doctrina Christiana Part 1*, 301.

76. On Milton's use of the word "organic" in this passage in relation to Aristotelian biology and psychology, see Sugimura, *Matter of Glorious Trial*, 125. On the instrumentality of Satan's influence, Augustine writes, "By virtue of his angelic stature and his superior nature, Satan made the serpent subject to him in spiritual wickedness, and, by abusing it as his instrument, had deceitful converse with the woman." See Augustine, *The City of God against the Pagans*, trans. R. W. Dyson (Cambridge: Cambridge University Press, 1998), 606.

77. See book 12, chapter 7 in Augustine, *The City of God against the Pagans*, 506. For an excellent discussion of this passage and the causality of the Fall, see chapter 8 of William Poole's *Milton and the Idea of the Fall* (Cambridge: Cambridge University Press, 2005), 146–157. Poole emphasizes the demonic pride of selfishness as the origin of evil in Milton's poem, but does not discuss the scene of Satan's insomnia in Heaven.

78. Hequembourg reads the serpent's temptation of Eve in light of the curious nature of Satanic speech, and notes the tendency for unfallen creatures to find themselves reproducing such speech with implications for the circuits of sin. Hequembourg, "Milton's 'Unoriginal' Voice."

79. James Kuzner, "Habermas Goes to Hell: Pleasure, Public Reason, and the Republicanism of *Paradise Lost*," *Criticism* 51, no. 1 (Winter 2009): 104–145, 118.

80. Fallon, *Milton among the Philosophers*, 208.

81. Sharon Achinstein, "Milton's Political Ontology of the Human," *ELH* 84, no. 3 (Fall 2017): 591–616.

82. Garrett Sullivan Jr., *Sleep, Romance and Human Embodiment: Vitality from Spenser to Milton* (Cambridge: Cambridge University Press, 2012), 120.

83. In her discussion of the numerous references to Hercules among Milton's works, Stella P. Revard suggests that this scene's condensation of "guilty wakenings" points to a "deeply human Hercules" (235) at odds with the Stuart monarchy's uses of the hero as an emblem for imperial power and sovereign identification. But Milton's incorporation of this more vulnerable Hercules, I would argue, also draws on Seneca's depiction of the hero's slumber and its Stoic ethical implications, which in turn shape Milton's poetics of somnolence and care across his epic poem. Stella P. Revard, "The Politics of Milton's Hercules," *Milton Studies* 37 (1996): 217–245.

84. Kerrigan observes that "what hair is for Samson, the potency derived from good nourishment is for Adam and other men." Kerrigan, *The Sacred Complex*, 204.

85. John Milton, *The Prose Works of John Milton: Volume III*, ed. J. A. St. John (London: George Bell and Sons, 1888), 133.

86. As Leah Whittington argues in her illuminating account of this scene's Homeric resonances and Milton's adaptations of classical supplication, Eve's physical lowering

and clasping of Adam's knees set into motion a transformation toward contrition and reconciliation through a mutual acceptance of the couple's shared sin before God. See Leah Whittington, *Renaissance Suppliants: Poetry, Antiquity, Reconciliation* (Oxford: Oxford University Press, 2016), 184–185.

87. Held, "Eve's 'Paradise Within' in *Paradise Lost*," 173.

88. Russell M. Hillier argues that Miltonic caritas is an integration of vertical and horizontal duties of love between God and humanity in "The Good Communicated: Milton's Drama of the Fall and the Law of Charity," *Modern Language Review* 103, no. 1 (January 2008): 1–21.

89. Milton, *Areopagitica*, 3.514, quoted in Schwartz, *Remembering and Repeating*, 37.

Coda

1. René Descartes, *Meditations on First Philosophy*, ed. John Cottingham (Cambridge: Cambridge University Press, 1996), 23.

2. Descartes, *Meditations on First Philosophy*, 56–57.

3. Descartes, *Meditations on First Philosophy*, 61.

4. Descartes echoes Plato when he suggests in a letter to Mersenne that to know something, it is "sufficient to touch it with one's thought." Quoted in Descartes, *Meditations on First Philosophy*, 32, footnote 1. See also my discussion of Plato's *Republic* and his use of the term *haptetai* to describe the encounter with Forms in chapter 1 under "Asleep in the Polis."

5. As Shapin writes, "There is Descartes's own testimony, repeated throughout his life and in a variety of settings, that medical prophylaxis, therapeutics and the extension of human life were central goals—even the most cherished goals—of his philosophical reform programme" (137). Steven Shapin, "Descartes the Doctor: Rationalism and Its Therapies," *British Journal for the History of Science* 33, no. 2 (2000): 131–154.

6. Margaret Cavendish, *Observations upon Experimental Philosophy*, ed. Eileen O'Neill (Cambridge: Cambridge University Press, 2001), 249–275.

7. Cavendish, *Observations upon Experimental Philosophy*, 250.

8. Anne Conway, *The Conway Letters*, ed. Marjorie Nicholson (Oxford: Clarendon Press, 1992), 237. Also quoted in O'Neill's introduction to Cavendish, *Observations upon Experimental Philosophy*, xviii.

9. O'Neill has done more than anyone in the past twenty years to show that Cavendish draws on numerous principles of Stoic philosophy in her conceptions of nature, matter, and causality, and so my argument here builds on many of her insights. My approach is unique, however, in attending to the connections between cosmology and ethics in Cavendish's thought through her appropriation of the Stoic concept of oikeiôsis. On Cavendish's Stoicism, see O'Neill's introduction to the *Observations upon Experimental Philosophy*, and Eileen O'Neill, "Margaret Cavendish, Stoic Antecedent Causes, and Early Modern Occasional Causes," *Revue Philosophique de la France et de l'Étranger* 203, no. 3 (2013): 311–326.

10. Thomas Stanley, *The History of Philosophy, in Eight Parts* (London: 1656), 60. The quotation is from part 2, chapter 3 of the eighth and final volume in Stanley's collection, titled "Of First Natural Appetite."

11. Cavendish, *Observations upon Experimental Philosophy*, 125

12. "Since natural knowledge and perception, is the ground and principle, not only of philosophy both speculative and experimental, but of all other arts and sciences, nay, of all the infinite particular actions of nature; I thought it not amiss to join to the end of this part, a full declaration of my opinion concerning the subject." Cavendish, *Observations upon Experimental Philosophy*, 137.

13. On *krasis* as the Stoic theory of total blending, see the discussion of Senecan Stoicism and *Hercules Furens* in chapter 2 under "*Krasis* and *Ira*."

14. Cavendish, *Observations upon Experimental Philosophy*, 127.

15. Cavendish, *Observations upon Experimental Philosophy*, 138.

16. Cavendish, *Observations upon Experimental Philosophy*, 149.

17. Cavendish, *Observations upon Experimental Philosophy*, 149.

Bibliography

Achinstein, Sharon. "Milton's Political Ontology of the Human." *ELH* 84, no. 3 (Fall 2017): 591–616.

Agamben, Giorgio. *Homo Sacer: Sovereign Power and Bare Life*. Translated by Daniel Heller-Roazen. Stanford, CA: Stanford University Press, 1998.

——. *State of Exception*. Chicago: University of Chicago Press, 2005.

——. *The Time That Remains: A Commentary on the Letter to the Romans*. Stanford, CA: Stanford University Press, 2005.

——. *The Use of Bodies*. Translated by Adam Kotsko. Stanford, CA: Stanford University Press, 2016.

Akrigg, G. P. V., ed. *Letters of King James VI and I*. Berkeley: University of California Press, 1984.

Aristotle. *De Anima*. Translated by Christopher Shields. Oxford: Oxford University Press, 2016.

——. *Metaphysics*. Translated by Richard Hope. New York: Columbia University Press, 1952.

——. *Nicomachean Ethics*. Translated by Sarah Broadie and Christopher Rowe. Oxford: Oxford University Press, 2002.

——. *The Works of Aristotle*. Edited by W. D. Ross. Oxford: Oxford University Press, 1931.

Augustine. *The City of God against the Pagans*. Translated by R. W. Dyson. Cambridge: Cambridge University Press, 1998.

——. *Confessions*. Translated by Henry Chadwick. Oxford: Oxford University Press, 2008.

——. *Corpus Christianorvm, Series Latina XXXVI: Sancti Avrelii Avgvstini*. Turnholt, BE: Typographi Brepols Editores Pontificii, 1954.

——. *Tractates on the Gospel of John 112–124*. Translated by John W. Rettig. Washington, DC: Catholic University of America Press.

Axton, Marie. *The Queen's Two Bodies: Drama and the Elizabethan Succession*. London: Royal Historical Society, 1977.

Badiou, Alain. *St Paul: The Foundation of Universalism*. Stanford, CA: Stanford University Press, 1997.

Bailey, D. J. T. "The Structure of Stoic Metaphysics." *Oxford Studies in Ancient Philosophy* 46 (Summer 2014): 253–309.

Baker, Howard. *Induction to Tragedy*. Baton Rouge: Louisiana State University Press, 1939.

Baldwin, T. W. *William Shakespeare's Small Latine & Lesse Greeke*. Urbana: University of Illinois Press, 1944.

Barbour, Reid. *English Epicures and Stoics*. Amherst: University of Massachusetts Press, 1998.

Batto, Bernard F. "The Sleeping God: An Ancient Near Eastern Motif of Divine Sovereignty." *Biblica* 68, no. 2 (1987): 153–177.

Bellamy, Elizabeth J., Patrick Cheney, and Michael Schoenfeldt, eds. *Imagining Death in Spenser and Milton*. London: Palgrave Macmillan, 2003.

Belsey, Catherine. "Senecan Vacillation and Elizabethan Deliberation: Influence or Confluence?" *Renaissance Drama, New Series, Vol. 6: Essays on Dramatic Antecedents* (1976): 65–88.

Berger Jr., Harry. "Sexual and Religious Politics in Book 1 of Spenser's *Faerie Queene*." *English Literary Renaissance* 34, no. 2 (2004): 201–242.

——. "The Spenserian Dynamics." *SEL: Studies in English Literature 1500–1900* 8 (1968): 1–18.

Blake, Liza, and Jacques Lezra, eds. *Lucretius and Modernity*. London: Palgrave Macmillan, 2016.

Blanchot, Maurice. *The Space of Literature*. Translated by Ann Smock. Lincoln: University of Nebraska Press, 1989.

Blanshard, Alastair. *Hercules: Scenes from a Heroic Life*. London: Granta, 2005.

Blumenberg, Hans. *Care Crosses the River*. Stanford, CA: Stanford University Press, 2010.

Bobonich, Chris, ed. *The Cambridge Companion to Ancient Ethics*. Cambridge: Cambridge University Press, 2017.

Boorde, Andrew. *A Compendyous Regyment or a Dyetary of Healthe*. London: Wyllyam Powell, 1567.

Boswell, Jackson Campbell. *Milton's Library: A Catalog of the Remains of John Milton's Library and an Annotated Reconstruction of Milton's Library and Ancillary Readings*. New York: Garland Publishing, 1975.

Braden, Gordon. *Renaissance Tragedy and the Senecan Tradition: Anger's Privilege*. New Haven, CT: Yale University Press, 1985.

Bradley, Henry. "Cursed Hebenon (Or 'Hebona')." *The Modern Language Review* 15, no. 1 (January 1920): 85–87.

Brakke, David. *Demons and the Making of the Monk: Spiritual Combat in Early Christianity*. Cambridge, MA: Harvard University Press, 2006.

——. "The Problematization of Nocturnal Emissions in Early Christian Syria, Egypt, and Gaul." *Journal of Early Christian Studies* 3, no. 4 (1995): 419–460.

Brandt, Reinhardt. "Self-Consciousness and Self-Care: On the Tradition of Oikeiosis in the Modern Age." *Grotiana* 22/23 (2001/2002): 73–92.

Brehier, Emile. *The History of Philosophy: The Hellenistic and Roman Age*. Translated by Wade Baskin. Chicago: University of Chicago Press, 1971.

Brooke, Christopher. *Philosophic Pride: Stoicism and Political Thought from Lipsius to Rousseau*. Princeton, NJ: Princeton University Press, 2012.

Browne, Sir Thomas. *The Works of Sir Thomas Browne*. Vol. 1. Edited by Charles Sayle. London: Grant Richards, 1904.

Bryant, Levi R. *Difference and Givenness: Deleuze's Transcendental Empiricism and the Ontology of Immanence*. Evanston, IL: Northwestern University Press, 2008.

Bullough, Geoffrey. *Narrative and Dramatic Sources of Shakespeare*. Vol. 7. London: Routledge and Kegan Paul, 1973.

Bushnell, Rebecca. *A Culture of Teaching: Early Modern Humanism in Theory and Practice*. Ithaca, NY: Cornell University Press, 1996.

Cadman, Daniel. "'The Very Nerves of State': Biopolitics and Sovereignty in Shakespeare's Vienna." In *Lectures de Measure for Measure de William Shakespeare*, edited by Delphine Lemonnier-Trexier and Guillame Winter. Rennes, FR: Presses Universitaires de Rennes, 2012.

Calvin, John. *Commentaries: Volume 8*. Edited by David Torrance and Thomas Torrance. Grand Rapids, MI: Eerdmans, 1959–1972.

——. *Institutes of the Christian Religion*. Translated by Henry Beveridge. Grand Rapids, MI: Eerdmans, 1989.

——. *Selected Works of John Calvin: Tracts and Letters*. Edited by Henry Beveridge and Jules Bonnet. 7 vols. Edinburgh: Calvin Translation Society, 1851.

Campana, Joe. *The Pain of Reformation*. New York: Fordham University Press, 2012.

Campana, Joe, and Scott Maisano, eds. *Renaissance Posthumanism*. New York: Fordham University Press, 2016.

Canguilhem, Georges. *The Normal and the Pathological*. Brooklyn, NY: Zone Books, 1989.

——. *A Vital Rationalist: Selected Writings from Georges Canguilhem*. Edited by François Delaporte. Brooklyn, NY: Zone Books, 1994.

Cassian, John. *The Conferences*. Translated by Boniface Ramsey. New York: Paulist Press, 1997.

Cavendish, Margaret. *Observations upon Experimental Philosophy*. Edited by Eileen O'Neill. Cambridge: Cambridge University Press, 2001.

——. *Philosophical Fancies*. London: J. Martin and J. Allestrye, 1653

——. *Philosophical and Physical Opinions*. London: J. Martin and J. Allestrye, 1655.

Chrysostom, John. *The Homilies of S. John Chrysostom, Archbishop of Constantinople, on the Epistles of St. Paul the Apostle to Timothy, Titus, and Philemon*. Oxford: J. Parker, 1843.

Cicero. *Cicero: On Old Age; On Friendship; On Divination*. Translated by W. A. Falconer. Loeb Classical Library 154. Cambridge, MA: Harvard University Press, 1923.

——. *On Ends*. Translated by H. Rackham. Loeb Classical Library 40. Cambridge, MA: Harvard University Press, 1914.

——. *On Moral Ends*. Edited by Julia Annas. Translated by Raphael Woolf. Cambridge: Cambridge University Press, 2001.

——. *Pro Archia. Post Reditum in Senatu. Post Reditum ad Quirites. De Domo Sua. De Haruspicum Responsis. Pro Plancio*. Translated by N. H. Watts. Loeb Classical Library 158. Cambridge, MA: Harvard University Press, 1923.

Clark, Arthur Melville. *Murder under Trust: Or, The Topical Macbeth and Other Jacobean Matters*. Edinburgh: Scottish Academic Press, 1981.

Conway, Anne. *The Conway Letters*. Edited by Marjorie Nicholson. Oxford: Clarendon Press, 1992.

Coolidge, John. *The Pauline Renaissance in England: Puritanism and the Bible*. Oxford: Clarendon Press, 1970.

Crary, Jonathan. *24/7: Late Capitalism and the Ends of Sleep*. London: Verso, 2013.

Cunliffe, John William. *The Influence of Seneca on Elizabethan Tragedy*. London: Macmillan, 1893.

Curran, Kevin. "Renaissance Non-humanism: Plants, Animals, Machines, Matter." *Renaissance Studies* 24, no. 2 (2009): 314–322.

Daston, Lorraine. *Against Nature*. Cambridge, MA: MIT Press, 2019.

De Grazia, Margreta. Hamlet *without Hamlet*. Cambridge: Cambridge University Press, 2007.

Deleuze, Gilles. *Essays Critical and Clinical*. Edited by Dan Smith. London: Verso, 1998.

——. *The Logic of Sense*. Translated by Mark Lester. New York: Columbia University Press, 1990.

Deleuze, Gilles, and Felix Guattari. *A Thousand Plateaus: Capitalism and Schizophrenia*. Minneapolis: University of Minnesota Press, 1987.

——. *What Is Philosophy?* Translated by Hugh Tomlinson and Graham Burchell. New York: Columbia University Press, 1994.

Descartes, René. *Meditations on First Philosophy*. Edited by John Cottingham. Cambridge: Cambridge University Press, 1996.

De Waal, Esther. *A Life-Giving Way: A Commentary on the Rule of St. Benedict*. Collegeville, MN: Liturgical Press, 1995.

Diogenes Laertius. *Lives of the Eminent Philosophers*. Edited by James Miller. Translated by Pamela Mensch. Oxford: Oxford University Press, 2018.

——. *Lives of Eminent Philosophers, Volume II: Books 6–10*. Translated by R. D. Hicks. Loeb Classical Library 185. Cambridge, MA: Harvard University Press, 1925.

Dollimore, Jonathan. *Radical Tragedy: Religion, Ideology and Power in the Drama of Shakespeare and His Contemporaries*. Durham: Duke University Press, 2003.

Dolven, Jeff. "Besides Good and Evil." *SEL: Studies in English Literature 1500–1900* 57, no. 1 (Winter 2017): 1–22.

——. *Scenes of Instruction in Renaissance Romance*. Chicago: University of Chicago Press, 2007.

——. *Take Care*. New York: Cabinet Books, 2017.

Donne, John. *Selected Prose*. Edited by Neil Rhodes. New York: Penguin Classics, 1987.

Donnelly, Phillip J. "'Matter' Versus Body: The Character of Milton's Monism." *Milton Quarterly* 33, no. 3 (1999): 79–85.

Dressler, Alexander J. "Matter, Language, and Attachment in Seneca's Moral Epistles." PhD diss., University of Washington, 2009.

Drummond, William of Hawthornden. *Poems and Prose*. Edited by Robert H. MacDonald. Edinburgh: Scottish Academic Press, 1976.

Dzelzainis, Martin. "*Paradise Lost* II.4 and Seneca's *Hercules Furens*." *Notes and Queries* 45 (1998): 49–50.

Engberg-Pedersen, Troels. *The Stoic Theory of Oikeiôsis: Moral Development and Social Interaction in Early Stoic Philosophy*. Aarhus, DK: Aarhus University Press, 1990.

Enterline, Lynn. *Shakespeare's Schoolroom: Rhetoric, Discipline, Emotion*. Philadelphia: University of Pennsylvania Press, 2012.

Erasmus, Desiderius. *The "Adages" of Erasmus: A Study with Translations*. Edited by Margaret Mann Phillips. Cambridge: Cambridge University Press, 1964.

——. *Enchridion Militis Christiani: An English Version*. Edited by Anne M. O'Donnell. Oxford: Oxford University Press, 1981.
——. *Praise of Folly*. New York: Penguin, 1978.
Esposito, Roberto. *Bios: Biopolitics and Philosophy*. Translated by Timothy Campbell. Minneapolis: University of Minnesota Press, 2008.
——. *Communitas: The Origin and Destination of Community*. Translated by Timothy Campbell. Stanford, CA: Stanford University Press, 2009.
——. "Community, Immunity, Biopolitics." *Angelekai* 18, no. 3 (2013): 83–90.
——. *Immunitas: The Protection and Negation of Life*. Translated by Zakiya Hanafi. Malden, MA: Polity, 2011.
Evans, Meredith. "Rumor, the Breath of Kings, and the Body of Law in *2 Henry IV*." *Shakespeare Quarterly* 60, no. 1 (Spring 2009): 1–24.
Fallon, Stephen. *Milton among the Philosophers: Poetry and Materialism in Seventeenth-Century England*. Ithaca, NY: Cornell University Press, 1991.
Fitch, John G. *Seneca's Hercules Furens: A Critical Text with Introduction and Commentary*. Ithaca, NY: Cornell University Press, 1987.
Foucault, Michel. *The Care of the Self: Volume 3 of the History of Sexuality*. Translated by Robert Hurley. New York: Vintage Books, 1988.
——. *The Hermeneutics of the Subject: Lectures at the Collège de France, 1981–1982*. Edited by Arnold Davidson. Translated by Graham Burchell. New York: Palgrave Macmillan, 2005.
——. *History of Madness*. Edited by Jean Khalfa. Translated by Jonathan Murphy and Jean Khalfa. New York: Routledge, 2006.
——. *The History of Sexuality, Volume 1: An Introduction*. New York: Vintage Books, 1990.
——. *Security, Territory, Population: Lectures at the Collège de France, 1977–1978*. Edited by Arnold Davidson. Translated by Graham Burchell. New York: Palgrave Macmillan, 2007.
Foxley, Rachel. "'Due Libertie and Proportiond Equalitie': Milton, Democracy, and the Republican Tradition." *History of Political Thought* 34, no. 4 (2013): 614–638.
Freud, Sigmund. "The Antithetical Meaning of Primal Words," in *Complete Works*, ed. James Strachey. Vol. 11. London: Hogarth Press, 1910.
Frye, Northrop. *Fables of Identity: Studies in Poetic Mythology*. New York: Harcourt, Brace, & World, 1963.
——. *Northrop Frye's Notebooks on Renaissance Literature*. In *Collected Works of Northrop Frye*, edited by Michael Dolzani. Toronto: University of Toronto Press, 2006.
The Geneva Bible: A Facsimile of the 1560 Edition. Madison: University of Wisconsin Press, 1969.
Gil, Daniel Juan. *Shakespeare's Anti-politics: Sovereign Power and the Life of the Flesh*. New York: Palgrave Macmillan, 2013.
Gless, Darryl. *Interpretation and Theology in Spenser*. Cambridge: Cambridge University Press, 2004.
Goldberg, Jonathan. *Endlesse Worke: Spenser and the Structures of Discourse*. Baltimore: Johns Hopkins University Press, 1981.
——. *James I and the Politics of Literature*. Baltimore: Johns Hopkins University Press, 1983.

——. *The Seeds of Things: Theorizing Sexuality and Materiality in Renaissance Representations*. New York: Fordham University Press, 2009.

Goldstein, Amanda Jo. *Sweet Science: Romantic Materialism and the New Logics of Life*. Chicago: University of Chicago Press, 2017.

Gotthelf, Allan, and James G. Lennox, eds. *Philosophical Issues in Aristotle's Biology*. Cambridge: Cambridge University Press, 1987.

Graver, Margaret. *Stoicism and Emotion*. Chicago: University of Chicago Press, 2007.

Gregory of Nyssa. *Dogmatic Treatises, Etc*. Edited by Phillip Schaff. New York: Christian Literature Publishing, 1892.

Grotius, Hugo. *The Most Excellent Hugo Grotius, His Three Books Treating of the Rights of War and Peace*. Translated by William Evats. London: Printed by M. W. for Thomas Basset and Ralph Smith, 1682.

Gundry, Robert H. *Soma in Biblical Theology*. Cambridge: Cambridge University Press, 1976.

Hadfield, Andrew. *Edmund Spenser: A Life*. Oxford: Oxford University Press, 2012.

Halliwell, Martin, and Andy Mousley. *Critical Humanisms: Humanist/Anti-humanist Dialogues*. Edinburgh: Edinburgh University Press, 2003.

Halpern, Richard. *The Poetics of Primitive Accumulation: English Renaissance Culture and the Genealogy of Capital*. Ithaca, NY: Cornell University Press, 1991.

Hamilton, A. C., ed. *The Spenser Encyclopedia*. Toronto: University of Toronto Press, 1990.

Hammill, Graham. *The Mosaic Constitution: Political Theology and Imagination from Machiavelli to Milton*. Chicago: University of Chicago Press, 2012.

Hammill, Graham, and Julia Reinhard Lupton, eds. *Political Theology and Early Modernity*. Chicago: University of Chicago Press, 2012.

Handley, Sasha. *Sleep in Early Modern England*. New Haven, CT: Yale University Press, 2016.

Happe, Peter. "The Restless Mind That Would Never Raging Leave: Jasper Heywood's *Thyestes*." *Medieval English Theater* 27 (2005): 16–33.

Hard, Fredrick. "Richard Haydocke and Alexander Browne: Two Half-Forgotten Writers on the Art of Painting." *PMLA* 55, no. 3 (September 1940): 727–741.

Harris, Jonathan Gil. *Untimely Matters in the Time of Shakespeare*. Philadelphia: University of Pennsylvania Press, 2009.

Hart, D. Bentley. "Matter, Monism, and Narrative: An Essay on the Metaphysics of *Paradise Lost*." *Milton Quarterly* 30, no. 1 (1996): 16–27.

Heidegger, Martin. *Being and Time*. Translated by John Macquarrie and Edward Robinson. New York: Harper Perennial, 1962.

Heil, Andreas, and Gregor Damschen, eds. *Brill's Companion to Seneca: Philosopher and Dramatist*. Leiden: Brill, 2013.

Held, Joshua R. "Eve's 'Paradise Within' in *Paradise Lost*: A Stoic Mind, a Love Sonnet, and a Good Conscience." *Studies in Philology* 114, no. 1 (2017): 171–196.

Heller-Roazen, Daniel. *The Inner Touch: Archaeology of a Sensation*. Brooklyn, NY: Zone Books, 2007.

Hequembourg, Stephen. "Milton's 'Unoriginal' Voice: Quotation Marks in *Paradise Lost*." *Modern Philology* 112, no. 1 (2014): 154–178.

Hibbert, Christopher. *The Virgin Queen*. London: Viking, 1990.

Hierocles. *Hierocles the Stoic: Elements of Ethics, Fragments and Excerpts*. Edited by Ilaria Ramelli. Translated by David Konstan. Atlanta: Society of Biblical Literature, 2009.

Hillier, Russell M. "The Good Communicated: Milton's Drama of the Fall and the Law of Charity." *Modern Language Review* 103, no. 1 (January 2008): 1–21.

Hillyer, Richard. *Divided between Carelessness and Care: A Cultural History*. New York: Palgrave Macmillan, 2013.

Hobbes, Thomas. *Leviathan*. Oxford: Oxford University Press, 1996.

Horkheimer, Max. *Eclipse of Reason*. Oxford: Oxford University Press, 1947.

Hunter, G. K. "Seneca and the Elizabethans: A Case Study in 'Influence.'" *Shakespeare Survey* 20 (1967): 11–26.

Hutson, Lorna, and Victoria Kahn, eds. *Rhetoric and Law in Early Modern Europe*. Edited by Lorna Hutson and Victoria Kahn. New Haven, CT: Yale University Press, 2001.

Jackson, Ken. "'All the World to Nothing': *Richard III*, Badiou, and Pauline Subjectivity." *Shakespeare* 1 (June 2005): 29–52.

——. "'Is It God or the Sovereign Exception?': Giorgio Agamben's *Homo Sacer* and Shakespeare's *King John*." *Religion and Literature* (Autumn 2006): 85–100.

James VI and I. *Correspondence of King James VI of Scotland with Sir Robert Cecil and Others in England, During the Reign of Queen Elizabeth*. Westminster, UK: J. B. Nichols and Sons for the Camden Society, 1861.

——. *Political Writings*. Edited by Johann P. Sommerville. Cambridge: Cambridge University Press, 1994.

Jonson, Ben. *The Case Is Altered*. Edited by William Selin. New Haven, CT: Yale University Press, 1917.

Kahn, Charles H. *The Art and Thought of Heraclitus: An Edition of the Fragments with Critical Commentary*. Cambridge: Cambridge University Press, 1979.

Kahn, Victoria. *The Future of Illusion: Political Theology and Early Modern Texts*. Chicago: University of Chicago Press, 2014.

Kantorowicz, Ernst H. *The King's Two Bodies: A Study in Medieval Political Theology*. Princeton, NJ: Princeton University Press, 1997.

Kaufman, Sheiba Kian. "Care." In *Entertaining the Idea: Shakespeare, Performance, and Philosophy*, edited by Lowell Gallagher, James Kearney, and Julia Reinhard Lupton. Toronto: University of Toronto Press, 2020.

Kerrigan, William. *The Sacred Complex: On the Psychogenesis of* Paradise Lost. Cambridge, MA: Harvard University Press, 1983.

Kirk, G. S. *Heraclitus: The Cosmic Fragments*. Cambridge: Cambridge University Press, 1954.

Klein, Jacob. "The Stoic Argument from *Oikeiôsis*." *Oxford Studies in Ancient Philosophy* 50 (2016): 143–200.

Kneidel, Gregory. *Rethinking the Turn to Religion in Early Modern English Literature: The Poetics of All Believers*. Basingstoke, UK: Palgrave Macmillan, 2008.

Knowles, Dom David. *The Monastic Order in England: A History of Its Development from the Times of St. Dunstan to the Fourth Lateran Council*. Cambridge: Cambridge University Press, 1940.

Kuzner, James. "Habermas Goes to Hell: Pleasure, Public Reason, and the Republicanism of *Paradise Lost*." *Criticism* 51, no. 1 (Winter 2009): 104–145

——. *Open Subjects: English Renaissance Republicans, Modern Selfhoods, and the Virtue of Vulnerability*. Edinburgh: Edinburgh University Press, 2011.

——. "Unbuilding the City: *Coriolanus* and the Birth of Republican Rome." *Shakespeare Quarterly* 58, no. 2 (Summer 2007): 174–199.

Langis, Unhae Park. "Humankindness / *King Lear* and the Suffering, Wisdom, and Compassion within Buddhist Interbeing." In *Literature and the Religious Experience*, edited by Matthew Smith and Caleb Spencer. London: Palgrave Macmillan, 2021.

Lemonnier-Texier, Delphine, and Guillame Winter, eds. *Lectures de Measure for Measure de William Shakespeare*. Rennes, FR: Presses Universitaires de Rennes, 2012.

Leonard, John. *Naming in Paradise: Milton and the Language of Adam and Eve*. Oxford: Oxford University Press, 1990.

Levine, Caroline. *The Heart and Stomach of a King: Elizabeth I and the Politics of Sex and Power*. Philadelphia: University of Pennsylvania Press, 1994.

Lieb, Michael. *The Dialectics of Creation: Patterns of Birth and Regeneration in* Paradise Lost. Amherst: University of Massachusetts Press, 1970.

Littlewood, C. A. J. *Self-Representation and Illusion in Senecan Tragedy*. Oxford: Oxford University Press, 2004.

Long, A. A., and D. N. Sedley, eds. *The Hellenistic Philosophers*. Vol. 1. Cambridge: Cambridge University Press, 1987.

Long, A. G., ed. *Plato and the Stoics*. Cambridge: Cambridge University Press, 2013.

Lucas, F. L. *Seneca and Elizabethan Tragedy*. Cambridge: Cambridge University Press, 1922.

Lupton, Julia Reinhard. *Citizen-Saints: Shakespeare and Political Theology*. Chicago: University of Chicago Press, 2005.

——. "The Pauline Renaissance: A Shakespearean Reassessment." *The European Legacy* 15 (2010): 215–220.

——. *Shakespeare Dwelling: Designs for the Theater of Life*. Chicago: University of Chicago Press, 2018.

——. *Thinking with Shakespeare: Essays on Politics and Life*. Chicago: University of Chicago Press, 2011.

Luther, Martin. *Commentary on Romans*. Translated by J. Theodore Muller. Grand Rapids, MI: Kregel Publications, 1976.

MacCulloch, Diarmaid. *The Later Reformation in England, 1547–1603*. New York: Palgrave Macmillan, 1990.

MacLure, Millar, and F. W. Watt, eds. *Essays in English Literature from the Renaissance to the Victorian Age, Presented to A.S.P. Woodhouse*. Toronto: University of Toronto Press, 1964.

Marcovich, M., ed. *Heraclitus: Greek Text with a Short Commentary*. Merida: Los Andes University Press, 1967.

Marlowe, Christopher. *The Complete Works of Christopher Marlowe*. Edited by Fredson Bowers. Vol. 1. Cambridge: Cambridge University Press, 1973.

Marshall, William H. "Calvin, Spenser, and the Major Sacraments." *Modern Language Notes* 74, no. 2 (1959): 97–101.

Martin, Wayne. "Stoic Transcendentalism and the Doctrine of *Oikeiôsis*." In *The Transcendental Turn*, edited by Sebastian Gardner and Matthew Grist, 342–368. Oxford: Oxford University Press, 2015.

McColley, Diane Kelsey. *Milton's Eve*. Urbana: University of Illinois Press, 1983.

McCrea, Adriana Alice Norma. *Constant Minds: Political Virtue and the Lipsian Paradigm in England, 1584–1650*. Toronto: University of Toronto Press, 1997.

Miernowski, Jan, ed. *Early Modern Humanism and Postmodern Antihumanism in Dialogue*. Cham, CH: Palgrave Macmillan: 2016.

Miles, Geoffrey. *Shakespeare and Constant Romans*. Oxford: Oxford University Press, 1996.

Miller, David Lee. "Spenser's Poetics: The Poem's Two Bodies." *PMLA* 101 (1986): 170–185.

Miller, Mark. *Philosophical Chaucer: Love, Sex, and Agency in the Canterbury Tales*. Cambridge: Cambridge University Press, 2004.

Miller, Nichole. *Violence and Grace: Exceptional Life between Shakespeare and Modernity*. Evanston, IL: Northwestern University Press, 2014.

Milton, John. *Complete Prose Works, Volume VIII: 1666–1682*. Edited by Don M. Wolfe. New Haven, CT: Yale University Press, 1982.

——. *The Complete Works of John Milton. Volume VIII: De Doctrina Christiana Parts 1 and 2*. Edited by John K. Hale and J. Donald Cullington. Oxford: Oxford University Press, 2012.

——. *John Milton: A Critical Edition of the Major Works*. Edited by Stephen Orgel and Jonathan Goldberg. Oxford: Oxford University Press, 1991.

——. *Paradise Lost: A Norton Critical Edition*. Edited by Gordon Teskey. New York: Norton, 2005.

——. *The Prose Works of John Milton*. Edited by J. A. St. John. Vol. 3. London: George Bell and Sons, 1888.

Miola, Robert. *Shakespeare and Classical Tragedy: The Influence of Seneca*. Oxford: Oxford University Press, 1996.

Montrose, Louis. *The Purpose of Playing: Shakespeare and the Cultural Politics of Elizabethan Theater*. Chicago: Chicago University Press, 1996.

Moore, Norman, MD. *The History of the Study of Medicine in the British Isles*. Oxford: Clarendon Press, 1908.

Motto, Anna Lydia, and John R. Clark. "Senecan Tragedy: A Critique of Scholarly Trends." *Renaissance Drama* 6 (1973): 219–235

Mulcaster, Richard. *Mulcaster's Elementarie*. Edited by E. T. Campagnac. London: Humphrey Milford for Oxford University Press, 1927.

Mullaney, Steven. "Mourning and Misogyny: *Hamlet, The Revenger's Tragedy*, and the Final Progress of Elizabeth I, 1600–1607." *Shakespeare Quarterly* 45, no. 2 (Summer 1994): 139–162.

Nagel, Thomas. *Mind and Cosmos: Why the Materialist Neo-Darwinian Conception of Nature Is Almost Certainly False*. New York: Oxford University Press, 2012.

Negarastani, Reza. *Cyclonopedia: Complicity with Anonymous Materials*. Melbourne: re.press, 2008.

Nelson, William, ed. *A Fifteenth Century School Book: From a Manuscript in the British Museum (Ms. Arundel 249)*. Oxford: Clarendon Press, 1956.

Nohrnberg, James. *The Analogy of the Faerie Queene*. Princeton, NJ: Princeton University Press, 1976.

Norbrook, David, Stephen Harrison, and Phillip Hardie, eds. *Lucretius and the Early Modern*. London: Oxford University Press, 2015.

O'Neill, Eileen. "Margaret Cavendish, Stoic Antecedent Causes, and Early Modern Occasional Causes." *Revue Philosophique de la France et de l'Étranger* 203, no. 3 (2013): 311–326.

Oram, William A. "Spenserian Paralysis." *SEL: Studies in English Literature 1500–1900* 41, no. 1 (2001): 49–70.

Orgel, Stephen. *The Illusion of Power: Political Theater in the English Renaissance*. Berkeley: University of California Press, 1975.

Palmer, Ada. *Reading Lucretius in the Renaissance*. Cambridge, MA: Harvard University Press, 2014.

Parker, Patricia. "Eve, Evening, and the Labor of Reading in *Paradise Lost*." *English Literary Renaissance* 9, no. 2 (Spring 1979): 319–342.

Passanante, Gerrard. *The Lucretian Renaissance: Philology and the Afterlife of Tradition*. Chicago: University of Chicago Press, 2011.

Paster, Gail Kern. *The Body Embarrassed: Drama and the Disciplines of Shame in Early Modern England*. Ithaca, NY: Cornell University Press, 1993.

——. *Humoring the Body: Emotions and the Shakespearean Stage*. Chicago: University of Chicago Press, 2004.

Paster, Gail Kern, Katherine Rowe, and Mary Floyd-Wilson, eds. *Reading the Early Modern Passions: Essays in the Cultural History of Emotions*. Philadelphia: University of Pennsylvania Press, 2004.

Paul, Henry. *The Royal Play of Macbeth*. New York: Palgrave Macmillan, 1950.

Pertile, Giulio. "'And All His Sences Stound': The Physiology of Stupefaction in Spenser's *Faerie Queene*." *English Literary Renaissance* 44, no. 3 (2014): 420–451.

——. *Feeling Faint: Affect and Consciousness in the Renaissance*. Evanston, IL: Northwestern University Press, 2019.

Plato. *Plato: Complete Works*. Edited by John M. Cooper. Indianapolis: Hackett Publishing, 1997.

——. *The Republic*. Translated by R. E. Allen. New Haven, CT: Yale University Press, 2006.

Plutarch. *Moralia, Volume XII: Concerning the Face Which Appears in the Orb of the Moon. On the Principle of Cold. Whether Fire or Water Is More Useful. Whether Land or Sea Animals Are Cleverer. Beasts Are Rational. On the Eating of Flesh*. Translated by Harold Cherniss and W. C. Helmbold. Loeb Classical Library 406. Cambridge, MA: Harvard University Press, 1957.

Polito, Roberto. "Sextus on Heraclitus on Sleep." In *Sleep*, edited by T. Wiedemann and K. Dowden, 53–70. Bari: Levante, 2003.

Poole, William. *Milton and the Idea of the Fall*. Cambridge: Cambridge University Press, 2005.

Quilligan, Maureen. *Incest and Agency in Elizabeth's England*. Philadelphia: University of Pennsylvania Press, 2005.

——. *The Language of Allegory: Defining the Genre*. Ithaca, NY: Cornell University Press, 1979.

Quitslund, Beth. "Despair and the Composition of the Self." *Spenser Studies* 17 (2003): 91–106.

Radice, Roberto. *Oikeiôsis: ricerche sul fondamento del pensiero Stoico e sulla sua genesi.* Milan: Vita e Pensiero, 2000.

Rand, Sebastian. "Organism, Normativity, Plasticity: Canguilhem, Kant, Malabou." *Continental Philosophy Review* 44 (2011): 341–357.

Reesing, John. "The Materiality of God in Milton's De Doctrina Christiana." *The Harvard Theological Review* 50, no. 3 (1957): 159–174.

Reich, Warren T. "History of the Notion of Care." *Encyclopedia of Bioethics*. New York: Palgrave Macmillan, 1995.

Reid, Jane Davidson. *The Oxford Guide to Classical Mythology in the Arts, 1300–1990s.* Oxford: Oxford University Press, 1993.

Revard, Stella P. "The Politics of Milton's Hercules." *Milton Studies* 32 (1996): 217–245.

——. *The War in Heaven:* Paradise Lost *and the Tradition of Satan's Rebellion*. Ithaca, NY: Cornell University Press, 1980.

Riley, Kathleen. *The Reception and Performance of Euripides's* Herakles. Oxford: Oxford University Press, 2008.

Robertson, Jean. "Macbeth on Sleep." *Notes and Queries* 14 (1967): 139–141.

Robinson, John A. T. *The Body: A Study in Pauline Theology*. Chicago: Allenson, 1952.

Rogers, John. *The Matter of Revolution: Science, Poetry, and Politics in the Age of Milton.* Ithaca, NY: Cornell University Press, 1996.

Rosenmeyer, Thomas G. *Senecan Drama and Stoic Cosmology*. Berkeley: University of California Press, 1989.

Rust, Jen. "Political Theology and Shakespeare Studies." *Literature Compass* 6, no. 1 (2009): 175–190.

Sakezles, Priscilla. "Aristotle and Chrysippus on the Physiology of Human Action." *The Society for Ancient Greek Philosophy Newsletter* (1996): 454.

Salles, Ricardo, ed. *God and Cosmos in Stoicism*. Oxford: Oxford University Press, 2009.

Santner, Eric. *The Weight of All Flesh: On the Subject-Matter of Political Economy.* Oxford University Press, 2015.

Schoenfeldt, Michael. *Bodies and Selves in Early Modern England: Physiology and Inwardness in Spenser, Shakespeare, Herbert and Milton*. Cambridge: Cambridge University Press, 1999.

Schwartz, Regina. *Remembering and Repeating: On Milton's Theology and Poetics.* Chicago: University of Chicago Press, 1993.

Scodel, Joshua. *Excess and the Mean in Early Modern English Literature*. Princeton, NJ: Princeton University Press, 2002.

Scodel, Ruth, ed. *Theater and Society in the Classical World*. Ann Arbor: University of Michigan Press, 1993.

Segal, Charles. *Interpreting Greek Tragedy: Myth, Poetry, Text*. Ithaca, NY: Cornell University Press, 1986.

Seneca. *Anger, Mercy, Revenge*. Translated by Robert A. Kaster and Martha C. Nussbaum. Chicago: University of Chicago Press, 2010.

——. *Epistles, Volume I: Epistles 1–65*. Translated by Richard M. Gummere. Loeb Classical Library 75. Cambridge, MA: Harvard University Press, 1917.

——. *Letters on Ethics*. Translated by Margaret Graver and A. A. Long. Chicago: University of Chicago Press, 2015.

——. *On Benefits*. Translated by Miriam Griffin and Brad Inwood. Chicago: University of Chicago Press, 2011.

——. *Seneca: His Tenne Tragedies*. Edited by Thomas Newton. New York: Alfred A. Knopf, 1927.

Shakespeare, William. *The Complete Pelican Shakespeare*. Edited by Stephen Orgel and A. R. Braunmuller. New York: Penguin Books, 2002.

Shapin, Steven. "Descartes the Doctor: Rationalism and Its Therapies." *British Journal for the History of Science* 33, no. 2 (2000): 131–154.

Shelton, Jo-Ann. "Problems of Time in Seneca's *Hercules Furens* and *Thyestes*." *California Studies in Classical Antiquity* 8 (1975): 257–269.

Shifflett, Andrew. *Stoicism, Politics and Literature in the Age of Milton*. Cambridge: Cambridge University Press, 1998.

Shuger, Debora. "'Gums of Glutinous Heat' and the Stream of Consciousness: The Theology of Milton's *Maske*." *Representations* 60 (Autumn 1997): 1–21.

——. *Political Theologies in Shakespeare's England: The Sacred and the State in* Measure for Measure. London: Palgrave Macmillan, 2001.

Silberman, Lauren. "'Perfect Hole': Spenser and Greek Romance." *Spenser Studies* 23 (2008): 283–291.

Simon, David Carroll. *Light without Heat: The Observational Mood from Bacon to Milton*. Ithaca, NY: Cornell University Press, 2018.

Skinner, Quentin. *Foundations of Modern Political Thought*. 2 vols. Cambridge: Cambridge University Press, 1978.

Soellner, Rolf. "The Madness of Hercules and the Elizabethans." *Comparative Literature* 10, no. 4 (1958): 309–324.

Southwell, Robert. *Collected Poems*. Edited by Peter Davidson and Anne Sweeney. Manchester, UK: Carcanet Press, 2007.

Spenser, Edmund. *The Faerie Queene*. Edited by Thomas P. Roche. New York: Penguin, 1987.

Stafford, Emma. *Herakles*. New York: Routledge, 2012.

Stanley, Thomas. *The History of Philosophy, in Eight Parts*. London: 1656.

Star, Christopher. *The Empire of the Self: Self-Command and Political Speech in Seneca and Petronius*. Baltimore: Johns Hopkins University Press, 2012.

Steadman, John M. "The 'Inharmonious Blacksmith': Spenser and the Pythagoras Legend." *PMLA* 79, no. 5 (1964): 664–665.

Strier, Richard. *The Unrepentant Renaissance: From Petrarch to Shakespeare to Milton*. Chicago: University of Chicago Press, 2011.

Sugg, Richard. *The Smoke of the Soul: Medicine, Physiology and Religion in Early Modern England*. New York: Palgrave Macmillan, 2013.

Sugimura, N. K. *"Matter of Glorious Trial": Spiritual and Material Substance in* Paradise Lost. New Haven, CT: Yale University Press, 2009.

Sullivan Jr., Garrett. *Memory and Forgetting in English Renaissance Drama: Shakespeare, Marlowe, Webster*. Cambridge: Cambridge University Press, 2005.

——. *Sleep, Romance, and Human Embodiment: Vitality from Spenser to Milton*. Cambridge: Cambridge University Press, 2012.

Sullivan Jr., Garrett, and Mary Floyd-Wilson, eds. *Geographies of Embodiment in Early Modern England*. Oxford: Oxford University Press, 2020.

Summit, Jennifer. "Renaissance Humanism and the Future of the Humanities." *Literature Compass* 9, no. 10 (2012): 665–676.

Teskey, Gordon. *Allegory and Violence*. Ithaca, NY: Cornell University Press, 1996.

——. *Delirious Milton: The Fate of the Poet in Modernity*. Cambridge, MA: Harvard University Press, 2006.

Thom, Johan C. *Cleanthes' Hymn to Zeus: Text, Translation, and Commentary*. Tübingen, DE: Mohr Siebeck, 2005.

Todd, Margo. *Christian Humanism and the Puritan Social Order*. Cambridge: Cambridge University Press, 1987.

Totaro, Rebecca. "Securing Sleep in *Hamlet*." *SEL: Studies in English Literature 1500–1900* 50, no. 2 (Spring 2010): 407–426.

Tuck, Richard. *Philosophy and Government 1572–1651*. Cambridge: Cambridge University Press, 1993.

Turner, Timothy A. "Othello on the Rack." *Journal for Early Modern Cultural Studies* 15, no. 3 (2015): 102–136.

Vatter, Miguel. *The Republic of the Living: Biopolitics and the Critique of Civil Society*. New York: Fordham University Press, 2014.

Vaughan, William. *Approved Directions for Health, Both Naturall and Artificial*. London: 1612.

Vogt, Katja. *Law, Reason, and the Cosmic City: Political Philosophy in the Early Stoa*. Oxford: Oxford University Press, 2007.

Wakelin, Daniel. *Humanism, Reading, and English Literature 1430–1530*. Oxford: Oxford University Press, 2007.

Warner, Charles Dudley, ed. *Library of World's Best Literature: An Anthology in Thirty Volumes*. New York: Warner Library, 1917.

Whittington, Leah. *Renaissance Suppliants: Poetry, Antiquity, Reconciliation*. Oxford: Oxford University Press, 2016.

Williams, Gareth. *The Cosmic Viewpoint: A Study of Seneca's* Natural Questions. New York: Oxford University Press, 2012.

Winston, Jessica. "Seneca in Early Elizabethan England." *Renaissance Quarterly* 59, no. 1 (2006): 29–59.

Wolfe, Jessica. "Homer, Erasmus and the Problem of Strife." In *Renaissance Papers*, edited by Thomas Hester and Christopher Cobb (Rochester: Boydell & Brewer), 1–32. 2003.

Woodbridge, Linda. "Resistance Theory Meets Drama: Tudor Seneca." *Renaissance Drama* 38 (2010): 115–139.

Woodhouse, A. S. P. "Notes on Milton's Views on the Creation: The Initial Phases." *Philological Quarterly* 28, no. 1 (January 1949): 211–236.

Zak, Gur. *Petrarch's Humanism and the Care of the Self*. Cambridge: Cambridge University Press, 2010.

Žižek, Slavoj. *The Monstrosity of Christ: Paradox or Dialectic*. Cambridge, MA: MIT Press, 2009.

——. *The Puppet and the Dwarf*. Cambridge, MA: MIT Press, 2003.

Index

Printed in the USA
CPSIA information can be obtained
at www.ICGtesting.com
CBHW021358040424
6381CB00011B/183/J

9 781501 764509